The Economics of E-Commerce and Networking Decisions

Also by Yew-Kwang Ng:

WELFARE ECONOMICS: Towards a More Complete Analysis

The Economics of E-Commerce and Networking Decisions

Applications and Extensions of Inframarginal Analysis

Edited by

Yew-Kwang Ng, Heling Shi and Guang-Zhen Sun
Department of Economics
Monash University
Australia

palgrave
macmillan

First published 2003 by
PALGRAVE MACMILLAN
Houndmills, Basingstoke, Hampshire RG21 6XS and
175 Fifth Avenue, New York, N. Y. 10010
Companies and representatives throughout the world

PALGRAVE MACMILLAN is the global academic imprint of the Palgrave Macmillan division of St. Martin's Press, LLC and of Palgrave Macmillan Ltd. Macmillan® is a registered trademark in the United States, United Kingdom and other countries. Palgrave is a registered trademark in the European Union and other countries.

ISBN 0–333–99932–0

This book is printed on paper suitable for recycling and made from fully managed and sustained forest sources.

A catalogue record for this book is available from the British Library.

Library of Congress Cataloging-in-Publication Data

The economics of e-commerce and networking decisions : applications and extensions of inframarginal analysis / edited by Yew-Kwang Ng, Heling Shi, and Guang-Zhen Sun.
p. cm.
Includes bibliographical references and index.
ISBN 0-333-99932-0 (cloth)
1. Electronic commerce. I. Title: Electronics of e-commerce and networking decisions. II. Ng, Yew-Kwang. III. Shi, Heling, 1965- IV. Sun, Guang-Zhen.

HF5548.32.E25 2003
381'.1–dc21 2003053276

10 9 8 7 6 5 4 3 2 1
12 11 10 09 08 07 06 05 04 03

Printed and bound in Great Britain by
Antony Rowe Ltd, Chippenham and Eastbourne

Contents

Notes on the Contributors

Andrew Field is Lecturer in the Department of Business Law and Taxation at Monash University, Australia. In addition to conducting research into the developing legal framework of electronic commerce, his research interests include public and private international law and commercial law generally.

Ke Li is Assistant Professor in Economics, St Joseph's University, USA, and Associate Professor at Nihon University Japan. His main research interests are property rights system, economic organization, economics of state, new economy, and economics of specialization.

Monchi Lio is Assistant Professor at National Sun Yat-sen University; his PhD is from National Taiwan University. His research interests are economic organization and uncertainty, economic history and empirical studies on transaction infrastructure.

Meng-Chun Liu is Research Fellow at Chung-Hua Institution for Economic Research, Taiwan. His PhD is from Monash University. His research interests are international trade, economic organization, economics of technological change, and empirical studies on transaction infrastructure.

Hayden Mathysen is a PhD candidate in the Department of Economics, Monash University, Australia. His PhD and principal research interests are in the spheres of bounded rationality, focal points and experimental coordination games.

Yew-Kwang Ng graduated with a BCom from Nanyang University (Singapore) in 1966 and a PhD from Sydney University in 1971. he has been a fellow of the Academy of Social Sciences in Australia since 1980. he has published refereed papers in economics, biology, mathematics, philosophy, and psychology, and articles in the popular press. Books published include *Welfare Economics* (1979), *Mesoeconomics: a Micro-Macro Analysis* (1986), *Social Welfare and Economic Policy* (1990), *Specialization and Economic Organization* (1993 with X. Yang), *Increasing Returns and Economics Analysis* (1998, co-edited with K. J Arrow and X. Yang), *Efficiency, Equality, and Public Policy: with a Case for Higher Public Spending* (Macmillan, 2000), *Welfare Economics: Towards a Complete Analysis* (Macmillan, forthcoming). He has also published a Kungfu Novel in Chinese serialized in *Nanyang Business Daily* (Malaysia) and as a book *The Unparalleled Mystery* (1994).

George Rivers is a continuing lecturer in the Department of Economics at Monash University. His research interests relate to the theory of the firm, including mergers and acquisitions, downsizing and transaction costs. He is currently a candidate in the degree of Doctor of Philosophy, which is in the process of being finalized. He is the joint author of Rivers and Ward 'Economics in the Business Environment'. He is also a director of the Master of Applied Economics and a member of the Faculty of Business and Economics Marketing Advisory Group. He has been involved with various consulting engagements including, most recently, cost–benefit work with the Department of Natural Resources and the Environment, The Victorian Qualifications Authority and The Royal Botanical Gardens.

Heling Shi is Senior Lecturer In Economics, Monash University. He has applied inframarginal economics in the areas of international trade and globalization, economics growth, industrialization, e-commerce, economics of property rights and the international comparison of living standards.

Guang-Zhen Sun is Logan Fellow in Economics at Monash University and Assistant Professor of Economics, the University of Macau. His current research interests are microeconomic analysis of the division of labour and evolutionary economics.

Wong Chee Kong completed his Master's degree at the Department of Economics, National University of Singapore. His research interests include the Chinese economy, the development of information technology and the Internet in China and the economics of network industry.

John Wong is Research Director of the East Asian Institute at the National University of Singapore. He was formerly Director of the Institute of East Asian Political Economy (1990–96). His research interests are on economics development of China, Asian NIEs and ASEAN economies, and other economic issues of East Asia. He has written more then ten books and published numerous articles and papers on China and other East Asian economies.

Dexin Yang is Associate Professor of Economics at Zhongnan University of Finance and Economics. His research interests are foreign direct investment and regional economic development.

Xiaokai Yang is Professor of Economics at Monash University. His 1993 book, *Specialization and Economic Organization*, with Yew-Kwang Ng, has been described by Ben-Ner, in *Journal of Institutional and Theoretical Economics* (1995, p. 571), 'as a veritable technical and intellectual *tour de* *force'*. Their new framework has spawned many research papers shedding new lights upon many economic issues.

Shuntian Yao is Associate Professor in Economics at Nanyang Business School, Nanyang Technological University of Singapore, and a Charter Member of the Game Theory Society. Yao's main research interests are in Game Theory and Mathematical Economics, having published articles in the *Journal of Economic Theory*, the *Economics Journal*, and the *Journal of Mathematical Economics and Games and Economic Behaviour*. Yao is involved in the research projects on Inframarginal Analysis in the Yang–Ng framework, having made some contributions to the theoretical foundations.

Yimin Zhao obtained his PhD in Economics from Monash University. Dr Zhao is currently providing economics consulting services to multinational enterprises in China and heading up the transfer-pricing unit of KPMG Shanghai. He was a research fellow in Monash University, with particular research interests in the areas of economics of specialization and imperfect competition.

Preface

This volume is a collection of selected revised papers, from the international conference on 'The Economics of e-Commerce and Networking Decisions' held at Monash University on 6–7 July 2001. The financial assistance to the conference of the following sponsors is gratefully acknowledged: Department of Economics – Faculty of Business and Economics, Monash University; Australian Research Council; Productivity Commission; and Law & Economics Consulting Group.

During the conference, Professor Paul Milgrom from Stanford University and Professor Yew-Kwang Ng, as keynote speakers, reviewed features of recent e-commerce phenomena and the relationship between e-commerce phenomena and inframarginal analysis of impersonal networking decisions especially in light of the division of labour decision, developed mainly by economists associated with the Department of Economics, Monash University. Other participants (from Australia, New Zealand, USA, Japan, China Mainland, Hong Kong, Macau, Taiwan, and Singapore) presented their papers on various aspects of the economics of e-commerce and inframarginal analysis of the network of division of labour.

An interesting dialogue during the conference may be reported. Xiaokai Yang expressed his admiration of the high EQ (emotional quotient) of Yew-Kwang Ng. The latter expressed his surprise, saying 'I always believe that I have very low EQ both in comparison to my IQ and in comparison to the EQ of my wife. My only possible explanation of your admiration must be that, while your IQ is higher than mine, your EQ may be even lower than mine!' As it turned out, Xiaokai proved his low EQ (absolutely as well as relatively) during the conference by failing to notify the Pro Vice-Chancellor for research (who was invited to open the conference) of a change in the opening time (advanced by half an hour), making the Pro Vice-Chancellor too late (while punctual for the original scheduled time) to open the conference. While Xiaokai has climbed to the towering heights with his theoretical analysis of networks, he had, on that day at least, almost completely cut off one of the most important network links in practice.

As an example of the low EQ of Kwang, the following true story may be told. He was visiting the Department of Economics, National University of Singapore (NUS) in the second half of 2002 when Professor X started his appointment there as the head of department. During a function of the graduate students, the two of them were sitting together and X mentioned to Kwang about the two ex-wives of X. A week or so later, while making the point on the importance of marriage to happiness during a seminar, Kwang suddenly (without prior foreknowledge) said something like this: "Our head of department, who is sitting right there, has two ex-wives. He may be able to share his experience with us later." Kwang immediately realized that the statements made might have been a mistake but comforted himself that X probably did not mind as he had volunteered the potentially sensitive information about himself to a new acquaintance in a fairly public place in the first place. Nevertheless, other participants of the seminar did not agree and had said privately (as Kwang later found out), "This will be the last time Yew-Kwang visits NUS!", implying that X would be so angry as to never appoint Kwang as a visiting professor again. Two weeks or so later, during a dinner in the presence of other distinguished guests, probably trying to exemplify the frankness (if not naivety) of Kwang, X said to the whole group, "He even disclosed matters of my private life in front of the whole seminar audience!" Kwang then tried to explain to X the basis of his mistake saying, "As you mentioned to me your two ex-wives....", thus disclosing the precise nature of the *faux pax* again in front of the distinguished guests! When Kwang apologized to X for his double mistakes the next day, X was rather gracious and asked him to forget about it. This is not the end of the story yet. Robert Owen, Professor of Economics at the University of Nantes, was also visiting the Department and told Kwang later, "I told X not to worry and explained that this may be a blessing in disguise, since the disclosure made known to all the graduate students (half of them being female) that X was available." To which, Kwang replied, "I hope that Professor X will get a third wife from among one of the graduate students. Then I might be able to come back to visit NUS after all!"

Another true story about Xiaokai may be told. Soon after the publication of Yang and Ng (*Specialization and Economic Organization: a New Classical Microeconomic Framework*, Amsterdam: North-Holland, 1993), Fischer Black (who would have shared a Nobel prize in economics had he not died earlier; also reputed to be one of a very few rich, if not the richest economist at the time) was impressed enough by the book (on his evaluation, see Black, *Exploring General Equilibrium,* Cambridge: MIT Press, 1995, pp. 255–6) to write Yang and Ng a letter. After the latter's response, he emailed Xiaokai asking him some questions and then also asked Xiaokai whether any financial support was needed for our research. Xiaokai replied to the question and said that he would come back to the question of financial assistance later when he would be less busy. Many weeks passed. Before Xiaokai could email Black regarding support for research, Black passed away. Xiaokai could have been given a huge sum of research funding by just writing that email in time!

Xiaokai Yang – a remarkable person? As one who, during the early stages of the Cultural Revolution, dared to challenge the Chinese communist authority even as a teenager (and was imprisoned for ten years for that; see

Yang and McFadden *Captive Spirits*, New York: Oxford University Press, 1997), no doubt about it! (Yew-Kwang Ng is absolutely sure that he admires Xiaokai Yang for his courage here much more than Xiaokai's admiration of Yew-Kwang's EQ, despite the interpersonal comparison involved!)

While this editorship is largely a joint product, Heling Shi is largely responsible for editing Section 2, while Guang-Zhen Sun for the other sections, and Yew-Kwang Ng for the overall coordination and the writing of the preface and introduction. (See, we do not just analyse but also practice division of labour.) All the selected papers have been refereed and revised. While the editors have tried to improve the quality and presentation of the papers, remaining mistakes as well as merits rest principally with the authors of the respective papers. Finally, we wish to thank Roland Cheo for meticulously undertaking the final stage of editing and putting the volume into camera-ready form.

1
Introduction

Yew-Kwang Ng

The widespread use of the Internet and the associated emergence of e-commerce have significantly changed our lives and are going to have an increasing impact on the world economy. With the increase of internet use and e-commerce, informational and transaction costs are reduced dramatically. As with any network (such as the telephone system), the greater the number of people using the Internet, the more useful it is to its users. Thus, with the expected explosion in the number of users in the near future, the benefits of internet use and e-commerce will increase dramatically. Just as in e-commerce, in the division of labour in the economy, transaction costs and networking effects also play important roles. On the one hand, the division of labour allows each individual to specialize more, tapping the economies of specialization. A larger network of division of labour allows more of such economies to be enjoyed. On the other hand, specialization necessitates more trade, which involves transaction costs. In fact, the optimal tradeoff between the economies of specialization through the network of division of labour and the transaction costs of the required exchanges is a central aspect of the Yang–Ng framework of inframarginal analysis (on which more below) of the network of division of labour and the associated economic organization and its evolution. As both e-commerce and economic organization are closely associated with transaction costs and networking effects, it is natural that both may be amenable to the same framework of analysis.

Classical economists, including Adam Smith, regarded the division of labour, to take advantage of the economies of specialization, as the principal economic mechanism for increasing the wealth of nations. However, with their focus on marginal analysis (comparing more or less of some variables, like how many apples to buy, how much labour to employ), orthodox economists after the neoclassical revolution have largely ignored the principal problem of classical economics. A group of researchers originating mainly from Monash University, led by Professors Xiaokai Yang and Yew-Kwang Ng (the defining work being their joint book *Specialization and Economic Organization*, 1993), 'attempt[s] to shift the focus back to specialization and the division of labour' (Smythe, *Journal of Economic Literature*, 1994, p. 691). (A more reader-friendly text is Yang, *Economics: the Neoclassical versus Neoclassical Approaches*, 2001.)

With specialization, one chooses to become either an accountant, an economist, or a lawyer rather than deciding how many hours of accounting work to do or how many hours to allocate to physics problems. One chooses between different corners of specialization. For such choices, marginal analysis is insufficient to give adequate guidance. Yang and Ng devised an analytical method to compare the different corners of specialization not only for an individual, but also for the whole economy. The focus in their work is on the tradeoff between the economies of specialization and transaction costs. It uses traditional marginal analysis as well as inframarginal analysis of total costs and benefits of the different corners. This allows the choice of different occupations (which good to produce, whether to become an employee, or whether to set up a firm), different degrees of specialization (how much home production is engaged), and, for the economy, different economic organizations or structures to be analysed at the fundamental level of individual utility maximization. Rather than assumed as exogenously given, degrees of specialization and organizational structures are outcomes of individual optimization and their interaction. Classical problems are analysed using modern mathematical economic tools. This analysis covers the emergence and enlargement of trade from autarky to globalization, economic growth, industrialization, urbanization, the emergence of firms and multinational corporations, the role of property rights, the effects of e-commerce and so on. It has conceptual as well as practical significance for many economic problems.

Professor James Buchanan calls the increasing returns from the economies of specialization made possible by the division of labour 'generalized increasing returns'. He also regards the work of the Monash group, Yang in particular, as the most exciting item of economic research in the world today. He organized a workshop at the Virginia Polytechnic and State University with NSF support in June 2002, with lectures by Yang, Ng and Heling Shi and others to an invited group of US economists and graduate students. More workshops have been held or are being planned in Australia and China.

The international symposium at Monash University in July 2001 focused on not only the inframarginal analysis of networking decisions but also its relevance for analysing and explaining e-commerce and its effects.

This volume is divided into four parts. Part I comprises keynote speeches at the conference. The chapter by Ng outlines the basics of the Yang–Ng framework of inframarginal analysis and its role in the analysis of the network of the division of labour and the associated evolution of economic organization. The internet revolution and the associated growth of e-commerce, through dramatically reducing the costs of transaction, may lead to a larger network of division of labour and higher economies of specialization. Examples (such as infrastructure provision, bundling sales, unusual high P/E ratios of many e-commerce companies, and the aggregate risk of coordination failure) are used to illustrate the differences between marginal analysis and inframarginal analysis.

The chapter by Yang provides a detailed and up-to-date review of the rapidly growing literature (including basic theoretical research, applied theories, and empirical studies) of inframarginal analysis of the division of labour, identifying its distinctive characteristics. It outlines major criticisms of this literature, including those emerging from the refereeing process. It then identifies those criticisms that have already been satisfactorily absorbed and those that have yet to be satisfactorily addressed by researchers into inframarginal analysis. Possible future developments are also discussed.

E-commerce and networking decisions

Part II comprises five chapters which cover quite diverse fields. The first chapter provides a framework linking the specific features of e-commerce with the recent literature on economics of transaction costs and the network of the division of labour. This is followed by two theoretical chapters examining two distinctive aspects of e-commerce: bundling sales and exchange intermediary. E-commerce raises various legal issues, and one of them is the validity of online contracts. The fourth chapter in this section provides a comparative study of the online contract legislations in several jurisdictions and concludes that remedies should be introduced to reduce the uncertainty on the legal status of online contracting. The final chapter in this part offers a case study on the adoption of e-commerce in China.

The first chapter, by Shi and Mathysen, is written from the business perspective, and argues that e-commerce will mainly influence transaction costs and therefore provides a convincing linkage to the existing literature on the economics of transactions costs. The essay classifies various forms of transaction costs in market exchange, such as search costs, consumer acquisition costs, uncertainty regarding quality, opportunistic behaviour, and negotiation costs. It also deals with agency costs within an organization, such as information distortion, monitoring and measurement costs, and the decrease in managerial capability. Moreover, their work illustrates that the adoption of e-commerce will affect these costs in different ways and to differing extents. Accordingly, e-commerce will affect the optimal organizational format. The authors push forward this transmission mechanism to explain some observations in the real world, such as the optimal size of the firm, vertical integration and horizontal expansion, the replacement of international trade by foreign direct investment, and so on.

The next chapter, by Yang, addresses a current controversy associated with e-commerce, that is, whether e-commerce will eliminate or reduce the role of entrepreneurs. Casual observations indicate the coexistence of two opposite trends: some middle persons permanently disappear, while some new species of middle persons emerge. Yang's chapter provides a theoretical foundation which predicts that the relative movement of transaction costs in markets is the driving force for the disappearance and emergence of the wholesaler–retailer–customer chain. So, it is not insightful to talk about whether e-commerce will reduce the role of middle persons or not; rather, understanding how e-commerce is going to relatively affect the efficiency of transaction in different markets offers much more predictive power.

Li's chapter constructs a general equilibrium model on bundling sales, which is regarded by the author as one of the more common business practices in e-commerce. Prior to this chapter, bundling sales have traditionally been regarded as a business strategy to exercise price discrimination and monopoly power. Bundling sales is not sustainable in a competitive environment. The author argues that with the existence of transaction costs in pricing a good, bundling sales can be used to reduce pricing costs. If the endogenous transaction costs of not pricing is lower than the exogenous transaction costs of pricing such a good, then not pricing a good, and hence bundling sales, will become the equilibrium phenomenon, regardless of the market structure – monopoly or competitive.

The contribution of Field is unique in that it documents the current legal status of online contracts under various jurisdictions. As an Australian, the author is very comforted to notice that the legislative programme adopted in Australia and the gradual introduction of the electronic transaction legislation would appear to place Australia in a position comparable to that of its trading partners. However, the author notices that the selfsame legislation in Australia, the *Electronic Transactions Act*, still leaves some basic questions of the law of contract unanswered. Much of the law of contract as applied in Australia is based on the Common Law as developed by the courts over the decades, bound by the doctrine of precedent; and so far, this law has not yet been applied in a legal contest by the said courts to an electronic contract formed over the Internet. So, the question hinges upon whether this law can be carried over to cover online contracts. The editors decided to include this essay in this economic theory-dominated volume because it provides a detailed case study showing how the uncertainty in legislation could significantly increase the transaction costs in using e-commerce to do business.

Wong and Wong use the survey data compiled by the China Internet Network Information Center (CNNIC) to present a snapshot of the utilization of e-commerce in China and report on the factors contributing to the rapid growth of e-commerce in China since then. Infrastructure development is regarded as being the single largest factor contributing to the exponential growth of the sector. However, some institutional flaws, especially the dominance of the rigid state-owned enterprises, the lack of financial strength of the private sector SMEs (small and medium-sized enterprises), and the prevailing business culture, are preventing the B2B and B2C e-commerce models from developing further. Given this point, the author is confident that the WTO accession will overcome these institutional obstacles to accelerate the adoption of e-commerce in China.

Impersonal networking and endogenous specialization

Part III is devoted to equilibrium analyses of the structure of the division of labour, which emerges from the interaction between the decentralized Walrasian decisions guided by price signals. The authors argue that a very important function of the market is to coordinate individuals' decisions in choosing their patterns of specialization, and that many issues, such as direct foreign investment and time allocation, can be well understood as one aspect or another of the progressive (international) division of labour.

The chapter by Sun, Yang and Yao develops an analytical framework with both increasing returns and transaction costs to show that an impersonal network of the division of labour emerges from the interactions between the Walrasian decisions of self-interested and *ex ante* identical individuals guided by price signals and that the emergent network structure of the division of labour is efficient. Within this analytical framework, the notion of the decentralized coordination of the division of labour by competitive markets (which has been a long-standing tradition in economics) can be resurrected in a modern body of formal analysis. The authors argue that a most important function of the market is to coordinate individuals' decisions in choosing their patterns of specialization in order to fully exploit the positive network effects of division of labour net of transaction costs. As such, their analysis may be seen as a starting point toward the theoretical foundation of the studies of impersonal networking decisions.

Although Sun, Yang and Yao's chapter, and some other theoretical analyses as well, may serve as a theoretical foundation for analysing many important issues, yet many interesting models with intra- and inter-firm division of labour among *ex ante* heterogeneous agents are still not tractable by the existing toolkit, thus presenting a technically challenging problem that needs to be overcome. The chapter by Sun develops a new method for identifying equilibria and conducting comparative statics of structures of the division of labour to fill this void. The method starts with the analysis of individuals' decisions on specialization under given price signals, and then solves for the equilibria and comparative statics in one step, resulting in a complete characterization of subspaces of parameters in which different structures of specialization occur in equilibrium. This approach proves particularly powerful in dealing with models with substitutions between markets (for products and those for labour) and/or *ex ante* heterogeneous agents. In addition, the new approach may help to analyse some theoretical issues in the new classical microeconomic framework.

While the contributions of Sun, Yang and Yao and Sun are both mainly theoretical, the chapter by Dexin Yang introduces an interesting analysis of how foreign direct investment may emerge from the international division of labour. To that end, the author develops a general equilibrium model, which combines the inframarginal theory of the firm developed by Yang and Ng on the one hand, and the international division of labour based on both exogenous and endogenous comparative advantages on the other. As such, a kind of unifying framework for analysing direct foreign investment may be developed.

Time allocation has long been a topic of interest to many theorists. The chapter of Lio addresses the implication of the progressive division of labour for time allocation by developing a model with endogenous specialization and the tradeoff between economies of specialization and transaction costs. This analysis shows that the level of the division of labour, the extent of the market, the level of specialization, productivity, the time spent on consumption activities, the consumption diversity, and per capita real income increase concurrently as transaction efficiency is improved. Perhaps more importantly, the author proves that, under certain conditions, a stronger desire for leisure could have a positive effect on productivity by promoting the development of division of labour if people have a strong preference for diversified consumption.

Transaction costs and division of labour

Although it is well known in the economics profession that transaction costs have profound implications for economic performance in general and for economic organization in particular, the appropriate way to measure and identify transaction costs for a given economy or a firm has long been controversial and still remains a challenging task. Some new efforts in furthering this goal are made in Part IV of this volume.

The contribution of Rivers introduces an indirect approach to the measurement of transaction costs, wherein some proxies are proposed to measure transaction costs associated with the exchange of intermediate goods (services), as well as those associated with the exchange of labour. His analysis begins with a category of transaction costs: *ex ante* or *ex post* costs of market exchange. The former consists of information (search) costs and contract negotiation costs and the latter classified as contract enforcement costs, coordination costs, external arbitration costs and holdup costs. For each subclass of transaction costs, some appropriate practical proxies are proposed. The identification and measurement of transaction costs are an important step towards a complete characterization of what is usually rather loosely referred to as 'transaction costs'.

Lio and Liu's empirical study regarding the relationship between transaction costs and economic structural changes related to the division of labour is complementary to Rivers' work. Specifically, their study empirically examines the urbanization theory of Yang and Rice, using a cross-country data set for 1996 obtained from the *2001 World Development Indicators CD-Rom* published by the World Bank. Their analysis shows that transaction efficiency has strong positive effects on the level of urbanization, strong negative effects on the share of the labour force in agriculture, and strong positive effects on per capita real income. A substantial positive relationship is found between the level of urbanization and per capita real income, while a substantial negative relationship is found between the share of the labour force in agriculture and per capita real income. That the division of labour mediates the positive relationship between transaction efficiency and per capita real income and induces economic structural changes, which is predicted by Yang and Rice's theory, is confirmed.

The contribution of Yang and Zhao is concerned with endogenous transaction costs and the division of labour. Their essay develops a general equilibrium model with alternating offer bargaining and endogenous specialization to investigate the interplay between the network effects of division of labour and endogenous transaction costs caused by strategic interactions. It skilfully demonstrates the negative effects of endogenous transaction costs on the division of labour and on welfare, and posits that the endogenous transaction cost problem may be nonetheless much less serious if players have incentives to care about their reputation. A surprising result produced by this model is that endogenous transaction costs and the level of the division of labour may increase side by side as an exogenous trading efficiency coefficient increases due to complicated interplays between endogenous and exogenous transaction costs and positive network effects of division of labour on aggregate productivity.

Part I

Keynote Speeches

2

Inframarginal Versus Marginal Analysis of Networking Decisions and E-Commerce*

Yew-Kwang Ng

1 What is the connection between e-commerce and the inframarginal analysis of networking decisions?

Many participants in this year's International Symposium of the Economics of e-Commerce and Networking Decisions may ask: what is the economics of e-commerce and networking decisions? After having had a look at the preliminary programme of the symposium, you may wonder what is meant by 'inframarginal analysis' and what is the relationship between inframarginal analysis and e-commerce? Some participants may think that this is a strange combination of two separate and distinct fields: one is a very business-oriented discussion about e-commerce in the real world and the other, a very academic economic analysis of networking decisions. Some may even think of this as a gimmick to sell boring economic theory by bundling it with the e-commerce stuff, which is of interest to many business economists. This speech addresses this concern and provides motivation for this symposium.

I know that many faculty members in business schools and in various departments of marketing, accounting, management, and other business-oriented fields do not like, and may actually hate, the field of economics. Not only is it claimed by many non-economics faculty members that economics is quite irrelevant to real businesses (and hence many businessmen can do very well without it) but also economics departments are losing potential students and high profile faculty members to business schools. As an economist myself, it is an overstatement to say that I am sympathetic to this view. However, as social scientists, perhaps we should ask ourselves: do they have some good reasons to feel this way? Might not our economics be missing something important in today's business world? My outline of inframarginal analysis may throw some light on this

* I am grateful to Heling Shi and Xiaokai Yang for assistance during the drafting of this chapter.

question. More ambitiously, the incorporation of the inframarginal analysis of networking decisions may make economics more relevant to the real world. (Even before this extension, economic analysis has much relevancy and is very important for practitioners in various business areas and beyond; see Lazear, 2000.)

Real business decisions can be categorized into two main classes: marginal decisions about resource allocation and inframarginal networking decisions. The latter includes such decisions as: which line of business does one engage in? Should one adopt a new method of production? The former includes: how much to produce? how much of an input to use? Inframarginal analysis is the total cost–benefit analysis across corner solutions in addition to the marginal analysis of each corner solution. If the optimum value of a decision variable takes on its upper or lower bound (usually zero), the optimal decision is a corner solution. In many cases, the inframarginal networking decision is much more important than the marginal decision. But since the 'marginal' revolution, economists have focused their attention on the marginal analysis of resource allocation. The following example illustrates why the inframarginal decision might be more important than the marginal decision.

Arthur and Betty both graduated around the same time. Arthur started working for a travel agency and ended up as a successful owner-manager of a travel agency with booming business. Betty bought and runs a corner shop. While business was initially good, it declined significantly with the shift of shopping habits towards supermarkets and shopping centres. She eventually could not make enough profits to pay her own living expenses and had to close down the business at a big loss. However, if we examine their individual marginal business decisions, we will agree that Betty is a better and more hard-working manager who made sure she ordered the right amount of each good, priced each good correctly, and was nice to her customers. Nevertheless, being in a line with declining demand, she could not survive even with the best decisions on all her marginal choices.

The problems of the division of labour and the resulting economies of specialization which give rise to further implications for the wealth of nations are at the core of classical mainstream economics represented by William Petty and Adam Smith. Although Adam Smith did not use the term 'network effects', he did appreciate the benefits of network effects of division of labour and specialization. He argued that the division of labour is limited by the extent of the market. Allyn Young (1928) spelt this out in the Young Theorem that not only is the division of labour dependent upon the extent of the market, but the extent of the market is also dependent on the level of division of labour. This circular causation is a common feature of network effects, just like the circular causation that the usefulness of an e-mail account is dependent on the number of people using e-mail accounts, while the number of people using e-mail accounts is dependent on the usefulness of an e-mail account.

When Alfred Marshall formalized neoclassical economics within a mathematical framework at the end of the nineteenth century, he assumed the dichotomy between pure consumers and pure producers to avoid the inframarginal analysis of corner solutions. In Marshall's framework, each consumer buys all goods from the market and does not choose her level of self-sufficiency (the reciprocal of which is the level of specialization), which determines the size of her trade network. Hence, the focus of economics shifted from the inframarginal analysis of specialization and trade networking decisions to the marginal analysis of resource allocation, with the network of division of labour given. By following this neoclassical framework, neoclassical development economics also departed from the then mainstream classical framework of economics. Hence, the inframarginal analysis of networking decisions lost the central position that it had occupied in classical economics.

Though inframarginal analysis had been used to analyse a number of problems in the 1950s, most economists still followed the Marshallian dichotomy between pure consumers and pure producers. The formal inframarginal analysis of networking decisions and its implications was not explored in greater detail until the late 1970s. A literature of inframarginal analysis of impersonal networking decisions emerged at the end of the 1970s and the 1980s. It has been rapidly growing since the publication of Yang and Ng (1993). (See Yang and S. Ng, 1998; Yang, 2001, and Yang's piece in this volume for surveys of these developments.) This literature shows that if a Smithian framework without the dichotomy between pure consumers and firms is adopted, an interior solution is never optimal and a corner solution is the rule rather than an exception. Hence, marginal analysis is not enough and inframarginal analysis is essential for investigating networking decisions.

This literature not only resurrects the spirit of classical mainstream economics in a modern body of inframarginal analysis, but also provides a new framework for the study of networking decisions. Hence it creates an opportunity to bring the study of networking decisions back to the core of modern mainstream economics. As is well known, e-commerce and the internet phenomena are characterized by networking decisions and network effects. The new literature of inframarginal analysis of networking decisions provides a powerful analytical instrument for the study of the economics of e-commerce and the Internet.

The essence of the Yang–Ng analysis is the tradeoff between economies of specialization made possible by the network of division of labour and the transaction costs of trade necessitated by specialization. Which network of the market and the related division of labour is efficient depends on this tradeoff. If transaction efficiency is low, the economies of specialization or the positive network effects of the market are outweighed by transaction costs, so that autarky or a low level of division of labour, which is associated with a small size of the network of the market, is efficient and will be chosen by the invisible hand. If transaction efficiency is improved, the level of division of labour and the related size of market network will increase.

Figure 2.1 gives an intuitive illustration of the evolution of the network of division of labour (a type of comparative statics of general equilibrium) where the number of goods and the population are assumed to be four in a symmetric version of the model. The lines in Figure 2.1 denote goods flows. The small arrows indicate the directions of goods flows. The numbers beside the lines signify the goods involved. A circle with number i denotes a person selling good i. Panel (a) denotes autarky where each person self-provides four goods, due to an extremely low transaction efficiency. Panel (b) denotes partial specialization where each person sells one good, buys one good, trades two goods, and self-provides three goods, as an improvement in transaction efficiency generates a partial division of labour. Panel (c) denotes complete specialization where each person sells and self-provides one good, buys three goods, and trades four goods, due to high transaction efficiency and/or large economies of specialization.

2 Inframarginal analysis of e-commerce and the network effects of division of labour

There are at least two distinct types of reactions from economists to many new e-commerce phenomena. One of them is represented by Shapiro and Varian (1999). They have noted that, confronted by the New Economy, many instinctively react by searching for a corresponding 'New Economics' to guide their business decisions. Executives charged with rolling out cutting edge software products or online versions of their magazines are

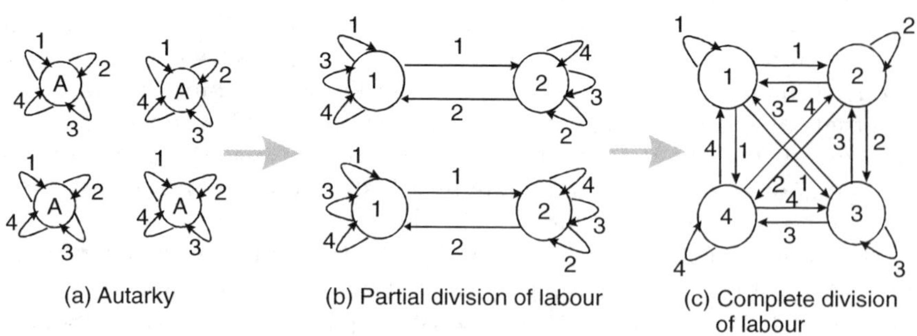

Figure 2.1 Evolution of the division of labour

tempted to abandon the classic lessons of economics, and rely instead on an ever-changing roster of trends, buzzwords, and analogies that promise to guide strategies in the information age. 'Not so fast,' say Carl Shapiro and Hal Varian. In their book, they warn managers, 'Ignore basic economic principles at your own risk. Technology changes. Economic laws do not.' According to this line of thinking, reinterpretation and application of the marginal analysis of information economics to e-commerce phenomena is all we need. On the other hand, many economists who contribute to the literature of inframarginal analysis of networking decisions disagree. According to them, marginal analysis works only for problems of resource allocation for a given pattern of network and is not sufficient for the analysis of networking decisions. Inframarginal analysis (total cost–benefit analysis across network patterns in addition to marginal analysis of resource allocation for a given pattern of network) is essential for networking decisions. I am an eclectic. I believe that traditional economics is still relevant for the new economy, but the power of economic analysis can be increased tremendously by combining traditional economics with the inframarginal analysis of the network of division of labour.

A very important difference between the traditional marginal analysis of the resource allocation and the inframarginal analysis of the division of labour and networking decisions is that the former takes the network of economic organizations or the degree of division of labour of the economy as given. The discussion of the benefits of e-commerce (for example, Bakos, 2001; Borenstein and Saloner, 2001) focuses on the benefits to consumers and producers due to the lower search costs and the likely higher degree of competition. I am not aware of any discussion of the lower transaction costs leading to a higher degree of division of labour and the resulting economies of specialization.

The improvement in transaction (including communication and transportation) efficiency may generate benefits in excess of the direct benefits, through the promotion of a higher degree of specialization. If transaction efficiency is very low (or transaction costs are very high), it may be optimal for everyone to be in autarky, self-producing all the goods needed. As transaction efficiency improves, it then becomes more optimal to buy some goods from others and sell the good one specializes in, but in general, to still have some goods self-produced and self-consumed. As transaction efficiency improves still further, the set of goods bought from others increases. Thus, the benefits of an improvement in transaction efficiency is not only directly translated into the reduction of transaction costs, but also in indirectly promoting the degree of specialization and the consequent tapping of the economies of specialization.

It may be thought that we are already in a fully specialized economy with virtually everyone having only one job or selling only one product. However, even in our era of increasing specialization, there is still much scope for increasing the degree of the division of labour. For one thing, traditional activities performed in the home are increasingly being replaced by alternatives provided through the market – for example, takeaway food and dining out, specialized carpet cleaning and gardening services. Secondly, further specialization can take place at the level of input usage by producers with the adoption of more specialized inputs and more roundabout methods of production. Thirdly, with lower market transaction costs, specialization between firms may replace specialization within a firm. This is especially characteristic of most small and medium-sized firms in Taiwan, which may specialize in producing only a certain input or a particular process, including the final assembly of a product. Thus, the development of e-commerce made possible by the Internet could lead to a much higher degree of division of labour and provide benefits through the economies of specialization. This benefit is analysed more effectively by inframarginal analysis.

Let me use some examples to illustrate the usefulness of inframarginal analysis of the network of division of labour. The first concerns the role of infrastructure. Even assuming that the costs of exclusion are negligible and that there is no free-rider problem, a private producer of an improvement in infrastructure (including the Internet) that reduces transaction costs may only be able to capture the direct benefits of lowering transaction costs, but unable to capture the indirect benefits of promoting more specialization (even in the absence of individual differences giving rise to different consumer surpluses). People will simply assess the direct benefits of lower transaction costs given the existing level of specialization in the economy. Not only will the benefits from a higher degree of specialization occur in the future, contingent on the appearance of new marketable goods, but this development is also assumed not to be affected by the improvement in the transaction efficiency of an individual herself. It is thus rational (even in conditions of full knowledge) to ignore the indirect benefits of higher transaction efficiency on the level of specialization. In other words, there are two public-good problems. The improvement in infrastructure to raise transaction efficiency may itself be a public good. However, even if this public-good problem can be overcome through excludability, there is another public-good problem. The higher transaction efficiency contributes to an increase in the level of specialization which is generally ignored by decision-makers. Even with perfect foresight, each individual does not take into account the benefits of a higher level of specialization because that level is determined by the general level of transaction efficiency prevailing across the whole economy. As such, ultimately it is not appreciably affected by the actions of any one individual or even any big firm. Even if I should correctly foresee that the widespread use of a new communication system will promote increased specialization and increase the number of new products available in the market, I will still not count the benefits of the availability of the new products in assessing the usefulness of the communication system in my decision-making. This is because the new products will be available even if I myself do not use the new communication system just as long as others do. This second level of the public-good problem is quite impossible to solve through exclusion, as the producers of the new set of products are typically different from the producer of the infrastructure. Thus, the indirect externality of infrastructure may then make its public provision or encouragement desirable. The Yang–Ng framework of inframarginal analysis is used in Ng and Ng (2001) to analyse the case for encouraging improvement in transaction efficiency over and above its direct benefits.

Another example is a common phenomenon in e-commerce: implicit bundling sale. An extensive literature of marginal, partial equilibrium analysis of bundling sale (Burstein, 1960; Stigler, 1963; Adams and Yellen, 1976; Schmalensee, 1984; McAfee, McMillan and Whinston, 1989; Whinston, 1990; Hanson and Martin, 1990; Varian, 1995, 1997; and Bakos and Brynjolfsson, 1999a, 1999b) has been developed. This literature focuses on bundling that is associated with monopoly power. Bakos and Brynjolfsson (1999b, p. 3) seem to suggest that bundling with zero prices of some services is a phenomenon of disequilibrium. It is certainly true that many disequilibrium phenomena occur, especially in the current flux of operators in the internet. However, a good of zero price implicitly bundled with goods of positive prices can be a general equilibrium phenomenon. A conventional market for petrol and air pump services may illustrate the point.

There are many petrol stations which sell petrol at competitive prices and provide air-pump services free of charge. This market strategy has been in place for a long time. The bundling of petrol and air-pump services must be an equilibrium phenomenon. In this market, all consumers' preferences for petrol and air-pump services might be very similar, so that the rationale for the type of bundling in the existing literature is irrelevant.[1] The intuition for this phenomenon is quite straightforward. Pricing of air-pump services and collection of related payment involves a transaction cost to consumers as well as to petrol stations (such as waiting time, inconvenience, and tangible resource cost for pricing and payment collection). If the production cost of such services can be added to the price of petrol which is complementary to air-pump services, then such transaction cost can be avoided. Bundling sale may incur endogenous transaction costs which are the distortions caused by individuals who use air pump services but do not buy petrol from the same petrol station. But as long as the reduction of exogenous transaction costs of the pricing of air pump service outweighs the increase in endogenous transaction cost, a competitive market will generate pressure to compel all petrol stations to implement such a bundling price structure. This may be called implicit bundling. Implicit bundling is closer to mixed bundling than the pure bundling investigated in the existing literature. Other implicit bundling cases include TV programmes (TV shows are free of charge and associated advertisements are paid at positive prices by companies selling goods to viewers of TV programmes) and an automobile company's marketing operation with positive prices of cars and free internet purchase services. (However, the case of TV also involves an additional aspect of advertising or marketing; see Wang et al. (2001) on marketing goods.) Here, the key point is that the prohibitively high pricing costs of some goods may result in zero prices of goods bundled with goods of positive prices even in the absence of monopoly power. Moreover, the market viability of additional goods made possible by bundling may have general equilibrium effects through enlarging the network of division of labour. Therefore, we need a general equilibrium model without monopoly power and with transaction costs and competitive (implicit) bundling. Using the Yang–Ng (1993) framework of inframarginal analysis, Li (2001) has formalized this story.

He tells the story by formulating the tradeoff between positive network effects of the division of labour on aggregate productivity and transaction costs. As suggested by Allyn Young (1928), network effect is a notion of general equilibrium. Not only the network size of division of labour depends on the extent of the market (the number of participants in the network of division of labour), but also the number of participants is determined by all individuals' participation decisions in the network of division of labour, which relate to their decisions of their levels of specialization. This circular causation, noted by Young, is of course an essential feature of general equilibrium, analogous to the circular causation between quantities and prices in the general equilibrium (each individual's quantities demanded and supplied depend on prices, while the equilibrium prices are determined by all individuals' decisions of quantities). Hence, marginal analysis of a partial equilibrium model, such as those in the existing literature of bundling, does not work for our task.

Moreover, since we need an assumption of a competitive market in order to investigate the network effects of division of labour, we are not confined to the strategic networking decisions that are associated with monopoly power. We need a general equilibrium model of impersonal networking decisions to investigate infinite feedback loops between network size of the division of labour, each person's participation decision, prices, quantities, and different markets. Yang (2001) and Sun et al. (1999) have drawn a distinction between the strategic networking decision and the impersonal networking decision. For the latter, each decision-maker is not concerned with whom she has a trade connection with. She is concerned with how many goods (and which set of goods for the case with non-symmetric preferences) she will trade and how many she will self-provide. Her decision in choosing the number of types of traded partners determines her trade network size and pattern. Impersonal networking decisions take place in a market where nobody can manipulate prices, so that implicit bundling with zero prices of some goods may emerge from competitive pressure and free entry.

Intuitively, Li's story can be told as follows. Suppose that an automobile manufacturer, such as Holden, sells automobiles and internet services for purchasing cars online. Automobiles are tangible goods which are easy to price, but internet services are intangible and very difficult to price. Holden can bundle these two goods together by providing free internet services and by adding the operating cost of internet services to the price of automobiles. If such bundling can save consumers' transaction costs incurred in a purchase in excess of the added cost to the price of automobiles, Holden will have a competitive edge compared to other automobile manufacturers who do not provide such bundled deals. Then the competitive pressure in the market may force all manufacturers to provide such bundled deals. Here, monopoly power, constant and independent valuations of one unit of good, non-resale, and other special assumptions used in the bundling literature are not needed. In addition, even if all individuals have *ex ante* identical utility functions, which allow for the substitution between goods, productivity gains from bundling may be generated by the network effects of division of labour. Without bundling, involvement of the good with prohibitively high transaction costs in a high level of division of labour and avoidance of direct pricing cost of such a good cannot coexist. Hence, positive network effects of division of labour on aggregate productivity cannot be fully exploited. With bundling, both of the tasks can be achieved at the same time. Therefore, network effects may be fully exploited and aggregate productivity may be promoted by the use of bundling. It is interesting to note that bundling in a competitive market has very important productivity implications even if all individuals have *ex ante* identical utility and production functions and substitution between different goods are non-trivial.

The inframarginal analysis of impersonal networking decisions can also be extended to explain the unusually high P/E ratios of many e-commerce companies. If positive network effects of e-commerce can be created by the founding of many e-commerce companies, but services provided by these companies are not easy to price directly, then the merger of e-commerce companies and other companies which sell tangible goods can indirectly price intangible e-commerce services via implicit bundling in e-commerce. The bundling of automobiles and internet purchase services is one such example. Other examples include the merger of the communication company, American Online (AOL) and Warner Brothers, which bundles intangible services of the AOL with tangible goods provided by Warner Brothers, and the online bookstore, Amazon.com, which bundles intangible e-commerce with tangible hard copies of books. Hence, some e-commerce companies can have unusually high P/E ratios since the market expects that such companies may merge with or be bought by other companies selling tangible goods at quite high share prices because of the possibility of significant network effects.

Another e-commerce phenomenon that has not been predicted by standard neoclassical marginal analysis is that as new internet technologies significantly improve the reliability and reduce the cost of each transaction, the risk of coordination failure of the network of division of labour and income share of transaction costs increase. This phenomenon is noted by Autor (2001) and Barber and Odean (2001), but they cannot find an appropriate analytical instrument to explain it. As Shapiro and Varian (1999) suggest, they rely on an ever-changing roster of trends, buzzwords, and analogies to verbally describe such a phenomenon. However, Shapiro and Varian's marginal analysis cannot help them either. As shown by Yang and Ng (1993) and Yang (2001), the use of marginal analysis does not help in explaining many impersonal networking decisions in conventional markets; neither does it formalize classical mainstream economics which focuses on network effects of the division of labour. The use of marginal analysis is even less suitable for handling e-commerce phenomena. Hence, this conference focuses on theories and applications of inframarginal analysis of impersonal networking decisions. This distinguishes our symposium from the Symposium of E-Commerce held in the US (see Borenstein and Saloner, 2001; Goolsbee, 2001; Autor, 2001; Barber and Odean, 2001; and Bakos, 2001). That symposium was characterized by verbal descriptions and marginal, partial equilibrium analysis. Lio (1998) and Yang and Wills (1990) have developed several models of impersonal networking decisions prior to that event. The use of inframarginal analysis in these models predicts the above e-commerce phenomenon. Their models specify the tradeoffs between positive network effects of the division of labour on aggregate productivity, coordination reliability of the network of the division of labour, exogenous transaction costs in specifying property rights, and endogenous transaction costs caused by imprecise specification and the enforcement of property rights. As the transaction cost coefficient is reduced by new internet technology, the scope for the tradeoff between economies of division of labour against transaction costs is enlarged, so that the equilibrium network size of division of labour increases. However, this expansion of network of interdependent specialists will increase the length of a series connection of many professional occupations. If there is a transaction risk for each trade connection, the aggregate risk of coordination failure of the trade network will increase with the number of connections. Thus, the aggregate risk of coordination failure may increase as a result of a decrease in the risk of coordination failure of each trade connection. However, as long as the positive network effects of division of labour outweigh the negative network effects of increasing risk of coordination failure, the network size of division of labour and aggregate risk of coordination failure may increase side by side. Also, the income share of transaction costs may increase as a result of the expansion of network of division of labour, driven by improvements in communication efficiency. Many other e-commerce phenomena can be much better explained by inframarginal analysis than by marginal analysis.

More generally, all information about inframarginal decisions (or about whether any pair of players are connected) is associated with the 'topological properties of an organism' which can be represented by a graph consisting of vertices (or nodes, points) and edges (or lines, curves). All information about marginal decisions of resource allocation relates to quantities of goods ('goods' used in the general sense), which is a non-topological property of an organism and can be represented by weights attached to edges of the graph. Hence, a weighted digraph can describe the topological as well as non-topological properties of an economic organism. Marginal analysis focuses on the non-topological properties of economic organisms, while inframarginal analysis focuses on the topological properties of economic organisms. The networking decision, which is essential for e-commerce, is an inframarginal decision.

It will be an exciting experience to learn about inframarginal analysis from the many sessions in this conference. Many papers presented in this conference will show the implications of inframarginal analysis for the studies of e-commerce and beyond.

Borenstein and Saloner (2001, p. 6) may be right that the 'key impediments to capturing the cost savings of e-commerce and the Internet will probably not involve technical issues, but rather inertial forces'. Similarly, it is inertia that allows academic journals to continue requiring the costly submissions of many single-sided, double-spaced hard copies of papers for publication rather than allowing electronic submissions (Ng, 2001). So, wake up and do something!

Note

1 As shown by Bakos and Brynjolfsson (1999a), benefit of bundling disappears as consumers' evaluations converge to the same value.

References

Adams, W. J. and Yellen, J. L. (1976) 'Commodity Bundling and the Burden of Monopoly', *Quarterly Journal of Economics*, 90, 3, 475–98.

Arrow, K., Ng, Y.-K. and Yang, X. (eds) (1998) *Increasing Returns and Economic Analysis* (London: Macmillan).

Autor, D. (2001) 'Wiring the Labour Market', *Journal of Economic Perspectives*, 15, 25–40.

Bakos, Y. (2001) 'The Emerging Landscape for Retail E-commerce', *Journal of Economic Perspectives*, 15, 69–80.

Bakos, Y., and Brynjolfsson, E. (1999a) 'Bundling Information Goods: Pricing, Profits and Efficiency', *Management Science*, 45, 12.

Bakos, Y., and Brynjolfsson, E. (1999b) 'Bundling and Competition on the Internet', Working Paper, Stern School of Business, New York University.

Barber, B. and Odean, T. (2001) 'The Internet and the Investor', *Journal of Economic Perspectives*, 15, 41–54.

Borenstein, S. and Saloner, G. (2001) 'Economics and Electronic Commerce', *Journal of Economic Perspectives*, 15, 3–12.

Buchanan, J. and Stubblebine, W. (1962) 'Externality', *Economica*, 29, 371–84.

Burstein, M. L. (1960) 'The Economics, of Tie-In Sales', *The Review of Economics and Statistics*, 42, 68–73.

Coase, R. (1946) 'The Marginal Cost Controversy', *Economica*, 13, 169–82.

Coase, R. (1960) 'The Problem of Social Cost', *Journal of Law and Economics*, 3, 1–44.

Goolsbee, A. (2001) 'The Implications of Electronic Commerce for Fiscal Policy (and Vice Versa)', *Journal of Economic Perspectives*, 15, 13–24.

Hanson, W., and Martin, R. K. (1990) 'Optimal Bundling Pricing', *Management Science*, 36(2) 155–74.

Lazear, E. P. (2000) 'Economic Imperialism', *Quarterly Journal of Economics*, 115, 99–146.

Li, K. (2001) 'A General Equilibrium Analysis of the Division of Labour: Violation and Enforcement of Property Rights, Impersonal Networking Decisions and Bundling Sale.' PhD Dissertation, Department of Economics, Monash University.

Lio, M. (1998) 'Uncertainty, Insurance, and Division of Labor', *Review of Development Economics*, 2, 76–86.

McAfee, R. P., McMillan, J., and Whinston, M. D. (1989) 'Multiproduct Monopoly, Commodity Bundling, and Correlation of Values', *Quarterly Journal of Economics*, 104, 371–83.

Ng, Y.-K. (2001) 'Paper Submission in the Electronic Age', *Newsletter of Royal Economic Society* (UK) July.

Ng, Y.-K. and Ng, S. (2001) 'Why it may be Desirable to Encourage Improvements in Transaction Efficiency: Economies of Specialization and Network Externalities', Paper for presentation to the Symposium on the Economics of e-Commerce and Networking Decisions, Monash University, July.

Petty, William (1671) *Political Arithmetics*, in C. H. Hull (ed.), *Economic Writings of Sir. William Petty* (New York: Augustus M. Kelley, 1963).

Petty, William (1683) *Another Essay on Political Arithmetics*, in C. H. Hull (ed.), *Economic Writings of Sir. William Petty* (New York: Augustus M. Kelley, 1963).

Schmalensee, R. (1984) 'Gaussian Demand and Commodity Bundling', *Journal of Business*, 57(1) s211–30, part 2.

Shapiro, C. and Varian, H. R. (1999) *Information Rules: a Strategic Guide to the Network Economy* (Boston, MA: Harvard Business School Press).

Smith, Adam (1776) *An Inquiry into the Nature and Causes of the Wealth of Nations*. Reprint, edited by E. Cannan (Chicago: University of Chicago Press, 1976).

Stigler, G. (1963) 'United States v. Leow's Inc.: a note on block booking', *Supreme Court Review*, 152–7.

Sun, G., Yang, X. and Yao, S. (1999) 'Theoretical Foundation of Economic Development Based on Networking Decisions in the Competitive Market', Harvard Center for International Development Working Paper No. 17.

Varian, H. L. (1995) 'Pricing Information Goods', in Proceedings of Scholarship in the New Information Environment Symposium, Harvard Law School.

Varian, H. L. (1997) 'Versioning Information Goods', accessed at http://www.sims.berkeley.edu/~hal/pages/sciam.html, 25/3/99.

Wang, J., Li, Y. S. and Ng, Y.-K. (2001) 'Marketing Goods', typescript.

Whinston, Michael (1990) 'Tying, Foreclosure, and Exclusion', *American Economic Review*, 80, 4, 837–59.

Yang, X. (2001) *Economics: New Classical versus Neoclassical Framework* (Oxford: Blackwell).

Yang, X. and Ng, Y.-K. (1993) *Specialization and Economic Organization: a New Classical Microeconomic Framework* (Amsterdam: North-Holland).

Yang, X. and Ng, S. (1998) 'Specialization and Division of Labor: a Survey,' in Arrow, Ng, and Yang, *Increasing Returns and Economic Analysis*.

Yang, X. and Wills, I. (1990) 'A Model Formalizing the Theory of Property Rights', *Journal of Comparative Economics*, 14, 177–98.

Young, Allyn (1928) 'Increasing Returns and Economic Progress', *The Economic Journal*, 152, 527–42.

3

A Review of the Literature of Inframarginal Analysis of Network of Division of Labour

Xiaokai Yang

The purpose of this chapter is twofold. First, it will provide an updated review of an emerging and rapidly growing literature of the inframarginal analysis of network of division of labour. Second, it will outline major comments and challenges against the core propositions in the literature, which have emerged during the refereeing process. Section 1 identifies those characteristics of the literature that distinguish it from other lines of research. Section 2 reviews basic theoretical research in this literature. Section 3 reviews applied theories in this literature. Section 4 reviews empirical studies of the literature and major assessments and criticisms of the literature. Section 5 reviews textbooks based on the literature.

1 An emerging and rapidly growing literature

The core of classical mainstream economics represented by William Petty (1671, 1683) and Adam Smith (1776) was about the development implications of the division of labour. Although classical economists did not know the term 'network effect', Smith did appreciate the nature of network effects, particularly of the benefits of division of labour and specialization. He proposed the theorem that the division of labour is limited by the extent of the market. In terms of modern economics, this theorem implies that individuals' decisions to choose their levels of specialization are determined by the benefits of division of labour, which are dependent on the number of participants in the network of division of labour (the extent of the market). This is just like the case where the use value of a telephone set is dependent on the number of telephone sets in use. Allyn Young (1928) spelt this out in the Young Theorem that not only does division of labour depend upon the extent of the market, but the extent of the market is also dependent on the level of division of labour. This circular causation is a common feature of network effects, just like the circular causation that the use value of a telephone set is dependent on the number of telephone sets in use, meanwhile the number of telephone sets in use is dependent on the use value of each telephone set. The circular causation is a typical characteristic of the notion of general equilibrium and the fixed point theorem. In a conventional general equilibrium model, the optimum quantities demanded and supplied are dependent on market prices while equilibrium prices are determined by all individuals' decisions about quantities. According to Smith and Young, each individual's decision of her level and pattern of specialization (or her networking decision) depends on the number of participants in the network of division of labour, while the number of participants is determined by all individuals' decisions of their levels and patterns of specialization. Hence, the Smith–Young theorem explores intimate relationships between the notions of general equilibrium and fixed point theorem, network effects, and division of labour.

As shown in Yang (2001), inframarginal analysis of individuals' networking decisions is essential for formalizing the classical economic thinking on network effects of division of labour. Here inframarginal analysis, a phrase coined by Buchanan and Stubblebine (1962), is the total cost–benefit analysis across corner solutions in addition to the marginal analysis of each corner solution. If the optimum value of a decision variable takes on its upper or lower bound, the optimal decision is a corner solution. If the optimum value takes on a value between its upper and lower bounds, it is an interior solution. Formally, inframarginal analysis relates to nonlinear programming, mixed integer programming, dynamic programming, control theory, and other nonclassical mathematical programming, while marginal analysis relates to classical mathematical programming which is confined to an interior solution.

The first decision a university freshman makes is to choose a major. If she chooses economics as her major, then she does not attend classes for chemistry or physics, but she takes classes in microeconomics, macroeconomics, and econometrics. We call such a decision an inframarginal decision, since values of decision variables discontinuously jump between zero and interior values as the student shifts between majors. An inframarginal decision is a type of decision about 'yes' or 'no', which is also called a networking decision since it determines which major (or occupation) and which group of individuals (specialized teachers and students in a particular major) one is connected to or not. After she has said 'yes' to a major and 'no' to other majors, she allocates her limited time between the fields to which she has said 'yes'. This decision of resource allocation for a given major (or occupation) is called a marginal decision since standard marginal analysis is applicable to this type of decision-making. Marginal decisions are about 'how much' after one has chosen a yes–no configuration. The aggregate outcome of all students' choices of their majors in a university generates division of students among majors and fields, which is analogous to a network pattern of division of labour in society. All information about inframarginal decisions (or about whether any pair of players are connected) is called 'topological properties of an organism', which can be represented by a graph consisting of vertices (or nodes, points) and edges (or lines, curves). All information about marginal decisions of resource allocation relates to quantities of goods which is a non-topological property of an organism and can be represented by weights attached to edges of the graph. Hence, a weighted directed graph (or digraph for short) can describe all topological as well as non-topological properties of an economic organism.

But when Alfred Marshall (1890) formalized classical economics within a mathematical framework at the end of the nineteenth century, he did not know about inframarginal analysis. He made an assumption of the strict dichotomy between pure consumers' decisions and firms' decisions to avoid inframarginal analysis of corner solutions. Within the neoclassical framework, each pure consumer must buy all goods from the market and cannot choose her level of self-sufficiency or its reciprocal, the level of specialization. As shown in Yang (2001, introductory chapter), the equilibrium topological properties of an economic organism under the assumption of dichotomy in the neoclassical framework are not well defined. Hence, the focus of economics shifted from inframarginal analysis of the network effects of the division of labour and topological properties of economic organisms to marginal analysis of resource allocation and non-topological properties of economic organisms. In terms of modern economic language, classical economics is about the functioning of the price system in carrying information about topological as well as non-topological properties of economic organisms. It paid more attention to the function of the price system in carrying information of topological properties (level of division of labour and extent of the market) than the function of the price system in carrying information of non-topological properties (resource allocation). However, neoclassical economics represented by Marshall has been exclusively occupied with the analysis of the latter.

Since the 1950s, economists have applied inframarginal analysis to various decision problems. However, many economists still follow Marshall's assumption of dichotomy between pure consumers and firms, under which the corner solution is exceptional and the interior solution is the rule and equilibrium topological properties of economic organisms are not well defined. Hence, implications of formal inframarginal analysis for investigating effects of network size of division of labour on economic development could not be fully explored until the late 1970s. The Wen Theorem (1998) in an emerging literature of inframarginal analysis of network of division of labour has shown that if a Smithian framework is adopted, the interior solution is never optimal and corner solution is a rule rather than an exception in the absence of the dichotomy between pure consumers and exogenously given firms. Hence, marginal analysis is not enough and inframarginal analysis is essential for exploring implications of network effects of the division of labour.

At the end of the 1970s, a literature of general increasing returns and network effects of division of labour emerged. Basic theories, applied theories, and empirical research of this literature developed rapidly in the 1990s. Yang and Ng (1993) covers many early models in this literature. Yang and Ng (1998) provide a survey of the literature. Yang (2001) includes an updated review of the rapidly growing literature. The models in this literature are characterized by the following three features:

1. Each decision-maker is a consumer-producer who applies marginal analysis to sort out resource allocation for each network pattern of trade and then applies total cost–benefit analysis to sort out the optimum trade pattern and level of specialization from many corner solutions. The two-step decision procedure is called inframarginal analysis. The optimum decision is always a corner solution and the interior solution is never optimal. If individuals are *ex ante* identical, positive network effects of division of labour on aggregate productivity can endogenously emerge as a consequence of individuals' decisions choosing different patterns of specialization and the existence of individual specific (local) increasing returns to specialization. If they are *ex ante* different, the positive network effects of division of labour on aggregate productivity may occur in the absence of economies of scale.
2. The production functions are specified for each consumer-producer and represent each person's capacity for learning by doing in all possible production activities. Hence, when a person sells her labour, it is a process in which she sells her production functions. This implies that an employer cannot simply pool all employees' labour into her production function. But rather, the production function of a firm is a combination of production functions of all employees and the employer. In a sense, this approach to specifying the production function is similar to the analytical framework for trade theory in which labour trade is not allowed between countries (or between different types of individuals). However, in the literature of endogenous specialization, hiring labour is allowed, though it is to specifically hire the production functions of the employee. The implication of this way to specify production conditions is that the aggregate production set may be nonconvex even if all individuals' production sets are convex. Hence, strong aggregation result (maximization of total profit of all firms by a central planner is equivalent to aggregate outcome of all individual firms' profit maximization) and marginal cost pricing in neoclassical economics no longer holds in the models of endogenous specialization. In the

literature of endogenous specialization, before individuals make their decisions, no firm exists. The institution of the firm emerges from the division of labour only if individuals have decided to choose a high level of division of labour and to use a labour market to coordinate the division of labour between the production of final goods and the production of intermediate goods. The production function for the firm emerges *ex post* as a combination of individual specific production functions only if individuals choose the labour market to coordinate the division of labour. The models have formalized Young's idea (1928, p. 539) that 'The mechanism of increasing returns is not to be discerned adequately by observing the effects of variations in the size of an individual firm or of a particular industry, for the progressive division of labour and specialisation of industries is an essential part of the process by which increasing returns are realized. What is required is that industrial operations be seen as an interrelated whole.' This 'interrelated whole' is a network of division of labour in modern economic terms. Hence, general increasing returns and network effects of division of labour are compatible with a competitive market. Several papers in the literature of endogenous specialization have shown that the Pareto optimum utility frontier might be different from the production possibility frontier because of the tradeoff between economies of division of labour and transaction costs. Also, marginal cost pricing no longer holds in the competitive equilibrium. This feature of the literature distinguishes it from all models with economies of scale.

3. Transaction costs have very important implications for the equilibrium network size of division of labour. As a unit transaction cost coefficient decreases, the equilibrium network size of division of labour is enlarged, aggregate productivity and social welfare increase, and total transaction costs increase. This invalidates the claim that the argument of transaction costs in this literature is a tautology.

2 Theoretical foundation of the literature

Three papers (Sun, Yang, and Zhou, 1998; Sun, Yang, and Yao, 1999; and Sun, 1999) have established the existence theorems, the first welfare theorem, and core and equilibrium equivalent theorem for a general class of general equilibrium models with impersonal networking decisions and endogenous structure of division of labour. These papers use weighted digraphs to describe the network of division of labour and resource allocation. They show that the general increasing returns are network effects of division of labour, which may exist in the absence of economies of scale within a firm. The network effects are caused by impersonal networking decisions which are compatible with the competitive market. The most important function of the market is to coordinate individuals' impersonal networking decisions and to utilize network effects of division of labour. The papers use Hildenbrand's (1974) approach to large economies with local increasing returns to synthesize the Arrow–Debreu model of resource allocation, which focuses on interactions between prices and quantities of goods, and recent literature of strategic networking decision (Katz and Shapiro, 1986; Jackson and Wolinsky, 1996; and Dutta and Mutuswami, 1997) which focuses on networking decisions and ignores interactions between quantities, prices and networking decisions.

These papers have explored general equilibrium mechanisms that simultaneously determine interdependent quantities (non-topological properties of organisms), prices, and topological properties (such as the degrees of connectedness, market integration, and asymmetry between the core and periphery) of organisms. They show that when individuals are capable of conducting inframarginal analysis, the equilibrium pattern of division of labour in the market place is Pareto optimal even if there are network effects of division of labour, local increasing returns in production, and transaction costs. The results have established the proposition that the price system can carry not only all information about non-topological properties (quantities consumed and produced or resource allocation) of economic organisms, but also all information about topological properties of economic organisms. The papers have satisfactorily addressed criticisms raised by referees in the early 1990s that network effects of the division of labour and increasing returns are not compatible with a competitive market. Such criticisms were the main hurdles for the literature to be widely accepted. They are completely silenced by the major pure theory research toward the end of the 1990s.

Sun, Yang, and Yao (1999) was the first paper to establish the existence theorem and the first welfare theorem for a general class of general equilibrium models with endogenous structure of division of labour and *ex ante* identical consumer-producers. Sun, Yang, and Zhou (1998) have established the first existence theorem and the first and second welfare theorems for a general class of models with *ex ante* different consumer-producers. This paper allows constant returns as well as increasing returns and has used the measurement theory, while Sun, Yang, and Yao's existence theorem does not need measurement theory to be proven. But in the models of these two papers there is no producer good. Sun (1999) has established the first existence theorem for a class of general models with *ex ante* different consumer-producers, and consumer and producer goods. He is currently working on the existence theorem for a class of models allowing trade in labour and institution of the firm.

Yang and Yao (2001) have developed the concept of Walrasian sequential equilibrium to formalize the notions of fundamental social and endogenous uncertainties, bounded rationality, and entrepreneurial discovery. It predicts that social sequential experiments with efficient as well as inefficient network patterns of division of labour can gradually acquire organization information for society as a whole. The experiment process is decentralized and based on individuals' bounded rationality. In this process, each individual never knows the others' characteristics, although all players collectively learn abstract organization information carried by price signals gradually. This paper proves an existence theorem of equilibrium for a general class of well-closed Walrasian sequential equilibrium models and avoids the recursive paradox in the presence of individual bounded rationality. This basic theoretical research shows that information asymmetry in a Walrasian sequential equilibrium model can be much more than in any game models with incomplete information. As Aumann (1997, p. 8) points out, the game models with incomplete information and information asymmetry involve super rationality rather than bounded rationality. Yang and Yao (2001) provide a new approach to studying individuals' bounded rationality which may generate socially rational outcomes.

Another important theorem that is essential for managing applied theories in this literature is the Wen Theorem (Wen, 1998) which claims that each consumer-producer never sells and buys the same goods, never produces and buys the same goods, and sells at most one good. Without this theorem, the number of possible corner solutions and the number of market structures which are combinations of corner solutions are too great to be manageable. The Wen Theorem significantly reduces the number of corner solutions that constitute the set of candidates for the optimum decision. However, the Wen Theorem may not hold if linear production functions with fixed learning costs are allowed. Recently, the Wen Theorem has been extended to the general Wen Theorem (Yao, 2002, see also Yang, 2001, chapter 13) by Yao which claims that although selling more than two goods is possible, the optimum decision can be achieved by selling at most one good.

Li and Sun (1998) have proved several theorems on the measurement of levels of division of labour and economies of division of labour. They have shown that the level of division of labour can be defined by the spectrum of a labour allocation matrix of each and every individual in society. Economies of division of labour need many variables to be well defined. Hence, economies of division of labour cannot be defined by the economies of scale of a single firm.

A technical obstacle for the mainstream acceptance of inframarginal analysis is that a multiple-step approach to handling many corner solutions and many corner equilibria is very complicated and cumbersome. Sun (2001) has developed an algorithm to solve for general equilibrium and its inframarginal comparative statics in one step. This algorithm may speed up acceptance of inframarginal analysis by a new generation of economists.

Yao is working on an existence theorem for a general class of dynamic general equilibrium models with endogenous network pattern of division of labour, developed by Yang and Borland (1991), Wen (1997), and Zhang (1997).

3 Applied theory research

With the sound theoretical foundation of inframarginal analysis of general increasing returns and network effects of division of labour, many applied theory papers have explored the implications of the new framework for trade theory (Cheng, Sachs, Yang, 2000a,b; Yang, 1994, 1996; G. Li, 2001; D. Yang, 2001; Cheng, Liu, and Yang, 2000; S. Ng, 1995; Yang and Zhang, 2000, forthcoming), growth theory (Borland and Yang, 1995; Yang and Borland, 1991; Wen, 1997; Zhang, 1997), development economics (Yang, 2003b; Sachs, Yang, and Zhang, forthcoming; Yang and Shi, 1992; Shi and Yang, 1995), the theory of endogenous externality, public goods, and endogenous transaction costs (Chu, 1997; Chu and Wang, 1998; Lio, 1996, 1998; Y.-K. Ng and S. Ng 2001a,b; Yang, 2000; Yang and Yeh, 2002; Fang and Zhu, 1999; Ng and Yang, 2000; Yang and Zhao, 2003; Liu and Yang, 2001), the theory of the firm and contract (Yang and Ng, 1995; Liu and Yang, 2000; Yang and Yeh, forthcoming; Yang, 2001; Sun, 2000), the economics of transaction costs (Yang, 1991, 1996; Lio, 1996, 1998), the economics of property rights (Yang and Wills, 1990; Lio, 1998), the economics of e-business and the Internet (Li, 2001), the economics of state (Li, 2001; Liu and Yang, 2001), monetary theory (Cheng, 1998, 1999; Yang and Ng, 1993), theory of capital and investment (Yang, 1999; Yang and Borland, 1991; Wen, 1997), theory of urbanization (Yang and Rice, 1994; Sun and Yang, 2000), theory of industrialization (Shi and Yang, 1995; Sun and Lio, 1996), theory of business cycles (Yang and Ng, 1993, ch. 18; Du, 2003), theory of insurance (Lio, 1998), theory of bounded rationality (Ng and Yang, 1997; Zhao, 1999), and theory of hierarchy (Shi and Yang, 1998; Yang, 2001, ch. 20).

The focus of these papers is on the effects of trading efficiency, which could be affected by the institution of the firm, hierarchical structure of transactions and contracts, money, the institution of government, opportunism (associated with moral hazard, adverse selection, cheating, stealing, and tariff), urbanization, insurance, structure of property rights and ownership, and bundling sales, on the network size of division of labour and interplays among equilibrium topological properties of economic organisms, prices, and resource allocation. For instance, inframarginal comparative statics of general equilibrium in the models show that as parameter values of trading efficiency and production conditions shift between parameter subspaces which demarcate various structures of division of labour, transactions, property rights, and contracts, the general equilibrium discontinuously jumps across the structures, resulting in endogenous changes in the level of division of labour, monetary regime, trade pattern, structure of property rights, transactions, contracts, and institution. Income share of transaction cost may increase in response to the emergence of money, improvements in trading efficiency, and evolution in division of labour that generates productivity progress. Aggregate reliability of the network of division of labour may decrease and aggregate risk of coordination failure of division of labour may increase as a consequence of the expansion of network of division of labour which generates productivity progress, as well as, a high degree of connectedness of an integrated market. Several dynamic models in this literature have explored spontaneous (or endogenous) co-evolution in division of labour, trading efficiency, number of traded goods, number of available goods, per capita income, optimum government tax rate, size of government revenue, and market integration.

Since much of the early applied theory research in this literature is reviewed in Yang and Y.-K. Ng (1993), Yang and S. Ng (1998), and Yang (2001), I shall concentrate on the recent work in this strand of the literature.

Recent inframarginal analysis of trade theory: Cheng, Sachs, and Yang (2000a) show that government trade policy regimes, equilibrium network size of division of labour, and aggregate productivity are interdependent in a Ricardian model. This paper shows that as transportation efficiency is improved, the general equilibrium discontinuously jumps from autarky to partial division of labour, where the country producing both goods would impose a tariff and the country producing a single good would prefer unilateral free trade. This is followed by a complete division of labour where both countries would negotiate on tariff rates to achieve free trade. In a model with three countries, the country which does not have a comparative advantage relative to the other two countries and/or which has low transaction efficiency may be excluded from trade. Cheng, Sachs, and Yang (1999, 2000b) have applied inframarginal analysis to the Heckscher–Ohlin (HO) model with exogenous technological as well as endowment comparative advantages to obtain similar results. Cheng, Liu, and Yang (2000) and Yang and Zhang (2000, 2003) have applied inframarginal analysis to models with endogenous as well exogenous comparative advantages to study the interplays between trade policy regime, dual structure, income distribution, and network size of division of labour. Sachs, Yang and Zhang (forthcoming) have applied inframarginal analysis to the Dixit–Krugman models to explain discontinuous jumps of trading patterns by interplays among endogenous and exogenous comparative advantages in technology, endowments, and transaction efficiencies. D. Yang (2001) and G. Li (2001) have applied inframarginal analysis to investigate the relationship between international trade, foreign direct investment, and the network size of division of labour.

Liu and Yang (2000), Sun (2000), and Zhang (2000, 2001) have formalized the theory of irrelevance of the size of the firm and found empirical evidence in support of this theory.

Inframarginal analysis of externality, public goods, and endogenous transaction costs (see Chu and Wang 1998; Y.-K. Ng and S. Ng, 2001a, b; and Ng and Yang 2000) have introduced externalities into models of endogenous specialization to investigate effects of externalities on the extent of the market and network size of division of labour. Yang (2000) and Yang and Yeh (2002) have introduced moral hazard into a model of endogenous specialization to investigate effects of the endogenous transaction costs caused by moral hazard on the extent of the market and network size of division of labour. Yang and Zhao (2003) in this volume use several game models to investigate interplays among endogenous and exogenous transaction costs caused by bargaining and network size of division labour. All of the models can predict concurrent increases in endogenous transaction costs, aggregate productivity, and the wealth of a nation as consequences of different patterns of evolution in the division of labour.

Yang (2000) absorbs recent criticisms of Hart's theory of incomplete contract by Maskin, Milgrom, and Homstrom. This paper introduces the concept of two-sided moral hazard into the Yang–Ng model of endogenous specialization and endogenous emergence of the firm. This model saves the essential story in the Grossman–Hart–Moore model by absorbing technical substance into the Maskin critique.

Fang and Zhu (1999), Yao (forthcoming), Sachs, Woo, and Yang (2001), and Li, Smyth, and Yao (forthcoming) report recent research on inframarginal analysis of transitional economics. They use models of endogenous specialization to analyse political economics, implicit and explicit corruption, and other issues in economic transition.

Li's paper (2001) and Heling Shi's chapter in this volume report recent research on inframarginal analysis of e-business and the Internet.

Liu and Yang (2001) and Li (2001) report recent research on formal equilibrium models and inframarginal analysis of the economics of the state.

Cheng (1998, 1999) reports recent research on the inframarginal analysis of monetary theory.

Yang (1999) reports recent research on the inframarginal analysis of the theory of capital and investment.

Sun and Yang (2000) report recent research on the inframarginal analysis of theory of urbanization which generates a rival prediction against the Fujita–Krugman type models of urbanization. The Sun–Yang model predicts that either positive or negative correlation between degree of urbanization, degree of industrialization, average size of firms, and aggregate productivity (or per capita real income) is possible, while the Fujita–Krugman model predicts a monotonically positive correlation between the variables.

Du (2003) reports recent research on the inframarginal analysis of business cycles. He has absorbed criticism of an earlier model of endogenous business cycles, endogenous growth, and endogenous evolution of division of labour by Blanchard, who claims that business cycles can be smoothed out by overlapping generations in a model of endogenous specialization and endogenous business cycles.

I am sure that this brief review of recent research of the scope of inframarginal analysis has overlooked many ongoing research projects. I have yet to be able to read several recent papers and to conduct a thorough search of ongoing PhD and masters theses and working papers in this literature. From e-mail messages that I have received, I understand that many such research projects are on going.

4 Assessment, challenges, and criticisms

In this section, I shall first outline major affirmative comments on the papers in the literature of inframarginal analysis of network of division of labour. I will then outline major challenges against and criticisms of the literature.

4.1 Major comments on literature review papers and general comments on this literature

James Buchanan's comments on Yang and S. Ng (1998): 'The paper is very important. The paper will be very informative to economists, regardless of their particular interests. ... The theme concerning the difference between economies of scale and specialisation of labour gives a new slant to a lot of the literature, and especially as the authors relate this to Marshall's influence in getting economists off the Smithian track' (Buchanan, 1998). Another referee of the paper (see Jeff Borland in K. Arrow et al., 1998) indicates:

> 'The paper is divided into three main sections. The first part reviews research on specialisation from the time of Adam Smith through to the publication of Samuelson's economic principles' text (1948). The second part provides a brief overview of models of specialisation which derive from neoclassical trade theory or are part of what has come to be known as the "new" trade or growth theory. The key identifying characteristic of these models is that changes in the division of labour are represented through changes in the number of goods in the economy. In the third part of the paper an extensive introduction to a new class of models of specialisation – of which Xiaokai Yang has been one of the pioneers – is presented. The distinguishing feature of this type of model is that changes in the division of labour are represented both in the number of goods in the economy and in individuals' level of specialisation in

production activities. Perhaps the best test of a survey is to ask – after reading it – whether there is a sufficiently substantial literature to warrant a survey. To both these questions the answer after reading Yang and Ng's paper would have to be resoundingly in the positive. The range of issues where specialisation appears to be relevant does not make it hard to accept Houthakker's (1956, p. 182) assertion that "there is hardly any part of economics that would not be advanced by a further analysis of specialisation.

Representative comments on the literature are Sherwin Rosen, Donald Smythe and Avner Ben-Ner's comments on Yang and Ng's book (1993). Rosen regards the book as 'First rate' (see a report of Professor A. Sinclair). Nobel prize nominee Fischer Black regarded the book as 'a brilliant book' (Black's letter to Ng and Yang). He stated (*Exploring General Equilibrium* (1995), pp. 255–6):

> Yang and Ng (1993) model growth as a process of increasing specialisation through learning about efficient ways to organize production and about specific production processes. Specialisation and roundabout production add to production efficiency by increasing transportation and bargaining costs. Comparative advantage is acquired, and it works between countries and within countries in the same way. Firms increase efficiency by reducing transaction costs. Contracting costs imply an optimal degree of vagueness in property rights; even many 'externalities' are endogenous and optimal. Money and credit are essential after specialisation reaches a certain point, but do not affect the evolution of the real economy. Even business cycles and unemployment are endogenous and optimal. All this is consistent with a general equilibrium approach to growth and business cycles...

Professor Donald Smythe, in his review of the book (*Journal of Economic Literature*, 1994, Vol. 32, pp. 691–2), states:

> This is an ambitious book. Although its authors claim their objective is merely to increase the variety of microeconomic frameworks, it ranges across topics in trade and growth, urban economics, comparative systems, industrial organization, and even macroeconomics. It argues for a complete reorientation of microeconomics away from problems of resource allocation toward problems of economic organization. ... This is an interesting and original book. Its motivation is sound, and its fundamental insights are compelling. Professors Yang and Ng have provided us with a refreshing new approach to microeconomics, one that has the potential to address many issues that have long resisted formal treatments.

Professor Avner Ben-Ner in his review of the book (*Journal of Institutional and Theoretical Economics*, 1995, vol. 151, pp. 571–2) states:

> This book represents a veritable technical and intellectual *tour de force*. Working their way up from a limited set of assumptions, the authors seek to provide a theoretical explanation for many economic phenomena; from the endogenous emergence of firms, to urbanization, to patterns of international trade, to the emergence of money, to the evolution of property rights, to transition in former communist countries, and much more. In addition, the authors attempt to test empirically some aspects of this theory. The book accomplishes many of these ambitious goals ... Readers will benefit from reading this book because it deals competently and in novel ways with core issues of economic organization. The authors skilfully model situations that other economists have found untractable, and show some of the best uses for economic theory.

An early referee report recognizes that the literature 'develops the concepts of competitive equilibrium and Pareto optimum in relation, not to resource allocation within a market structure, but to the development of market structures'.

In contrast to some referees' view that the implication of transaction efficiency for the division of labour is a tautology, a referee states:

> The authors observe that increased transaction efficiency (lower costs per unit traded) can actually result in higher total transaction costs, since production becomes more specialized. Of course these higher costs are outweighed by the increased production efficiency. This is worth emphasizing, since it contrasts with the literature that emphasizes the reduction in resources used in transacting associated with 'introducing money'. In fact, a short numerical illustration of the levels of per capita utility and total transaction costs attained for specific production function parameters and various levels of transaction efficiency could emphasize this central theme: that the main gains from monetization come not from reduction in resources spent on transacting, but rather come from the more efficient structure of production that is induced.

In summary, recently rapid development of the literature of inframarginal analysis of network of division of labour seems to have satisfactorily absorbed Stigler's following criticism of mainstream economics. Stigler (1976) writes:

> The last of Smith's regrettable failures is one for which he is overwhelmingly famous – the division of labour. How can it be that the famous opening chapters of his book, and the pin factory he gave immortality,

> can be considered a failure? Are they not cited as often as any passages in all economics? Indeed, over the generations they are. The failure is different: almost no one used or now uses the theory of division of labour, for the excellent reason that there is scarcely such a theory. ... there is no standard, operable theory to describe what Smith argued to be the mainspring of economic progress. Smith gave the division of labour an immensely convincing presentation – it seems to me as persuasive a case for the power of specialisation today as it appeared to Smith. Yet there is no evidence, so far as I know, of any serious advance in the theory of the subject since his time, and specialisation is not an integral part of the modern theory of production. (*Journal of Political Economy*, 1976, vol. 84, pp. 1209–10)

4.2 Comments on inframarginal analysis of the theory of the firm

The model of Yang and Ng (1995) is regarded by a referee as 'to capture a number of the arguments for the existence of firms, including (i) the reduction of transactions costs, (ii) division of labour (increasing returns to specialisation), (iii) substituting factor for product markets, (iv) replacing a market for knowledge and managerial intangibles with a market in commodities'. The paper is considered by the referee as to 'formulate and demonstrate consistency of a model with these characteristics'. The referees regard the strand of the literature as 'a small, but rapidly growing, literature that aims at placing the theory of economic organization in the context of the evolution of the division of labour, using formal methods and choosing a general equilibrium/maximization point of departure'.

4.3 Comments on inframarginal analysis of urban economics

A referee of Yang and Rice (1994) states: 'Yang and Rice present a nice model which explains the development of cities on the basis of the tradeoff between transactions costs and goods specific increasing returns in production ... I like the basic idea of the paper. As the authors claim, this is the first paper to develop a full model of the emergence of cities due to a reduction in transactions costs, combined with scale economics. Broadly speaking, the economic mechanism of the paper rings true.' Another referee states: 'The paper presents a general equilibrium model which explains the emergence of urban concentrations as transaction costs of trade decline. The driving force is the economies of scale associated with a division of labour.' It is interesting that the referee notes the difference between this literature and models of urbanization based on economies of scale. He states as follows:

> The paper is similar in some respects to the recent works of Krugman on the formation of cities while differing in some others. Both are concerned with explaining the emergence of urban concentrations and in

both, economies of scale, transport costs, and exogenous immovable rural sector play a key role. However, the two approaches differ from one another in the specification of the economies of scale. In Krugman, these economies are realized within the firm, in Yang and Rice, these economies result from the division of labour.

4.4 Comments on the inframarginal analysis of development economics and endogenous growth

The referee of Yang (1990) states: 'This paper follows an approach that is quite original. The author assumes that increasing returns are present at the level of the individual but that these do not extend to collections of individuals. Thus, for each individual there is a productive advantage to specialisation in a single task, but there is no tendency for firms to become arbitrarily large. The resulting equilibrium is essentially one with competition, but with specialisation in production. What makes this paper different from papers that simply start from an assignment of workers to different specialized tasks is that the specialisation is an endogenous outcome of the model. Thus, it can consider the determinants of the degree of specialisation.' Edward Schuh, in his Fellow's Address in 1991 Annual Meeting of American Agricultural Economics Association (p. 13), assesses Yang and Borland's paper (1991) as follows.

> Contrary to models which exogenously fix the level of specialisation of an individual agent, the Yang–Borland model can explain why an economy evolves from autarky to a state in which there is a highly developed division of labour between individuals in a firm, between firms, and between countries. Moreover, the evolution of the division of labour they examine enlarges the extent of the market, speeds up the accumulation of human capital, and raises trade dependence and endogenous comparative advantage.

The referees for the *Journal of Political Economy* state:

> This paper develops a model of economic growth and labour specialisation that is capable of generating a pattern of evolution from autarky to labour specialisation. I found many aspects of the paper innovative ... Understanding the economics of the division of labour is certainly important. This paper presents a structure where this division changes through time. It is a nice feature since we can explore what variables speed or retard the rate at which economies develop. Another interesting feature is that population is held fixed in the model. Division of labour is driven by forces other than population change. In most of the static models of division of labour, population is the key variable.

A *QJE* referee states that: 'The present paper attempts to model changes in economic organization by highlighting the tension between the dynamic increasing returns attainable with the division of labour and the increased transactions costs that specialized individuals must incur. I find the central theme of the paper interesting and, to the best of my knowledge, original.' Another referee for the *International Economic Review* states that: 'This paper is a promising combination of two different forms of increasing returns. The first, which he labels increasing returns to specialisation, is a static effect. The second is a more familiar form of learning by doing. The essence of the argument is as follows. Depending on the parameters of the economy, the static model can lead to different configurations of trade and specialisation because of a tradeoff between the gains from specialisation and the costs of executing trades in the market. By imposing a form of learning by doing in a dynamic model, the author can consider the possibility of evolution in the structure of the economy, for example from one with autarky, to one with trade between individuals who specialize in different goods.'

A referee of Shi and Yang (1995) states:

> This paper presents a simple general equilibrium model with economies of specialisation and transactions costs. The individual agents make decisions simultaneously as consumers and producers. The model is basically static but it is capable of explaining a wide variety of phenomena associated with the industrialization process. The paper itself is original, provocative, and technically competent.

Two *QJE* referees of the paper mentioned:

> This is a very interesting and promising line of research. The use of corner equilibria in conjunction with increasing returns seems to me capture important aspects of the economy ... This paper presents a general equilibrium model to explain several concurrent phenomena in the industrialization process: an increase in productivity, an increase in trade, an increase in the roundaboutness in production, and an increase in division of labour. The most innovative feature of the model is to allow various production configurations. The model is creative and interesting, and the analysis is done very nicely.

An *AER* referee states:

> The paper sets up an interesting model in which the presence of increasing returns technologies and various possibilities for how intermediate goods and labour can be used to produce final output yields a model that can speak to the issue of how improvements in

transactions technologies can lead to economic development. More importantly, the model explicitly examines how the division of labour changes with development and actually identifies different aspects of the division of labour: the level of specialisation of individuals, the degree of diversity of professions, and the degree of roundaboutness in production.

4.5 Comments on the inframarginal analysis of trade theory

Smythe's review of Yang and Ng's book indicates

> The tradeoff between economies of specialisation and transaction costs is the recurring theme. And an analysis of how the tradeoff changes as transaction efficiency improves provides the basis for understanding the process of evolution within many of the models. To give some idea of the scope, readers will find, among many other contributions, an endogenous theory of international trade, a formalization of Coase's theory of the firm, and a theory of technological change based on the evolution of the division of labour.

The referees of Yang (1996) state: The main contribution of the paper is as follows. It adopts a simple formal model that considers the factors such as transaction costs and learning efficiency in the determination of supply and demand of commodities. This contrasts sharply with traditional (for example, Marshall's) view on supply-demand. The results obtained also have interesting applications, providing insightful explanations on a number of phenomena (for instance, trading pattern, economic growth) in international trade.

4.6 Comments on the inframarginal analysis of the economics of property rights and transaction costs

A referee of Yang and Wills (1990) writes, 'The accomplishment of this paper is the formal derivation of a relationship between the extent of private property rights and the gains from specialisation. Since the days of Adam Smith, economists have argued that specialisation in production is welfare enhancing. Other economists have pointed out that specialisation is privately profitable only to the degree that property rights are well defined and enforced. The author of this paper shows, in a fairly abstract general equilibrium model, that stronger property rights require a greater expenditure of resources on property right enforcement. These same resources, however, could have been used to produce more goods as a result of economies of specialisation. But increased specialisation implies more transactions and a greater probability that rights will be violated. Thus, a trade off between property protection and gains from specialisation exists. This idea is not new, but this paper is one of the few attempts to model formally the idea. The paper provides a starting point for others on this important topic – the economics of property rights.'

> Professor Avner Ben-Ner in his review on Yang and Ng (1993) states: The models developed in this book focus on the relationship between specialisation and transaction costs and the associated decisions of individuals regarding what to produce and what to buy. Thus this book by Yang and Ng belongs to the New Institutional Economics, especially to the literature that focuses on transaction costs and the boundaries between firms and markets. These authors' emphasis on specialisation gives their framework a unique flavour which distinguishes them from Coase, Williamson and others. The endogenization of the choice of specialisation and therefore of what to produce and what to buy sets Yang and Ng apart from much of the industrial organization and organizational economics literature, from which the authors draw many of their modelling techniques.

4.7 Comments on the inframarginal analysis of the theory of capital

Referees of Yang (1999) point out that 'Contrary to "old" and "new" neoclassical growth theories, investment in physical and human capital or in the innovation of new products do no automatically increase future productivity "if the investment were not used to develop the right level and pattern of division of labour". Yang sets out to formalize the connection between the division of labour and capital as emphasized by Smith (1776) and Young (1928) within a modern intertemporal general equilibrium approach with corner solutions. They, as consumer-producers, choose endogenously between self-production of food (tractors) and buying these goods from specialized producers. Specialization allows productivity enhancing learning by doing but needs saving (investment) in food to provide the means of consumption for the tractor producer. The author's work alone and in collaboration with others (Borland and Yang 1991; Yang and Ng, 1993) is innovative and important. Contrary to the Hicks–Arrow–Debreu version of intertemporal general equilibrium, there is no complete (exogenous) specialization between households and firms but in Yang's approach the consumer-producer is the basic economic unit which chooses – dependent on transaction costs, the economies of specialization and roundaboutness and fixed learning costs of specialized production – the efficient degree of division of labour. It enriches in an interesting and substantially important way the range of the core of modern economic theory (optimization and market clearing). Basic classical economic insights such as the dependence of the division of labour on the extent of the market and the reverse (Young, 1928) and the role of savings and capital investment in consumer goods to make possible the specialization on producing learning costs intensive means of production can be reconstructed within a unique theoretical approach.'

4.8 Comments on the inframarginal analysis of monetary theory

The referees of chapter 17 of Yang and Ng (1993) and Cheng (1999) state: in this paper, a model is constructed to capture the relationship between specialization in production and monetary exchange ... If transactions costs are sufficiently large relative to the gains from exploiting economies of scale, then autarky results. However, if transactions costs are low enough, then an equilibrium can be supported where markets open in sequence, and exchange is supported using credit. I like the idea here very much. Existing explicit treatments of the role of money, for example Kiyotaki and Wright (1989), simply takes specialization as given. There are many interesting coordination issues which could be studied in the context of a model where there is joint determination of specialization and monetary arrangements ... This paper presents a model within which it is possible to determine endogenously the patterns of production and consumption that is specialization and at the same time to analyse the interaction between specialization and the use of money. This is a very interesting set of questions, that many economists have been discussing and debating for years, and I think it is well worth attempting to provide formal models that bear on these issues. I think that the paper makes a contribution ... This paper contributes to the recent literature on the economic factors which give rise to monetary exchange. In particular, it focuses on the importance of the specialization of labour in a multi-stage production process involving both intermediate goods and a final consumption good. The paper develops a model in which all agents are ex ante identical and specialization is endogenous rather than exogenously imposed. This is contrasted with other works which impose specialization. With this, the paper establishes a positive relationship between returns to specialization/transaction efficiency and division of labour. Given partial or full specialization, there will be no 'double coincidence' of supply and demand in bilateral trades. Thus there is a role for commodity and fiat money. In the case of complete division of labour, an enforceable credit system leads to fiat money equilibria and no-enforceability leads to commodity money equilibria. It is also shown that the introduction of fiat money improves productivity and improves transactions efficiency. In solving the model, the authors employ a neoclassical structure in determining number of agents specializing in a particular productive activity and relative prices. They impose both market clearing and utility equalisation. This is an innovative methodology which circumvents the more difficult bilateral bargaining problems which persist in search theoretic models of money. This is a timely paper given the current interest in developing explicit microfoundations of money as a medium of exchange. Its primary contribution is not in identifying what factors are important in determining the emergence of money but rather the mechanism by which they provide a role of money. They show that a multi stage production process leads to endogenous specialization and division of labour which then naturally leads to a role for money. Both commodity and fiat money demand are thus linked to fundamentals such as transaction efficiency and economies of specialization through the individuals decision of specialization instead of imposing these decisions exogenously. They also show that one of the factors that determine which commodity will emerge as money depends upon the stage of the good in the production process.

4.9 Comments on the inframarginal analysis of the theory of business cycles and unemployment

A referee of chapter 18 of Yang and Ng (1993) states that 'This work presents a dynamic general equilibrium model that can generate business cycles with unemployment. The structure of the economy is such that business cycles with unemployment can result from the actions of utility maximizing agents in the economy. Hence they can be interpreted as an evidence of market success instead of market failure. The paper shows that if the framework with consumer-producers, economies of specialization and transactions costs developed by Yang (1991) and Yang and Borland (1991) is modified to allow for job shifting costs and durable producer goods, then the framework will be able to generate a dynamic equilibrium with business cycles and unemployment. Moreover, this equilibrium will be Pareto superior to that with no unemployment.' Another referee states: 'The method of computing the equilibrium is innovative. It involves a global comparison of corner solutions instead of a local and marginal approach.'

4.10 Comments on theoretical foundation of the inframarginal analysis of division of labour

A referee of Sun, Yang, and Yao (1999) states as follows: This paper aims at providing an analytical framework for the study of the specialization and the division of labour in a general equilibrium model with increasing returns and transaction costs. The equilibrium network of impersonal interactions is obtained endogenously in a world in which households are both consumers and producers. A model is provided in which the existence of an efficient equilibrium network is shown to exist. The question addressed here is certainly interesting and connects with the classical tradition about the division of labour and the extent of the markets. The approach followed to analyse this problem is perfectly right, when the authors avoid dissociating the agents in their roles as consumer and producers. The two theorems that show the existence and the efficiency of an equilibrium are correct ... The question addressed here is interesting and the approach of consumers-producers agents pertinent. Finding that even with identical agents a complex network of interactions may emerge is a relevant step forward in this line of research.

The main criticisms of the models in the literature in the early 1990s are as follows.

1. The models are too idiosyncratic and too non-mainstream, so that the referee does not know which literature the paper can be located to. This is a very strategic way to reject new ideas that the referee is unfamiliar with or does not like. But it also indirectly acknowledges the originality of the work. This kind of complaint has been silenced since the middle of the 1990s when several referees acknowledged the 'emerging literature' and 'rapidly growing literature'.
2. Some reviewers of models without firms complain that this kind of models is relevant only to pre-industrialization economies. The publication of several papers on the institution of the firm and endogenous number of links and number of producer goods in roundabout production chain in this literature has silenced such complaints. It becomes plausible that it is the advantage of this kind of model that it can explain the emergence and evolution of the institution of the firm and emergence of new goods as *ex post* production functions (*ex post* means they can be seen in equilibrium only after individuals have made decisions) discontinuously jumps between various structures of division of labour in response to shifts of parameter values between parameter subspaces which demarcate the structures. New *ex post* production function for a new type of the firm or a new type of good may emerge from such inframarginal jumps.
3. Some referees complained that transaction costs are exogenous in this kind of models. More than ten papers have incorporated endogenous transaction costs (distortions caused by bargaining power, moral hazard, adverse selection, externality, and other opportunisms) into the models in response to such legitimate complaints (Chu, 1997, Chu and Wang, 1998; Lio, 1997, 1998; Yang, 2000; Yang and Yeh, 2002; Fang and Zhu, 1999; Ng and Yang, 2000; Yang and Zhao, 2000; Liu and Yang, 2001). These models have shown that interesting tradeoffs exist between endogenous transaction costs, exogenous transaction costs, and positive network effects of division of labour on aggregate productivity which can be used to tell many relevant real business stories that standard neoclassical models cannot explain. For instance, several of the models predict concurrent increases in productivity, level of division of labour, and endogenous transaction costs in response to emergence of insurance or to improvements in transportation efficiency.
4. Several referees claim that all stories in this literature can be told by general equilibrium models with global economies of scale (Dixit and Ethier type of models of monopolistic competition). One may claim that this kind of complaint does not constitute a legitimate

challenge to the new literature. If we respect the goodwill of the referees, we can see that it is not easy to appreciate the distinction between the notion of network effects of division of labour and economies of scale of a firm. Undoubtedly, the algebra of inframarginal analysis is very tedious and cumbersome (so many corner solutions and even much more combinations of corner solutions which constitute possible market structures must be counted). Many economists are understandably reluctant to invest in such a risky business with high investment costs. Most referees and editors are not familiar with the new literature. Most editors of leading journals send papers to writers in the rival literature for reviewing. Only a few editors send papers of this type of literature to major contributors to this selfsame literature.

5. Some referees cannot accept the assumption that a person's labour is not allowed to be an input into another person's production function or that many workers' labour is not allowed to be pooled into the production function of the firm. In this literature, when a person founds a firm, she will hire an employee's production function, rather than hire his labour. Much clearer justification for such an assumption is needed. With this specific feature, aggregate production sets might not be convex even if individuals' production sets are convex. Not only do strong aggregation results of production decisions, which hold in an Arrow–Debreu model, not hold here, but also the marginal productivity principle no longer holds as well.

Recent empirical research in this literature may address the scepticism found in (4). The Dixit-type models with global economies of scale and monopolistic competition predict several types of scale effects: (a) a positive correlation between population size, productivity, and the average size of firms; (b) a positive correlation between total factor productivity or per capita real income and average size of firms; (c) a positive correlation between the degree of urbanization and the average size of firms; (d) a positive correlation between the degree of industrialization and the average size of firms. All the postulated positive correlations have been conclusively rejected by empirical evidence (Liu and Yang, 2000; Murakami, Liu and Otsuka, 1996; Zhang, 2000, 2001; National Research Council, 1986; Dasgupta, 1995). Recently common business practice of downsizing, outsourcing, disintegration, contracting out, and franchising (Hart, 1995; Liu and Yang, 2000) rejects the scale effects too. The evidence is consistent with the theory of irrelevance of the size of the firm formalized in the literature of endogenous specialization (Liu and Yang, 2000; Sun, 2000). This theory states that the average size of firms and productivity (or per capita real income) increase together if division of labour develops within each firm, and that the average size of firms decreases and productivity goes up if division of labour develops among firms.

Also, neoclassical saving fundamentalism (a positive correlation between investment or saving rate and growth rate) has been conclusively rejected by empirical evidence provided by Jones (1995a,b). Jones' empirical evidence is consistent with the model of investment in the literature of endogenous specialisation (Yang, 1999; Borland and Yang, 1991). In addition, the positive correlation between income share of transaction cost, per capita real income, and level of division of labour, predicted by models in the literature of endogenous specialisation is supported by empirical evidence (North, 1985). The positive correlation between degree of commercialisation, per capita real income, and transaction efficiency in specifying and enforcing property rights, predicted by the models in the literature of endogenous specialisation has been supported by empirical evidence (Yang, Wang, and Wills, 1992). More empirical evidence supports the prediction of the literature about positive correlation between development performance and an index of institution quality that affects trading efficiency (Barro, 1997; North, 1958; North and Weingast, 1989; Gallup and Sachs, 1998; Sachs and Warner, 1995; Easton and Walker, 1997; Gwartney, Lawson and Block, 1996; Frye and Shleifer, 1997; Yang, Wang, and Wills, 1992).

5 Teaching and textbooks

Two textbooks (Yang, 2001, 2003) that teach the inframarginal analysis of general increasing returns and network effects of division of labour are intended to provide a systematic and overarching pedagogical vehicle to educators. The books not only provide a comprehensive review of this new literature, comparing it with related branches of mainstream economics, but also teach inframarginal analysis step by step. Several workshops have been organized to teach inframarginal analysis of network of division of labour in the United States, China, Taiwan, and Australia. One of the workshops that is currently organized by James Buchanan invites leading mainstream economists as discussants of key lectures which contribute to the literature of inframarginal analysis of network of division of labour. Their critical discussion of the lectures exposes students to challenging debates, criticisms and defences of new ideas. This may resurrect the spirit of classical mainstream economics in a modern body of new mainstream economics.

Assessment reports of the textbooks recognize them as 'doing a nice job of classifying and specifying the foundation for a new pedagogical way of thinking about economics'. A reviewer states: The strength of the work is its intellectual quality, its breadth, its connection of current ideas with those in the history of thought, and its logical organization. It is truly impressive. There are no comparable books. He is establishing a whole new field. Yes, I do foresee a growing interest in new classical economics – I think it may well be the wave of the future.' Another reviewer is not so positive. He states: 'This is an interesting book which I enjoyed reading. It carries the message that the "new classical economics" is a better description of our environment than the neoclassical economics. The arguments are presented clearly, persuasively and in an interesting way. I would recommend this book to any good economics library and, no doubt, it will be acquired by many economists and economics teachers. In short, the book is quite revolutionary and has a high intellectual quality but even with growing interest in new classical economics I do not foresee its taking off in the near future.' One of the reviewers claims that, 'the book is in some ways a remarkable tour de force. I feel that such an overarching point of view lends a greater sense of purpose and unity to the book.'

Other reviewers also recognize 'the most outstanding feature of the ms. is its nice theoretical coherence' and 'the real value of this text is that it brings considerable analytic machinery to bear on important problems.'

More textbooks for undergraduate students, with only limited mathematics, should be developed. Graphical approaches to inframarginal analysis of network of the division of labour is more intuitive and easier to teach than traditional demand and supply curves in marginal analysis of resource allocation, since topological properties of economic organisms are closely related to graphical properties of economic organisms, which are much easier to describe using graphs than non-topological properties of economic organisms (such as quantities of goods).

There are many ongoing PhD dissertations and master theses related to the literature of the inframarginal analysis of network of the division of labour in Australian, American, Chinese, and Taiwanese universities. A much better and more effective international teaching network and greater facilities are badly needed for coordinating the teaching and graduate research programs in this field. The quality of some dissertations and theses are not very high since very little timely and qualified supervision is available to many students in this field. The Research Centre of Increasing Returns and Economic Organization at Monash University has been set up to organize regular international workshops and conferences and to develop core curriculum and regular teaching programs. The Society of Inframarginal Economics was set up in 2002. This society has set up a refereed journal *Division of Labor and Transaction Costs – A Journal of the Society of Inframarginal Economics* and a book series *Increasing Returns and Inframarginal Economics*, both published by the World Scientific Publishing Company. The book series includes three subseries: a research monograph series, a graduate and undergraduate textbook series, and a readings and paper collection series. A specialized website www.inframarginal.com was set up in 2000 which provides updated information on all programs and projects related to the new literature.

References

Aumann, Robert J. (1997) 'Rationality and Bounded Rationality', *Games & Economic Behavior*, 21, 2–14.

Barro, R. (1997) *Determinants of Economic Growth* (Cambridge, MA: MIT Press).

Black, F. (1995) *Exploring General Equilibrium* (MIT Press).

Borland, Jeff (1998) 'Comments on Xiaokai Yang and Siang Ng's chapter 'Specialization and Division of Labor: a Survey', in K. Arrow, Y.-K. Ng, and Xiaokai Yang (eds), *Increasing Returns and Economic Analysis* (London, Macmillan).

Borland, J. and Yang, X. (1995) 'Specialization, Product Development, Evolution of the Institution of the Firm, and Economic Growth', *Journal of Evolutionary Economics*, 5, 19–42.

Borland, J. and Yang, X. (1992b) 'Specialization and a New Approach to Economic Organization and Growth', *American Economic Review*, 82, 386–91.

Borland, J. and Yang, X. (1995) 'Specialization, Product Development, Evolution of the Institution of the Firm, and Economic Growth', *Journal of Evolutionary Economics*, 5, 19–42.

Buchanan, James (1998) 'Comments on Xiaokai Yang and Siang Ng's chapter "Specialization and Division of Labor: a Survey" ' in K. Arrow, Y.-K. Ng and Xiaokai Yang (eds), *Increasing Returns and Economic Analysis* (London: Macmillan).

Buchanan, J. (1994) 'The Return to Increasing Returns,' in J. Buchanan and Y. Yoon, (eds), *The Return to Increasing Returns* (Ann Arbor: The University of Michigan Press).

Buchanan, James M. and Stubblebine, W. Craig (1962) 'Externality', *Economica*, 29, 371–84.

Buchanan, J. and Yoon, Y. (eds) *The Return to Increasing Returns* (Ann Arbor: The University of Michigan Press).

Cheng, W. (1998) 'Specialization and the Emergence and the Value of Money', in K. Arrow, Y.-K. Ng, and X. Yang (eds), *Increasing Returns and Economic Analysis* (London: Macmillan).

Cheng, W. (1999) 'Division of Labor, Money, and Economic Progress', *Review of Development Economics*, 3, 354–67.

Cheng, W., Sachs J. an Yang, X. (1999) 'An Inframarginal Analysis of the Heckscher–Ohlin Model with Transaction Costs and Technological Comparative Advantage', Harvard Center for International Development Working Paper No. 9.

Cheng, W., Sachs, J. and Yang, X. (2000a) 'An Inframarginal Analysis of the Ricardian Model', *Review of International Economics*, 8, 208–20.

Cheng, W., Sachs, J. and Yang, X. (2000b) 'A General Equilibrium Re-appraisal of the Stolper–Samuelson Theorem', *Journal of Economics*, 66, 1–18.

Cheng, W., Liu, M. and Yang, X. (2000) 'A Ricardo Model with Endogenous Comparative Advantage and Endogenous Trade Policy Regime', *Economic Record*, 76, 172–82.

Chu, C. (1997) 'Productivity, Investment in Infrastructure, and Population Size: Formalizing the Theory of Ester Boserup', *Review of Development Economics*, 1, 294–304.

Chu, C. and Tsai, Y. (1998) 'Productivity, Investment in Infrastructure, and Population Size: Formalizing the Theory of Ester Boserup', in K. Arrow, Y.-K. Ng, and X. Yang (eds), *Increasing Returns and Economic Analysis* (London: Macmillan).

Chu, C. and Wang, C. (1998) 'Economy of Specialization and Diseconomies of Externality', *Journal of Public Economics*. 69, 249–61.

Dasgupta, Partha (1995) 'The Population Problem: Theory and Evidence', *Journal of Economic Literature*, 33, 1879–1902.

Du, J. (2003) 'Endogenous, Efficient Long-run Cyclical Unemployment, Endogenous Long-run Growth, and Division of Labor', *Review of Development Economics*, 7, 266–78.

Dutta, Bhaskar and Mutuswami, S. (1997) 'Stable Networks,' *Journal of Economic Theory*, 76, 322–44.

Easton, Stephen and Michael, Walker (1997) 'Income, Growth, and Economic Freedom', *American Economic Review, Papers and Proceedings*, 87, 328–32.

Fang, Xinghai and Zhu, Tian (1999) 'Institutional Imperfection and Transition Strategies,' *Economic Systems*, 23, 331–48.

Frye, Timothy and Shleifer, Andrei (1997) 'The Invisible Hand and the Grabbing Hand', *American Economic Review, Papers and Proceedings*, 87, 354–8.

Gwartney, J., Lawson, R., and Block, W. (1996) *Economic Freedom of the World: 1975–1995.* (Vancouver, BC: Fraser Institute).

Gwartney, J. and Lawson, R. (1997) *Economic Freedom of the World: 1997 Annual Report* (Vancouver, BC: Fraser Institute).

Hadley, G. (1964) *Nonlinear and Dynamic Programming* (Reading: Addison-Wesley).

Hart, O. (1995) *Firms, Contracts, and Financial Structure* (Oxford: Clarendon Press).

Hildenbrand, Werner (1974) *Core and Equilibria of a Large Economy* (Princeton, NJ: Princeton University Press).

Katz, M. and Shapiro, C. (1985) 'Network Externalities, Competition, and Compatibility', *American Economic Review*, 75, 424–40.

Katz, M. and Shapiro, C. (1986) 'Technology Adoption in the Presence of Network Externalities', *Journal of Political Economy*, 94, 822–41.

Jackson, M. and Wolinsky, A. (1996) 'A Strategic Model of Social and Economic Networks', *Journal of Economic Theory*, 71, 44–74.

Jones, C.I. (1995a) 'Time Series Tests of Endogenous Growth Models', *Quarterly Journal of Economics*, 110, 695–525.

Jones, C.I. (1995b) 'R & D-Based Models of Economic Growth', *Journal of Political Economy*, 103, 759–784.

Li, C. and Sun, G. (1998) 'A Note on the Measurement of the Extent of Division of Labor for Simple Production Economies', Discussion Paper, Department of Economics, Monash University.

Li, Guoqiang (2001) 'The Emergence of the Multinational Enterprise – A Model Formalizing Dunning's Eclectic Paradigm'. A paper presented in International Symposium of Economics of e-Commerce and Networking Decisions, at Monash University.

Li, Ke, R. Smyth and S. Yao (forthcoming) 'Institionalized Corruption and Privilege in China's Socialist Market Economy: a General Equilibrium Analysis', *Pacific Economic Review*.

Li, Ke, (2001) 'A General Equilibrium Analysis of the Division of Labour: Violation and Enforcement of Property Rights, Impersonal Networking Decisions and Bundling Sale', PhD Thesis, Department of Economics, Monash University.

Lio, M. (1996) 'Three Assays on Increasing Returns and Specialization: a Contribution to New Classical Microeconomic Approach', PhD Dissertation, Department of Economics, the National Taiwan University.

Lio, M. (1998) 'Uncertainty, Insurance, and Division of Labor', *Review of Development Economics*, 2, 76–86.

Liu, Meng-Chun (2001) 'Two Approaches to International Trade, Development and Import Protection', PhD Dissertation, Department of Economics, Monash University.

Liu, Pak-Wai and Yang, Xiaokai (2000) 'The Theory of Irrelevance of the Size of the Firm', *Journal of Economic Behavior and Organization*, 42, 145–65.

Liu, Wai-Man, and Yang Xiaokai, (2001) 'Good Capitalism versus Bad Capitalism: Effects of Political Monopoly of the Ruling Elite on the Extent of the Market, Income Distribution, and Development', Department of Economics Discussion Papers, No. 01/01, ISSN 1441–5429, Monash University.

Marshall, Alfred (1890) *Principles of Economics*, 8th edition (New York: Macmillan, 1948).

Murakami, Naoki, Liu, Deqiang, and Otsuka, K. (1996) 'Market Reform, Division of Labor, and Increasing Advantage of Small-scale Enterprises: the Case of the Machine Tool Industry in China', *Journal of Comparative Economics*, 23, 256–77.

National Research Council (1986) *Population Growth and Economic Development: Policy Questions* (Washington, DC: National Academy of Sciences Press).

Ng, S. (1995) 'Economic Openness and Growth', PhD dissertation, Department of Economics, Monash University.

Ng, Yew-Kwang and Ng Siang, (2001a) 'Specialization, Network Externalities, and Work Ethics', Working Paper, Department of Economics, Monash University.

Ng, Yew-Kwang and Ng Siang, (2001b) 'Why It May Be Desirable to Encourage Improvements in Transaction Efficiency: Economies of Specialization and Network Externalities', Working Paper, Department of Economics, Monash University.

Ng, Y.-K. and Yang, X. (2000) 'Effects of Taxation on the Extent of the Market and Network Size of Division of Labor', Working Paper, Department of Economics, Monash University.

Ng, Y.-K. and Yang, X. (1997) 'Specialization, Information, and Growth: a Sequential Equilibrium Analysis', *Review of Development Economics*, 1, 257–74.

North, Douglass (1958) 'Ocean Freight Rates and Economic Development', *Journal of Economic History*, 18, 537–55.

North, D. (1986) 'Measuring the Transaction Sector in the American Economy', in S. Eugerman and R. Gallman (eds), *Long Term Trends in the American Economy* (Chicago: University of Chicago Press).

North, Douglass and Weingast, Barry (1989) 'Constitutions and Commitment: the Evolution of Institutions Governing Public Choice in Seventeenth-Century England', *Journal of Economic History*, XLIX, 803–32.

Petty, William (1671) *Political Arithmetics*, in C. H. Hull (ed.), *Economic Writings of Sir. William Petty*, reissued (New York: Augustus M. Kelley, 1963).

Petty, William (1683) *Another Essay on Political Arithmetics*, in C. H. Hull (ed.), *Economic Writings of Sir. William Petty*, reissued (New York: Augustus M. Kelley, 1963).

Sachs, J., Yang, X. and Zhang, D. (2000) 'Trade Pattern and Economic Development when Endogenous and Exogenous Comparative Advantages Coexist', *China Economic Review*, 11, 189–209.

Sachs, J., Yang, X. and Zhang, D. (2001) 'Patterns of Trade and Economic Development in the Model of Monopolistic Competition', *Review of Development Economics*, forthcoming.

Sachs, J. and Warner, A. (1995) *Natural Resources and Economic Growth* (Cambridge, MA: Harvard University mimeo) (January).

Sachs, J. Wing Thye Woo, and Xiaokai Yang (2000) 'Economic Reforms and Constitutional Transition', *Annals of Economics and Finance*, 1, 260–74.

Shi, H. and Yang, X. (1995) 'A New Theory of Industrialization' *Journal of Comparative Economics*, 20, 171–89.

Shi, H., and Yang, X. (1995) 'Centralised Hierarchy within a Firm vs. Decentralised Hierarchy in the Market', in K. Arrow, Y.-K. Ng, and X. Yang (eds), *Increasing Returns and Economic Analysis* (London: Macmillan).

Smith, Adam (1776) *An Inquiry into the Nature and Causes of the Wealth of Nations*, reprint, edited by E. Cannan (Chicago: University of Chicago Press, 1976).

Smythe, D. (1994) 'Book Review: Specialization and Economic Organization: a New Classical Microeconomic Framework', *Journal of Economic Literature*, 32, 691–2.

Sun, Guangzhen (1999) 'Increasing Returns, Roundabout Production and Urbanization: a General Equilibrium Analysis of the Division of Labour', PhD Dissertation, Department of Economics, Monash University.

Sun, Guangzhen (2000) 'The Size of the Firm and Social Division of Labour', *Australian Economic Papers*, 39, 263–77.

Sun, Guangzhen (2001) 'A general method for identifying the equilibrium structure of the division of labor', mimeo, Department of Economics, Monash University.

Sun, G. and Lio, M. (1996) 'A General Equilibrium Model Endogenizing the Level of Division of Labor and Variety of Producer Goods', Working Paper, Department of Economics, Monash University.

Sun, G. and Yang, X. (2002) 'Evolution in Division of Labor, Urbanization, and Land Price Differentials between the Urban and Rural Areas', *Australian Economic Papers*, 42, 164–84.

Sun, G., Yang, X, and Yao, S. (1999) 'Theoretical Foundation of Economic Development Based on Networking Decisions in the Competitive Market', Harvard Center for International Development Working Paper No. 17.

Sun, Guang-Zhen, Yang, Xiaokai, and Zhou, Lin (1998) 'General Equilibria in Large Economies with Endogenous Structure of Division of Labor', Working Paper, Department of Economics, Monash University.

Wen, M. (1997) 'Infrastructure and Evolution in Division of Labor', *Review of Development Economics*, 1, 191–206.

Wen, M. (1997) 'Division of Labor in Economic Development', PhD dissertation, Department of Economics, Monash University.

Wen, M. (1998) 'An Analytical Framework of Consumer-Producers, Economies of Specialisation and Transaction Costs', in K. Arrow, Y.-K. Ng and X. Yang (eds), *Increasing Returns and Economic Analysis* (London: Macmillan).

Yang, Dexin (2001) 'Division of Labour and the Emergence of International Trade and Foreign Direct Investment', a paper presented in International Symposium of Economics of e-Commerce and Networking Decisions at Monash University.

Yang, X. (1994) 'Endogenous vs. Exogenous Comparative Advantages and Economies of Specialization vs. Economies of Scale', *Journal of Economics*, 60, 29–54.

Yang, X. (1999) 'The Division of Labor, Investment, and Capital', *Metroeconomica*, 50, 301–24.

Yang, X. (2000) 'Incomplete Contingent Labor Contract, Asymmetric Residual Rights and Authority, and the Theory of the Firm', Seminar Paper, Department of Economics, Monash University

Yang, X. (2001) *Economics: New Classical Versus Neoclassical Frameworks* (Cambridge, MA: Blackwell).

Yang, X. (2003a) *Development Economics: Inframarginal Versus Marginal Analyses* (Cambridge, MA: Blackwell).

Yang, X. (2003b) *Economic Development and the Division of Labor* (Cambridge, MA: Blackwell).

Yang, X. and Borland, J. (1991) 'A Microeconomic Mechanism for Economic Growth', *Journal of Political Economy*, 99, 460–82.

Yang, X. and Ng, Y.-K. (1993) *Specialization and Economic Organization: a New Classical Microeconomic Framework* (Amsterdam: North-Holland).
Yang, X. and Ng, Y.-K. (1995) 'Theory of the Firm and Structure of Residual Rights', *Journal of Economic Behavior and Organization*, 26, 107–28.
Yang, X. and Ng, S. (1998) 'Specialization and Division of Labor: a Survey', in K. Arrow, Y.-K. Ng, and Xiaokai Yang (eds), *Increasing Returns and Economic Analysis* (London: Macmillan).
Yang, X. and Rice, R. (1994) 'An Equilibrium Model Endogenizing the Emergence of a Dual Structure between the Urban and Rural Sectors', *Journal of Urban Economics*, 25, 346–68.
Yang, X. and Shi, H. (1992) 'Specialization and Product Diversity', *American Economic Review*, 82, 392–8.
Yang, X. and Wills, I. (1990) 'A Model Formalizing the Theory of Property Rights', *Journal of Comparative Economics*, 14, 177–98.
Yang, X. and Yeh, Y. (2002) 'A General Equilibrium Model with Endogenous Principal–Agent Relationship', *Australian Economic Papers*, 41, 15–36.
Yang, X., Wang, J., and Wills, I. (1992) 'Economic Growth, Commercialization, and Institutional Changes in Rural China, 1979–1987', *China Economic Review*, 3, 1–37.
Yang, X. and Yao, S. (2001) 'Walrasian Sequential Equilibrium, Bounded Rationality, and Social Experiments', Discussion Paper, Department of Economics, Monash University.
Yang, X. and Zhang, D. (1999) 'International Trade and Income Distribution', Harvard Center for International Development Working Paper No. 18.
Yang, X. and Zhang, D. (2003) 'International Trade and Income Distribution', *Journal of Economics*, 78, 163–90.
Yang, X. and Zhao, Y. (2003) 'Endogenous Transaction Costs and Division of Labour' in Conference Proceedings on Inframarginal Analysis of Networking Decisions and E-commerce.
Yao, S. (2002) 'Walrasian Equilibrium Computation, Network Formation, and the Wen Theorem', *Review of Development Economics*, 6, 415–27.
Young, Allyn (1928) 'Increasing Returns and Economic Progress', *The Economic Journal*, 38, 527–42.
Zhang, J. (1997) 'Evolution in Division of Labour and Macroeconomic Policies', *Review of Development Economics*, 1, 236–45.
Zhang, Yongsheng (2000) 'Irrelevance of the Size of the Firm: Theory and Empirical Evidence', PhD Dissertation, Department of Economics, Renmin University.
Zhang, Yongsheng (2001) 'Scale Effects Versus the Theory of Irrelevance of the Size of the Firm: Empirical Evidence,' a paper presented in International Symposium of Economics of e-Commerce and Networking Decisions, July, at Monash University.
Zhao, Y. (1999) 'Information, Evolution of the Institution of the Firm, and the Optimal Decision Horizon', *Review of Development Economics*, 3, 336–53.

Part II
E-Commerce

4

E-Commerce, Transaction Cost, and the Network of Division of Labour: a Business Perspective

Heling Shi and Hayden Mathysen*

1 Introduction

In the US and other industrialized economies multinational conglomerates continue to dominate the economy. The wave of corporate mergers and consolidations seemingly indicate this trend may continue. Yet evidence exists of another phenomenon that is emerging: large corporate leviathans are participating in a spate of corporate downsizing and vertical disintegration. What adds an element of paradox to this new phenomenon is that it is occurring in an economy that has been booming for three years and expanding for nine. After successive years of economic expansion since 1991, the spate of corporate downsizing remains unabated. The paradoxical incidence of downsizing in an economic boom has been explained away by cyclical factors external to the economy, such as an inflated dollar, an Asian economic downturn and a Russian economic crisis. It is believed that these external factors may have fuelled the intensity of price competition and cost cutting in the domestic economy, and thus have precipitated a wave of downsizing. In early 1998, when cyclical-induced downsizing was highlighted in *Business Week* as the cause, it was supplemented by an explanation that firms *expected* slow profit growth throughout 1998. This supplementary explanation is suggested to reinforce the conjecture that even the *expectation* of cyclical swings was enough to initiate corporate downsizing during an economic boom. Research by Budros (1999) supports this explanation. The attempt by many US companies to enhance organizational efficiency and/or effectiveness through downsizing has been discovered by Budros to be consistent with expectations of lower growth prospects. However, in early 1998, Fortune's Business Confidence Index provided *contradictory evidence* on expectations of growth and business confidence. Despite tremors of an Asian downturn, business confidence remained strong in the early months of 1998.

* Correspondence to: Dr Heling Shi, Department of Economics, Monash University, Clayton, 3168. Australia. e-mail: he-ling.shi@buseco.monash.edu.au

Given the contradictory evidence, can expectations of slower growth satisfactorily explain why US corporations possess a renewed zeal for downsizing? Probably not. While the Asian downturn fuelled expectations of slower profit growth and the Russian crisis dented business confidence in 1998, these concerns were transitory and gradually paled into insignificance when US economic activity did not falter. In 1999, restructuring and downsizing continued apace despite the boom. For instance, layoff announcements were hitting record levels, which is evidence of business restructuring (Melcher, 1999). Moreover, the American Management Association's latest annual survey of nearly 1,200 major companies discovered that in mid-1999 a quarter of respondents said they had actually downsized in the previous twelve months (Koretz, 2000).

The evidence suggests that structural, rather than expectational phenomena are at work, and these phenomena are by no means insignificant. Parallel to the spate of corporate downsizing and vertical disintegration in the US economy, is the emergence of the Internet Revolution. Net-driven growth is accelerating and may well explain the structural transformation in an economy characterized by a continuous wave of corporate downsizing. Not only are new online firms entering the fray, but established brand name companies are also embracing the net. The revolution of the Internet and the emergence of e-commerce have induced companies to rapidly restructure their operations in order to reach new operational efficiencies through their business-to-business commerce over the Internet. The emergence of e-commerce has introduced fundamental and dramatic changes to the way corporations conduct business. For instance, consider the impact of the net on supply and distribution networks. The chief economist at Morgan Stanley Dean Witter, Stephen Roach, calculates that by 2005 the e-commerce combination of business-to-business and business-to-consumer will reduce the labour force in the distribution sector of the economy by 35 per cent. This works out to be marginally more than a one per cent increase in the overall corporate profit share of GDP (Farrell, 2000).

Due to the precipitous decline in transaction costs from internet-based commerce it may be efficient for firms to restructure themselves around e-commerce. The radical transformation in the way business is conducted today entails the fundamental restructuring of existing operations which may involve downsizing and vertical disintegration. The intuition behind the impact of e-commerce on transaction costs and the concomitant wave of vertical disintegration and downsizing is illustrated formally by Liu and Yang (2000)'s research into the size of the firm and transaction costs. As transaction efficiency is higher in the exchange of intermediate goods than that for labour, then organizing division of labour between more specialized firms and individuals is more efficient than organizing the division of labour within the entity of the firm. Consequently, with the increase in the level of specialization of firms and the rise in the division of labour between micro-businesses and individuals, the average employment levels of firms decline. The dynamics of this model have had some empirical support. Malone and Laubacher (1998) reveal that in 1973, Fortune 500 companies employed one in five US workers. At the time of writing, that ratio has fallen to one in ten.

If it is relatively cheaper to conduct transactions internally, the size of the firm increases. However, if it is relatively cheaper to conduct transactions between separate firm entities, firm size remains small or shrinks. The advent of e-commerce drives the transaction efficiency of intermediate goods higher, reducing the cost of inter-firm exchange and hence precipitating a wave of downsizing and vertical disintegration. Internet commerce permits the instant and inexpensive sharing and dissemination of information among many people in many locations (Malone and Laubacher, 1998). The centralized decision-making and expensive bureaucracies previously necessary to collate, process as well as disseminate information and coordinate actions within a large conglomerate, have become outmoded and inefficient. Micro-entities, even on an individual level, can effectively manage themselves, as electronic networks enable fluid coordination and exchange between independent micro-entities. E-commerce not only permits fluid business-to-business exchange. Electronic networks also allow micro-businesses to tap into the separate global reservoirs of information, expertise and financing previously enjoyed only by large firms, whilst retaining the beneficial attributes of leanness, flexibility and creativity: the very essence of a small firm.

Despite the increasing numbers of vertical disintegrations, large industrial organizations continue to dominate the world economy. The life of these conglomerates appears to be sustained by a concurrent wave of horizontal mergers and acquisitions. In the years 1998 to 2000 examples of horizontal merger mania abound. For example, British Airways allies with American Airlines which in turn allies with US Airways, Compaq buys Digital Electronic Corporation, Citibank merges with Travellers, Daimler Benz acquires Chrysler, and so on. The phenomena of vertical disintegration and horizontal alliances (mergers) are occurring simultaneously. The latter can also be attributed to the evolution of online technology, which has produced a decline in agency cost within a firm. With the introduction of intranet or e-mail within the entity of the firm there is far greater fluidity and less distortion to the flow of information between the CEO and the firm's employees. No longer must important pieces of information flow through the distortionary filters of each successive hierarchical layer before reaching the CEO. Information is passed directly from employees to the top layer of management, via the intranet, which raises the efficacy of management control and performance monitoring. The diseconomies of large-scale production attributed to agency cost are now attenuated or eliminated. The enhanced ability of managers to control conglomerates effectively without the significant agency cost diseconomies has led to a spate of alliances, mergers and acquisitions. Horizontally integrated firms, utilizing the technology of the intranet, do not incur the substantial transaction costs in monitoring the performance of their employees. This enables higher returns to horizontal alliances and mergers.

This chapter investigates the impact of e-commerce on market exchange and transaction costs. Section 2 provides a theoretical foundation – inframarginal analysis – to investigate the impacts of e-commerce on the network division of labour. Section 3 examines the prospects of e-commerce, particularly its prospects for exchange facilitation. Section 4 underscores the impact of e-commerce on the many transaction costs that exist in goods (services) markets and in labour exchange. It also unveils the relationship between e-commerce, transaction costs and business restructuring. Section 5 concludes the paper by presenting some broad forecasts for the future of e-commerce.

2 Inframarginal analysis of e-commerce

A popular slogan in the recent literature of e-commerce is that 'E-commerce will cut out the middlemen and generate a phenomenon called "disintermediation".' Lucking-Riley and Spulber (2001) observed that popular discussions often suggest that efficiencies in B2B (Business to Business) e-commerce are obtained by disintermediation – that is, by cutting out the middlemen and supplanting presumably costly intermediaries with direct transactions. They have noted that 'however, less expensive intermediation and lower transactions costs do not necessarily mean fewer intermediaries. If B2B e-commerce encourages outsourcing to replace some transactions previously internal to the firm, or if firms can use intermediaries to outsource some of their current external purchasing and sales efforts, or if firms can employ specialized intermediaries to avoid inefficient one-on-one direct meetings between companies and their suppliers, the end result would be a greater number of intermediaries' (Lucking-Riley and Spulber, 2001). Their intuition hasn't been so far formalized by marginal analysis; we believe that this is due to the inherited shortcomings of marginal analysis, for the following reasons.

Firstly, the phenomena noted by Lucking-Riley and Spulber are associated with the expansion of the network of division of labour which is generated by discontinuous shifts of individuals across different network patterns of transactions and division of labour. As suggested by Allyn Young (1928), evidence of a network effect is a notion of general equilibrium. Not only does the network size of division of labour depend on the extent of the market (the number of participants in the network of division of labour), but also the number of participants is in itself determined by all individuals' participation decisions in the network of division of labour, which relate to their decisions of their own levels of specialization. This circular causation, noted by Young, is an essential feature of general equilibrium, analogous to the circular causation between quantities and prices in the fixed point theorem (each individual's quantities demanded and supplied depend on prices, while the equilibrium prices are determined by all individuals' decisions of quantities). Marginal analysis, based on a given pattern of division of labour, does not appropriately explain this observation centralizing around the expansion of the network division of labour.

Secondly, the phenomena noted by Lucking-Riley and Spulber and their intuitive explanation are associated with an endogenously determined hierarchical structure of transactions and the various interplays between the hierarchical structure of transactions and network size of division of labour. In an extensive literature of endogenous hierarchy or spanning, the number of layers of a hierarchical organism is endogenized by formulating various trade-offs (see Borland and Eichberger, 1998, for a recent review of this literature). Disintermediation implies that the number of layers in the transaction hierarchy will be reduced. To assess the validity of this prediction, we need to understand the intimate relationship between the number of layers of a transaction hierarchy and the endogenously determined hierarchical structure of the network of division of labour. Shi and Yang (1998) and Yang (2001) have explored the features of such interplays. Using an inframarginal analysis of general equilibrium network hierarchy of division of labour and related transactions, they show that the number of layers of hierarchical structure of division of labour is positively related to the number of layers of hierarchical structure of transactions. The two numbers increase side by side as trading efficiency is improved. On the other side, Yang and Hogbin (1990) show that as trading efficiency is improved, the equilibrium number of layers of a hierarchy of cities and trade network decreases. Hence, whether disintermediation will occur as a result of improvement of trading efficiency associated with the utilization of e-commerce, will ultimately be determined by which of the two counterforces dominates.

More generally, according to inframarginal analysis pertaining to the theory of the irrelevance of firm size (Liu and Yang, 2000), if e-commerce improves the trading efficiency of goods and services more significantly than the trading efficiency of labour, then the expansion of e-commerce may encourage outsourcing, contracting out, franchising, downsizing, and, ultimately, disintegration. On the other hand, if e-commerce improves the trading efficiency of goods and services less significantly than the trading efficiency of labour, the opposite trend will happen, as is intuitively noted by Lucking-Riley and Spulber (2001).

3 E-commerce and market exchange

The emergence of the online market has resulted in lower costs and a far more fluid alternative to the traditional modes of market exchange. Not only does the online market promote competition due to low entry costs, but, in addition, the ease of market exchange itself presents enormous possibilities for trade growth. The unprecedented contribution of online markets in facilitating exchange may ultimately spawn the evolution of new markets.

Industrialization in the eighteenth and nineteenth centuries was driven on by the invention of the steam engine which enabled the transit of agents between population centres and between markets. Even though the steam train and other automotive devices greatly facilitated trade, the reduction in transaction costs was achieved by successively reducing the costs of travelling the same physical distances. However, advances in the information and communication industry enable virtual transactions to *replace* and hence overcome the physical distance between people. These faster and more reliable modes of communication enable large and dispersed groups of people to coordinate their disparate activities. Each of these innovations (developments) in the space of a century has not only facilitated market exchange but has also provided the impetus for the evolution of new markets.

The arrival of the Internet and e-commerce perhaps represents the zenith of two-and-a-half centuries' progress in mitigating the physical distances between people and markets. The unique properties of e-commerce permit unprecedented gains in market transaction efficiency. The properties of e-commerce include, first, properties of non-synchronization between buyer and seller. Buyers and sellers do not need to be present at the same place or at the same time to effect market exchange. Secondly, that of repetition; information is readily available anytime and anywhere, usually at zero cost to the user. Thirdly, information is bi-directional. That is, e-commerce enables two-way communication between buyer and seller. Fourthly, and perhaps most importantly, the market is global by design. There are no political and geographical impediments to online trade, market exchange can be easily effected between agents across political borders and across oceans. The historical problem of overcoming physical distance in order to engage in market exchange has been eliminated through e-commerce.

Parallel to these revolutionary developments, the vast improvement in communication and transaction efficiency enabled the emergence of large, complex organizations. With more reliable and faster communication and transportation choices, these industrial conglomerates could effectively market their goods and services both nationally and internationally. The owners of these corporations also had the means to coordinate the activities of large groups of people across the globe. In the latter half of the twentieth century, strong growth in trade enabled these industrial conglomerates to grow to immense proportions, each with their own extensive portfolio of activities and businesses.

At the same time, significant improvements in transaction efficiency in intermediate and final goods markets, due to online trade, have initiated a wave of vertical disintegration. With online trade smaller business entities can now achieve the same or better levels of transaction efficiency without being encumbered by rigid and unwieldy hierarchical bureaucracies that characterize vertically integrated conglomerates.

4 E-commerce and its impact on transaction cost

Table 4.1 represents the taxonomy of different sources of transaction cost and the effect e-commerce has on these traditional sources of transaction cost.

Search cost (pre-purchase information cost)

The first transaction cost incurred before market exchange is the buyer's search cost. This is the cost of acquiring the requisite information on pricing and availability of the good or service before making the purchase. E-commerce is able to substantially curtail both the resource and cost of search (in this instance the explicit cost of both purchasing the information, the cost of travelling to the place of exchange and the cost of time devoted to search) incurred by the consumer. Searching on the Internet covers virtual distance instead of physical distance, eliminating the transaction cost involved in travelling physical distances. Moreover, the explicit and opportunity cost of gathering information in order to effect exchange has been significantly reduced due to the availability of online information. The telephone inquiry, in principle, could serve the same purpose in eliminating physical-distance-type transaction costs. However, the telephone inquiry requires temporal synchrony between parties. That is, because telephone inquiry requires interaction between parties. For information to be imparted, both buyer and seller must be on the telephone at the same time, making this search process costly. E-commerce does not require temporal synchronization between buyer and seller.

Seller's search cost on consumers' preference

Online commerce not only produces a unilateral reduction in transaction cost for the buyer, the seller also experiences a decline in search costs. More specifically, the search cost on consumers' preference (consumer acquisition cost) declines. In the conduct of business, sellers incur a substantial cost in attempting to discover the true preferences of consumers. Such information is valuable because it provides better, more specific services to their clientele and enables the firm to exercise price discrimination and therefore increases the firm's profit margin. Typically, a firm expends one-third of its resources on marketing, where a large proportion of these resources are channelled to efforts in collating and deciphering consumer preferences for its good or

Table 4.1 The impact of e-commerce on transaction cost

Sources of transaction cost		*Effects of e-commerce*
Goods and Services Market		
Search cost (pre-purchase information cost)	Buyer's search cost on price and availability	Will be significantly reduced
	Seller's search cost on consumer's preference (Consumer acquisition cost)	Will be significantly reduced
Accuracy of pre-purchase information	Buyer's information	More accurate for standardized goods and services, but not so for others
	Seller's information	More accurate
Uncertainty on quality of goods and services		Repeated purchase reveal true information Addition of information externality of informed purchasers
Asset specificity and opportunistic behaviour		*Ex-post* opportunistic behaviour will be subject to the positive externality generated by the informed party. This reduces the incentive of holding out behaviour and therefore increases the level of specialised investment of the upstream party.
Negotiation cost		Auction (non-personal) market to replace person-to-person negotiation
Labour market		
Diminishing marginal productivity of management		Intranet (as opposed to the Internet) enhances the ability of managers to monitor the performance of the subordinates.
Information distortion		The usage of groupware (such as Lotus Notes or Novell Groupwise) smoothes out the information flow and potentially reduces information distortion.

service. Without the large-scale, direct interaction offered by the Internet, where preferences are easily signalled, obtaining consumers' preferences through more traditional means is costly. Companies utilizing conventional methods of eliciting consumer preferences (such as surveys) require dedicated marketing departments. E-commerce may, to some degree, reduce seller search cost on consumers' preference. For instance, through the purchase of a book over the Internet, the consumers' preferred topic is automatically revealed to the seller. If consumers order several similar books over a short time horizon there is quite an accurate revelation of consumer preferences. The seller could therefore specifically target advertising and promotions of certain products (services) to a particular clientele. The online bookstore, Amazon.com, has been particularly active in using this automatically collated online information to run more specific advertisements.

Accuracy of pre-purchase information

The Internet is a vehicle for the dissemination of vast volumes of information. However, the information that is imparted online can be either more or less accurate than information exchanged through traditional direct interaction. The Internet does not have a clear advantage in informational accuracy; the relative accuracy of online information depends on the nature of the goods and services that are traded. The information imparted online to the buyer may be more accurate than traditional exchange when one trades in standardized goods (services). The buyer can sift through the seller's online information, but will have access to additional information, and impartial reviews of the product (service) at other online locations.

However, for non-standardized goods and services that may contain hidden information, online information may be less accurate. Moreover, in markets with asymmetric information such as the used car market, online information may not only be less accurate but the information may also be insufficient. Markets with asymmetric information problems and markets for non-standardized goods and services both require more direct interaction to reveal hidden information.

As a whole, the accuracy of the seller's information has overall been enhanced through online trade. The direct revelation of consumer preferences through online purchases is far more accurate than the indirect traditional measures designed to elicit consumer preferences, such as surveys.

Uncertainty over the quality of goods and services

Another transaction cost hindering the fluidity of market exchange is the uncertainty over the quality of goods and services. Again the ease in relaying pertinent information online reduces this type of transaction cost. The repeated online purchase of goods and services by established clients and/or new customers reveals accurate information on the quality of goods and services. Furthermore, numerous websites (such as online auction sites) offer both product (service) reviews and evaluations of the sellers. Product (service) reviews, seller evaluations and repeated sales can be observed by prospective clients, which allay both quality concerns and concerns of opportunistic behaviour on the part of the seller.

Analogous with the literature on incomplete markets for information (see, for example, Grossman and Stiglitz, 1976) new online consumers are in a position to observe the movements of informed online purchasers. Thus, if the market was segmented into informed and uninformed purchasers, the fluidity of information transmission enables uninformed purchasers to observe the transactions of the informed. Repeated purchases of the goods and services by these informed consumers disclose the true information of successful online exchange, and reduce the uncertainty surrounding the quality of goods and services traded on the Internet. The generation of positive information externalities by informed purchasers online also prevents opportunistic behaviour on the part of suppliers. Given the many avenues that facilitate the transfer of information online – for example, online discussion groups – informed parties can easily pass on their assessment of traders to the uninformed parties. The transaction cost of opportunistic behaviour (interpreted by Williamson (1985) as 'self-interest seeking with guile') may involve a firm with considerable bargaining power reneging or defaulting on their contractual obligations, particularly if contracts are incomplete. The transaction cost of opportunistic behaviour could also entail calculated attempts by one party to mislead, distort, disguise or otherwise confuse the contracting party. Given that *ex post* opportunistic behaviour will be subject to the positive informational externality generated by the informed party and that incidences of opportunistic behaviour are easily disseminated online, there is less incentive to cheat the contracting party. Firms will not engage in opportunistic behaviour because they risk the disintegration of their reputation capital if informed purchasers expose their dubious practices. Fewer incidences of opportunistic behaviour and greater adherence to contractual obligations are likely to generate overall higher levels of investment, since firms that enter into contracts can now pursue their plans with greater certainty.

Negotiation cost

Typically, negotiation between buyer and seller entails an opportunity cost of time. The opportunity cost of time involved in negotiation is eliminated by internet-based auctions. For example, with the purchase of standardized intermediate inputs, negotiation cost can be avoided by transacting online. However, internet auctions can only effectively replace person-to-person negotiation to the extent that products are standardized. The internet auction is not an effective substitute to trade in non-standardized goods and services, which may possess hidden information. In such a scenario, direct person-to-person negotiation is more efficient.

Job market search

Analogous to the market for goods and services, the fluidity of the online hiring and selling of generic labour units, such as process workers, may reduce the transaction costs that exist in the labour market. For instance, job searching, negotiating, and contracting will be easier using e-commerce. Understandably, however, for less homogenous positions in the labour force, such as general management positions (which is synonymous to trade in non-standardized goods and services), e-commerce will not have a significant impact on the saving of transaction costs in this sphere of the labour market. Because of the specificity of management skills and the possibility of hidden information direct interaction between parties is necessary, even though the costs of executing such transactions may be high.

Agency cost within an organization

The ability of management to monitor and control a firm effectively is subject to diminishing returns. That is, as the firm continues to grow in size the efficacy of management monitoring and control progressively diminishes while agency cost increases. Eventually diseconomies of firm size may emerge as management encounters increasing difficulty in monitoring the performance of its employees. The introduction of the intranet (a network within an organization, as opposed to the Internet) enhances the ability of management to monitor the performance of those managed. Firstly, the intranet eliminates the need for cumbersome hierarchical layers of management as a means of transmitting and deciphering information for those at the top. Secondly, the intranet is revolutionary in that it enables management to have continued and direct access to information from employees on the shop or factory floor. Thirdly, not only does it remove the distortionary informational filters that typically reside in the hierarchical chain, but it also enhances the ability of managers to directly monitor every employee, which in turn enables the manager to exercise greater leverage and control over the firm's future. An example of improving management monitoring and hence reducing agency cost within the firm is through the utilization of groupware (such as Lotus Notes or Novell Groupwise). Groupware smoothes out the information flow and potentially reduces the information distortion.

The intranet unleashes new possibilities for managers to effectively monitor and control even the largest industrial behemoth. The spate of horizontal alliances and mergers is a potential manifestation of the increasing efficacy of management monitoring and control – a product of intranet technology. The intranet-induced erosion in the cost of principal–agent monitoring significantly raises the threshold size of the firm at which diseconomies emerge. This means that CEOs can effectively conduct and monitor the operations of large horizontally integrated firms through intranet-based communication.

5 Some broad forecasts

The implications of e-commerce for market exchange and the economy in general are multifaceted. E-commerce is likely to facilitate and promote the fluidity of exchange in many ways. As well as providing an impetus to greater competition, it removes the barriers to entry that typically exist in physical markets.

Given the existence of consumer caution, it is likely that business-to-business transactions will dominate the e-commerce scene in the future. This may be due to the fact that the opportunity cost of time engaged in search and in physical market exchange is far greater and more explicit for firms. Moreover, purchases of standardized intermediate inputs are voluminous, so uncertainty over the quality of one or two items may not be an issue if there are significant savings in transaction costs. The parallelism between booming business-to-business e-commerce and vertical disintegration manifests itself through a wholesale shift from internally sourced intermediate goods production to fluid online purchase of intermediate goods from outsourced vendors. Because the causality can run both ways, either from business-to-business e-commerce to vertical disintegration or vice versa, the two phenomena act as mutual reinforcements. As evidenced by strong growth in online business-to-business exchange, Hof and Smith (2000) observe that investors are fleeing e-tail stocks and are flocking to new business-to-business websites. The clear attraction of investors to online firms that conduct business-to-business exchange is that they can boast real sales, clear cost savings for customers and can demonstrate a more definite path to profits than e-tailers, who must spend millions to effectively market their goods and services to fickle consumers.

The decline in transaction costs in both search and market exchange may be initiating the current spate of vertical disintegration. If the transaction efficiency for intermediate goods is higher than that for labour, it is more efficient to organize the division of labour between specialized firms rather than organizing the division of labour within the entity of a single firm. With e-commerce generating greater transaction efficiencies in the market for intermediate goods (services), it is optimal for firms to vertically disintegrate, which is exactly the phenomenon we are witnessing.

However, with no fall in transaction costs in the trade of management services and non-standardized commodities, the sourcing of management services and the production of non-standardized goods (services) may remain within the entity of the firm. Moreover, due to the specificity of skills (attributes) and the existence of potentially hidden information, trade in management services and non-standardized goods (services) is likely to be conducted through traditional mediums of exchange such as direct interaction, rather than through online exchange.

The increasing frequency of horizontal mergers, acquisitions and alliances may highlight the possible impact of intranet technology on decisions to horizontally integrate. The intranet's ability to enhance monitoring and control by management will continue to make horizontal integration a viable proposition. Moreover, due to the vast improvement in managerial supervision and control, the intranet will accentuate the importance of managerial skill and initiative. The performance of the firm will hinge increasingly upon managerial adroitness in monitoring and control. Less able managers and their firms are likely to be taken over quickly by better-run firms.

E-commerce is also likely to initiate stronger growth in foreign direct investment. Given that a vast intricate web of different transaction costs plague the business of exporting and importing, multinational enterprises are in a position to trade these previously exported (imported) commodities online at a significantly lower transaction cost. Therefore, it may be efficient to replace importing (exporting) intermediaries with multinational enterprises that produce the same commodities domestically and trade them online at a fraction of the original transaction cost.

References

Budros, A. (1999) 'A Conceptual Framework for Analyzing Why Organizations Downsize', *Organization Science*, 10, 1, 69–81.

Borland, Jeff and Eichberger, Jurgen (1998) 'Organizational Form outside the Principal–Agent Paradigm', *Bulletin of Economic Research*, 50, 201–27.

Farrell, C. (2000) 'Death of the Dot-Coms? Don't Bet on it. Reality is setting in, and competition is rising, but the battle for customers has just begun', *Business Week*.

Grossman, S. and Stiglitz, J. (1976) 'Information and Competitive Price Systems', *American Economic Review*, 66, 2, 246–53.

Hof, R. and Smith, G. (2000) 'E-Investors Embrace Business-to-Business', *Business Week*, 3671, 6 April.

Koretz, G. (2000) 'Hire Math: Fire 3, Add 5. Why job churning is on the rise', *Business Week*, 3672, 13 March.

Liu, P. and Yang, X. (2000) 'The theory of irrelevance of the size of the firm', *Journal of Economic Behavior & Organization*, vol. 42.

Lucking-Riley, D. and Spulber, D. (2001) 'Business-to-Business Electronic Commerce', *Journal of Economic Perspectives*, 15, 55–68.

Madigan, K. (1999) 'This Economy Has Fuel Injection. A tank full of corporate cash could keep the expansion going', *Business Week*, Iss. 3640, 2 August.

Malone, T. and Laubacher, R. (Sep./Oct. 2000) 'The dawn of the E-lance Economy', *Harvard Business Review*, 76, 5.

Melcher, R. (1999) 'Go Ahead, Lay Me Off, Losing a job is no big worry in today's growing economy', *Business Week*, Iss. 3640, 2 August.

Shi, Heling, and Yang, Xiaokai (1998) 'Centralized Hierarchy within a Firm and Decentralized Hierarchy in the Market', in Kenneth Arrow, Yew-Kwang Ng and Xiaokai Yang (eds), *Increasing Returns and Economic Analysis* (London: Macmillan), 145–69.

Williamson, O. (1985) *The Economic Institutions of Capitalism – Firms, Markets, Relational Contracting* (London: Collier Macmillan Publishers).

Yang, X. and Hogbin, B. (1990) 'The Optimum Hierarchy', *China Economic Review*, 2, 125–40.

Yang, Xiaokai (2001) *Economics: New Classical versus Neoclassical Frameworks* (Cambridge, MA: Blackwell).

5
An Equilibrium Model of Hierarchy

Xiaokai Yang

1 Introduction

The purpose of this chapter is twofold. First, I extend the received partial equilibrium analysis of hierarchical models to a general equilibrium context. Second, the equilibrium model of hierarchy will be used to explore the relationship between the hierarchical structure of economic organization and the level of division of labour.

There are three separate literatures based on hierarchy. The first relates to multiple layers of principal–agent relationships and related endogenous transaction costs caused by moral hazard and other opportunism (see Tirole, 1986; Laffont, 1990; Bac, 1996; Bag, 1997; MacLeod and Malcomson, 1988; Calvo and Wellisz, 1978, 1979; Hart and Holmstrom, 1987; Sappington, 1991; Holmstrom and Milgrom, 1995; among others). Milgrom and Roberts (1992) provide a comprehensive review of this literature up to 1991. Bolton and Scharfstein (1998) and Gibbons (1998) provide recent surveys of the literature. The second literature studies a series connection of elements that involves the tradeoff between reliability of and gains from the series connection (see Sah, 1991; Sah and Stiglitz, 1988, 1991; Kremer, 1993). The models in the two literatures do not necessarily involve a choice of the optimum pyramidal structure with a series connection of many layers and parallel connections between the elements in any two neighbouring layers. The third literature based on hierarchical models focuses on the tradeoffs that determine the efficient number of layers in a pyramidal structure and efficient spanning. This literature is reviewed by Borland and Eichberger (1998), Spanjers (1997), and van Zandt (1995).[1] In the current chapter, I will develop a general equilibrium model that bridges the theoretical gap between the third literature of hierarchy and the literature of endogenous specialization.

Pyramidal hierarchies can be classified into one of two types: a one way hierarchy or a network hierarchy. A library is an example of a *one way hierarchy*: For example, a person uses a library catalogue system to look for a book at the bottom layer of this system, he searches from the top layer, in this instance, categories, to the bottom layer – books. I refer to such a hierarchy as a one way hierarchy because the search process flows in a single direction from top to bottom. Among other examples of one way hierarchies are the military command system, an English dictionary, a hierarchical screening process in a tournament involving many contestants, and a packaging system of some standard commodities. Further the example of the dictionary, the top of the hierarchy of the dictionary is its user. The next layer is divided into 26 letters used for the first letter of words. Each of the letters is divided into 26 letters used for the second letter of the words at the next layer, and so on. In the tournament example, a large number of groups (of contestants) are pitted against each other the first round tournament separately. The winners of the first round tournament then compete separately against a smaller number of groups in the second round of the tournament, and so on. In the packaging system example, goods are packaged in large numbers of small boxes which are packaged yet again into a smaller number of larger boxes which are later put in a few containers, which are then carried by a cargo ship.

A postal system is a hierarchy based on a network. The bottom of the hierarchy consists of many people whose mail is delivered to one another through the higher layers of the hierarchy (for example, a postal centre in large cities and post offices in medium-sized cities and small towns). The function of such a hierarchy is to improve the efficiency of each element at the bottom level through communication with one another through the higher layers. I refer to such a hierarchy as a network hierarchy since communications are two-way – both from bottom to top and from top to bottom. Other examples of network hierarchies are the wholesale and retail distribution network, the telephone network, and the management systems of a large companies.

An alternative way of classifying pyramidal hierarchies is to look at the structure of decision-making. If a decision-maker at the top of a hierarchy can choose the number of layers and other structural features of the hierarchy, then the hierarchy is referred to as a *centralized hierarchy*. If no individual decision-maker can consciously choose the number of layers of a hierarchy, then the hierarchy is referred to as a *decentralized hierarchy*. A hierarchical structure of cities and a wholesale and retail network in the marketplace are typical decentralized hierarchies (Muller-Hagedorn, 1995).

Relevant case studies in business, such as the case studies of the McCormick harvesting machine company and the Ford motor company in Dicke (1992), document the fact that a keen understanding of the impact of the number of hierarchical layers in the wholesale and retail network on the level of division of labour in production (and thereby productivity) is crucial for a business to be successful. In many such businesses, the hierarchical structure of transactions is associated with a symmetrical market relationship between the franchiser and franchisee rather than the asymmetrical ownership relationship between the employer and employee. The intrinsic relationship between the hierarchical structure of transactions and the hierarchical structure of the division of labour is highlighted in the growing literature of endogenous specialization. A recent survey of this literature is found in Yang and Ng (1998).

The papers of Carter (1995) and Bolton and Dewatripont (1994) investigate the relationship between the level of division of labour and a hierarchical structure of information communication. In these very interesting papers, there is a tradeoff between economies of specialization in handling information and communication costs caused by the division of labour between professional managers, salesmen, and producers or specialists processing different information. Economies of specialization are not well specified as features of production functions in Carter's model where benefits of specialization are represented by values of some exogenously given parameters. Hence, the efficient balance of the tradeoff between economies of division of labour and communication costs is not achieved via choosing output and input levels in production process (of goods or information). The flow of logic between the assumptions on values of parameters and the final conclusion based on comparative statics of choice of organization structure is too short. In Bolton and Dewatripont's model, economies of specialization in processing information are specified as a feature of processing functions of information. But both models are decision models for a firm in which utility functions and consumption of goods are not specified. A general equilibrium model is needed to investigate a mechanism that simultaneously determines many interdependent endogenous variables: the level of division of labour, the number of layers and number of elements at each layer of a pyramidal hierarchy, transaction efficiency, total transaction costs, quantities of goods and services that are produced and consumed, and prices. As Allyn Young (1928) stated, 'not only the division of labour is dependent on the extent of the market, but also the extent of the market is determined by the level of division of labour.' Furthermore, in a model with endogenous specialization and endogenous structure of a pyramidal hierarchy, the equilibrium number of layers of the hierarchical structure of wholesale and retail network is dependent upon the level of division of labour. As shown in the literature of endogenous specialization (see Yang and Ng (1993) for instance), the equilibrium level of division of labour in society is determined by the level of division of labour in transacting activities which in turn determines transaction efficiencies. However, in a model of endogenous specialization and endogenous hierarchy, the number of layers in a hierarchical structure of transactions affects the level of division of labour in transacting activities and thereby affecting transaction efficiencies. Therefore, not only is the number of layers of hierarchy dependent on the level of division of labour, but also the level of division of labour is determined by the number of layers in the hierarchy. The circular causation and infinite feedback loops between many endogenous variables that characterize an organization structure in the market implies that the notion of general equilibrium (a fixed point) is needed to identify a mechanism to simultaneously determine all of the interdependent variables.

This chapter will develop a general equilibrium model to simultaneously endogenize the network pattern of division of labour and the number of layers in a pyramidal structure of transactions. Because of the tradeoff between the degree of endogenization and tractability of the model, I do not specify uncertainties in communication in the model. The models of endogenous specialization with transaction risk and moral hazard and with an exogenous hierarchical structure of transactions are discussed by Lio (1996, 1998).

Each individual, as a consumer, prefers diverse consumption and, as a producer, prefers specialized production of goods and transaction services due to a fixed learning cost which generates economies of specialization in each activity. Moreover, trade will incur transaction costs. The tradeoff between economies of specialization and transaction costs can be used to endogenize the level of division of labour. A low level of division of labour involves only trade between neighbours and a high level of division of labour involves trade between neighbours as well as between non-neighbours. Assume that trade with an individual's neighbour is a transacting activity that is distinguishable from trade with non-neighbours. Then, there are three possible levels of specialization in transacting activities if the level of division of labour in producing goods is sufficiently high: (i) self-provision of two types of transaction services by producers of goods; (ii) supply of one type of transaction service by partially specialized middlemen and self-provision of the other type of transaction service by each person; and (iii) supply of each type of transaction service by completely specialized middlemen. In case (iii), a middleman may specialize in mediating transactions between local middlemen who take care of trade between neighbours. This implies that a hierarchical structure of wholesale and retail distribution networks may emerge from a high level of division of labour. Two tradeoffs exist: (i) a tradeoff between economies of specialization in producing goods and transaction costs; and (ii) a tradeoff between economies of specialization in transacting activities and transaction costs in delivering transaction services which can then be used to simultaneously endogenize the number of layers of a hierarchical structure of transactions and the level of division of labour in production and transaction activities. The first tradeoff entails endogenization of each individual's level of specialization and the number of his trading partners. Hence, as the number of trading partners increases due to the higher level of specialization, a new transacting activity for trade between non-neighbours endogenously emerges and thereby creates scope for a hierarchical structure of transactions to emerge from the second tradeoff.

We draw a distinction between the quantities of the same good or service that are self-provided, sold, and purchased. This distinction leads to corner solutions of consumer-producer optimization problems. Using the Kuhn–Tucker approach to corner solutions, it can be shown that each individual sells at most one good and does not simultaneously buy and sell nor simultaneously buy and self-provide the same good. The combinations of individuals' corner solutions that are consistent with this condition generate many candidates for the general equilibrium which satisfy the market-clearing conditions but not all conditions for full utility maximization of individuals.

We can identify four types of market structures as candidates for the general equilibrium. The first is autarky where no market exists. The second is the partial division of labour where each partially specialized producer of goods self-provides transaction services. This structure of transactions is symmetric, and no hierarchy exists. The third is associated with the division of labour between partially specialized producers of goods and partially specialized producers of one type of transaction service where each middleman has two producers of goods as trading partners, but each producer of goods has only one trading partner. The simplest hierarchy of transactions with two layers emerges from a higher level of division of labour between the production of goods and the production of transaction services. The fourth is a complete division of labour where everybody trades all four goods and all types of transaction services, and each professional middleman specializes in a single transacting activity. A retail middleman specializes in local business between neighbours and a wholesale middleman specializes in trade between local communities. There are three layers of the hierarchy of transactions: the top consists of the wholesale agents; the middle layer consists of the retail agents; the bottom consists of specialist producers of goods. In the three-layer decentralized hierarchy, the producers of goods are more peripheral than the retail middlemen who are in turn more peripheral than wholesale middlemen.

Comparative statics of equilibrium show that the equilibrium is autarky if the degree of economies of specialization is sufficiently small and if the transaction cost coefficient for a unit of transaction service is sufficiently large, since in this case transaction costs outweigh economies of specialization generated by the division of labour. As the transaction cost coefficient is slightly lowered and/or the degree of economies of specialization increases, the general equilibrium shifts to the partial division of labour with partially specialized producers of goods where there is no middleman. If the transaction cost coefficient is further lowered and/or the degree of economies of specialization further increases, the general equilibrium entails a hierarchical structure of transactions with two layers where there is a division of labour between producers and middlemen. If the transaction cost coefficient is extremely small and the degree of economies of specialization is sufficiently high a hierarchy of three layers emerges from a high level of division of labour between wholesale and retail business and between producers and middlemen. As the transaction cost coefficient is reduced, the division of labour evolves, resulting in an increase in productivity, the extent of the market, the degree of endogenous comparative advantage, the degree of diversity of economic structure, and in trade dependence.

Section 2 of this chapter describes the model which has consumer-producers, economies of specialisation, and transaction costs. Section 3 investigates individuals' decision problems and different market structures. In section 4 the comparative statics of the general equilibrium are used to explore the implications of the model for endogenizing the number of layers of a decentralized hierarchy and the level of division of labour.

2 A model with consumer-producers, economies of specialization, and transaction costs

Consider an economy with a set of consumer-producers and four consumer goods. The set is a continuum with mass *M*. Each consumer-producer's self-provided amount of good i is x_i. The respective amounts of good i sold and purchased in the market are x_i^s and x_i^d respectively. Fraction $1 - T_i$ of a shipment of good i disappears in transit because of transaction costs. Thus, $T_i x_i^d$ is the amount a person receives from the purchase of good i.[2] An individual's consumption of good i is $x_i + T_i x_i^d$. The utility function is identical for all individuals:

$$U = \Sigma_i^4 = 1\ (x_i + T_i x_i^d). \tag{5.1}$$

We assume that utility is 0 if the amount of any goods consumed is non-positive. It is assumed that the residential location of individuals is exogenously given. We further assume, for simplicity, that a local community consists of at most three types of occupation configurations. A pair of individuals who are in different communities are called non-neighbours.[3] Suppose the coefficient T_i equals the quantity of the transaction service for delivering good i. T_i consists of only T_{in} if trade takes place between neighbours where T_{in} denotes the quantity of the transaction service for delivering good i between neighbours. If trade takes place between non-neighbours in the absence of the division of labour between wholesale and retail middlemen, T_i consists of two components T_{in} and T_{io}, where T_{io} denotes the quantity of the transaction service for delivering good i between non-neighbours. If a seller of a good buys a good through both wholesale and retail businessmen from another community (see Figure

5.1(4c)), the two types of transaction services for neighbours will be needed. First the good purchased will be procured from an original seller by the local middleman who resides in the same community as the seller. Then the local middleman delivers the good to the wholesaleman who then delivers the good to the retail middleman in the local community of the ultimate buyer. Let n denote a service for neighbours provided by the middleman in the same community of the ultimate buyer and n' denote a service for neighbours provided by a middleman in the same community of the original seller. T_i consists of T_{in}, T_{io}, and $T_{in'}$ if a good is delivered by both wholesale and retail middlemen between non-neighbours. Because of the assumption of iceberg transaction cost coefficient, T_i, it is a coefficient of receiving rate as well as compounded quantity of transaction services. With the assumption, a transfer of goods from a middleman and the ultimate buyer can be considered as a delivery with an added transaction service in the absence of resale of goods. This avoids the formidable problem of indices of sources and origins of a delivery.

Transaction services can be either self-provided or purchased. Each consumer-producer's self-provided amount of transaction service of good i is t_{ij}, where $j = n, n', o$, letters n and n' stand for neighbour and o stands for non-neighbour. The respective amounts of transaction service sold and purchased in the market are t_{ij}^s and t_{ij}^d. Fraction 1-k of a delivery of transaction service purchased disappears in transit because of transaction costs of the services. Thus, kt_{ij}^d is the amount a person receives from the purchase of transaction service t_{ij}^d and the definition for T_i is given as follows.

$T_i = T_{in} = (t_{in} + kt_{in}^d)$ if trade occurs between neighbours (5.2a)

$T_i = T_{in}\, T_{io} = (t_{in} + kt_{in}^d)(t_{io} + kt_{io}^d)$ if trade occurs between non-neighbours in the absence of division of labour between wholesale and retail middlemen; (5.2b)

$T_i = T_{in}\, T_{io}\, T_{in'} = (t_{in} + kt_{in}^d)(t_{io} + kt_{io}^d)(t_{in'} + kt_{in'}^d)$ if trade occurs between non-neighbours through both wholesale and retail middlemen[4] (5.2c)

where it is assumed that $k \in [0,1]$. The transaction services n, o, and/or n' are connected in series when trade occurs between non-neighbours since the service will not be completed if either the delivery of a good within a local community or its delivery between local communities fails to complete. The production functions for the four goods and various services and endowment constraint are the same for each consumer-producer, given by

$$x_i + x_i^s = L_{ix} - A, \qquad A \in [0,1] \tag{5.3a}$$

$$t_{ij} + t_{ij}^s = L_{ij} - A, \tag{5.3b}$$

$$\Sigma_i L_{ix} + \Sigma_i \Sigma_j L_{ij} = 1, \tag{5.3c}$$

$$L_{ix}, L_{ij} \in [0,1],\ i = 1,2,3,4,\ j = n,o$$

where $x_i + x_i^s$ is the output level of good *i*, $t_{ij} + t_{ij}^s$ is the output level of type *j* transaction service for good i, L_{ix} is a person's labour share in producing good i, which I term his *level of specialization in producing good i*. L_{ij} is a person's level of specialization in producing type j service for good i. Each consumer-producer is endowed with one unit of labour. Parameter A is a fixed learning cost in producing a good or a type of service. A larger A is associated with a greater *degree of economies of specialization* since division of labour and specialization can avoid more duplicated fixed learning cost as A increases.

Later one will see that the *ex ante* identical individuals can choose between becoming different specialists with various patterns and level of specialization and becoming self-sufficient as they choose different levels of specialization and different professions. Endogenous comparative advantage, which is defined by Yang and Borland (1991) as the difference in labour productivity between a buyer and a seller of a good, will emerge from the *ex ante* identical individuals if they choose different levels of specialization in different activities. Such endogenous comparative advantages do not exist if they choose the same level of specialization in each and every activity.

It is assumed that values of all decision variables are non-negative. This implies that they might be 0 and thus non-linear programming is essential in solving for an individual's decision. I assume that there is free entry for all individuals into any sector and the population size M is large. These assumptions imply that *ex ante* identical individuals treat prices parametrically.

The specification of physical conditions of the model formalizes the following tradeoffs which give rise to the emergence of a hierarchy from a high level of division of labour. If a person has a low level of specialization, such that he has no more than two producers of goods as trading partners, then he needs to trade with only his neighbours. If his level of specialization in producing goods is high, then he will need the services of both his neighbours and his non-neighbours. This implies that a higher level of specialization in producing goods creates a scope for a higher level of division of labour in producing the two types of services.

Several subtle tradeoffs, however, complicate the story. If there is a division of labour between producers of three goods, then three producers can constitute an integrated local business community where they trade only with neighbours. If there is a division of labour between producers and a local retail middleman, then the local community can contain only two types of producers in addition to the middleman. This implies that only two goods are traded between neighbours and trading three goods will involve non-neighbours. This implies the tradeoff between economies of specialization in production and economies of specialization in trading. That is, trading three goods, which increases a person's level of specialization in producing goods, requires spending time on one additional transaction service for non-neighbours which reduces his level of specialization in producing goods. This implies, on the other hand, that each local middleman can buy at most two goods from neighbours and has to buy goods from non-neighbours if he trades three goods. The emergence of wholesale middlemen will enlarge the scope for trading among all participants in the model. But a wholesalesman has to buy all his consumption goods from non-neighbouring producers of goods through local middlemen because his neighbours are retail middlemen who do not produce goods for sale. Each transfer of goods between different middlemen and between middlemen and original seller or ultimate buyers involve transaction costs and the division of labour between wholesale and retail middlemen increases the number of such transfers that are essential for a good to reach its ultimate consumer. Hence, another tradeoff exists between economies of specialization in producing transaction services and the transaction cost in delivering such services. An improvement in transaction efficiency in delivering the services and/or an increase in the degree of economies of specialization will enlarge the scope for the market to efficiently tradeoff one benefit against others among the opposing forces. Therefore, the level of division of labour and the number of layers of the hierarchy of transactions can be explained by the two parameters.

3 Configurations and market structures

In this section I investigate the relationship between individuals' decisions about their levels and patterns of specialization and the organizational pattern of transactions for society as a whole. It is assumed that each consumer-producer maximizes his utility with respect to the quantities of goods produced, traded, and consumed by him for a given set of relative prices of traded goods subject to the budget constraint, production functions, and endowment constraint. Combinations of zero and non-zero values of 36 decision variables x_i, x_i^s, x_i^d, t_{ij}, t_{ij}^s, t_{ij}^d ($i = 1,2,3,4$ and $j = n,o$) generate $2^{36} = 68{,}719{,}476{,}736$ profiles of zero and non-zero variables and thereby one interior solution and $2^{36} - 1$ corner solutions. Wen (1998) has proven a theorem for a broad class of models of endogenous specialization that each consumer-producer does not simultaneously buy and sell nor simultaneously buy and self-provide the same goods; also he sells only one good at most. Because of the assumption of iceberg transaction costs, a delivery of goods from a middleman to a buyer does not involve resale of the good although it adds a transaction service factor to the good. This ensures that this theorem is applicable to the model. Using this theorem, the interior solution and many corner solutions can be ruled out from the set of candidates for the optimal decision. A profile of zero and non-zero variables that is compatible with the Wen Theorem and compatible with the individuals' budget constraints is referred to as a *configuration.*

A combination of configurations that is compatible with the market-clearing condition is called a market structure, or simply a *structure.* Free entry and competition among *ex ante* identical utility maximizers will establish utility equalization and market-clearing conditions for each structure. The utility equalization and market-clearing conditions determine a set of relative prices for the traded goods and the numbers of individuals selling different goods. The set defines a *corner equilibrium* for each structure. I will show that general equilibrium is one of the corner equilibria. In this section, individuals' corner solutions and the corner equilibrium are solved for each structure. Then the general equilibrium is defined and then identified in the next section as follows:[5]

1. Structure and configuration (1), depicted in Figure 5.1(1) where a circle represents a consumer-producer and lines with arrows represent the flow of goods. In structure (1), each individual self-provides all four goods and is referred to as *autarky.*

2. Structure (2a) is depicted in Figure 5.1(2a) where a symbol *i* in a circle represents good or service *i* sold by the circle which denotes an individual. This structure consists of two different configurations. One configuration is denoted by the circle with the number 1. A person choosing this configuration sells good 1, buys good 2, and self-provides goods 1, 3, and 4 and service *n.* Another configuration is denoted by the circle with the number 2. A person choosing this configuration sells good 2, buys good 1, and self-provides goods 2, 3, and 4 and service *n.* For this structure there is no middleman and each person produces four types of goods and services, trades two goods, and needs only one type of neighbour as his trading partner. Hence, no transaction services for non-neighbours are needed.

3. Structure (2b) is depicted in Figure 5.1(2b). This structure consists of three different configurations. One configuration is denoted by the circle with the number 1. A person choosing this configuration sells good 1, buys good 2 and service *n,* and self-provides goods 1, 3 and 4. The second configuration is denoted by the circle with the number 2. A person choosing this configuration sells good 2, buys good 1 and service *n,* and self-provides goods 2, 3, and 4. The third configuration is denoted by the circle with the letter *n.* A person choosing this configuration sells service *n,* buys goods 1 and 2, and self-provides goods 3 and 4 and service *n.* This structure is referred to as *low partial division of labour with a hierarchy of two layers* where there is a division of labour between producers of goods and middlemen. A simple hierarchical structure of transactions emerges from the low level of division of labour where a middleman is the centre of a local business community and producers of goods are peripheral and have to trade with each other through that middleman. Each person produces three

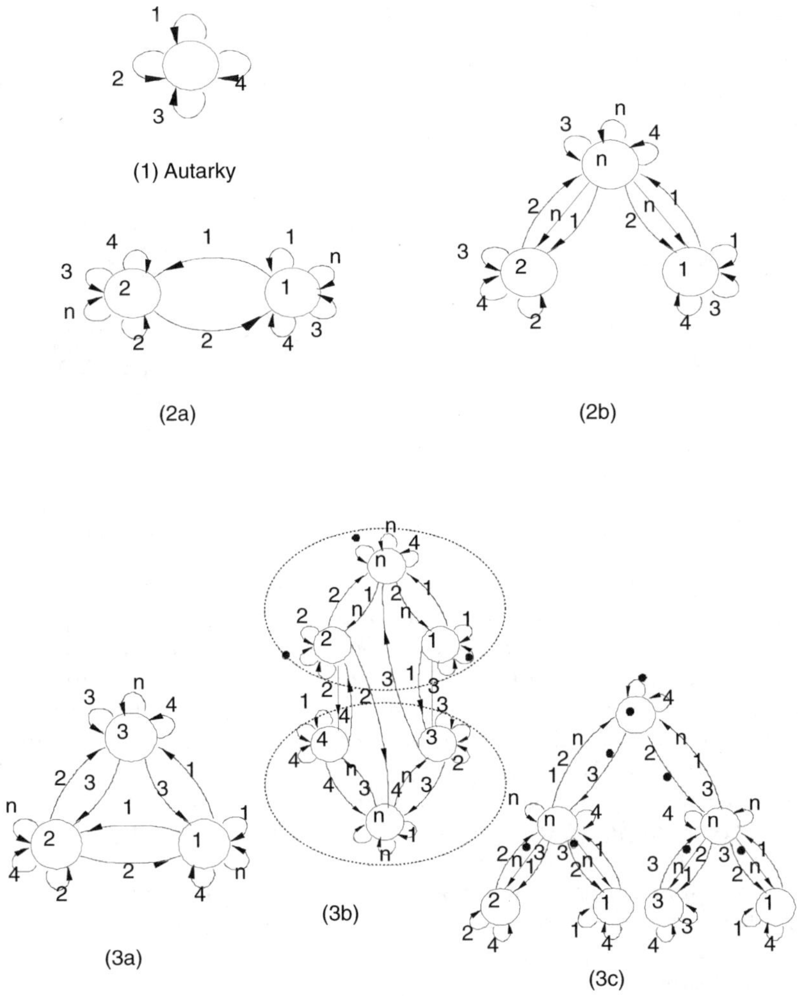

Figure 5.1 Emergence of a hierarchical structure of the market

goods and trades three types of goods and services. Each seller of goods has one type of neighbouring seller of goods and a middleman has two types of producers of goods as trading partner(s). Hence, services for non-neighbours are not needed and the division of labour in producing different transaction services cannot take place.

4. Structure (3a) is depicted in Figure 5.1(3a) where a circle with letter *i* represents a configuration which sells good *i*, buys goods *j* and *r*, and self-provides goods *i* and *s* ($s \neq i,j,r$). In this structure consisting of three

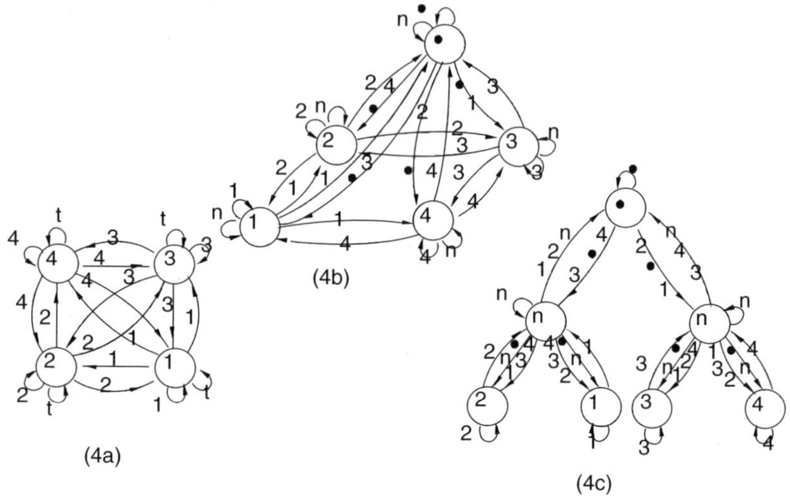

Figure 5.1 Emergence of a hierarchical structure of the market – *Continued*

configurations, each individual produces three types of goods and services, trades three goods, and has two types of neighbouring sellers of goods as his trading partners. Hence, transaction services for non-neighbours are not needed. Note that there are at most three types of neighbours in a local community by assumption. This structure is referred to as a *high partial division of labour in production without hierarchy* where there is no division of labour between producers of goods and middlemen.

5. Structure (3b) is depicted in Figure 5.1(3b) where a circle with *i* represents a configuration which sells good i, buys goods *j* and *r* and service *n*, self-provides goods *i* and *s* ($s \neq i,j,r$), and service *o*. A circle with the letter *n* represents a middleman who sells service *n*, buys three goods, and self-provides one good and services *o* and *n*. In this structure, each person produces three types of goods and services and trades 4 types of goods and services.

Two dashed circles in Figure 5.1(3b) denote two local communities. Individuals in the same community are neighbours and they need transaction service for non-neighbours if they buy goods from another community. For this structure, there is a division of labour between producers of goods and middlemen, but there is no division of labour in producing different transaction services. Here, the theorem in Yang (1991) is used to exclude those configurations in which a middleman sells two types of services or a producer sells more than one good. Since the level of specialization of each producer of goods is higher than in structure (2b), each seller of goods produces one less good than in (2b) and he has a type of neighbouring producer of goods, a neighbouring middleman, and a type of non-neighbour producer of goods as his trading partners. Hence, services for both neighbours and non-neighbours are needed.

6. Structure (3c) is depicted in Figure 5.1(3c) where a circle with letter *i* represents a configuration which sells good *i*, buys goods *j* and *r* and services *n* and *o*, self-provides goods *i* and good 4. A circle with letter *o* represents a wholesale middleman who sells service *o*, buys goods 1, 2, and 3 and service *n*, and self-provides good 4 and service *o*. A circle with letter *n* represents a retail middleman who sells service *n*, buys goods 1, 2, and 3 and service *o*, and self-provides good 4 and service *n*. Here, a wholesale middleman trades goods and services indirectly with the producers of goods through the retail middlemen. Each producer of goods must buy a local retail middleman's service as well as a distant retail middleman's service if he buys goods from non-neighbours. In this structure consisting of five configurations, each individual produces two types of goods and services and trades five types of goods and services. This structure is referred to as *high partial division of labour with a hierarchy of three layers* where there is a division of labour between producers of goods and middlemen as well as between wholesale and retail middlemen, so that a hierarchical structure of transactions involves three layers. Since the level of specialization of each producer of a good is higher than in structures (2a), (2b), or (3b), such a producer trades with a neighbour-producer of goods and a non-neighbour producer of goods. Hence, services for both neighbours and non-neighbours are needed. This implies that a higher level of division of labour in producing goods creates more scope for a division of labour between middlemen (see Marshall, 1890, pp. 256 and 264). It is interesting to see that specialization in producing transaction services is featured with diversity of goods flows handled by those professional middlemen.

7. Structure (4a), depicted in Figure 5.1(4a), is analogous to (3a), except that each person buys good 4 from a specialist producer instead of self-providing it. There is no middleman in this structure.

8. Structure (4b), depicted in Figure 5.1(4b), is analogous to (3b) except that each person buys all goods from specialist producers without self-provision of goods. This structure is referred to as *complete division of labour in production with a hierarchy of two layers* where there is a complete division of labour between producers of goods with the assistance of partially specialized middlemen but there is no division of labour in providing different transaction services.

9. Structure (4c), depicted in Figure 5.1(4c), is analogous to (3c) except that each person buys good 4 from a specialist producer instead of self-providing it. This structure is referred to as *complete division of labour in transactions and production with a hierarchy of three layers*.

There are many symmetrical structures which generate the same per capita real income as in the corresponding structures listed earlier. For instance, in a structure analogous to (2a), each individual has the same level of specialization as in structure (2a) but goods 1 and 3 instead of goods 1 and 2 are traded. Those structures are excluded from our consideration. Furthermore, I will not consider structures which involve profiles of zero and non-zero variables that are not configurations because they are incompatible with the Kuhn–Tucker conditions.

Letting the number of individuals selling good *i* be M_i, a product of M_i and individual supply (demand), given by the individual optimal decisions, yields the market supply of (or demand for) each traded good. Equilibrating the market demand to the market supply yields the market-clearing conditions for each market structure. Furthermore, free entry will ensure utility equalization through individuals' behaviour of maximizing utilities. The market-clearing and utility equalization conditions determine the relative prices of traded goods and the numbers of individuals choosing different configurations. The set of relative prices and numbers defines a *corner equilibrium* in each structure. The concept of a corner equilibrium for a structure is an analogue of a corner solution for an individual configuration. A corner equilibrium is not a general equilibrium unless each individual's utility is maximized with respect to configurations because a corner solution is not an optimal decision unless it maximizes an individual's utility. Let us investigate these nine structures one by one.

Structure (1) In this structure there is only one autarkical configuration. The individual decision problem for this configuration is

$$\max_{L_i}: \quad U = x_1x_2x_3x_4 = (L_1 - A)(L_2 - A)(L_3 - A)(1 - L_1 - L_2 - L_3 - A) \tag{5.4a}$$

$$\text{s. t.} \quad x_i = L_i - A, \quad i = 1, 2, 3, 4 \qquad \text{(production function)}$$
$$L_1 + L_2 + L_3 + L_4 = 1 \qquad \text{(endowment constraint)}$$

The solution is

$$L_i = 1/4, \quad i = 1, 2, 3, 4, \qquad U(1) = [(1/4) - A]^4 \tag{5.4b}$$

where $U(1)$ is the per capita real income in autarky which is positive iff $A < 1/4$ since the amount of each goods consumed is not-positive for $A \geq 1/4$.

Structure (2a) In this structure there are two different configurations. The decision problem for a person who sells good 1, buys good 2, and self-provides goods 1, 3, and 4 and service n is

$$\max_{L_i,\, x_1^s}: \quad U_1 = x_1(t_{2n}x_2^d)x_3x_4 = (L_1 - A - x_1^s)(1 - L_1 - L_3 - L_4 - A)(L_3 - A)(L_4 - A)p_1x_1^s/p_2 \tag{5.5a}$$

$$\text{s. t.} \quad x_1 + x_1^s = L_1 - A, \; x_i = L_i - A, \; i = 3,4 \qquad \text{(production functions of goods)}$$

$t_{2n} = L_{2n} - A,$ (production function of service)
$L_1 + L_2 + L_3 + L_{2n} = 1$ (endowment constraint)
$p_1 x_1^s = p_2 x_2^d$ (budget constraint)

where p_i is the price of good i. Note that all transactions here are between neighbours because it will be shown that each person has only one type of producer of goods as his trading partner in this structure. The solution is given by

$$L_1 = (2 - 3A)/5, \quad L_i = (1 + A)/5, \quad i = 3,4,n, \tag{5.5b}$$
$$x_1^s = (1 - 4A)/5, \qquad x_1 = x_3 = x_4 = t_{2n} = (1 - 4A)/5,$$
$$x_2^d = p_1(1 - 4A)/5p_2 \quad U_1(p) = p_1[(1 - 4A)/5]^5 p_2$$

where $U_1(p)$ is the indirect utility function for this configuration. x_1^s is an individual's supply function of good 1 and x_2^d is his demand function for good 2. The decision problem for the configuration which sells good 2, buys good 1, and self-provides goods 3 and 4 and service n is symmetric to (5.5). The solution to the decision problem for the symmetric configuration is

$$L_2 = (2 - 3A)/5, \quad L_i = (1 + A)/5, \; i = 3,4,n, \quad x_2^s = (1 - 4A)/5$$
$$x_2 = x_3 = x_4 = (1 - 4A)/5, \quad x_1^d = p_2(1 - 4A)/5p_1$$
$$t_{2n} = (1 - 4A)/5, \qquad U_2(p) = p_2[(1 - 4A)/5]^5 p_1$$

where $U_2(p)$ is the indirect utility function for this configuration. x_2^s is an individual's supply function of good 2 and x_1^d is his demand function for good 1. The market-clearing and utility equalization conditions for structure (2a) are

$$M_1 x_1^s = M_2 x_1^d \tag{5.7a}$$
$$U_1(p) = U_2(p) \tag{5.7b}$$

where M_i is the number of individuals selling good i and x_1^s, x_1^d, and $U_i(p)$ are given in (5.5b) and (5.6). Due to Walras' Law, the market-clearing condition for good 2 is not independent of (5.7a). Inserting the solutions to the individual decision problems into the relevant variables in (5.7), the corner equilibrium in structure (2a) is found as:

$$p_1/p_2 = M_1/M_2 = 1, \quad U(2a) = [(1 - 4A)/5]^5 \tag{5.8}$$

where $U(2a)$ is the per capita real income in structure (2a). Note that $M_1/M_2 = 1$ implies that each producer of good i has one producer of good j as his unique trading partner. It is straightforward that $U(2a) < U(1)$, which implies that the corner equilibrium in (2a) cannot be the general equilibrium.

Repeating this procedure, I have solved for the corner equilibria in the other seven structures. The per capita real income, relative prices, the numbers of individuals selling different goods, and level of specialization for individuals choosing different configurations are listed in Table 5.1. The algebraic treatment for establishing the results in Table 5.1 is in the Appendix at the end of this chapter.

In Table 5.1, M_i is the number of individuals selling good (or service) i, p_i is the price of good (or service) i, and L_i is the level of specialization for a person selling good (or service) i, $i = 1,2,3,4, n,o$. M is the population size, k is the transaction efficiency of transaction services, and A is the fixed learning cost in each activity which relates to the degree of economies of specialization. In the notation for a structure ij (i = 1,2,3,4 and j = a,b,c), letter i represents a level of specialization in producing goods and letter j represents a level of specialization in producing transaction services and related hierarchical structure of transactions. Each individual does not trade if $i = 1$; he trades two goods if $i = 2$, trades three goods if $i = 3$, and trades four goods if $i = 4$. If $j = a$, there is a division of labour in producing goods but no division of labour exists between the production of goods and the production of transaction services, so that no hierarchical structure of organization exists. If $j = b$, there is a division of labour between the production of goods and the production of transaction services but no division of labour exists in producing different transaction services, so that the number of layers of the hierarchy of transactions is 2. If $j = c$, there is a division of labour between the production of goods and the production of transaction services as well as between different transaction services, so that the number of layers of the hierarchy of transactions is three.

From the individual decision problems in this section, one can see the effects of our method of specifying production functions on individual demand and supply, indirect utility functions, and the theory of equilibrium. Firstly, individual demand depends on individual supply while demand and supply are two sides of the division of labour. Demand and supply functions and indirect utility functions are not continuous across structures. Secondly, an individual not only solves for the efficient resource allocation for a given pattern and level of specialization, but also chooses a configuration in order to find the efficient pattern and level of specialization. The indirect utility function and *ex post* production functions differ from configuration to configuration despite *ex ante* identical utility and production functions for all individuals. A corner equilibrium in this chapter is equivalent to a general equilibrium in neoclassical microeconomics. A corner equilibrium determines an efficient allocation of resources for a given level of division of labour and a given number of layers of a hierarchy of transactions. However, for our model, the general equilibrium will determine the efficient level of division of labour and the efficient number of layers of a hierarchy of transactions. Many economic

Table 5.1 Corner equilibria in nine market structures

Structure	*Per capita real income U*	*Corner equilibrium relative prices*	*Number of different specialists*	*Level of specialization*
(1)	$[(1-4A)/4]^4$			
(2a)	$[(1-4A)/5]^5$	$p_1/p_2 = 1$	$M_1 = M_2 = M/2$	$L_1 = L_2 = (3-7A)/5$
(2b)	$k^{2/3}(1-3A)^{16/3}/5^{10/3}6^2$	$p_1/p_n = (1-3A)^{1/6}5^{5/3}/36k^{1/3}$, $p_1/p_2 = 1$	$M_n = M[1 + 12k^{1/3}/5^{2/3}(1-3A)^{1/6}]^{-1}$, $M_1 = M_2 = 6k^{1/3}M_n/[12k^{1/3} + 5^{2/3}(1-3A)^{1/6}$	$L_1 = L_2 = (3-4A)/5$, $L_n = (2-3A)/3$
(3a)	$[(1-3A)/6]^6$	$p_1/p_2 = p_1/p_3 = 1$	$M_1 = M_2 = M_3 = M/3$	$L_1 = L_2 = (1-A)/2$
(3b)	$k^{3/4}[(1-3A)/9]^{9/4}$ $[(1-4A)/7]^{21/4}$			
(3c)	$k^3(1-2A)^{58/7}$ $8^{-48/7}10^{-10/7}$	$p_1/p_2 = p_1/p_3 = 1$, $p_n/p_o = [8^8k(1-2A)^2 10^{-10}]^{1/7}$, $p_1/p_n = k^{-2/7}$	$M_o = 5M/[5 + 12p_o(1/p_n + 1/p_1)]$, $M_1 = M_2 = M_3 = 4p_oM_o/5p_1$, $M_n = 12p_oM_o/5p_n$	$L_1 = L_2 = L_3 = (6-5A)/7$, $L_n = (7-6A)/8$, $L_o = (9-8A)/10$
(4a)	$[(1-3A)/8]^8$	$p_1/p_2 = p_1/p_3 = p_1/p_4 = 1$	$M_1 = M_2 = M_3 = M_4 = M/4$	$L_1 = L_2 = L_3 = L_4 = (1-A)/2$
(4b)	$[k(1-2A)^{11}/8^8 12^3]^{4/5}$	$p_1/p_2 = p_1/p_3 = p_1/p_4 = 1$, $p_1/p_o = [(1-2A)^4 8^8/k12^3]^{1/5}$	$M_o = M/[1 + 2^3 3^{7/5}/(1-2A)^{4/5}]$, $M_1 = M_2 = M_3 = M_4 = 3^{7/5}2k^{1/5}M_o/(1-2A)^{4/5}$	$L_1 = L_2 = L_3 = L_4 = (5-2A)/8$, $L_o = (2-A)/3$
(4c)	$k^{56/11}(1-A)^{592/55}$ $10^{-48/11}11^{-4}12^{-12/5}$	$p_1/p_2 = p_1/p_3 = p_1/p_4 = 1$, $p_1/p_n = 11[k^3(1-A)10^{10}]^{-1/11}$, $p_n/p_o = 10(1-A)^{1/5}12^{-6/5}$	$M_o = M[1 + 5p_o(1/3p_1 + 4/11p_n)]^{-1}$, $M_1 = M_2 = M_3 = M_4 = 5p_oM_o/12p_1$, $M_n = 20p_oM_o/11p_n$	$L_1 = L_2 = L_3 = L_4 = L_n = L_o = 1$

phenomena can be explained by changes in organizational patterns of division of labour even if utility and production functions are *ex ante* identical for all individuals. Therefore, I refer to this approach as organization-oriented while neoclassical microeconomics is resource-allocation-oriented.

4 The general equilibrium and its comparative statics

A *general equilibrium* is defined as a fixed point that satisfies the following two conditions: (i) each individual maximizes his/her utility with respect to configurations and quantities of goods consumed, produced, and traded for a given set of relative prices of traded goods and a given set of numbers of individuals choosing different configurations, subject to his/her production functions, endowment constraint, and budget constraint; (ii) the set of relative prices of traded goods and the set of numbers of individuals choosing different configurations equate the market demand for each traded good to its market supply and equalize all individuals' utility levels.[6] By comparing per capita real income in all structures, the corner equilibrium with the maximum per capita real income can be identified. I refer to this corner equilibrium as the Pareto optimum corner equilibrium. Because of multiple corner equilibria, the following proposition is needed.

Proposition 1
A Pareto optimum corner equilibrium is a general equilibrium and all non-Pareto optimum corner equilibria are not general equilibria.

The proof of this proposition is in the Appendix and a more general proof for a broad class of models of endogenous specialization can be found in Sun, Yang, and Yao (1998). By comparing the per capita real incomes in the nine corner equilibria, the general equilibrium is identified as in the following table where the equilibrium structures for different values of k and A are shown in the bottom entries. In Table 5.2, the values of $k_1 \equiv (164.79(1 - 4A)^6/(1 - 3A),^{8}$ $k_2 \equiv 5^5(1 - 3A)/6,^{6}$ $k_3 \equiv 39.88(1 - 3A)^{16/7}/(1 - 2A),^{174/49}$ $k_4 \equiv .46(1 - 2A),^{18/77}$ $k_5 \equiv 47.10(1 - 2A)^{3.97}/(1 - A),^{5.15}$ $k_6 \equiv \{10^{48/11}11^4[(1 - 2A)^{11}/8^8]^{4/5}/12^{24}(1 - A)^{592/55}\}^{55/236}$, $k_5 > k_4$ for $A \in (.40, .44)$, and $k_3 > k_2$ for $A \in (.32, .33)$. Structure (1) is that of autarky, structure (2b) is one of low partial division of labour in production and transactions with a hierarchy of two layers, (3a) is a non-hierarchical high partial division of labour in production, (4b) shows the complete division of labour in producing goods with a hierarchy of two layers, (3c) describes high partial division of labour with a hierarchy of three layers, (4c) is the complete division of labour in production and transactions with a hierarchy of three layers. The algebraic working for establishing the results in Table 5.2 is in the Appendix. Note that the level of division of labour in producing goods is higher in (4b) where four goods are traded than in (3c) where three goods are traded, but the level of division of labour in producing transaction services is higher in (3c) where there is a division of labour between wholesale and retail middlemen, than in (4b) where there is only one type of middleman. The level of division of labour for the whole economy is roughly the same for the two structures since each person in both structures produces two types of goods and/or services. Also, the level of division of labour is roughly the same between (2b) and (3a) which has a higher level of division of labour in production but a lower level of division of labour in transactions than in (2b). But the level of division of labour in (4c) is higher than in (4b) and (3c) which have a higher level of division of labour than in (2b) and (3a) which, in turn, have a higher level of division of labour than in structure (1).[7]

There are two types of comparative statics of the general equilibrium. Table 5.2 summarizes the comparative statics of the first type, which imply that the general equilibrium will discontinuously jump from one corner equilibrium to another when parameters change and reach some critical values. The comparative statics of the second type, which can be derived from Table 5.1, imply that the equilibrium relative prices and the equilibrium numbers of different specialists will continuously change within a certain structure if parameters continuously change within the ranges defined by the critical values which are given by the comparative statics of the first type. The second type of comparative statics are similar to the comparative statics of neoclassical general equilibrium which show how resource allocation and relative prices change in response to parameter changes for a given pattern of division of labour and for a given hierarchical structure of transactions. One cannot find a neoclassical counterpart of the first type of comparative statics which show that how pattern and level of division of labour and hierarchical structure of transactions change in response to parameter changes.

Table 5.2 implies that if the transaction efficiency coefficient k is held as a constant, the level of division of labour and the number of layers of the hierarchy of transactions increases as the fixed learning cost A increases. If A is held as a constant, the level of division of labour and the number of layers of the hierarchy of transactions increases as transaction efficiency for delivering transaction services is improved.

Table 5.2 General Equilibrium and Its Inframarginal Comparative Statics

$A \in$	(0, .22)	(.22, .24)		(.24, .32)		(.32, .33)			(.33, .4)		(.40, .44)			(.44, .5)		(.5, 1)
k		$< k_1$	$> k_1$	$< k_2$	$> k_2$	$< k_2$	$\in (k_2, k_3)$	$> k_3$	$< k_4$	$> k_4$	$< k_4$	$\in (k_4, k_5)$	$> k_5$	$< k_6$	$> k_6$	
Structure	1		2b	3a	2b	3a	2b	3c	4b	3c	4b	3c	4c	4b	4c	

The comparative statics of the first type are summarized in the following proposition.

Proposition 2
If the degree of economies of specialization in producing goods and transaction services are sufficiently small and a transaction cost coefficient for delivering transaction service is large, then the general equilibrium is one of autarky in which no market and hierarchical pattern of organization should exist. If the degree of economies of specialization and transaction efficiency are sufficiently great, then the general equilibrium is a hierarchical structure of transactions with three layers, which is based on the complete division of labour in producing various goods and transaction services. As the degree of economies of specialization increases and/or as the transaction cost coefficient for delivering transaction services falls, the level of division of labour and the number of layers of the hierarchy of transactions increase.

Proposition 2 is more understandable if Figure 5.1 and Table 5.2 are consulted as you read it.

Sun et al. (1998) show that for a broad class of equilibrium models of endogenous specialization the general equilibrium is Pareto optimal. This implies that a competitive market will sort out not only the efficient resource allocation for a given pattern of organization, but also the efficient level of division of labour and efficient hierarchical structure of transactions, due to individuals' horizontal and vertical free mobility across professions and across layers, both horizontal and vertical.

The evolution of the division of labour and the number of layers of the hierarchy based on the comparative statics in this chapter is exogenous because it never occurs in the absence of the exogenous evolution of transaction efficiency and the degree of economies of specialization. Endogenous evolution of the division of labour is investigated in Yang and Borland (1991), Wen (1997), and Zhang (1997). Here, endogenous evolution is a spontaneous evolutionary process that is not driven by any exogenous change in parameters, while exogenous evolution *is* driven by such exogenous changes. If the number of goods is 100 instead of four, and/or if producer goods are introduced into the model, and/or parameters k and A are different across goods and services, then a much richer story of incessant exogenous evolution of the division of labour and hierarchical structure of wholesale and retail networks will be predicted by an extended version of the model. Shi and Yang (1998) show that as the number of layers of the hierarchy increases to a very large number, a hierarchy within a firm which is part of the market hierarchy may emerge from a high level of division. In such circumstances, a theory of centralized hierarchy cum decentralized hierarchy is needed.

It is shown in the Appendix to this chapter that each individual's level of specialization, the degree of endogenous comparative advantage, the extent of the market, and labour productivity of traded goods increase with the level of division of labour and the number of layers of the hierarchy of transactions which can be raised by increases in the degree of economies of specialization and/or in transaction efficiency.

5 Conclusion

A framework consisting of consumer-producers, economies of specialization, and transaction costs has been used to formalize the tradeoff between the transaction costs in delivering transaction services and economies of specialization in producing transaction services in addition to the tradeoff between transaction costs and economies of specialization in producing goods in this chapter. The comparative statics of the general equilibrium based on corner solutions involves shifts of the general equilibrium across several corner equilibria. Having introduced a distinction between transaction services for neighbours and those for non-neighbours, the emergence of retail and wholesale middlemen and a hierarchical structure of transactions from exogenous evolution of division of labour is endogenized. This is driven by an increase in the degree of economies of specialization and/or in transaction efficiency in delivering transaction services. In the exogenous evolution of the division of labour and pyramidal hierarchy of transactions, the following variables: productivity, the extent of the market, trade dependence, the degree of endogenous comparative advantage, the degree of diversity of economic structure, and each person's level of specialization, all concurrently increase.

As shown in this chapter, the function of the market is not only to sort out the efficient resource allocation decision, but also to sort out the efficient level of division of labour and the efficient number of layers of the hierarchy of transactions problem. Free horizontal and vertical mobility of individuals across professions and across layers of the hierarchy is crucial for the efficiency of the invisible hand.

Notes

1 See also Williamson (1967), Calvo and Wellisz (1978, 1979), Keren and Levhari (1979, 1983, 1989), Radner (1992, 1993), Qian (1994), and Rosen (1982).

2 Later, it will be clear that T_i is always between 0 and 1 due to the assumption of unitary endowment of labour for each person.

3 If a more realistic assumption is made that each producer of goods has more than two neighbours, a much more complicated and intractable model is needed to endogenize the level of division of labour and the number of layers of hierarchy.
4 If a person buys transaction service with a non-neighbour from a wholesale middleman, he receives this service from a local retail middleman who receives it from the wholesale middleman. This will become clear when various trade structures are spelt out.
5 All structures with two or more layers in this model are called by Bolton and Dewatripont (1994) a regular pyramidal network in which each producer of goods trades with other producers via a middleman. They show that in their model the efficient networks are pyramidal and that a pyramidal network of conveyor belt type may be efficient under a certain condition. In our model, nonpyramidal structures A, (2a), (3a), and (4a) may be efficient and conveyor belt does not occur in equilibrium.
6 Sun, Yang, and Yao (1999) provides a proof of the existence theorem of general equilibrium in the kind of models in this chapter. In addition, Spanjers (1997) provides an existence theorem of general equilibrium hierarchy.
7 Structures (2a), (3b), or (4a) might be general equilibria if the fixed learning cost is much smaller in producing transaction services than in producing goods.

References

Bac, M. (1996) 'Corruption and Supervision Costs in Hierarchies', *Journal of Comparative Economics*, 22, 99–118.

Bag, P. K. (1997) 'Controlling Corruption in Hierarchies', *Journal of Comparative Economics*, 25, 322–44.

Bolton, P. and Dewatripont, M. (1994) 'The Firm as a Communication Network', *Quarterly Journal of Economics*, 109, 809–39.

Bolton, Patrick, and Scharfstein, David (1998) 'Corporate Finance, the Theory of the Firm, and Organization', *Journal of Economic Perspectives*, 12, 95–114.

Borland, Jeff and Eichberger, Jurgen (1998) 'Organizational Form outside the Principal–Agent Paradigm', *Bulletin of Economic Research*, 50, 201–27.

Calvo, G. and Wellisz, S. (1978) 'Supervision, Loss of Control and the Optimal Size of the Firm', *Journal of Political Economy*, 86, 943–52.

Calvo, G. and Wellisz, S. (1979) 'Hierarchy, Ability and Income Distribution', *Journal of Political Economy*, 87, 991–1010.

Carter, M. (1995) 'Information and the Division of Labour: Implications for the Firm's Choice of Organisation', *Economic Journal*, 105, 385–97.

Dicke, Thomas (1992) *Franchising in America – the Development of a Business Method, 1840–1980* (Chapel Hill: University of North Carolina Press).

Gibbons, Robert (1998) 'Incentives in Organization', *Journal of Economic Perspectives*, 12, 115–32.

Hart, O. and Holmstrom, B. (1987) 'The Theory of Contracts', in T. Bewley (ed.), *Advances in Economic Theory* (Cambridge: Cambridge University Press).

Holmstrom, B. and Milgrom, P. (1995) 'The Firm as an Incentive System', *American Economic Review*, 84, 972–91.

Keren, M. and Levhari, D. (1979) 'The Optimum Span of Control in a Pure Hierarchy', *Management Science*, 25, 1162–72.

Keren, M. and Levhari, D. (1983) 'The Internal Organization of the Firm and the Shape of Average Costs', *Bell Journal of Economics*, 13, 474–86.

Keren, M. and Levhari, D. (1989) 'Decentralization, Aggregation, Control Loss and Costs in a Hierarchical Model of the Firm', *Journal of Economic Behavior and Organization*, 11, 213–36.

Kremer, Michael (1993) 'The O-ring Theory of Economic Development', *Quarterly Journal of Economics*, 108, 551–75.

Laffont, J. J. (1990) 'Analysis of Hidden Gaming in a Three Level Hierarchy', *Journal of Law and Economic Organization*, 6, 301–24.

Lio, M. (1996) 'Three Assays on Increasing Returns and Specialisation: A Contribution to New Classical Microeconomic Approach', PhD Dissertation, Department of Economics, the National Taiwan University.

Lio, M. (1998) 'Uncertainty, Insurance, and Division of Labour', *Review of Development Economics*, 2, 76–86.

MacLeod, W. and Malcomson, J. (1988) 'Reputation and Hierarchy in Dynamic Models of Employment', *Journal of Political Economy*, 96, 832–81.

Marshall, Alfred (1890) *Principles of Economics*, 8th edition (New York: Macmillan, 1948).

Milgrom, P. and Roberts, J. (1992) *Economics, Organization and Management* (Englewood Cliffs: Prentice-Hall).

Muller-Hagedorn, Lothar (1995) 'The Variety of Distribution Systems', *Journal of Institutional Economics*, 151, 186–202.

Qian, Y. (1994) 'Incentives and Loss of Control in an Optimal Hierarchy', *Review of Economic Studies*, 61, 3, 527–44.

Radner, R. (1992) 'Hierarchy: the Economics of Managing', *Journal of Economic Literature*, 30, 1382–1415.

Radner, R. (1993) 'The Organization of Decentralized Information Processing', *Econometrica*, 61, 1109–46.

Rosen, S. (1982) 'Authority, Control, and the Distribution of Earnings', *Bell Journal of Economics*, 13, 311–23.

Sah, R. (1991) 'Fallibility in Human Organizations and Political Systems', *Journal of Economic Perspectives*, 5, 67–88.

Sah, R. and Stiglitz, J. (1988) 'Committees, Hierarchies and Polyarchies', *The Economic Journal*, 98, 451–70.

Sah, Raj and Stiglitz, Joseph (1991) 'The Quality of Managers in Centralized versus Decentralized Organizations', *Quarterly Journal of Economics*, 106, 289–95.

Sappington, D. (1991) 'Incentives in Principal–agent Relationships', *Journal of Economic Perspectives*, 5, 45–66.

Shi, H. and X. Yang (1998) 'Centralised Hierarchy within a Firm vs. Decentralised Hierarchy in the Market', in K. Arrow, Y.-K. Ng, and X. Yang (eds), *Increasing Returns and Economic Analysis* (London: Macmillan).

Spanjers, W. (1997) *Hierarchically Structured Economies: Models with Bilateral Exchange Institutions*. Theory and Decision Library, Series C (Dordrecht: Kluwer Academic Publishers).

Sun, G., Yang, X. and Yao, S. (1999) 'Theoretical Foundation of Economic Development Based on Networking Decisions in the Competitive Market', Harvard Centre for International Development Working Paper No. 17.

Tirole, J. (1986) 'Hierarchies and Bureaucracies: On the Role of Collusion in Organizations', *Journal of Law and Economic Organization*, 2, 181–214.

Van Zandt, T. (1995) 'Hierarchical Computation of the Resource Allocation Problem', *European Economic Review*, 39, 700–8.

Wen, M. (1997) 'Infrastructure and Evolution in Division of Labour', *Review of Development Economics*, 2.

Wen, M. (1998) 'An Analytical Framework of Consumer-Producers, Economies of Specialisation and Transaction Costs', in K. Arrow, Y.-K. Ng and X. Yang (eds), *Increasing Returns and Economic Analysis* (London: Macmillan).

Williamson, O. (1967) 'Hierarchical Control and Optimum Firm Size', *Journal of Political Economics*, 75, 123–38.

Yang, X. and Borland, J. (1991) 'A Microeconomic Mechanism for Economic Growth', *Journal of Political Economy*, 99, 460–82.

Yang, X. and Ng, Y.-K. (1993) *Specialization and Economic Organization: a New Classical Microeconomic Framework* (Amsterdam: North-Holland).

Yang, X. and Ng, S. (1998) 'Specialisation and Division of Labour: a Survey', in K. Arrow, Y.-K. Ng, and X. Yang (eds), *Increasing Returns and Economic Analysis* (London: Macmillan).

Young, Allyn (1928) 'Increasing Returns and Economic Progress', *The Economic Journal*, 38, 527–42.

Zhang, J. (1997) 'Evolution in Division of Labour and Macroeconomic Policies', *Review of Development Economics*, no. 2, 236–45.

Appendix: proof of propositions 1 and 2

This appendix first proves proposition 1, then works out the algebra in order to solve for the corner equilibria in the structures other than (1) and (2a). Then the results in Table 5.2 and proposition 2 are established. Finally, it is proved that the extent of the market, labour productivity, the degree of endogenous comparative advantage, and the degree of diversity increase as the level of division of labour and the number of layers of the hierarchy of transactions increase.

1 Proof of proposition 1

It is straightforward that the Pareto optimum corner equilibrium is a general equilibrium because it satisfies two conditions for a general equilibrium. I need therefore to prove only the second statement of proposition 1. Assume, for example, that the Pareto optimum corner equilibrium is in structure 2a and that other structures have non-Pareto optimum corner equilibria. Suppose all individuals are in the corner equilibrium in structure 2b where corner equilibrium prices are $p = (p_1, p_2)$ and corner equilibrium utility level is $u(2b)$. All individuals know that they can choose any one out of all configurations. Each individual can insert the corner equilibrium prices p of structure 2b into indirect utilities of the configurations in structure 3c. If these utilities are greater than $u(2b)$, then individuals have an incentive to switch from their assigned configuration in structure 2b to an alternative configuration that is in structure 2a.

In structure 2a, there are two configurations. The indirect utility functions in the configurations are

$$u_1(p) = u_x(p_{12}) \qquad (A5.1)$$
$$u_2(p) = u_y(p_{21})$$

where $u_1(p)$ and $u_2(p)$ are indirect utility functions for configurations (1/2) and (2/1), respectively under the corner equilibrium prices in structure 2b and $\partial u_i/\partial p_{ij} > 0$.

Let q be the corner equilibrium prices in structure 2a and replace p_{ij} by q_{ij} in (A5.1); the utility equalization conditions in structure 2a is:

$$u_1(q) = u_2(q) = u(2a) \qquad (A5.2)$$

where $u(2a)$ is a constant depending on all the parameters. Recalling that $u(2b)$ is the corner equilibrium utility in structure 2b; the assumption that structure 2a is the Pareto optimum corner equilibrium implies that $u(2a) > u(2b)$.

Individuals will compare the utilities in the configurations of structure 2a under prices of structure 2b, i.e. $u_1(p)$ and $u_2(p)$ with $u(2b)$. If any one of the following inequalities holds, then individuals have an incentive to shift to a configuration of structure 2a from their assigned configuration in structure 2b under the prices in structure 2b, which means that structure 2b is not a general equilibrium.

$$u_1(p) > u(2b) \qquad (A5.3)$$
$$u_2(p) > u(2b)$$

where $u_i(p)$ is utility for a configuration in structure 2a under the corner equilibrium relative price p in structure 2b.

Because $u(2a) > u(2b)$ by assumption, one of the two inequalities in (A5.3) will hold if the corresponding one of the two semi-inequalities in (A5.4) holds.

$$u_1(p) \geq u_1(q) = u(2a) > u(2b) \qquad \text{(A5.4)}$$
$$u_2(p) \geq u_2(q) = u(2a) > u(2b)$$

where the equalities are based on the utility equalization condition (A5.2). One of (A5.4) holds if one of (A5.5a) and (A5.5b) holds because $\partial u_i/\partial p_{ij} > 0$.

$$p_{12} \geq q_{12} \qquad \text{(A5.5a)}$$
$$p_{21} \geq q_{21} \qquad \text{(A5.5b)}$$

It is straightforward that at least one of (A5.5) must hold for any p and q. This implies that individuals have an incentive to shift to at least one configuration in structure 2a from structure 2b under corner equilibrium prices in 2b if $u(2b) < u(2a)$. That is, the non-Pareto optimum corner equilibrium in structure 2b is not a general equilibrium. Since I have used the assumption $u(2a) > u(2b)$ in the deduction, I cannot prove that individuals have an incentive to deviate from structure 2a if 2a is the Pareto optimum corner equilibrium.

We can similarly eliminate any of the other non-Pareto optimum corner equilibria. Therefore, Proposition 1 has been established. Q.E.D.

The intuition behind this deduction is straightforward. Since the effects of relative prices on the utility of individuals selling different goods are of different signs, if the prices in structure 2b differ from those in structure 2a and individuals do not prefer some configurations in structure 2a under the prices of structure 2b when 2a is Pareto superior to 2b, then they must prefer another configuration in 2a under the prices of 2b. This means that the utility in this configuration under prices of structure 2b is greater than the maximum utility in structure 2b. Hence, individuals will have an incentive to shift from 2b to this configuration in 2a under the prices of structure 2b.

2 Algebra for solving for the corner equilibria that is not detailed in the chapter

The corner equilibrium in structure (2b) In structure (2b), there are three different configurations. The decision problem for a person who sells good 1, buys good 2 and service n, and self-provides goods 1, 3, and 4 is as follows

$$\underset{L_i,\, x_1^s}{\text{Max:}} \quad U_1 = x_1(kt_{2n}{}^d x_2{}^d)x_3x_4 = k(L_1 - A - x_1{}^s)(1 - L_1 - L_3 - L_4 - A)(L_3 - A)(L_4 - A)p_1x_1{}^s/p_2$$

$$\text{s. t.} \quad x_1 + x_1{}^s = L_1 - A,\ x_i = L_i - A,\ i = 3, 4 \qquad \text{(production function of goods)}$$
$$L_1 + L_3 + L_4 = 1 \qquad \text{(endowment constraint)}$$
$$p_1x_1{}^s = p_2x_2{}^d + p_nt_{2n}{}^d \qquad \text{(budget constraint)}$$

where k is the transaction efficiency coefficient in delivering transaction service and p_i is the price of good (or service) i. Note that all transactions here are between neighbours because I will show that each person has only one type of producer of goods as his trading partner in this structure. The solution is

$L_1 = (3 - 4A)/5$, $L_i = (1 + 2A)/5$, $i = 3,4$, $x_1^s = 2(1 - 3A)/5$
$x_1 = x_3 = x_4 = (1 - 3A)/5, x_2^d = p_1(1 - 3A)/5p_2$
$t_{2n}^d = p^1(1 - 3A)/5p_n$, $U_1(p) = kp_1^2[(1 - 3A)/5]^5/p_2p_n$

where $U_1(p)$ is the indirect utility function for this configuration, x_1^s is an individual's supply function of good 1, t_{2n}^d is his demand function for service n, and x_2^d is his demand function for good 2. The decision problem for the configuration which sells good 2, buys good 1 and service n, and self-provides goods 3 and 4 is symmetric to the above problem. The symmetry and utility equalization condition between the two symmetric configurations implies $p_1 = p_2$.

The decision problem for a person who sells service n, buys goods 1 and 2, and self-provides goods 3 and 4 is the following:

Max: $U_n = (t_{1n}x_1^d)(t_{2n}x_2^d)x_3x_4$
s. t. $t_{1n} + t_{2n} + t_n^s = L_n - A$, $x_i = L_i - A$, $i = 3, 4$ (production functions of services, goods)
$L_n + L_3 + L_4 = 1$ (endowment constraint)
$p_nt_n^s = p_1x_1^d + p_2x_2^d$ (budget constraint)

The solution is therefore:

$L_n = (2 - 3A)/3$, $L_i = (1 + 3A)/6$, $i = 3,4$, $t_n^s = (1 - 3A)/3$
$t_{1n} = t_{2n} = x_3 = x_4 = (1 - 3A)/6$, $x_1^d = p_n(1 - 3A)/6p_1$ $x_2^d = p_n(1 - 3A)/6p_2$
$U_n(p) = p_n^2[(1 - 3A)/6]^6/p_2p_1$

where $U_n(p)$ is the indirect utility function for this configuration, t_n^s is an individual's supply function of service n, x_i^d is his demand function for good i.

The market-clearing and utility equalization conditions for structure (2b) are

$M_1x_1^s = M_2x_1^d(2) + M_nx_1^d(n)$,
$M_2x_2^s = M_1x_2^d(1) + M_nx_2^d(n)$
$U_1(p) = U_2(p) = U_n(p)$

where M_i is the number of individuals selling good or service i and x_i^s, x_i^d, and $U_i(p)$ are given by the solutions of individual decision problems. (j) after x_i^d denotes the quantity of good i demanded by a person selling good j. Due to Walras' Law, the market-clearing condition for service n is not independent of the above equations. The three equations give the corner equilibrium in structure (2b) as listed in Table 5.1. Note that $M_1 = M_2$ implies that each producer of good i has only one producer of good j as his one of trading partners.

The algebra for solving for the corner equilibrium in structures (3a) is analogous to that for (2a), which is given in (5)–(8). The algebra required for solving for the corner equilibrium in structures (3b) is analogous to that for (2b).

The corner equilibrium in structure (3c) In structure (3c), there are six different configurations. The decision problem for a person who sells good 1, buys goods 2 and 3, and services n and o, and self-provides goods 1 and 4 is as follows:

Max: $U_1 = x_1[(kt_{2n}^d)x_2^d][(kt_{3n}^d)(kt_{3o}^d)(kt_{3n'}^d)x_3^d]x_4$
s. t. $x_1 + x_1^s = L_1 - A$, $x_4 = L_4 - A$, (production functions of goods)

$$L_1 + L_4 = 1 \qquad \text{(endowment constraint)}$$
$$p_1 x_1^s = p_2 x_2^d + p_3 x_2^d + p_n(t_{2n}^d + t_{3n}^d) + p_{n'} t_{3n'}^d \qquad \text{(budget constraint)}$$

where each t_{ij}^d involves a transaction cost $(1 - k)t_{ij}^d$, n is the service bought from a local retail middleman and n′ is the service for non-neighbours bought from a retail middleman who is in another community. The solution is thus,

$$L_1 = (7 - 6A)/8, \quad L_4 = (1 + 6A)/8, \quad x_1^s = 3(1 - 2A)/4$$
$$x_1 = x_4 = (1 - 2A)/8, \quad x_2^d = p_1(1 - 2A)/8p_2, \quad x_3^d = p_1(1 - 2A)/8p_3,$$
$$t_{2n}^d = t_{3n}^d = p_1(1 - 2A)/8p_n, \quad t_{3n'}^d = p_1(1 - 2A)/8p_{n'},$$
$$t_{3o}^d = p_1(1 - 2A)/8p_o, \quad U_1(p) = k^4 p_1^6[(1 - 2A)/8]^8/p_n^2 p_{n'} p_o p_2 p_3$$

where $U_1(p)$ is the indirect utility function for this configuration. The symmetry between services n and n′ and the utility equalization condition imply $p_n = p_{n'}$. The decision problem for the configuration which sells good 2, buys goods 1 and 3, and services n and o, and self-provides good 4 and the configuration which sells good 3, buys goods 1 and 2, and services n and o, and self-provides good 4 are symmetric to the above decision. The symmetry and utility equalization conditions between the three symmetric configurations imply $p_1 = p_2 = p_3$.

The decision problem for a person who sells service n, buys goods 1, 2, and 3, and service o, and self-provides good 4 and service n is

$$\text{Max:} \quad U_n = (t_{1n}x_1^d)(t_{2n}x_2^d)[(kt_{3n'}^d)(kt_{3o}^d)x_3^d]x_4$$
$$\text{s. t.} \quad t_{1n} + t_{2n} + t_n^s = L_n - A, \; x_4 = L_4 - A \qquad \text{(production functions of services, goods)}$$
$$L_n + L_4 = 1 \qquad \text{(endowment constraint)}$$
$$p_n t_n^s = p_1 x_1^d + p_2 x_2^d + p_3 x_3^d + p_o t_{3o}^d + p_n t_{3n'}^d \qquad \text{(budget constraint)}$$

The solution is

$$L_n = (7 - 6A)/8, \quad L_4 = (1 + 6A)/8, \quad t_n^s = 5(1 - 2A)/8$$
$$t_{1n} = t_{2n} = x_4 = (1 - 2A)/8, \quad x_1^d = p_n(1 - 2A)/8p_1 \quad x_2^d = p_n(1 - 2A)/8p_2$$
$$x_3^d = p_n(1 - 2A)/8p_3, \quad t_{3n'}^d = p_n(1 - 2A)/8p_{n'} \quad t_{3o}^d = p_n(1 - 2A)/8p_o$$
$$U_n(p) = k^2 p_n^5[(1 - 2A)/8]^8/p_1 p_2 p_3 p_o p_{n'}$$

where $U_n(p)$ is the indirect utility function for this configuration.

The decision problem for a person who sells service o, buys goods 1, 2, and 3, and service n, and self-provides good 4 and service o is given by:

$$\text{Max:} \quad U_o = [(kt_{1n}^d)t_{1o}^d x_1^d][(kt_{2n}^d)t_{2o}x_2^d][(kt_{3n}^d)t_{3o}x_3^d]x_4$$
$$\text{s. t.} \quad t_{1o} + t_{2o} + t_{3o} + t_o^s = L_o - A, \quad x_4 = L_4 - A \qquad \text{(production functions of services, goods)}$$
$$L_o + L_4 = 1 \qquad \text{(endowment constraint)}$$
$$p_o t_o^s = p_1 x_1^d + p_2 x_2^d + p_3 x_3^d + p_n(t_{1n}^d + t_{2n}^d + t_{3n}^d) \qquad \text{(budget constraint)}$$

The solution is as follows:

$$L_o = (9 - 8A)/10, \quad L_4 = (1 + 8A)/10, \quad t_o^s = 3(1 - 2A)/5$$
$$t_{1o} = t_{2o} = t_{3o} = x_4 = (1 - 2A)/10, \quad x_1^d = p_o(1 - 2A)/10p_1$$

$$x_2^d = p_o(1-2A)/10p_2$$
$$x_3^d = p_o(1-2A)/10p_3, \quad U_o(p) = k^3 p_o^6[(1-2A)/10]^{10}/p_1 p_2 p_3 p_n^3$$

where $U_o(p)$ is the indirect utility function for this configuration.
The market-clearing and utility equalization conditions for structure (3c) are given by:

$$M_1 x_1^s = M_2 x_1^d(2) + M_3 x_1^d(3) + M_n x_1^d(n) + M_o x_1^d(o),$$
$$M_2 x_2^s = M_1 x_2^d(1) + M_3 x_2^d(3) + M_n x_2^d(n) + M_o x_2^d(o),$$
$$M_3 x_3^s = M_1 x_3^d(1) + M_2 x_3^d(2) + M_n x_3^d(n) + M_o x_3^d(o),$$
$$M_n t_n^s = M_1[t_{2n}^d(1) + t_{3n}^d(1) + t_{3n'}^d(1)] + M_2[t_{1n}^d(2) + t_{3n}^d(2) + t_{3n'}^d(2)] + M_3[t_{1n}^d(3) + t_{2n}^d(3) + t_{1n'}^d(3)] + M_o t_{3n}^d(o),$$
$$U_1(p) = U_2(p) = U_3(p) = U_n(p) = U_o(p),$$

where M_i is the number of individuals selling good or service i. (j) after x_i^d or t_{in}^d denotes the quantity of good i demanded by a person selling good j. Due to Walras' Law, the market-clearing condition for service o is not independent of the above equations. Due to the symmetry between services n and n′, a distinction is drawn between them, so that M_n is the number of individuals who sell n and n′. The five equations give the corner equilibrium in structure (3c) as listed in Table 5.1.

The algebra for solving for the corner equilibria in (4a), (4b), and (4c) is analogous to that for (2a), (3b), and (3c), respectively. It can be obtained from the author upon request.

Now, let us prove proposition 1 using the results in Table 5.1. It is straightforward from Table 5.1 that utility levels generated by corner equilibria in structures (2a) and (3b) cannot be greater than that in structure (1) and that U(4a) < U(3a). Hence, the three structures (2a), (3b), and (4a) cannot be general equilibrium. The set of candidates for the equilibrium is narrowed down to structures (1), (2b), (3a), (3c), (4b), and (4c). It is obvious that U(4c) is positive and all other structures yield non-positive utility if $A \in (0.5,1)$ since the amount of each good consumed in any of the other structures is non-positive for $A \in (0.5,1)$. Hence,

(A1) Structure (4c) is the general equilibrium if $A \in (.5,1)$.

Also, only structures (3c), (4b), and (4c) among the candidates yield positive utility if $A \in (.33,.5)$. A comparison between U(3c), U(4b), and U(4c) yields

(A2) U(4c) > U(3c) iff $k > k_5$, but $k_5 > 1$ if $A < .40$, so that U(3c) > U(4c) for $A < .4$.
(A3) U(3c) > U(4b) iff $k > k_4$, but $k_4 > k_5$ for $A > .44$.
(A4) U(4c) > U(4b) iff $k > k_6$, but $k_6 > 1$ if $A < .36$, so that U(4b) > U(4c) for $A < .36$.

where the assumption $k \in [0,1]$ is used and k_4, k_5 and k_6 are given in Table 5.2. (A2) implies that U(3c) > U(4c) and thereby (4c) cannot be the equilibrium if $A < .40$. (A2) and (A3) imply that U(3c) is either smaller than U(4b) for $k < k_4$ or smaller than U(4c) for $k > k_4$ if $A >. 44$. Hence, (3c) cannot be equilibrium for $A > .44$.

Therefore, (A2)–(A4), together with the fact that U(1), U(2b), U(3a) are non-positive for $A > 1/3$, implies the following:

(A5) For $A \in (.44,.5)$, (4b) is the equilibrium if $k < k_6$ and (4c) is the equilibrium if $k > k_6$;
For $A \in (.40, .44)$ (4b) is the equilibrium if $k < k_4$, (3c) is the equilibrium if $k \in (k_4, k_5)$, and (4c) is the equilibrium if $k > k_5$;
For $A \in (.33, .4)$, (4b) is the equilibrium if $k < k_4$ and (3c) is the equilibrium if $k > k_4$.

A comparison between U(1), U(2b), U(3a), U(3c), U(4b), and U(4c) yields

(A6) $U(2b) > U(1)$ iff $k > k_1$, but $k_1 > 1$ for $A < .22$, so that $U(1) > U(2b)$ for $A < .22$
(A7) $U(3c) > U(2b)$ iff $k > k_3$, but $k_3 > 1$ for $A < .32$, so that $U(2b) > U(3c)$ for $A < .32$
(A8) $U(3a) > U(1)$ iff $A > .24$,
(A9) $U(3c) > U(3a)$ iff $k > k_7$, but $k_7 > 1$ for $A < .24$, so that $U(3a) > U(3c)$ for $A < .24$.
(A10) $U(4b) > U(2b)$ iff $k > k_8$, but $k_8 > 1$ for $A < .33$, so that $U(2b) > U(4b)$ for $A < .33$.

where k_1 and k_3 are given in Table 5.2, $k_7 \equiv \{8^{48/7}10^{10/7}[(1-4A)/4]^4/(1-2A)^{58/7}\}^{1/3}$, $k_8 \equiv (1-3A)^{40}[12^3 8^8/(1-2A)^{11}]^6/5^{25}6^{15}$. (A2), (A6), (A7), (A8), and (A10) together implies

(A11) For $A \in (0,.22)$, $U(1) > U(2b) > U(3c) > U(4c)$, $U(1) > U(2b) > U(4b)$, and $U(1) > U(3a)$. Hence, structure (1) is the equilibrium;

(A2), (A7), (A8), and (A9) together imply

(A12s) For $A \in (.22,.24)$, $U(2b) > U(3c) > U(4c)$, $U(2b) > U(4b)$, and $U(1) > U(3a)$. Hence, (1) is the equilibrium if $k < k_1$ and (2b) is the equilibrium if $k > k_1$;

(A2), (A7), (A10), together with a comparison between U(3a) and U(2b), implies

(A13) For $A \in (.24,.32)$, $U(3a) > U(1)$, $U(2b) > U(3c) > U(4c)$, $U(2b) > U(4b)$. Hence, (2b) is the equilibrium if $k < k_2$ and (3a) is the equilibrium if $k > k_2$.

where k_2 is given in Table 5.2. (A4), (A10), together with the fact that U(1) is non-positive for $A > .25$, implies

(A14) For $A \in (.32,.33)$, $U(2b) > U(4b) > U(4c)$, so that (3a) is the equilibrium if $k < k_2$, (2b) is the equilibrium is $k \in (k_2,k_3)$, and (3c) is the equilibrium if $k > k_3$.

(A1)–(A14) are sufficient for establishing the results in Table 5.2 and proposition 1.

3 Concurrent increases in productivity, trade dependence, and comparative advantages

Now, let us work out the comparative statics of the first type that can generate the concurrent economic phenomena discussed at the end of section 4.

Level of specialization A comparison of individuals' levels of specialization in producing goods which are sold, (given in Table 5.1), across structures, yields

(A15) $L_x(3c) > L_x(3a)$ iff $3 - 10A(3c) > -7A(3a)$

where A(3c) is a value of A that ensures (3c) as a candidate for the equilibrium and A(3a) is that for (3a). The inequality (A15) holds if

(A16) $3 - 10\text{Max}\{A(3c)\} > -7\text{Min}\{A(3a)\}$.

From Table 5.2, it can be seen that Max{A(3c)} = .44 and Min{A(3a)} = .24. Plugging the values back into (A16) establishes the inequality. Hence, $L_x(3c) > L_x(3a)$. Following an analogous line of reasoning, the following claim can be established.

(A17) $L_n(4c) > L_n(3c), L_n(4b) > L_n(2b) > L_n(1)$
$L_o(4c) > L_o(3c) > L_o(2b) > L_o(1)$
$L_x(4c) > L_x(3c), L_x(4b) > L_x(2b), L_x(3a) > L_x(1)$.

(A17) can be used to work out the comparative statics of the first type for other variables which depend on individuals' level of specialization.

Labour productivity Labour productivity of traded good (or service) i increases as the economy shifts from structure (1) to (2b) or (3a), followed by (4b) or (3c), and finally ending up with (4c) because the level of specialization of goods and services sold increase with such shifts and because of the existence of economies of specialization (which implies that labour productivity increases with the level of specialization).

Degree of endogenous comparative advantage Endogenous comparative advantage is defined by Yang and Borland (1991) and Yang and Ng (1993) as a difference in labour productivity of a good between its sellers and buyers. Since a buyer's labour productivity of a good is non-positive (that is, he/she does not produce the good), the difference in labour productivity between the sellers and buyers of a good increases as the sellers' labour productivity of the good increases. Hence, (A17) can be used to establish the statement that the degree of endogenous comparative advantage increases as the level of division of labour increases.

The extent of the market and trade dependence The extent of the market is defined as a product of both the population size and per capita value of all traded goods. Since only labour is the productive factor and each person is endowed with one unit of labour in the model, the value of the good produced by a person for sale in terms of labour can be represented by his labour share in producing the good, which is his level of specialization. The extent of the market is thus the weighted average of the values of different goods produced by individuals for sale. The weights are the population shares of individuals selling different goods. Irregardless of the values of the weights, the weighted average increases if the levels of specialization of individuals choosing different configurations increase. Hence, (A17) can be used to show that the extent of the market increases as division of labour evolves from (1) to (2b) or (3a), followed by (4b) or (3c), and finally ending up with (4c). Indeed, (A17) implies that the levels of specialization of all individuals choosing different configurations increase as division of labour and the number of layers of the hierarchy evolve. Since each person's level of specialization in producing the good which (in turn is sold by him) is his income share of the traded good (also termed his trade dependence), therefore trade dependence increases as division of labour and the number of layers exogenously evolve.

Degree of diversity of economic structure It is obvious that the number of markets for different goods, the number of professional configurations which are distinctive from each other, and the degree of asymmetry between the middleman on the top of the hierarchy and peripheral producers on the bottom, all increase as division of labour and the number of layers evolve. This implies the degree of diversity of economic structure increases as division of labour and the number of layers evolve.

6
A General Equilibrium Model with Impersonal Networking Decisions and Bundling Sales

Ke Li

1 Introduction

The purpose of this chapter is to investigate the function of a particular type of bundling sales in exploiting the network effect of the division of labour, and in promoting increases in productivity. First we shall survey the existing literature on bundling and tying sales. Then, we move on to consider some common internet phenomena which cannot be predicted by the existing approaches. Finally, we will formulate the effects of bundling sales on the network size of the division of labour by drawing from the literature on endogenous specialization and the network effect of division of labour.

There have been a number of extensive studies on bundling and tying sales: Burstein (1960), Stigler (1963), Adams and Yellen (1976), Schmalensee (1984), McAfee, McMillan, and Whinston (1989), Whinston (1990), Hanson and Martin (1990), Varian (1995, 1997), and Bakos and Brynjolfsson (1999a, b). These studies focus on bundling and tying associated with monopoly power. A few assumptions are made in these studies. Each consumer consumes at most one unit of goods and has constant valuation of this one unit. Resale of goods is not allowed. In addition, differentiated prices cannot be directly charged for individuals with differentiated valuations of goods because of the unobservability of such valuations. The assumptions imply that utility is not stated as a function of amounts of all consumption goods and that no substitution between goods is allowed (or with so-called independent valuations). Hence, interesting interactions and feedback loops between consumption quantities, prices, income, production decisions, and substitution between goods, which are the focus of standard general equilibrium analysis, are not investigated in these studies. With these rather special assumptions, it is easy to see that bundling can impose indirect price discrimination under a uniform price of a bundle of goods even if no monopoly power exists. Bakos and Brynjolfsson (1999a, b) have nicely presented this conclusion about the function of bundling.

From the literature surveyed, research results on the welfare effects of bundling are inconclusive. Adams and Yellen (1976) emphasize that adverse effects of bundling on welfare derive from monopoly power rather than bundling itself. Bowman (1957), Blair and Kaserman (1978), Grimes (1994), Delong (1998), Chae (1992), Fishburn, Odlyzko and Siders (1997), Varian (1995), Chuang and Marvin (1999), and Bakos and Brynjolfsson (1997, 1999a, b) highlight the positive welfare effects of bundling. Matutes and Regibeau (1992), Tirole (1989), and Martin (1999) pay attention to adverse welfare effects of tying sale. Whinston (1990) shows that the welfare effects of tying in an oligopoly regime are ambiguous.

As reviewers of some of the literature have pointed out, many internet and e-business phenomena are inconsistent with the particular assumptions made. For instance, there are more than a thousand e-mail or search engine providers, and each bundles its services. Some services are charged positive prices (very likely lower than marginal cost) and others are provided free of charge. Resale of such services is possible. Quantities of such services can be any integer number, for instance each person may get several e-mail accounts from different providers. In addition, substitution between services is not trivial, that is, a consumer's valuation of a service is not constant, and a consumer's utility is a function of quantities of such services and other goods.

Bakos and Brynjolfsson (1999b, p. 3) defend their position by arguing that bundling sales with zero prices of some services is a phenomenon of disequilibrium. We disagree. Goods of zero prices implicitly bundled with goods of positive prices can be a general equilibrium phenomenon.

A conventional market for petrol and air-pump services illustrates our point. Many petrol stations sell petrol at competitive prices and provide air-pump services free of charge. This market structure has been in place for a long time. The bundling of petrol and air-pump services must be regarded as a general equilibrium phenomenon. In this market, consumers' preferences for petrol and air-pump services might be very similar, so the rationale for the type of bundling is irrelevant.[1] However, the reason for this phenomenon is actually quite straightforward. The pricing of air-pump services and collection of related payments involve a transaction cost to consumers as well as to petrol stations – waiting time, inconvenience, and tangible resource cost for pricing and payment collection. If the production cost of such services can be added to the price of petrol, which is complementary to air-pump services, then the transaction cost can be avoided. It is true that the bundling sale may incur endogenous transaction costs, distortions caused by individuals who use air-pump services but do not buy petrol from the same petrol station. But as long as the reduction of exogenous transaction costs outweighs the increase in endogenous transaction costs, a competitive market will generate pressure on petrol stations to implement such a bundling price structure. We call this phenomenon 'implicit bundling', which charges a positive price of a good and zero price of another good without an explicit bundle. Implicit bundling is closer to mixed bundling than the pure bundling investigated in the existing literature. There are other examples of implicit bundling. TV programmes are free of charge, and associated advertisements are paid at positive prices by companies selling goods to viewers of TV programmes. An automobile company may market cars with positive prices of cars and free internet purchase services.

The key point is that competition pressure and prohibitively high pricing costs of some goods are essential for zero prices of goods bundled with goods of positive prices. Therefore, we need to construct a model without monopoly power that takes into account transaction costs and competitive (implicit) bundling. This chapter attempts to formulate a model using general equilibrium analysis, with specified *ex ante* identical utility and production functions for all individuals. We shall also analyse the tradeoff between the positive network effect of the division of labour on aggregate productivity on the one hand, and transaction costs on the other. As suggested by Allyn Young (1928), the network effect is a notion of general equilibrium. Not only does the network size of the division of labour depend on the extent of the market (the number of participants in the network of division of labour), but the number of participants is also determined by all individuals' participation decisions in the network of division of labour, which relate to the decisions of their levels of specialization. This circular causation, as noted by Young, is of course an essential feature of general equilibrium, analogous to the circular causation between quantities and prices in the fixed point theorem (that is, each individual's quantities demanded and supplied depend on prices, while the equilibrium prices are determined by all individuals' decisions of quantities). Hence, the partial equilibrium approach adopted in existing studies on bundling is not workable.

Moreover, since we assume a competitive market for investigating the network effect of the division of labour, we are not confined to the strategic networking decision associated with monopoly power. We need a general equilibrium model of impersonal networking decisions to investigate infinite feedback loops between network size of division of labour, each person's participation decision, prices, quantities, and different markets. Yang (2001) and Sun, Yang, and Yao (1999) have drawn a distinction between the strategic networking decision and the impersonal networking decision. In the latter case, each decision-maker is not concerned about whom he makes a trade connection with. He is more concerned about how many goods he will trade and how many he will self-provide. This concern is related to the number and categories of alternative trading partners, which would determine the size and pattern of his trade network.

Impersonal networking decisions take place in a market where nobody can manipulate prices, so that implicit bundling with zero prices of some goods may emerge from competitive pressure and free entry. Such impersonal networking decisions generate a network effect of the division of labour that is not a network externality, since it is reasonable to assume that each individual is capable of conducting inframarginal analysis (total cost–benefit analysis across corner solutions in addition to marginal analysis of each corner solution). This means that each individual is not only capable of choosing locally optimum resource allocation for a given trade network pattern using standard marginal analysis, but can also select a globally optimal trade network pattern by comparing several locally optimum values of objective functions. Formally, inframarginal analysis is non-linear programming. Coase (1946, 1960), Buchanan and Stubblebine (1962), and Yang (2001) have shown that a lot of so-called network externalities can be internalized as individuals' inframarginal decisions. They are only considered externalities by many economists in the naive assumption that individuals are not capable of inframarginal analysis. On the contrary, studies in Yang and Ng (1998) and Yang (2001) have amply demonstrated that marginal cost pricing does not work when individuals conduct inframarginal analysis. Hence, non-marginal cost pricing is compatible with a competitive market with increasing returns and impersonal networking decisions.

In this chapter, we specify a general equilibrium model with a continuum of *ex ante* identical consumer-producers who prefer diverse consumption and specialized production due to economies of specialization in the production of three goods. There is a tradeoff between transaction costs and the positive network effect of division of labour on aggregate productivity. Hence, if the transaction cost coefficient for a unit of goods traded is very large, the positive network effect is outweighed by transaction costs. Therefore, individuals choose autarky where market, institution of the firm, and bundling sales do not occur. As the transaction cost coefficient decreases, the general equilibrium discontinuously jumps to a higher level of division of labour. Markets emerge from the division of labour. However, if the transaction cost coefficient for labour is less than that for goods, the institution of the firm and the related labour market emerge from the division of labour. Otherwise, markets for various goods will be used to organize the division of labour in the absence of the institution of the firm and the related labour market. If the transaction cost coefficient for a good is extremely large and the equilibrium level of the division of labour is sufficiently high, then this good will be implicitly bundled with other goods to avoid the prohibitively high pricing cost, while getting this good involved in the large network size of division of labour and commercial production.

Let us paint a scenario. Suppose an automobile manufacturer, such as General Motors, offers automobiles and internet services for purchasing cars online. Automobiles are tangible goods which are easy to price, but internet services are intangible and very difficult to price. General Motors can bundle two goods together by providing free internet services and by adding the operation cost of internet services to the price of automobiles. If such bundling can save consumers' transaction costs incurred in a purchase deal with negligible added cost to the price of automobiles, General Motors will obtain a competitive edge over other automobile manufacturers which do not provide such a bundled deal. Competitive pressure in the market will eventually compel all manufacturers to provide such a bundled deal. Here, monopoly power, constant and independent valuations of one unit of good, non-resale, and other artificial assumptions are not needed. In addition, even if all individuals have an *ex ante* identical utility function that allows substitution between goods, productivity gains from bundling may be generated by the network effect of the division of labour. Without bundling, the prohibitively high transaction cost coefficient of the good in a high level of division of labour, will militate against the direct pricing cost of such a good. Hence, the positive network effect of the division of labour on aggregate productivity cannot be fully exploited. With the bundling, both can be achieved at the same time. Therefore, the network effect can be fully exploited and aggregate productivity can be promoted by the bundling. Interestingly enough, therefore, bundling in a competitive market has very important productivity implications, even if every individual has an *ex ante* identical utility function and substitution between different goods are non-trivial.

Section 2 of this chapter will be a description of the proposed model. Section 3 solves equilibrium problems and reports main findings from statistical implications. The final section delivers the conclusion.

2 A model with impersonal networking decisions and bundling sales

Consider an economy with a continuum of consumer-producers of mass M. This condition implies that the population size is very large. It avoids the integer problem of the numbers of different specialists, which may lead to non-existence of equilibrium with the division of labour.[2] Each consumer-producer has identical, non-satiated, continuous, and rational preference represented by the utility function

$$u = f(x^c, y^c) \tag{6.1}$$

where $x^c \equiv (x + x^d)$ and $y^c \equiv (y + y^d)$ are the amounts of the two final goods that are consumed, x and y are the amounts of the two goods that are self-provided, x^d and y^d are the amounts of the two goods that are purchased from the market, and $f(.)$ is continuously increasing and quasi-concave. For simplicity, it is assumed that $f(.) = (x^c)^\alpha \cdot (y^c)^{1-\alpha}$

Each consumer-producer's production functions are

$$x^p = x + x^s = (z + z^d)^\beta \, . \, l_x \text{ and } \beta \in (0,1) \qquad (6.2)$$
$$y^p = y + y^s = \text{Max } \{0, l_y - b\} \text{ and } \beta \in (0,1)$$
$$z^p = z + z^s = \text{Max } \{0, l_z - b\} \text{ and } b \in (0, 1)$$

where x^p and y^p are the amounts of the two final goods produced, z^p is the amount of the intermediate good produced, z^d is the amount of the intermediate good purchased from the market, x^s, y^s and z^s are the amounts of the three goods sold, b is a fixed learning and training cost in producing goods y and z and the parameter β represents the elasticity of output of good x with respect to input level of intermediate good z. It is implied by $\beta + 1 > 1$ that there are increasing returns in producing the final good x.

The endowment constraint for each individual endowed with one unit of working time is given as

$$l_x + l_y + l_z = 1 \qquad (6.3)$$

where l_i is the amount of labour allocated to the production of good i. This system of production implies that each individual's labour productivity increases as he narrows down his range of production activities. It is shown by Yang (2001, chapter 2) that the aggregate production schedule for three individuals discontinuously jumps from a low profile to a high profile as each person jumps from producing three goods to a production pattern in which at least one person produces only one good (specialization). The difference between the two aggregate production profiles is considered a positive network effect of division of labour on aggregate productivity. This network effect implies that each person's decision of level of specialization, or gains from specialization, depends upon the number of participants in a large network of division of labour, while this number is determined by all individuals' decisions in choosing their levels of specialization.[3] The economy of specialization is individual-specific, since learning by doing must be achieved through individually specific practice and cannot be transferred between individuals. Hence, labour endowment constraint is specified for each individual, so that increasing returns are localized.

The budget constraint for an individual is,

$$k_x p_x x^s + k_y p_y y^s + k_z p_z z^s = p_x x^d + p_y y^d + p_z z^d \text{ and } k_i \in (0, 1) \qquad (6.4)$$

where p_i is the price of good i. The fraction $1 - k_i$ of a good sold disappears in transit due to an iceberg transaction cost, whereas k_i is a trading efficiency coefficient, which represents the conditions governing transactions,[4] and relates to transportation conditions and the general institutional environment affecting trading efficiency. We assume that if labour trade occurs, the fraction $1 - g_i$ of the amount of labour employed to produce good i disappears in transit from the employee to the employer due to all kinds of transaction costs in labour trade (shirking, measurement cost of quantity and quality of labour, and anticipated moral hazard). Hence, g_i is the trading efficiency coefficient of labour employed to produce good i.

Due to the continuum number of individuals and the assumption of localized increasing returns in this large economy, a Walrasian regime prevails. The specification of the model generates a tradeoff between economies of division of labour and transaction costs. The decision problem for an individual involves deciding what and how much to produce for self-consumption, to sell and to buy from the market. In other words, the individual chooses nine variables x_i, x_i^s, x_i^d, y_i, y_i^s, y_i^d, z_i, z_i^s, $z_i^d \geq 0$. Hence, there are $2^9 = 512$ possible corner and interior solutions.

3 Corner solutions in a configuration and corner equilibrium in a structure

Since corner solutions are allowed in our model, the standard marginal analysis of interior solutions is not workable. We require a three-step inframarginal analysis. In the first step, a set of candidates for an individual's optimum decision is identified by ruling out inefficient interior and corner solutions. Possible network structures of the division of labour and related transactions can then be identified as combinations of corner solutions. This first step of inframarginal analysis is carried out in subsection 3.1. We then solve for all possible corner solutions and the local equilibrium in each market structure that is a combination of compatible corner solutions, using marginal analysis. The second step is performed in subsection 3.2. Finally, we will use total cost–benefit analysis to discover the conditions under which a local equilibrium becomes a general equilibrium. This final step is carried out in subsection 3.3.

3.1 Configurations and structures

The set of candidates for each individual's optimum decision includes many corner and interior solutions. In order to narrow down the list of the candidates, Yang and Ng (1993) and Wen (1998) employ the Kuhn–Tucker conditions to establish the following lemma:

> LEMMA 1. *Each individual sells at most one good, but does not buy and sell the same good, nor buys and self-provides the same good at the same time.*

We define a *configuration* as a combination of zero and positive variables that are compatible with Lemma 1. When labour trade and bundling are allowed, there are 19 configurations from which the individuals can choose. A combination of all individual's configurations constitutes a *market structure,* or *structure* for short. Let us examine all structures that might occur in equilibrium. The structures are represented in Figure 6.1.

Autarkic Structure A

Structure A consists of all individuals choosing configuration A (self-sufficiency or autarky) where an individual produces all the three goods for self-consumption. Configuration A is defined by $x, y, z > 0$ and $x^s = x^d = y^s = y^d = z^s = z^d = 0$.

Structures with partial division of labour: P_A, P_B and FP_B

Structure P_A is a division of the population between configurations (xz/y) and (y/x). A person choosing configuration (xz/y) produces goods x and z, buys good y, and sells good x. It is defined by $x, x^s, z, y^d > 0$, $z^s = z^d = y = y^s = x^d = 0$. A person choosing configuration (y/z) produces good y, buys good x, and sells good y. It is defined by $y, y^s, x^d > 0$, $x = x^s = z = z^s = z^d = y^d = 0$. Note that structure P_A involves trade of goods x and y, so that trading efficiency coefficients k_x and k_y appear in this structure.

Structure P_B is a division of the population between configuration (zx/y) and (yx/z). A person choosing configuration (zx/y) produces goods x and z, buys good y, and sells good z. It is defined by $x, z, z^s, y^d > 0$, $x^s = x^d = y = y^s = z^d = 0$. A person choosing configuration (yx/z) produces goods x and y, buys good z, and sells good y. It is defined by $x, y, y^s, z^d > 0$, $x^s = x^d = y^d = z = z^s = 0$. Note that structure P_B involves trade of goods z and y, so that trading efficiency coefficients k_z and k_y appear in this structure.

Structure FP_B is a division of the population between configuration (l_zx/y) and (yx/l_z). An individual choosing configuration (l_zx/y) produces goods x and z, buys good y, and sells labour for producing intermediate good z. It is defined by $x, z, l_z, y^d > 0$, $x^s = x^d = y = y^s = z^s = z^d = 0$. A person choosing configuration (yx/l_z) produces goods x and y, sells good y, and employs labour to produce good z. It is defined by $x, y, y^s, l_z > 0$, $x^s = x^d = y^d = z^s = z^d = 0$. Note that structure FP_B involves trade of good y and labour l_z, so that trading efficiency coefficients k_y and g_z appear in this structure.

Structures with complete division of labour: CD, FD_A, FT_A and FT_B

Structure CD without the institution of the firm is a division of the population among configurations (x/yz), (z/xy) and (y/x). An individual choosing configuration (x/yz) in structure CD produces and sells good x and buys goods y and z. It is defined by $x, x^s, y^d, z^d > 0$, $x^d = y = y^s = z = z^s = 0$. An individual choosing configuration (y/x) in structure CD produces and sells good y and buys good x. It is defined by $y, y^s, x^d > 0$, $x = x^s = y^d = z = z^s = z^d = 0$. An individual choosing configuration (z/xy) in structure CD produces and sells good z and buys goods x and y. It is defined by $z, z^s, x^d, y^d > 0$, $z^d = x = x^s = y = y^s = 0$. Note that structure CD involves trade

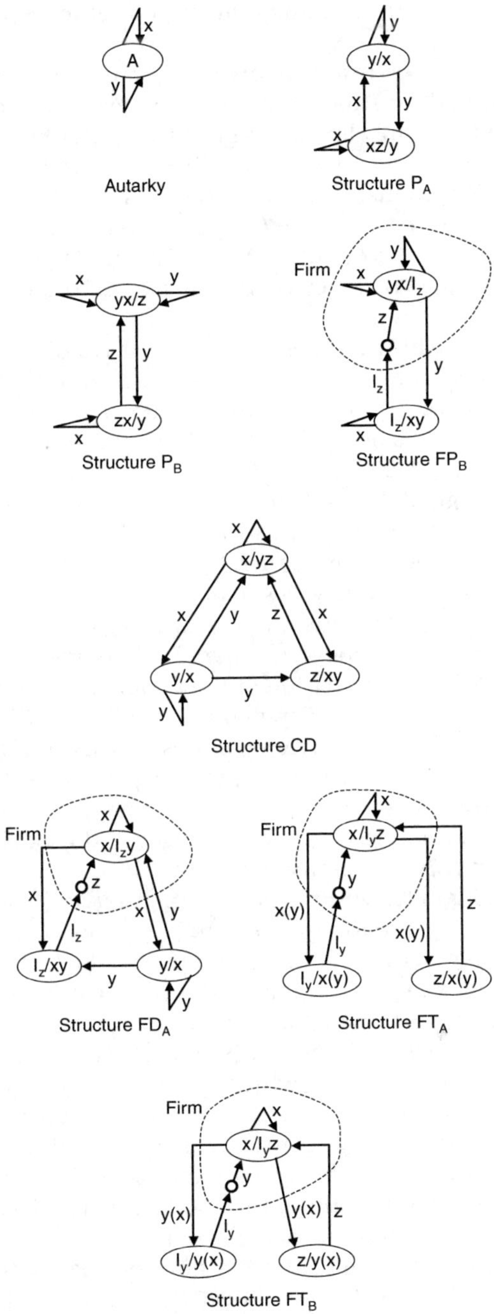

Figure 6.1 Configurations and structures

of goods x, y, and z, so that trading efficiency coefficients k_x, k_y, and k_z appear in this structure.

Structure FD_A with the firm is a division of the population among configurations ($z/l_x y$), (l_x/xy) and (y/x). An individual choosing ($z/l_x y$) produces and sells good z, hires labour to produce x, and buys good y. It is defined by $z, y^d, l_x, x^s > 0, x^d = y = y^s = z^s = z^d = 0$. An individual choosing (l_x/xy) sells labour for producing x and buys goods x and y. It is defined by 0 $x^d, y^d, l_x > 0, x^s = y = y^s = z = z^s = z^d = 0$. Configuration (y/x) is the same as in structure CD. Note that structure FD_A involves trade of goods x, y, and labour l_x, so that trading efficiency coefficients k_x, k_y, and g_x appear in this structure.

Structure FT_A with the firm and the bundling sales is a division of the population among configurations ($x/l_y z$), ($l_y/x(y)$) and (z/x(y)). An individual choosing ($x/l_y z$) produces good x, employs labour to produce y, and sells x that is bundled with y. It is defined by $x, x^s, l_y, Z^d, y^s > 0, x^d = y^d = z = z^s = 0$. An individual choosing ($l_y/x(y)$) sells labour for producing y, buys good x, and gets the bundled good y. It is defined by $x^d, l_y, y^d > 0, x = x^s = y = y^s = z = z^s = z^d = 0$. An individual choosing (z/x(y)) produces and sells z, buys good x, and gets the bundled good y. It is defined by $z, z^s, x^d, y^d > 0, x, = x^s = y = y^s = z^d = 0$. Note that structure FT_A involves trade of goods x, z, and labour l_y, so that trading efficiency coefficients k_x, k_z, and g_y appear in this structure. Good y is not directly priced though it is bundled with good x.

The mirror structure FT_B is a division of the population among configurations ($x/l_y z$), ($l_y/y(x)$) and (z/y(x)). Configuration ($x/l_y z$) in FT_B is symmetric to ($x/l_y z$) in structure FT_A. An individual choosing this configuration produces good x, hires labour for producing y, sells y, which is bundled with good x. The difference between FT_A and FT_B is that good x is priced and good y is not in the former, while good y is priced and good x is not in the latter. Configuration ($l_y/y(x)$) is symmetric to ($l_y/x(y)$) in structure FT_A, but good y is priced and good x is not. Configuration (z/y(x)) is symmetric to (z/x(y)) in structure FT_A, but good y is priced and good x is not. Note that structure FT_B involves trade of goods y, z, and labour l_y, so that trading efficiency coefficients k_y, k_z and g_y appear in this structure. Good x is not directly priced though it is bundled with good y.

According to Sun, Yang, and Zhou (1998)[5] a general equilibrium exists for a general class of models – of which the model in this chapter is a special case – under the assumptions that the set of individuals is a continuum, preferences are strictly increasing and rational; and both local increasing returns and constant returns are allowed in production and transactions. A general equilibrium in this model is defined as a set of relative prices of goods and all individuals' labour allocations and trade plans, such that (1) each individual maximizes his utility, that is, the consumption bundle generated by his labour allocation and the trade plan maximizes his utility function for given prices, and (2) all markets clear.

Since the optimum decision is always a corner solution and the interior solution is never optimal according to Lemma 1, we cannot use standard marginal analysis to solve for a general equilibrium. We adopt a three-step approach instead. The first step is to narrow down the set of candidates for the optimum decision and to identify configurations that have to be considered. We can identify structures from compatible combinations of configurations. In the second step, each individual's utility maximization decision is solved for a given structure. Both the utility equalization condition between individuals choosing different configurations and the market-clearing conditions are used to solve for the relative prices of traded goods and the numbers (measure) of individuals choosing different configurations. The relative prices and numbers, and associated resource allocation are referred to as a corner equilibrium for this structure.

General equilibrium occurs in a structure where, given corner equilibrium relative prices in the structure, no individual has an incentive to deviate from his chosen configuration in this structure. In the third step, we substitute the corner equilibrium relative prices into the utility function for each constituent configuration in the given structure to compare the utility between this configuration and any alternative configurations. This comparison is called a total cost–benefit analysis. The total cost–benefit analysis yields the conditions under which the utility in each constituent configuration of this structure is not less than any alternative configuration. With the existence theorem of general equilibrium proved by Sun, Yang, and Zhou (1998) we can completely partition the parameter space into subspaces, within each of which the corner equilibrium in a structure is a general equilibrium. As parameter values shift between the subspaces, the general equilibrium will discontinuously jump between structures. The discontinuous jumps of structure and all endogenous variables are called inframarginal comparative statics of general equilibrium. The three steps constitute an inframarginal analysis. The corner equilibria in the structures are solved in the following subsection.

3.2 Corner solution in a configuration and corner equilibrium in a structure

In this subsection, we first use two examples to illustrate how marginal analysis can be conducted to solve for the corner solution in each configuration and for the corner equilibrium in each structure. The first example is the corner solution in configuration A that is the corner equilibrium in autarkic structure A.

Autarky is a structure where each individual chooses configuration A. An individual's decision problem in A is

$$\text{Max: } u_A = x^{\alpha} \cdot y^{1-\alpha}$$

subject to the following constraints:

$$x = z^{\beta} \cdot l_x$$
$$y = l_y - b$$
$$z = l_z - b$$
$$l_x + l_y + l_z = 1$$

The solution is:

$$l_x = \frac{\alpha \cdot (1-2b)}{1+\alpha\beta}$$
$$l_y = \frac{(1-\alpha)\cdot(1-2b)+b\cdot(1+\alpha\beta)}{1+\alpha\beta}$$
$$l_z = \frac{\alpha\beta\cdot(1-b)+b}{1+\alpha\beta}$$
$$u_A = \frac{\beta^{\alpha\beta}\cdot(1-\alpha)^{1-\alpha}\cdot(1-2b)^{1+\alpha\beta}\cdot\alpha^{\alpha(1+\beta)}}{(1+\alpha\beta)^{1+\alpha\beta}}$$

where u_A is per capita real income in structure A.

Next, we consider the corner equilibrium in structure FT_A with bundling sales and the institution of the firm. This structure involves the division of the population among configurations $(x/l_y z)$, $(l_y/x(y))$ and $(z/x(y))$. An individual choosing $(x/l_y z)$ is the employer of a firm. He specializes in producing good x, and hires labour to produce final good y. He sells good x, buys intermediate good z and labour, and bundles good y with good x, which means good y is not directly priced, and people can obtain some amount of good y when they buy good x from the market. The ratio of the amounts of the two goods bundled is chosen by the employer under competition pressure in the market.

In structure FT_A, the decision problem for an individual choosing configuration $(x/l_y z)$ is

$$\text{Max: } u_{FTA1} = x^{\alpha} \cdot y^{1-\alpha}$$

subject to the following constraints:

$$x + x^s = (z^d)^{\beta} \cdot l_x \text{ and } l_x = 1$$
$$Y^s = g_y \cdot L_y - b \text{ and } L_y = 1$$
$$y^s = h \cdot x^s$$
$$y + y^s = N \cdot Y^s$$
$$k_x p_x x^s = p_z z^d + w \cdot N \cdot L_y$$

where g_y is again the transaction efficiency coefficient for labour hired to produce good y, N is the number of workers hired by the employer to produce good y, w is the wage rate, and h is the bundling ratio between goods y and x. In order to distinguish interflow of goods from market trade flow, we use capitalized decision variables to denote internal flow. Hence, Y^s is the internal transfer of good y produced by an employee to the employer and y^s is the amount of good y provided free of charge by the firm. Here, x is priced and y is not. We assume $h = e \cdot (p_x/w)$. This implies that an individual selling x, buying labour, and bundling y with x, must choose the bundling ratio $h = y/x$ according to p_x/w. For a small relative market price p_x/w he must give away a small amount of y for each unit x sold. Otherwise, a small value of p_x/w may not be enough to cover the production cost of y which is not directly priced. Here, e is as given to the owner of the firm, later we can use the Yao Theorem[6] to derive the real optimal bundling ratio of goods x and y. In addition, l_x is the decision variable of the employer, while l_y is an employee's decision variable u_{FTA1} is the utility for x specialist-employers choosing (x/l_yz). The solution to the decision problem yields the demand function for labour and good z, supply function of good x, and indirect utility function for configuration (x/l_yz).

Similarly, an employee choosing configuration ($l_y/x(y)$) has the decision problem

$$\text{Max: } u_{FTA2} = (x^d)^\alpha \cdot (y^d)^{1-\alpha}$$

subject to the following constraints:

$$y^d = h \cdot x^d$$
$$w \cdot L_y = p_x \cdot x^d \text{ and } L_y = 1$$

The solution of this problem yields the demand for goods x and y, supply of labour, and indirect utility function for configuration ($l_y/x(y)$).

An individual choosing configuration (z/x(y)) has the decision problem

$$\text{Max: } u_{FTA3} = (x^d)^\alpha \cdot (y^d)^{1-\alpha},$$

subject to the production function, endowment constraint, and budget constraint:

$$z^s = l_z - b \text{ and } l_z = 1$$
$$y^d = h \cdot x^d$$
$$k_z p_z z^s = p_x x^d$$

The solution to this problem yields the demand for goods x and y, supply of good z, and indirect utility function for configuration (z/x(y)).

The two utility equalization conditions across three configurations yield the corner equilibrium relative prices of goods x and z and labour:

$$\frac{w}{p_z} = k_z(1-b) \text{ and}$$

$$\frac{w}{p_x} = [\frac{k_x(g_y-b)\cdot k_z\cdot\beta}{(1-\alpha)\cdot(1-\beta)+\alpha\beta}]^{\frac{\beta}{1-\beta}}\cdot\frac{\alpha^\alpha\cdot(1-\beta)\cdot[(1-\alpha).(\alpha-\beta)+\alpha\beta]^{(1-\alpha)+\frac{\beta}{1-\beta}}}{(1-\alpha)^{1-\alpha}}$$

According to the Yao Theorem, maximizing utility with respect to *e* yields the optimal value

$$e = \frac{k_x(1-\alpha)^2\cdot(g_y-b)}{(1-\alpha)\cdot(1-\beta)+\alpha\beta}$$

The two independent market-clearing conditions for goods x and z (the other market-clearing condition not being independent due to Walras' Law) yield the corner equilibrium relative numbers of specialists producing goods x, y, and z

$$\frac{M_x}{M_z} = \{[\frac{(1-\alpha)\cdot(\alpha-\beta)+\alpha\beta}{(1-\alpha)\cdot(1-\beta)+\alpha\beta}]^{(1-\alpha)\frac{\beta}{1-\beta}}\cdot\frac{\alpha^\alpha\cdot(1-\beta)\cdot[(g_y-b)\cdot\beta]^{\frac{\beta}{1-\beta}}\cdot}{(1-\alpha)^{1-\alpha}.k_x{}^{\frac{1-2\beta}{1-\beta}}}\}^{\frac{1}{1-\beta}}\cdot(\frac{k_z^2}{1-b})^{\frac{\beta}{1-\beta}}$$

$$\frac{M_y}{M_x} = [\frac{(1-\alpha)\cdot(\alpha-\beta)+\alpha\beta}{(1-\alpha)\cdot(1-\beta)+\alpha\beta}]\cdot\frac{(1-\alpha+\alpha\beta)}{\beta} - [\frac{k_x(g_y-b)\cdot k_z\cdot\beta}{(1-\alpha)\cdot(1-\beta)+\alpha\beta}]^{\frac{\beta}{1-\beta}}\cdot$$

$$\frac{\alpha^\alpha\cdot(1-\beta)\cdot[(1-\alpha)\cdot(\alpha-\beta)+\alpha\beta]^{(1-\alpha)+\frac{\beta}{1-\beta}}}{(1-\alpha)^{1-\alpha}}$$

where M_x is the number of x specialist-employers choosing (x/l_yz), M_z is the number of specialist producers of good z choosing ($z/x(y)$), and M_y is the number of employees choosing ($l_y/x(y)$). The relative numbers of specialists, together with the population size identity $M_x + M_z + M_y = M$, yield the corner equilibrium numbers of different specialists. Plugging relative prices into an indirect utility function of any of three configurations yields the per capita real income in this structure:

$$u_{FTA} = \alpha^\alpha\cdot(1-\beta)\cdot(1-\alpha)^{1-\alpha}\cdot(kz\cdot\beta)^{\frac{\beta}{1-\beta}}\cdot\{\frac{k_x(g_y-b)\cdot[(1-\alpha)\cdot(\alpha-\beta)+\alpha\beta]}{(1-\alpha)\cdot(1-\beta)+\alpha\beta}\}^{(1+\alpha)+\frac{\beta}{1-\beta}}$$

In Structure FT_A a firm produces both goods x and y, and sells x with good y bundled. The percentage *h* of goods x and y is dependent on the relative price of good x and labour, and *e*. Note that good y is bundled through the purchase of good x, therefore transaction costs in directly pricing good y is avoided.

Following this procedure, we can solve for corner equilibria in all structures. The results are summarized in Tables 6.1 and 6.2.

$$P_{FPB} = \frac{P_y}{w} = \{\frac{(1+\alpha\beta)^{\frac{1-a}{a}} \cdot k_y \cdot [g_z(1-b)\cdot(1-\alpha) - b(1+\alpha\beta)]}{(\alpha\beta)^{\frac{1-\alpha}{\alpha}} \cdot (1-\alpha)\cdot(1-b)^{\frac{1}{\alpha}}}\}^{\frac{\alpha\beta}{(1-\alpha)\cdot(1-\alpha+\alpha\beta)}}$$

$$M_{FPB} = \frac{M_z}{M_y} = \{\frac{(1+\alpha\beta)^{\frac{1-\alpha}{\alpha}} \cdot k_y \cdot [g_z(1-b)\cdot(1-\alpha) - b(1+\alpha\beta)]}{(\alpha\beta)^{\frac{1-\alpha}{\alpha}} \cdot (1-\alpha)\cdot(1-b)^{\frac{1}{\alpha}}}\}^{\frac{\alpha\beta}{(1-\alpha).(1-\alpha+\alpha\beta)}} \cdot [\frac{(1+\alpha\beta)^2}{(1-\alpha)\cdot(1-b)^2}]$$

$$P_{FTA1} = \frac{w}{p_x} = [\frac{k_x(g_y-b)\cdot k_z \cdot \beta}{(1-\alpha)\cdot(1-\beta)+\alpha\beta}]^{\frac{\beta}{1-\beta}} \cdot \frac{\alpha^{\alpha}\cdot(1-\beta)\cdot[(1-\alpha)\cdot(\alpha-\beta)+\alpha\beta]^{(1-\alpha)+\frac{\beta}{1-\beta}}}{(1-\alpha)^{1-\alpha}}$$

$$M_{FTA1} = \frac{M_x}{M_z} = \{[\frac{(1-\alpha)\cdot(\alpha-\beta)+\alpha\beta}{(1-\alpha)\cdot(1-\beta)+\alpha\beta}]^{(1-\alpha)+\frac{\beta}{1-\beta}} \cdot \frac{\alpha^{\alpha}\cdot(1-\beta)\cdot[(g_y-b)\cdot\beta]^{\frac{\beta}{1-\beta}}}{(1-\alpha)^{1-\alpha}\cdot k_x^{\frac{1-2\beta}{1-\beta}}}\}^{\frac{1}{1-\beta}} \cdot (\frac{k_z^2}{1-b})^{\frac{\beta}{1-\beta}}$$

$$M_{FTA2} = \frac{M_y}{M_x} = [\frac{(1-\alpha)\cdot(\alpha-\beta)+\alpha\beta}{(1-\alpha)\cdot(1-\beta)+\alpha\beta}] \cdot \frac{(1-\alpha+\alpha\beta)}{\beta} - [\frac{k_x(g_y-b).k_z.\beta}{(1-\alpha).(1-\beta)+\alpha\beta}]^{\frac{\beta}{1-\beta}} \cdot \frac{\alpha^{\alpha}\cdot(1-\beta)\cdot[(1-\alpha)\cdot(\alpha-\beta)+\alpha\beta]^{(1-\alpha)+\frac{\beta}{1-\beta}}}{(1-\alpha)^{1-\alpha}}$$

$$P_{FTB1} \frac{w}{p_y} = [\frac{k_y(g_y-b)\cdot k_z \cdot \beta}{(1-\alpha)\cdot(1-\beta)+\alpha\beta}]^{\frac{\beta}{1-\beta}} \cdot \frac{\alpha^{\alpha}\cdot(1-\beta)\cdot[(1-\alpha)\cdot(\alpha-\beta)+\alpha\beta]^{(1-\alpha)+\frac{\beta}{1-\beta}}}{(1-\alpha)^{1-\alpha}}$$

$$M_{FTB1} = \frac{M_x}{M_z} = \{[\frac{(1-\alpha)\cdot(\alpha-\beta)+\alpha\beta}{(1-\alpha)\cdot(1-\beta)+\alpha\beta}]^{(1-\alpha)+\frac{\beta}{1-\beta}} \cdot \frac{\alpha^{\alpha}\cdot(1-\beta)\cdot[(g_y-b)\cdot\beta]^{\frac{\beta}{1-\beta}}}{(1-\alpha)^{1-\alpha}\cdot k_y^{\frac{1-2\beta}{1-\beta}}}\}^{\frac{1}{1-\beta}} \cdot (\frac{k_z^2}{1-b})^{\frac{\beta}{1-\beta}}$$

$$M_{FTB2} = \frac{M_y}{M_x} = [\frac{(1-\alpha)\cdot(\alpha-\beta)+\alpha\beta}{(1-\alpha)\cdot(1-\beta)+\alpha\beta}] \cdot \frac{(1-\alpha+\alpha\beta)}{\beta} - [\frac{k_x(g_y-b)\cdot k_z\cdot\beta}{(1-\alpha)\cdot(1-\beta)+\alpha\beta}]^{\frac{\beta}{1-\beta}} \cdot \frac{\alpha^{\alpha}\cdot(1-\beta)\cdot[(1-\alpha)\cdot(\alpha-\beta)+\alpha\beta]^{(1-\alpha)+\frac{\beta}{1-\beta}}}{(1-\alpha)^{1-\alpha}}$$

Table 6.1 Relative price and number of specialists

Structure	*Relative prices*	*Relative number of specialists*
A	N/A	N/A
P_A	$\frac{P_x}{P_y}=\frac{k_y^{\alpha}\cdot(1+\beta)^{1+\beta}}{k_x^{1-\alpha}\cdot\beta^{\beta}\cdot(1-b)^{\beta}}$	$\frac{M_x}{M_y}=\frac{\alpha\cdot k_y^{1-\alpha}}{(1-\alpha)\cdot k_x^{\alpha}}$
P_B	$\frac{P_y}{P_z}=(\frac{k_z^{1-\alpha}}{k_y^{\alpha\beta}})^{\frac{1}{1-\alpha+\alpha\beta}}$	$\frac{M_z}{M_y}=\frac{\alpha\beta\cdot k_y^{\frac{1-\alpha}{1-\alpha+\alpha\beta}}}{(1-\alpha)\cdot k_z^{\frac{\alpha\beta}{1-\alpha+\alpha\beta}}}$
FP_B	$\frac{P_y}{w}=P_{FPB}$	$\frac{M_z}{M_y}=M_{FPB}$
CD	$\frac{P_x}{P_z}=(\frac{1-b}{1-\beta})^{1-\beta}\cdot\frac{k_z^{1-\beta}}{\beta^{\beta}\cdot k_x^{1-\alpha+\alpha\beta}}$ $\frac{P_z}{P_y}=\frac{k_y^{\alpha}}{k_z}$	$\frac{M_y}{M_x}=\frac{(1-\alpha)+\alpha\beta(1-k_x\cdot k_z\cdot k_y^{1-\alpha})}{\alpha\cdot(1-\beta)\cdot k_x^{1-\alpha}}$ $\frac{M_x}{M_z}=\frac{(1-\beta)}{\beta\cdot k_z\cdot k_x^{\alpha}}$
FD_A	$\frac{w}{P_y}=k_y^{\alpha}\cdot(g_z-b)$ $\frac{w}{P_x}=k_x^{1-\alpha+\alpha\beta}\cdot(1-\beta)^{1-\beta}\cdot\beta^{\beta}\cdot(g_z-b)^{\beta}$	$\frac{M_x}{M_z}=\frac{g_z\cdot(1-\beta)}{\beta\cdot k_x^{\alpha}}$ $\frac{M_y}{M_x}=\frac{k_x^{\alpha}\cdot(1-\alpha)}{k_y^{1-\alpha}\cdot\alpha\cdot(1-\beta)}$
FT_A	$\frac{w}{P_z}=k_z(1-b)$ $\frac{w}{P_x}=P_{FTA1}$	$\frac{M_x}{M_z}=M_{FTA1}$ $\frac{M_y}{M_x}=M_{FTA2}$
FT_B	$\frac{w}{P_z}=k_z(1-b)$ $\frac{w}{P_y}=P_{FTB1}$	$\frac{M_x}{M_z}=M_{FTB1}$ $\frac{M_y}{M_x}=M_{FTB2}$

3.3 General equilibrium and its inframarginal comparative statics

We now consider the third step in inframarginal analysis. With the results from the first two steps, we partition the parameter space into subspaces, within each of which a particular structure occurs in equilibrium.

For any given structure, each individual can plug the corner equilibrium prices into his indirect utility functions for all configurations, including those that are not in this structure. He has no incentive to deviate from a constituent configuration in this structure if this configuration generates a utility value that is not less than those of alternative configurations under

Table 6.2 Per capita real income in different structures

Structure	*Per capita real income, u*
A	$\dfrac{\beta^{\alpha\beta}\cdot(1-\alpha)^{1-\alpha}\cdot(1-2b)^{1+\alpha\beta}\cdot\alpha^{\alpha(1+\beta)}}{(1+\alpha\beta)^{1+\alpha\beta}}$
P_A	$\dfrac{\alpha^{\alpha}\cdot(1-\alpha)^{1-\alpha}\cdot(1-b)^{1+\alpha\beta}\cdot\beta^{\alpha\beta}\cdot(k_x\cdot k_y)^{\alpha(1-\alpha)}}{(1+\beta)^{\alpha(1+\beta)}}$
P_B	$u_{PB=}\dfrac{\alpha^{\alpha}\cdot(1-\alpha)^{1-\alpha}\cdot(1-b)^{1+\alpha\beta}\cdot(\alpha\beta)^{\alpha\beta}\cdot(k_z\cdot k_y)^{\frac{\alpha\beta(1-\alpha)}{1-\alpha+\alpha\beta}}}{(1+\alpha\beta)^{1+\alpha\beta}}$
FP_B	$u_{FPB}=\{\dfrac{(1+\alpha\beta)^{\frac{1-\alpha}{\alpha}}\cdot k_y\cdot[g_z(1-b)\cdot(1-\alpha)-b(1+\alpha\beta)]}{(\alpha\beta)^{\frac{1-\alpha}{\alpha}}\cdot(1-\alpha)\cdot(1-b)^{\frac{1}{\alpha}}}\}^{\frac{\alpha\beta}{(1-\alpha)\cdot(1-\alpha+\alpha\beta)}}\cdot$ $[\dfrac{(1-\alpha)^{1-\alpha}\cdot\alpha^{\alpha+\beta}\cdot(1-b)^{1+\beta}\cdot\beta^{\beta}}{(1+\alpha\beta)^{1+\beta}}]$
CD	$\alpha^{\alpha}\cdot(1-\alpha)^{1-\alpha}\cdot(1-b)^{1-\alpha+\alpha\beta}\cdot\beta^{\alpha\beta}\cdot(1-\beta)^{\alpha(1-\beta)}\cdot k_z^{\alpha\beta}\cdot k_x^{\alpha(1-\alpha+\alpha\beta)}\cdot k_y^{\alpha-(1-\alpha)}$
FD_A	$\alpha^{\alpha}\cdot(1-\alpha)^{1-\alpha}\cdot(g_z-b)^{1-\alpha+\alpha\beta}\cdot\beta^{\alpha\beta}\cdot(1-\beta)^{\alpha(1-\beta)}\cdot k_y^{\alpha(1-\alpha)}\cdot k_x^{\alpha(1-\alpha+\alpha\beta)}$
FT_A	$u_{FTA}=\alpha^{\alpha}\cdot(1-\beta)\cdot(1-\alpha)^{1-\alpha}\cdot(k_z\cdot\beta)^{\frac{\beta}{1-\beta}}\cdot$ $\{\dfrac{k_x(g_y-b)\cdot[(1-\alpha)\cdot(\alpha-\beta)+\alpha\beta]}{(1-\alpha)\cdot(1-\beta)+\alpha\beta}\}^{(1-\alpha)+\frac{\beta}{1-\beta}}$
FT_B	$u_{FTB}=\alpha^{\alpha}\cdot(1-\beta)\cdot(1-\alpha)^{1-\alpha}\cdot(k_z\cdot\beta)^{\frac{\beta}{1-\beta}}\cdot$ $\{\dfrac{k_y(g_y-b)\cdot[(1-\alpha)\cdot(\alpha-\beta)+\alpha\beta]}{(1-\alpha)\cdot(1-\beta)+\alpha\beta}\}^{(1-\alpha)+\frac{\beta}{1-\beta}}$

the corner equilibrium values of prices in this structure. Each individual can conduct such total cost–benefit analysis across configurations. Letting indirect utility in each constituent configuration not be smaller than in any alternative configurations, we can obtain a system of semi-inequalities that involves only parameters. This system of semi-inequalities defines a parameter subspace within which the corner equilibrium in this structure is the general equilibrium. This total cost–benefit analysis is very tedious and cumbersome. Fortunately, the Yao Theorem can simplify it. The Yao Theorem states that in an economy with a continuum of *ex ante* identical consumer-producers having rational and convex preferences and production functions displaying individual specific economies of specialization, a Walrasian general equilibrium exists, and it is the Pareto optimum corner equilibrium. Here the Pareto optimum corner equilibrium is the corner equilibrium that generates the highest per capita real income. Since our model in this chapter is a special case of the above-mentioned general class of models, the individuals have no incentive to deviate from their chosen constituent configurations in a structure if and only if the individuals' corner equilibrium utility value in this structure is no lower than those in any other corner equilibria. With the Yao Theorem, we then compare corner equilibrium per capita real incomes across all structures, and the comparison partitions the five-dimension (α, β, g, b, k) parameter space into several subspaces, within each of which one corner equilibrium is the general equilibrium. As parameter values shift between different subspaces, the general equilibrium discontinuously jumps between corner equilibria. This is referred to as inframarginal comparative statics of general equilibrium.

In order to obtain an analytical solution of the inframarginal comparative statics, we consider the economy with $\alpha = \beta = 0.5$. A close examination of per capita real incomes in different structures, given in Table 6.2, generates the results in Table 6.3, in which trading efficiency coefficients in an entry positively correlate to per capita real income in a structure associated with the column.

From Table 6.2, we see that as any trading efficiency coefficient in the second row tends to zero, the per capita real income in the corresponding structure in the first row in Table 6.3 goes to zero. For instance, per capita real income in structure FD_A positively depends on trading efficiencies of goods x and y, k_x, k_y, and trading efficiency of labour employed to produce x, g_z. The per capita real income converges to zero as any of k_x, k_y, g_z tends to zero. Since per capita real income in autarkic structure A is independent of the trading efficiency coefficients, if all trading efficiency coefficients are sufficiently close to zero, per capita real income in autarky will be greater than that in any other structures with trade. Also, we can see from Table 6.3 that a structure with partial division of labour (P_A, P_B, or FP_B) involves trading efficiency coefficients of two types of goods and/or labour, while a structure with complete division of labour (three goods are involved in commercialized production) involves trading efficiency coefficients of three types of goods and/or labour. Hence, as trading efficiencies of more types of goods and labour are improved, the general equilibrium will discontinu-

Table 6.3 Trading efficiency coefficients that positively affect per capita real income in a structure

A	P_A	P_B	FP_B	CD	FD_A	FT_A	FT_B
n/a	k_x, k_y	k_z, k_y	g_z, k_y	k_x, k_y, k_z	k_x, k_y, g_z	k_x, k_z, g_y	k_z, k_y, g_y

ously jump from autarky to partial division of labour, followed by the complete division of labour. Hence, the first conclusion from the total cost–benefit analysis of per capita real income in various structures is that trading efficiency determines the general equilibrium network size of division of labour.

The second conclusion from the third step of inframarginal analysis is that the institution of the firm is a way to replace trade of goods with trade of labour. As we can see from Table 6.3, all structures with the firm (FP_B, FD_A, FT_A, FT_B) involve the trading efficiency coefficient of labour employed to produce good i, g_i. Per capita real incomes in all structures without the firm (P_A, P_B, CD) are independent of the trading efficiency of labour. Hence, if the trading efficiency is higher for labour than that for goods, the institution of the firm and related labour market will be used to more efficiently organize the division of labour. Otherwise, the markets for goods will be used to organize the division of labour in the absence of the institution of the firm and related labour market. This formalizes the theory of Coase (1937) and Cheung (1983), and is consistent with the inframarginal analysis of the theory of the firm by Yang and Ng (1995) and the model formalizing the theory of irrelevance of size of firm developed by Liu and Yang (2000).

A third conclusion can be obtained by drawing a comparison between structures with the firm and bundling (FT_i, i = A, B) and those with the firm and without bundling (FP_B, FD_A). A comparison between structures FD_A and FT_A shows that if trading efficiency is prohibitively low for good y (k_y tends to zero), then not only is a structure without the firm (such as structure CD) inadequate to coordinate the complete division of labour with three goods involved in commercialized production, even structures with the firm (FD_A, FD_B) are inadequate to coordinate the complete division of labour in the absence of bundling. This is because structures CD and FD_A involve the marketing and pricing of good y, while structure FT_A with bundling avoids the direct pricing of good y while getting good y involved in commercialized production.

In order to make results more concrete, we explicitly solve for general equilibrium and its inframarginal comparative statics for some specific ranges of parameter values.

We first assume that k_y, the trading efficiency of good y, is near zero. From Tables 6.2 and 6.3, we see that this implies zero per capita real incomes in structures P_A, P_B, CD, FD_A and FT_B, since per capital real incomes in these structures are positively dependent on k_y and they fall to zero as k_y tends to zero. Hence, the set of candidates for the equilibrium structure consists of structures A and FT_A, in which per capita real incomes are independent of k_y. As shown in Tables 6.2 and 6.3, per capita real income in structure A is independent of trading efficiency, per capita real income in structure FT_A depends on k_x, k_z, and g_y. Therefore, when k_x, k_z, and g_y are very small, the general equilibrium is the corner equilibrium in structure A. When k_x and k_z are large, the general equilibrium is the corner equilibrium in structure FT_A. The inframarginal comparative statics of general equilibrium are summarized in Table 6.4.

The inframarginal comparative statics in Table 6.4 indicate that as trading efficiencies increase from very small to very large values, the general equilibrium discontinuously jumps from autarky to the division of labour. Due to prohibitively low trading efficiency of good y, the division of labour must be organized via the institution of the firm that sells good x and provides good y free of charge. A particular structure with the firm and bundling can be used to avoid trade of a particular type of labour. Structure FT_A can be used to avoid trade of labour employed to produce good x. Suppose that good y is an intangible good (such as an information good) whereas good x is tangible. Hence the output and input of producing x are easy to measure, but measurement of the output and input of producing y could be prohibitively expensive. For instance, if the labour employed to produce good y is chiefly the intellectual effort expended in thinking and research, the quantity and quality of such efforts are probably expensive to measure. Under the circumstances, the bundling in structure FT_A avoids the direct pricing of output and input of the activity producing the information good y.

As shown in Yang and Ng (1995) the institution of the firm can indirectly price intangible intellectual properties via claims to residual rights of the firm. However, the model in this paper demonstrates that the institution of the firm coupled with bundling enlarges the scope for such indirect pricing of intellectual properties. From Table 6.4, we can see that the institution of the firm is inadequate to indirectly price all input and output of the activity producing good y in the absence of implicit bundling. Hence, without implicit bundling, the division of labour and commercialized production of information goods becomes impossible, so the positive network effect of such commercialised production through specialisation cannot be fully exploited.

In order to compare the roles of structures with and without bundling, we consider the case with $k_x \to 0$. The inframarginal comparative statics of general equilibrium within this range of parameter values are summarized in Table 6.5.

The inframarginal comparative statics in Table 6.5 indicate that, as trading efficiencies increase from very low to very high levels, the general

Table 6.4 General equilibrium and its inframarginal comparative statics as $k_y \to 0$

Trading efficiency of goods	k_x *and* k_z *are small*	k_x *and* k_z *are large*
Equilibrium structure	A	FT_A

Table 6.5 General equilibrium and its inframarginal comparative statics as $k_x \to 0$

Trading efficiency of good	k_y, k_z *are small*	k_y *and* k_z *are neither large nor small*		k_y *and* k_z *are large*
Trading efficiency of labour	g_y, g_z are small	g_y, g_z are small	g_z is neither large nor small	FT_B
Equilibrium structure	A	P_B	FP_B	

equilibrium shifts from autarky to the partial division of labour, then to the complete division of labour. The partial division of labour is coordinated by the institution of the firm and the related labour market if trading efficiency for labour is high. Otherwise, it is organized by the markets for goods in the absence of the firm and the related labour market. The complete division of labour can be organized only via the institution of the firm selling good y with good x bundled, due to the prohibitively low trading efficiency of good x. A comparison between Tables 6.4 and 6.5 shows that direct pricing of a good (x or y) must be avoided via bundling if the trading efficiency of the particular good is extremely low.

Following Sun, Yang, and Yao (1999)[7] it can be shown that the general equilibrium in our model is Pareto optimal. This first welfare theorem in our model with impersonal networking decisions and endogenous network size of division of labour implies that the market functions to coordinate impersonal networking decisions and fully utilize the network effect of the division of labour on aggregate productivity, net of transaction costs. Bundling in a competitive market is an effective way to promote the division of labour and increase productivity. This, together with the inframarginal comparative statics of equilibrium given in Tables 6.4 and 6.5, leads to the following proposition:

> PROPOSITION 1. *The absolute level of transaction efficiency of goods and labour determines the level of division of labour. As transaction efficiency is improved, the equilibrium level of division of labour increases. The ratio of transaction efficiency for labour to that for goods, determines if the division of labour is organized by the labour market and the institution of the firm. Bundling sales can be used to avoid direct pricing of output and input of the activity with the lowest transaction efficiency, while getting this activity involved in the division of labour and thereby promoting the division of labour and productivity progress. Bundling sales based on impersonal networking decisions have no adverse effects on welfare per se.*

Proposition 1 implies that the antitrust legislation should focus on attempts to block free entry into the market rather than on bundling sales itself, because according to Proposition 1 and the Yao Theorem, bundling sales promotes the division of labour and increases the aggregate productivity if it occurs in equilibrium. Bundling does not generate distortions in a competitive market.

Following Yang (2001), it is easy to prove that the marginal cost price no longer holds in a structure with division of labour, and that the aggregate production schedule discontinuously jumps to a higher level as the network of division of labour expands. Owing to the tradeoff between transaction costs and the positive network effect of division of labour on aggregate productivity, the equilibrium and Pareto optimum may be different from the PPF. As trading efficiency is improved, the equilibrium network size of division of labour enlarges, and the equilibrium and Pareto optimum become closer to the PPF.

4 Concluding remarks

This chapter develops a Walrasian general equilibrium model based on impersonal networking decisions and investigates the role of bundling sales in a competitive market and e-business. Several features distinguish our model of bundling from other models in the literature. In our model there is no monopoly power, and substitution between different goods and the resale of goods are both allowed. An *ex ante* identical utility function is specified for all individuals whose valuation of each good does not hold constant. Each individual can choose the size and pattern of his trade network by choosing his level of specialization subject to impersonal prices. Hence, the gain to each individual's level of specialization depends on the number of participants in the network of division of labour, while the number of participants depends on each individual's participation decision in the network, in turn determined by the decision of his level of specialization. Since individuals are capable of carrying out inframarginal analysis in choosing a utility maximizing trade network from the possible corner solutions, the equilibrium network size and pattern of division of labour is Pareto efficient, despite the network effect of division of labour on aggregate productivity.

The institution of the firm coupled with bundling sales can function to involve the activity with the lowest trading efficiency with the division of labour and commercial production, while avoiding direct pricing of the outputs and inputs of this activity. Implicit bundling coupled with the institution of the firm can provide a greater scope for indirectly pricing goods with the lowest trading efficiency, than the institution of the firm alone. In our model, the complete division of labour can be organized by the trade of three types of goods and labour. But there are six types of goods and labour: x, y, z, l_x, l_y, l_z. Hence, a competitive market will find a three-element combination from six elements to maximize the positive network effect of division of labour on aggregate productivity, net of total transaction costs. Note that the total equilibrium value of the transaction cost may increase, as a consequence of the evolving division of labour caused by improvements in trading efficiency. For instance, as trading efficiency is improved, the general equilibrium jumps from autarky, where transaction cost is zero and aggregate productivity is lower than the PPF, to the division of labour where total transaction cost is positive and aggregate productivity is higher.

Since the general equilibrium in our model is always Pareto optimal so long as nobody can block free entry into any sector and nobody can manipulate relative prices and the numbers of specialists, the policy implications of our model are straightforward. Bundling in a competitive market is efficient, and it ensures that the network effect of division of labour can be fully exploited when goods involved in the network of division of labour are associated with prohibitively high transaction costs. Hence, bundling in a competitive market can promote aggregate productivity by enlarging the scope for trading off the network effect of the division of labour on aggregate productivity, against transaction costs. Bundling per se cannot be a source of distortions in a competitive market. Bundling may generate-distortions only if it is used in connection with monopoly power. Hence, in antitrust cases such as *United States* v. *Microsoft*, attention should be placed on the possible blockage of free entry in an attempt to gain monopoly power, rather than the allegedly adverse effects of bundling per se on welfare. To business practitioners, our model suggests that the successful bundling of intangible e-business with some tangible 'brick-and-mortar' business is a key to commercial viability of e-business companies.

We can usefully extend our model by making the assumption that the seller of a bundle of goods cannot choose the bundling ratio, an assumption quite relevant to real e-business. We may assume that each buyer of implicitly bundled goods must allocate resources to use those goods that are free of charge. Hence, it is the buyer rather than the seller who chooses the bundling ratio subject to her resource endowment constraint. When a firm sells information goods via a website, it usually cannot choose the bundling ratio of goods with positive prices and goods free of charge. We surmise that, with this assumption, the extended model will confirm the results of this chapter.

Notes

1 As shown by Bakos and Brynjolfsson (1999a), the benefit of bundling disappears as consumers' evaluations converge to the same value.
2 See Sun, Yang, and Zhou (1998).
3 This is the Young theorem, see Young (1928).

4 The specification of the iceberg transaction cost is a common practice in the equilibrium models with tradeoff between increasing returns and transaction costs: see Krugman (1995). This specification avoids the notoriously formidable index sets of destinations and origins of trade flows.
5 See also Yang (2001, chapter 13).
6 See Yang (2001, p. 156).
7 See also Yang (2001).

References

Adams, W. J. and Yellen, J. L. (1976) 'Commodity Bundling and the Burden of Monopoly', *Quarterly Journal of Economics*, 90, 3, 475–98.

Bakos, Y. and Brynjolfsson, E. (1999a) 'Bundling Information Goods: Pricing, Profits and Efficiency', *Management Science*, 45, 12, 1613–1630.

Bakos, Y. and Brynjolfsson, E. (1999b) 'Bundling and Competition on the Internet', Working Paper, Stern School of Business, New York University.

Blair, R. and Kaserman, D. (1978) 'Vertical Integration Tying and Antitrust Policy', *American Economic Review*, 68, 397–402.

Bowman, Jr, W. S. (1957) 'Tying Arrangements and the Leverage Problem', *Yale Law Journal*, 67, 1, 19–36.

Buchanan, James M. and Stubblebine, W. Craig (1962) 'Externality', *Economica*, 29, 371–84.

Burstein, M. L. (1960) 'The Economics of Tie-In Sales', *The Review of Economics and Statistics*, 42, 68–73.

Chae, S. (1992) 'Bundling Subscription TV Channels: a Case of Natural Bundling', *International Journal of Industrial Organization*, 10, 2, 213–30.

Chuang, John Chung-I. and Sirbu, Marvin A. (1999) 'Optimal Bundling Strategy for Digital Information Goods: Network Delivery of Articles and Subscriptions', *Information Economics and Policy*, 11, 2, 147–76.

Coase, Ronald (1937) 'The Nature of the Firm', *Economica*, 4, 386–405.

Coase, Ronald (1946) 'The Marginal Cost Controversy', *Economica*, 13, 169–82.

Coase, Ronald (1960) 'The Problem of Social Cost,' *Journal of Law and Economics*, 3, 1–44.

Fishburn, P. C., Odlyzko, A. M. and Siders, C. (1997) 'Fixed Fee versus Unit Pricing for Information Goods: Competition, Equilibria and Price Wars', conference on Internet Publishing and Beyond: Economics of Digital Information and Intellectual Property, Cambridge, MA, 23–5 January.

Grimes, W. S. (1994) 'Antitrust Tie-in Analysis after Kodak: Understanding the Role of Masher Imperfections', *Antitrust Law Journal*, 62, 2, 263–325.

Hanson, W., and Martin, R. K. (1990) 'Optimal Bundling Pricing', *Management Science*, 36, 2, 155–74.

Hirsch, M., Magill, M. and Mas-Colell, A. (1990) 'A Geometric Approach to a Class of Equilibrium Existence Theorems', *Journal of Mathematical Economics*, 19, 1–2, 95–106.

Kim, Hee-Su (1996) 'Equilibrium and Efficiency in Auctions of Complementary Goods Without Bundling', *Economics Letters*, 52, 1, 49–54.

Liu, Pak-Wai and Yang, Xiaokai (2000) 'The Theory of Irrelevance of the Size of the Firm', *Journal of Economic Behavior and Organization*, 42, 145–65.

Martin, S. (1999) 'Strategic and Welfare Implications of Bundling', *Economics Letters*, 62, 3, 371–6.

Matutes, Carmen and Regibeau, Pierre (1992) 'Compatibility and Bundling of Complementary Goods in a Duopoly,' *Journal of Industrial Economics*, 40, 1, 37–54.

McAfee, R. P., McMillan, J., and Whinston, M. D. (1989) 'Multiproduct Monopoly, Commodity Bundling, and Correlation of Values', *Quarterly Journal of Economics*, 104, 371–83.

Schmalensee, R. (1984) 'Gaussian Demand and Commodity Bundling', *Journal of Business*, 57, 1, 211–30, part 2.

Stigler, G. (1963) 'United States v. Leow's Inc.: a Note on Block Booking', *Supreme Court Review*, 152–7.

Sun, G., Yang, X and Yao, S. (1999) 'Theoretical Foundation of Economic Development Based on Networking Decisions in the Competitive Markets', Harvard Center for International Development Working Paper no. 17.

Varian, H. L. (1995) 'Pricing Information Goods', in Proceedings of Scholarship in the New Information Environment Symposium, Harvard Law School.

Varian, H. L. (1996) 'Differential Pricing and Efficiency', http://www.sims.berkeley.edu/ ~hal/pages/sciam.html, 25/3/99.

Varian, H. L. (1997) 'Versioning Information Goods', http://www.sims.berkeley.edu/ ~hal/pages/ sciam.html, 25/3/99.

Varian, H. L. (2000) 'Buying, Sharing and Renting Information Goods', Working Paper, School of Information Management and Systems, University of California, Berkeley.

Whinston, Michael (1990) 'Tying, Foreclosure, and Exclusion', *American Economic Review*, 80, 4, 837–59.

Yang, X. (2001) *Economics: New Classical versus Neoclassical Frameworks* (Cambridge, MA: Blackwell).

Yang, X. and Ng, Y.-K. (1995) 'Theory of the Firm and Structure of Residual Rights', *Journal of Economic Behavior and Organization*, 26, 107–28.

Yang, X. and Ng, S. (1998) 'Specialization and Division of Labour: a Survey', in K. Arrow, Y.-K. Ng, and Xiaokai Yang (eds), *Increasing Returns and Economic Analysis* (London: Macmillan), 3–63.

Appendix: the corner equilibria of different market structures

A1 Partial division of labour: P_A

Structure P_A consists of two configurations, (xz/y) and (y/x). In the structure P_A, given that $x, x^s, z, y^d > 0$, $z^s = z^d = y = y^s = x^d = 0$, an individual in configuration (xz/y) has the decision problem

$$\text{Max: } u_{PA1} = (x^{\alpha}) \cdot (y^d)^{1-\alpha}$$

subject to the following constraints:

$$\begin{aligned}
&x + x^s = z^{\beta} \cdot l_x \text{ and } \beta \in (0,1)\\
&z = l_z - b \text{ and } b \in (0,1)\\
&l_x + l_z = 1\\
&k_x \cdot p_x \cdot x^s = p_y \cdot y^d
\end{aligned}$$

where u_{PA1} is the utility for an individual in configuration (xz/y). The equations of constraints state an individual's budget constraint, endowment constraint, and the production function.

Similarly, an individual in configuration (y/x) has the decision problem

$$\text{Max: } u_{PA2} = (x^d)^{\alpha} \cdot y^{1-\alpha}$$

subject to the following constraints:

$$\begin{aligned}
&y + y^s = l_y - b \text{ and } b \in (0,1)\\
&l_y = 1\\
&k_y \cdot p_y \cdot y^s = p_x \cdot x^d
\end{aligned}$$

where u_{PA2} is the utility for an individual in configuration (y/x).

Using the utility equalization condition and market-clearing conditions, the price of good x in terms of good y, and the relative number of individuals selling good x to individuals selling good y are given by:

$$\frac{P_x}{P_y} = \frac{k_y^{\alpha} \cdot (1+\beta)^{1+\beta}}{k_x^{1-\alpha} \cdot \beta^{\beta} \cdot (1-b)^{\beta}} \text{ and}$$

$$\frac{M_x}{M_y} = \frac{\alpha \cdot k_y^{1-\alpha}}{(1-\alpha) \cdot k_x^{\alpha}}$$

The real per capita income in this structure is therefore

$$u_{PA} = \frac{\alpha^{\alpha} \cdot (1-\alpha)^{1-\alpha} \cdot (1-b)^{1+\alpha\beta} \cdot \beta^{\alpha\beta} \cdot (k_x . k_y)^{\alpha(1-\alpha)}}{(1+\beta)^{\alpha(1+\beta)}}$$

A2 Partial division of labour: P_B

Similarly, in structure P_B the decision problem for an individual with configuration (zx/y) is

$$\text{Max: } u_{PB1} = x^{\alpha} \cdot (y^d)^{1-\alpha}$$

subject to the following constraints:

$$x = z^{\beta} \cdot l_x \text{ and } \beta \in (0,1)$$
$$z + z^s = l_z - b \text{ and } b \in (0,1)$$
$$l_x + l_z = 1$$
$$k_z \cdot p_z \cdot z^s = p_y \cdot y^d$$

where u_{PB1} is the utility for an individual in configuration (zx/y). The equations of constraints state an individual's budget constraint, endowment constraint, and the production function.

An individual in configuration (yx/z) has the decision problem

$$\text{Max: } u_{PB2} = x^{\alpha} \cdot y^{1-\alpha}$$

subject to the following constraints:

$$x = (z^d)^{\beta} \cdot l_x \text{ and } \beta \in (0,1)$$
$$y + y^s = l_y - b \text{ and } b \in (0,1)$$
$$l_x + l_y = 1$$
$$k_y \cdot p_y \cdot y^s = p_z \cdot z^d$$

The utility equalization condition and market-clearing conditions yield a set of relative prices and relative number of specialists, and the per capita real income in this structure.

$$\frac{P_y}{P_z} = \left(\frac{k_z^{1-\alpha}}{k_y^{\alpha\beta}}\right)^{\frac{1}{1-\alpha+\alpha\beta}}$$

$$\frac{M_z}{M_y} = \frac{\alpha\beta \cdot k_y^{\frac{1-\alpha}{1-\alpha+\alpha\beta}}}{(1-\alpha)\cdot k_z^{\frac{\alpha\beta}{1-\alpha+\alpha\beta}}}$$

$$u_{PB} = \frac{\alpha^{\alpha}\cdot(1-\alpha)^{1-\alpha}\cdot(1-b)^{1+\alpha\beta}\cdot(\alpha\beta)^{\alpha\beta}\cdot(k_z \cdot k_y)^{\frac{\alpha\beta(1-\alpha)}{1-\alpha+\alpha\beta}}}{(1+\alpha\beta)^{1+\alpha\beta}}$$

A3 Partial division of labour with the institution of the firm: structure FP_B

Structure FP_B is a division of the population between configuration (l_zx/y) and (yx/l_z). Given that $x, z, l_z, y^d > 0$, $x^s = x^d = y = y^s = z^s = z^d = 0$, an individual in configuration (l_zx/y) has the decision problem

Max: $u_{FPB1} = x^{\alpha} \cdot (y^d)^{1-\alpha}$

subject to the following constraints:

$$x = z^{\beta} \cdot l_x \text{ and } \beta \in (0,1)$$
$$z = l_z - b \text{ and } b \in (0,1)$$
$$l_x + l_z + L_z = 1$$
$$w \cdot L_z = P_y \cdot y^d$$

Similarly, A person choosing configuration (yx/l_z) produces goods x and y, sells good y, and employs labour to produce good z. It is defined by $x, y, y^s, l_z > 0$, $x^s = x^d = y^d = z^s = z^d = 0$. An individual in configuration (yx/l_z) has the decision problem

Max: $u_{FPB2} = x^{\alpha} \cdot y^{1-\alpha}$

subject to the following constraints:

$$y + y^s = l_y - b$$
$$x = (z^d)^{\beta} \cdot l_x \text{ and } \beta \in (0,1)$$
$$l_x + l_z = 1$$
$$z^d = N \cdot z^s$$
$$z^s = g_z \cdot L_z - b$$
$$k_y \cdot p_y \cdot y^s = w \cdot N \cdot L_z$$

The utility equalization condition and market-clearing conditions yield the price of good y in term of labour to produce good z, and the number of individuals selling good y relative to that of individuals selling labour to produce good z:

$$\frac{P_y}{w} = \{\frac{(1+\alpha\beta)^{\frac{1-\alpha}{\alpha}} \cdot k_y \cdot [g_z(1-b)\cdot(1-\alpha) - b(1+\alpha\beta)]}{(\alpha\beta)^{\frac{1-\alpha}{\alpha}} \cdot (1-\alpha)\cdot(1-b)^{\frac{1}{\alpha}}}\}^{\frac{\alpha\beta}{(1-\alpha)\cdot(1-\alpha+\alpha\beta)}}$$

$$\frac{M_z}{M_y} = \{\frac{(1+\alpha\beta)^{\frac{1-\alpha}{\alpha}} \cdot k_y \cdot [g_z(1-b).(1-\alpha) - b(1+\alpha\beta)]}{(\alpha\beta)^{\frac{1-\alpha}{\alpha}} \cdot (1-\alpha)\cdot(1-b)^{\frac{1}{\alpha}}}\}^{\frac{\alpha\beta}{(1-\alpha)\cdot(1-\alpha+\alpha\beta)}} \cdot [\frac{(1+\alpha\beta)^2}{(1-\alpha)\cdot(1-b)^2}]$$

The per capita real income in this structure is therefore

$$u_{FPB} = \{\frac{(1+\alpha\beta)^{\frac{1-\alpha}{\alpha}} \cdot k_y \cdot [g_z(1-b)\cdot(1-\alpha) - b(1+\alpha\beta)]}{(\alpha\beta)^{\frac{1-\alpha}{\alpha}} \cdot (1-\alpha).(1-b)^{\frac{1}{\alpha}}}\}^{\frac{\alpha\beta}{(1-\alpha)\cdot(1-\alpha+\alpha\beta)}} \cdot [\frac{(1-\alpha)^{1-\alpha} \cdot \alpha^{\alpha+\beta} \cdot (1-b)^{1+\beta} \cdot \beta^{\beta}}{(1+\alpha\beta)^{1+\beta}}]$$

A4 Complete division of labour without the firm: structure CD

There are three configurations (x/yz), (z/xy) and (y/x) in this structure, where an individual produces only one of good x, y or z, and sells the good in exchange for others. The decision problems for the individuals under different configurations are given as below respectively,

In configuration (x/yz)
Max: $u_{CD1} = x^{\alpha}\cdot(y^d)^{1-\alpha}$
s.t. $x + x^s = (z^d)^{\beta} \cdot l_x$ and $\beta \in (0,1)$
$l_x = 1$
$k_x \cdot p_x \cdot x^s = p_y \cdot y^d + p_z \cdot z^d$

In configuration (z/xy),
Max: $u_{CD2} = (x^d)^{\alpha}\cdot(y^d)^{1-\alpha}$
s.t. $z^s = l_z - b$ and $b \in (0,1)$
$l_z = 1$
$k_z \cdot p_z \cdot z^s = p_x \cdot x^d + p_y \cdot y^d$

In configuration (y/x),
Max: $u_{CD3} = (x^d)^{\alpha} \cdot y^{1-\alpha}$
s.t. $y + y^s = l_y - b$ and $b \in (0,1)$
$l_y = 1$
$k_y \cdot p_y \cdot y^s = p_x \cdot x^d$

The utility equalization condition and market-clearing conditions yield a set of relative prices and relative number of specialists:

$$\frac{p_z}{p_y} = \frac{k_y^{\alpha}}{k_z} \text{ and } \frac{p_x}{p_z} = (\frac{1-b}{1-\beta})^{1-\beta}\cdot\frac{k_z^{1-\beta}}{\beta^{\beta}\cdot k_x^{1-\alpha+\alpha\beta}}$$

$$\frac{M_y}{M_x} = \frac{(1-\alpha)+\alpha\beta(1-k_x\cdot k_z\cdot k_y^{1-\alpha})}{\alpha.(1-\beta)\cdot k_x^{1-\alpha}} \text{ and } \frac{M_x}{M_z} = \frac{(1-\beta)}{\beta\cdot k_z\cdot k_x^{\alpha}}$$

The per capita real income in this structure is therefore

$$u_{CD} = \alpha^{\alpha} \cdot (1-\alpha)^{1-\alpha} \cdot (1-b)^{1-\alpha+\alpha\beta} \cdot \beta^{\alpha\beta} \cdot (1-\beta)^{\alpha(1-\beta)} \cdot k_z^{\alpha\beta} \cdot k_x^{\alpha(1-\alpha+\alpha\beta)} \cdot k_y^{\alpha(1-\alpha)}$$

A5 Complete division of labour with the firm: structure FD_A

Structure FD_A consists of three individual configurations (x/l_zy), (l_z/xy) and (y/x). Given that $x, x^s, y^d, l_z > 0$, $x^d = y = y^s = z = z^s = 0$, an individual in configuration (x/l_zy) has the decision problem

Max: $u_{FDA} = x^{\alpha} . (y^d)^{1-\alpha}$

His budget constraint and production functions are

$x + x^s = (Z^d)^{\beta} \cdot l_x$ and $\beta \in (0,1)$
$l_x = 1$
$z^s = g_z \cdot L_z - b,\quad g_z \in (0,1)$ and $b \in (0,1)$
$L_z = 1$

$$Z^d = N.z^s$$
$$k_x \cdot p_x \cdot x^s = p_y \cdot y^d + w \cdot N \cdot L_z$$

where g_z is the transaction efficiency coefficient for labour hired to produce the intermediate good z. It encompasses all the costs that relate to the measurement of efforts to produce the intermediate good z in terms of quantity and quality. In essence, the measurement costs can be explained as pricing costs. Quantity N is the number of workers hired by the employer. In this configuration, l_x is the decision variable to the employer, while L_z is as given because it is bought from the labour market. An individual in configuration (x/l_zy) possesses the utility u_{FDA1}, and he is the employer in this structure FD_A.

Similarly, an individual in configuration (l_z/xy) has the decision problem

$$\text{Max: } u_{FDA2} = (x^d)^{\alpha} \cdot (y^d)^{1-\alpha}$$

The budget constraint and the production functions are:

$$L_z = 1$$
$$w \cdot L_z = p_x \cdot x^d + p_y \cdot y^d$$

The individual who chooses this configuration is the employee of this structure. Moreover, an individual in configuration (y/x) has the decision problem

$$\text{Max: } u_{FDA3} = (x^d)^{\alpha} \cdot y^{1-\alpha}$$

The budget constraint and the production functions are

$$y + y^s = l_y - b \text{ and } b \in (0,1)$$
$$l_y = 1$$
$$k_y \cdot p_y \cdot y^s = p_x \cdot x^d$$

The utility equalization condition and market-clearing conditions yield the set of prices of good x and y in terms of labour to produce good z, and the number of individuals selling goods x and y relative to that of individuals selling labour to produce good z:

$$\frac{w}{p_y} = k_y^{\alpha} \cdot (g_z - b)$$

$$\frac{w}{p_x} = k_x^{1-\alpha+\alpha\beta} \cdot (1-\beta) \cdot \beta^{\beta} \cdot (g_z - b)^{\beta}$$

$$\frac{M_x}{M_z} = \frac{g_z \cdot (1-\beta)}{\beta \cdot k_x^{\alpha}} \text{ and } \frac{M_y}{M_x} = \frac{k_x^{\alpha} \cdot (1-\alpha)}{k_y^{1-\alpha} \cdot \alpha \cdot (1-\beta)}$$

The per capita real income in this structure is therefore

$$u_{FDA} = \alpha^{\alpha} \cdot (1-\alpha)^{1-\alpha} \cdot (g_z - b)^{1-\alpha+\alpha\beta} \cdot \beta^{\alpha\beta} \cdot (1-\beta)^{\alpha(1-\beta)} \cdot k_y^{\alpha(1-\alpha)} \cdot k^{\alpha(1-\alpha+\alpha\beta)x}$$

A6 Bundling sales and the institution of the firm: structure FT_B

Structure FT_B is characterized by bundling sales and the institution of the firm, and involves the division of population among configurations $(x/l_y z)$, $(l_y/y(x))$ and $(z/y(x))$. In Structure FT_B, a firm specializes in producing good x, and also hires labour to produce another final good y. However, an owner of the firm only sells good y in exchange for intermediate good z and labour employed to produced good y; it bundles good x with good y, which means good x is not directly priced, and people can obtain some amount of good x when they buy good y from the market. The ratio of the amounts of the two goods is set up in a bundling sale.

In structure FT_B, an individual in configuration $(x/l_y z)$ has the decision problem

$$\text{Max: } u_{FTB1} = x^{\alpha} \cdot y^{1-\alpha}$$

subject to the following constraints:

$$x + x^s = (z^d)^{\beta} \cdot l_x \text{ and } \beta \in (0,1)$$
$$l_x = 1$$
$$Y^s = g_y \cdot L_y - b, \quad g \in (0,1) \quad \text{and} \quad b \in (0,1)$$
$$L_y = 1$$
$$x^s = h \cdot y^s$$
$$y + y^s = N \cdot Y^s$$
$$k_y \cdot p_y \cdot y^s = p_z \cdot z^d + w \cdot N \cdot L_y$$

where g_y is again the transaction efficiency coefficient for labour hired to produce good y, and N is the number of workers hired by the employer to produce good y. In order to distinguish the interflow of goods from market trade flow, we use capitalized decision variables to denote internal flow. Hence, Y^s is internal transfer of good y produced by an employee to the employer and y^s is the amount of good y sold by the firm. h is the bundling ratio between the bundled good y and the final good x which is for sale. Here, we assume $h = e.(p_x/w)$. This implies that an individual selling y, buying labour, and bundling x with y, must choose the bundling ratio $h = x/y$ according to p_y/w. For a small market value of p_y/w he must give away a small amount of x for each unit y sold. Otherwise, a small value of p_y/w may not be enough to cover the production cost of x which is not directly priced. Here, e is as given to the owner of the firm, later we can use the Yao Theorem to rule out the real optimal bundling ratio of goods y and x. In addition, l_x is the decision variable to the employer, while L_y is as given because it is bought from the labour market. u_{FTB1} is the utility for an individual in configuration $(x/l_y z)$, and he is the employer in this structure FT_B.

The solution to the decision problem yields demand function for labour and good z, supply function of good x, and indirect utility function for configuration $(x/l_y z)$.

Similarly, an employee choosing configuration $(l_y/y(x))$ has the decision problem

$$\text{Max: } u_{FTB2} = (x^d)^{\alpha} \cdot (y^d)^{1-\alpha}$$

subject to the following constraints:

$$x^d = h \cdot y^d$$
$$L_y = 1$$
$$w \cdot L_y = p_y \cdot y^d$$

The solution of this problem yields the demand for goods x and y, supply of labour, and indirect utility function for configuration (l_y/y(x)).

An individual choosing configuration (z/y(x)) has the decision problem

$$\text{Max: } u_{FTB3} = (x^d)^\alpha \cdot (y^d)^{1-\alpha}$$

subject to the production function, endowment constraint, and budget constraint:

$$z^s = l_z - b$$
$$l_z = 1$$
$$x^d = h \cdot y^d$$
$$k_z p_z z^s = p_y y^d$$

The solution to this problem yields the demand for goods x and y, supply of good z, and indirect utility function for configuration (z/y(x)).

The utility equalization conditions across three configurations yield the corner equilibrium relative prices of goods x and z and labour.

$$\frac{w}{p_z} = k_z(1-b)$$

$$\frac{w}{p_y} = [\frac{k_y(g_y - b) \cdot k_z \cdot \beta}{(1-\alpha)\cdot(1+\beta)+(\alpha\beta)}]^{\frac{\beta}{1-\beta}} \cdot \frac{\alpha^\alpha \cdot (1-\beta) \cdot [(1-\alpha)\cdot(\alpha-\beta)+\alpha\beta]^{(1-\alpha)\frac{\beta}{1-\beta}}}{(1-\alpha)^{1-\alpha}}$$

According to the Yao Theorem, maximizing utility with respect to *e* yields the optimal value

$$e = \frac{k_y(1-\alpha)^2 \cdot (g_y - b)}{(1-\alpha)\cdot(1-\beta)+\alpha\beta}$$

The two independent market-clearing conditions for goods x and z (the other market-clearing condition being not independent due to Walras' Law) yield the corner equilibrium relative numbers of specialists producing goods x, y, and z

$$\frac{M_x}{M_z} = \{[\frac{(1-\alpha)\cdot(\alpha-\beta)+\alpha\beta}{(1-\alpha)\cdot(1-\beta)+\alpha\beta}]^{(1-\alpha)+\frac{\beta}{1-\beta}} \cdot \frac{\alpha^\alpha \cdot (1-\beta) \cdot [(g_y - b)\cdot\beta]^{\frac{\beta}{1-\beta}}}{(1-\alpha)^{1-\alpha} \cdot k_y^{\frac{1-2\beta}{1-\beta}}}\} \cdot (\frac{k_z^2}{1-b})^{\frac{\beta}{1-\beta}}$$

$$\frac{M_x}{M_z} = [\frac{(1-\alpha)\cdot(\alpha-\beta)+\alpha\beta}{(1-\alpha)\cdot(1-\beta)+\alpha\beta}] \cdot \frac{(1-\alpha+\alpha\beta)}{\beta} - [\frac{k_y(g_y - b)\cdot k_z \cdot \beta}{(1-\alpha)\cdot(1-\beta)+\alpha\beta}]^{\frac{\beta}{1-\beta}} \cdot \frac{\alpha^\alpha \cdot (1-\beta) \cdot [(1-\alpha)\cdot(\alpha-\beta)+\alpha\beta]^{(1-\alpha)+\frac{\beta}{1-\beta}}}{(1-\alpha)^{1-\alpha}}$$

where M_x is the number of x specialist-employers choosing (x/l_yz), M_z is the number of specialist producers of good z choosing (z/y(x)), and M_y is the number of employees choosing (l_y/y(x)). The relative numbers of specialists, together with the population size identity $M_x + M_z + M_y = M$, yield the corner equilibrium numbers of different specialists. Plugging relative prices into an indirect utility function of any of three configurations yields the per capita real income in this structure:

$$u_{FTB} = \alpha^{\alpha}\cdot(1-\beta)\cdot(1-\alpha)^{1-\alpha}\cdot(k_z\cdot\beta)^{\frac{\beta}{1-\beta}}\cdot\{\frac{k_y(g_y-b)\cdot[(1-\alpha)\cdot(\alpha-\beta)+\alpha\beta]}{(1-\alpha)\cdot(1-\beta)+\alpha\beta}\}^{1-\alpha+\frac{\beta}{1-\beta}}$$

In Structure FT_B a firm produces both goods x and y, and sells y with good x bundled. The percentage *h* of goods x and y is dependent on the relative price of good y and labour, and the wage rate *w* of labour hired to produce good y, and *e*. Note that obtaining good x is bundled through the purchase of good y, therefore we need not take the transaction costs of good x into account separately from good y. In other words, we suppose there is no extra transaction cost to obtain good x when good x is bundled with good y.

7

Legislation, Electronic Commerce and the Common Law: the Growing Legislative Framework, How it Compares Internationally and its Failings in Australia

Andrew Field

1 Introduction

In reflecting upon a dichotomy which pervades the 'brave new world'[1] of the Internet and electronic commerce conducted within the global communications network, the following report written in 1999 and taken from an English website provides a nice illustration:

> The Queen has opened the last session of the British Parliament this century ...
>
> Seated on the Throne in the House of Lords, the Upper Chamber of the Westminster Parliament, the Queen unveiled the Government's programme for the next 12 months. The audience of ermine-clad Lords was joined by members of the House of Commons, summoned to hear the Queen's speech. She told Parliament that there are 28 planned pieces of legislation in the Government's third Parliament session ...
>
> [The Queen said]: 'To prepare Britain as a dynamic, knowledge-based economy, my Government will introduce a Bill to promote electronic commerce and electronic government, improving our ability to compete in the digital marketplace'.[2]

Just as the British Government must still rely on centuries-old mechanisms to introduce a legislative regime for electronic trade and contracting online in the twenty-first century, so too the introduction of legal regimes for other aspects of electronic transactions has to struggle with some age-old issues.

In Australia, it is clearly essential to meet the challenge of providing a legal framework for online contracts. The exponential growth reported in this sector dictates that this must be a priority. Specifically, whereas in 1996 global trade over the Internet was estimated at US$3 billion, the figure is now estimated in the hundreds of billions of dollars.[3] Locally, the Internet's promise of conquering the historical trade barrier of 'the tyranny of distance' has made electronic commerce a major area of development in Australia. This growth has been reflected over the last few years: Australia's online trade in 1997 was estimated at A$61 million, but in 2001 it was estimated at A$1.3 billion, and possibly as much as A$10 billion by 2003.[4] There are a lot of contracts being made online!

Despite the figures demonstrating the growth of electronic commerce, for some time there has been a question as to how far legislation provides a sound legal basis for contracting online. Uncertainties about how the law applies to transactions conducted over the Internet present one of the biggest hurdles to the adoption of electronic commerce by businesses and consumers alike.[5] Such uncertainties exist in a number of areas. A review of state and federal government legislative initiatives of the last couple of years reveals a series of measures designed to address these uncertainties. The results have been both positive and negative.[6]

The purpose of this chapter is threefold. Firstly, it will provide an outline of the progress of legislative measures introduced in Australia to assist in securing a legal regime and legal certainty in the making of contracts online. This essentially involves a discussion of the Commonwealth Government's *Electronic Transactions Act* 1999, and an update on the progress of the other versions of this legislation introduced by the various Australian state governments. It will be noted that flaws can be found in this legislative approach and programme. Secondly, this chapter will also make a brief comparison of this programme with the legislative measures introduced by other national governments. In this context, it will be found that the Australian legislative approach compares quite favourably. Nevertheless, flaws do exist in the Australian legislation. The third undertaking of this chapter is to identify and discuss one of the significant failings of the legislation, specifically taking into account those areas where such legislation is silent and a thousand years of common law would appear to still cover the field, a problem which only *sounds* innocuous.

2 *Electronic Transactions Act* 1999 (Cth)

The legislative programme of the Australian Government was prompted by a basic concern as to whether or not a contract formed online – a 'virtual contract' as some might be tempted to term it – is valid. The programme has been spearheaded by the *Electronic Transactions Act* 1999 (Cth). There is nothing terribly complex about this piece of legislation. It is a relatively short act of only three parts and 16 sections. However, nearly a year passed between the release of a draft of the Act and its receiving the royal assent in December 1999. In addition, the preliminary consultation process which preceded this Act can be traced back at least two years prior, to the time when the Information Industries Taskforce said the introduction of such legislation was 'urgent' if Australian industries were not to be placed at an international trading disadvantage through lack of confidence in the legal recognition of electronic communications.[7]

This consultation process reached an early peak with the Report of the Electronic Commerce Expert Group. Although the Expert Group noted, despite some doubts, that online contracts were probably valid,[8] for the purposes of legal certainty it recommended the adoption of legislation based on the Model Law prepared by the United Nations Commission on International Trade Law ('UNCITRAL')[9] in 1996. The adoption by the Commonwealth Government of this recommendation has given the resulting legislation a degree of international conformity, which should allow Australian traders to hold their own against international competitors.

(i) The general rule

The *Electronic Transactions Act* is directed at one basic issue: the validity of electronic communications. For example, does the fact that a contract is concluded by a series of electronic impulses in binary form deprive it of the necessary characteristics required to make the contract binding? As the Attorney-General Daryl Williams stated when introducing the bill:

> As current Australian legislation neither recognises nor denies the validity of electronic communications, the Bill establishes the basic rule that a transaction is not invalid because it took place by means of an electronic communication.[10]

Section 8 is the key provision of the Act, because it addresses this question. Section 8(1) states:

> For the purposes of a law of the Commonwealth, a transaction is not invalid because it took place wholly or partly by means of one or more electronic communications.

The section embodies the fundamental principle of technological or media neutrality which underlies the Act. Furthermore the section is clearly meant to be read broadly, section 5 defining 'transaction' to include non-commercial transactions. Thus the Act provides the legal basis for electronic information or communication under a law of the Commonwealth.

(ii) Requirements under laws of the Commonwealth: writing, signatures and the production and retention of documents

The rule of technological neutrality between paper and electronic media is expanded upon under Part 2 Division 2 of the Act, which comprises sections 9, 10, 11 and 12.

(a) Writing and signatures

Sections 9 and 10 similarly provide for legal recognition of electronic equivalents of writing and signatures. With regard to writing, the general rule under section 9 is that if under a law of the Commonwealth a person is required or permitted to give information in writing, that requirement is taken to be met if the person gives the information by means of an electronic communication. This rule operates with the following provisos:

1. In all cases – where at the time the information was given, it had been reasonable to expect that the information would be readily accessible so as to be usable for subsequent reference.
2. If the information is required or permitted to be given to a Commonwealth entity or a person acting on its behalf, and that entity requires or permits that the information be given in accordance with a particular technology by means of a particular kind of electronic communication, then the entity's requirement has been met.
3. If the information is required or permitted to be given to a Commonwealth entity or a person acting on its behalf, and that entity requires or permits that particular action be taken by way of verifying the receipt of information, then the entity's requirement has been met.
4. If the information is required or permitted to be given to a person who is neither a Commonwealth entity nor a person acting on behalf of such an entity, then the person to whom the information is required or permitted to be given must have consented to the information being given by way of electronic communication.

As an illustration of what 'giving information' means, section 9(5) goes on to provide a broad definition which includes, for example, matters such as making an application, lodging a claim, serving a notification, lodging an objection and giving a statement of reasons.

Section 10 deals with electronic signatures. In the light of some regimes proposed locally and overseas which go into some detail as to the methods and technologies utilized in the creation of an electronic signature, the brevity of this section appears as something of a letdown. Section 10 does no more than provide that where the signature of a person is required, that requirement is met in relation to an electronic communication, with the following provisos:

1. In all cases, a method must have been used to identify the person and to indicate that person's approval of the information communicated.
2. In all cases, having regard to all relevant circumstances at the time the method must have been as reliable as was appropriate for the purposes for which it was communicated.
3. In cases where the signature is required to be given to a Commonwealth entity or a person acting on its behalf and that entity requires that the method used as mentioned in paragraph (a) above is in accordance with particular information technology requirements, then the entity's requirement has been met.
4. If the signature is required to be given to a person who is neither a Commonwealth entity nor a person acting on behalf of such an entity, then the person to whom the signature is required to be given must have consented to the requirement being met by way of the method mentioned in paragraph (a) above.

Of course, beyond actually allowing for the use of signatures, section 10 still leaves a number of unanswered questions, which only time will answer. However, it is a fair prediction that much case law in the future might be devoted to the question of what signature method is 'as reliable as was appropriate' with regard to all the relevant circumstances.

(b) Production and retention of documents

Sections 11 and 12 have the potential to be of very practical value, as they deal with the storage and production of documents. Section 11 provides that if under a law of the Commonwealth a person is required or permitted to produce a document which is in the form of paper, an article or other material, that requirement is met if the person produces, by means of an electronic communication, an electronic form of document, with the following provisos:

1. In all cases, the method of generating the electronic form of the document provided a reliable means of assuring the maintenance of the integrity of the information contained in the document.
2. In all cases, at the time the communication was sent it was reasonable to expect the information contained in the electronic form of the document would be readily accessible so as to be usable for subsequent reference.
3. If the document is required or permitted to be produced to a Commonwealth entity or a person acting on its behalf, and the entity requires that the document be produced in electronic form in

accordance with particular information technology requirements by means of a particular kind of electronic communication, then the entity's requirement has been met.

4. If the document is required or permitted to be produced to a Commonwealth entity or a person acting on its behalf, and the entity requires that particular action be taken to verify the receipt of the document, then the entity's requirement has been met.
5. If the person to whom the document is required or permitted to be produced is neither a Commonwealth entity nor a person acting on behalf of such an entity, then the person to whom the document is required or permitted to be produced must have consented to the production, by means of an electronic communication, of an electronic form of the document.

Section 12, which deals with the retention of information, is significant insofar as it marks a statutory embodiment of the much anticipated future of information storage. It provides that if, under a law of the Commonwealth, there is a requirement for information to be recorded, or a written document or electronic communication to be retained, that requirement will be met having regard to factors including:

(a) the maintenance of the integrity of the stored information;
(b) any provision that might require storage on a particular kind of storage device;
(c) ready access to the information for subsequent reference; and
(d) the inclusion of additional information identifying such matters as the origin, destination, and time of dispatch and receipt of the communication.

Sections 11 and 12 of the Act herald a new era in record-keeping, so long anticipated in this information age. They have the potential to see the end of all sorts of paper record-keeping, from the shoebox filled with receipts retained for the tax audit, to the rented storage facilities containing thousands of paper files, which can be a substantial drain on business revenues. However, for a number of reasons – not least of which is a vigilant suspicion of the technologies presently employed for data storage – it is unlikely that paper records will be abandoned in the short term, even if the information they contain is merely a backup for information stored electronically. However, the legislation indicates that a change is in sight.

(iii) Other provisions

Significantly, the Act also defines the time and place of dispatch and receipt of electronic communications, the importance of which can be seen in a multitude of commercial situations. Specifically, section 14(1) states that if an electronic communication enters an information system outside the control of the originator, then the dispatch occurs when it enters that information system. Similarly, section 14(3) states that if an addressee of such a communication has designated an information system for the purpose of receiving communications, receipt will occur when the communication enters that system. Conversely, if the addressee has not so designated an information system, then receipt will only occur when the communication comes to the attention of the addressee, according to section 14(4).

(iv) Limitations of the Act

As it was first introduced, the Act had a twofold limitation. In most respects, this will lapse – and in important respects has lapsed – into historical obscurity. However, these limitations are worth recalling, as they are perhaps indicative of the Government's less than enthusiastic approach to the legislation. Firstly, despite the recommendation in the ECEG Report that the Commonwealth had adequate power under the Constitution to enact comprehensive legislation by which all State and Commonwealth legislation could be read, the *Electronic Transactions Act* 1999 is limited in all of its provisions to matters arising 'under a law of the Commonwealth'. On the face of it, this alone represents a significant limitation of the application of the Act, especially when it is recalled that most matters of contract law are under the ambit of State law.

Furthermore, under section 5(2), 'law of the Commonwealth' was further limited to mean only 'a law of the Commonwealth specified in the regulations' until 1 July 2001. It is interesting to observe exactly what pieces of legislation were exposed to the electronic age under the Regulations. By way of two sets of Regulations, over three hundred different 'laws of the Commonwealth' were designated as being subject to the Act. Although this sounds impressive, an examination of the Regulations reveals that the laws nominated are designated by sections, or by Parts of Acts, and only very occasionally by the whole Act. Among the Acts specified in their entirety there are some that beg the question why they were nominated. For example, the relevance of the *Treaty of Peace (Germany) Act* 1919 to present-day Australia and electronic commerce might well be doubted, yet it was one of the Acts nominated. With the passing of 1 July 2001, the purview of the *Electronic Transactions Act* 1999 is now determined on the basis of an 'opt-out' scheme, the Regulations specifying which laws of the Commonwealth the Act will *not* apply to.

It suffices to say that the legislation brought under the Act prior to 1 July 2001 reminds the author of the British Royal Navy 'pressgangs' of the eighteenth century, strong-arming unwilling volunteers into service. The legislation to which the Act was allowed to apply was very much a piecemeal affair. Conversely, the days leading up to 1 July 2001 – when the 'opt-in' system would change to an 'opt-out' system – also seemed like a last-minute scramble to get off a sinking ship. For example, the *Electronic Transactions Amendment Regulations 2001 (No. 2)* dated 13 June 2001 specified a series of laws of the Commonwealth to which the Act *did not* apply after 1 July 2001, setting out some one hundred and fifty-seven laws. Perhaps these events accurately reflect the feelings of the Government towards electronic commerce: overtly positive, but tinged with uncertainty, hesitancy, and a preference for non-participation.

3 State legislation

Because of the limitations of the Commonwealth legislation, the introduction of legislation by the states will have the most significant impact on electronic commerce. It was agreed upon by the various Australian state governments that the Commonwealth Act would form the model for a uniform scheme of state legislation. However, the present position is somewhat surprising.

Historically, it was the state governments which led the way towards the introduction of a legal framework for electronic transactions. For example, the former Victorian Minister for Multimedia, Alan Stockdale, strongly advocated the introduction of such legislation, initially producing a draft of state legislation on the basis that the Commonwealth was slow to act, even holding the position that Victoria would enact its own laws if necessary. However, contrary to this background, at present the states are generally failing to fill this legislative gap. Only New South Wales, Victoria and Tasmania have their respective versions of the legislation in force, and the vast void of uncertainty still covers most of Australia.

The *Electronic Transactions Act* (2000) (NSW), the *Electronic Transactions (Victoria) Act* 2000 (Vic), and the *Electronic Transactions Act* 2000 (Tas) need not be discussed at length. All three Acts were introduced to their respective Parliaments in 2000, and their passage and assent were unremarkable. Essentially, even though the numbering of the sections in the Acts varies for no obvious reason, they basically reproduce Part 2 of the Commonwealth Act, with the distinction that they are not limited to laws of the Commonwealth.

There are a few significant differences. Firstly, whereas the Commonwealth legislation commences as essentially an 'opt-in' scheme (and remained so until July 2001) and applied only to designated laws, the state legislation could be described as an 'opt-out' regime from the outset. For example, in section 7 of the *Electronic Transactions (Victoria) Act* 2000, the general rule is restated that a transaction is not invalid merely because it took place by means of an electronic communication. It is then noted that this general rule is subject to the regulations, which may exclude its effect from either a specified transaction or class of transactions or a specified law of the jurisdiction. As an indication of what matters might be excluded, at the time of writing the *Electronic Transactions (Victoria) Regulations 2000* states that section 7 will not apply to wills, codicils or any other testamentary instruments, or to any transaction requiring personal service of documents or information (for example, summonses and warrants).[11]

One other significant difference in Victoria is that the legislation came into force on 1 September 2000. In other words, the Victorian legislation had general application almost a year before the Commonwealth legislation.

4 Electronic transactions legislation in other jurisdictions

As was noted above, the Australian legislative scheme is based on the UNCITRAL Model Law. UNCITRAL completed work on development of the Model Law in 1996. Its purpose was to encourage national legislators to enact legislation and provide them with a set of internationally acceptable rules, the adoption of which would promote a degree of international uniformity as well as the legal certainty much sought after. However, it was also considered that any legislation derived from the Model Law should be fairly broad, in recognition of the fact that any specific technologies employed in meeting the problems of electronic commerce would almost certainly become outdated as technology advanced – a danger which was clearly apparent with new advances appearing with practically every passing week through the 1990s[12] and which can still be observed to a similar degree. With this in mind, it would appear that the broadly worded Australian legislation well satisfies these requirements. Nevertheless it might be asked how prompt the legislative action of Australia has been, compared with the efforts of other national governments.

Because of the leadership of the United States in the IT revolution, mention should be made of its developments. Most of the legislative action in the United States has been undertaken by the state legislatures. By the end of 2000, some 43 of the 50 states had enacted electronic commerce legislation of some kind. The lead was taken by the Federal Government with its *Electronic Signatures in Global and National Commerce Act*, which is in turn based upon the *Uniform Electronic Transactions Act* (US) as drafted by the National Conference of Commissioners on Uniform State Laws.[13] The Commissioners observed:

> The need for certainty as to the scope and applicability of this Act is critical, and makes any sort of a broad, general exception based on notions of inconsistency with existing writing and signature requirements unwise at best. The uncertainty inherent in leaving the applicability of the Act to judicial construction of this Act with other laws is unacceptable if electronic transactions are to be facilitated.[14]

Section 7 of the *Uniform Electronic Transactions Act* sets out to resolve this basic issue by stating:

(a) A record or signature may not be denied legal effect or enforceability solely because it is in electronic form.
(b) A contract may not be denied legal effect or enforceability solely because an electronic record was used in its formation.
(c) If a law requires a record to be in writing, an electronic record satisfies the law.
(d) If a law requires a signature, an electronic signature satisfies the law.

Generally, however, the various US state governments have taken a number of different approaches. As one recent commentator has written:

> The Utah legislation is very detailed and has been described as an infrastructure approach – it not only gives legal effect to digital signatures but also regulates the operations of certification authorities. The legislation is technology specific because it only recognises public key cryptography. On the other hand, in California the legislation deals very briefly with public entities and is supported by extensive regulations. The Californian legislation recognised authentications technology other than public key cryptography. In relation to the private sector in California, the legislature has adopted the *Uniform Electronic Transactions Act* (US) ... The Massachusetts approach is a minimalist one. The legislation simply gives digital signatures legal effect but does not cover the infrastructure that will be needed to support digital signatures. The Illinois proposal is an attempt to partially combine the minimalist approach with a technology specific approach.[15]

In contrast, the legislative bodies of member countries of the European Community have been prompted not merely by the encouragement of UNCITRAL but also by Directive Number 2000/31/EC of the European Parliament 'On Certain Legal Aspects of Information Society Services, in Particular Electronic Commerce, in the Internal Market'. The purpose of this directive is to encourage member states to adopt legislation reflecting its aims. Consistent with UNCITRAL's approach, the directive essentially was a brief missive (only 24 Articles), and includes the all-important statement that 'Member States shall ensure that their legal system allows contracts to be concluded by electronic means'.[16]

That there is still some hesitancy in introducing new legal measures among all of the Europeans is shown by the example of Great Britain. The *Electronic Communications Act 2000* (UK) appears to be more concerned with establishing approval mechanisms for the provision of cryptography (which is the substance of Part I). In Part II, the 'facilitation of Electronic

Commerce' is mostly undertaken through the wide-ranging power conferred on the 'appropriate Minister' to make orders modifying any enactment or subordinate legislation to 'facilitate the use of electronic communications'.[17] Evidently, this piecemeal approach is not entirely compelling, and it is perhaps significant that when the Parliament of the Isle of Man (a British dependency) introduced its own *Electronic Transactions Act* 2000, it chose to base it on the Australian model.[18]

Conversely, mention should be made of the Republic of Ireland's innovative *Electronic Commerce Act* 2000.[19] Not only does it give legal recognition to electronic communications and information in electronic form (section 9), it also addresses other basic legal questions still remaining in Australia and most other common law jurisdictions. Sections 12 and 13 are not exceptional; they give recognition to electronic writing and electronic signatures respectively. Section 19 is more novel, appearing to go a little further than most comparable enactments by providing that 'an electronic contract shall not be denied legal effect, validity or enforceability solely on the grounds that it is wholly or partly in electronic form'. Moreover, section 14 indicates how signatures which are required to be witnessed might achieve validity if executed electronically. Section 16 indicates what conditions need to be satisfied if a document is to be executed under seal electronically, a matter barely considered in most jurisdictions.

Closer to Australian shores, there was a fear in the late 1990s that Australia was falling behind its near neighbours. Specifically, in 1997 the report of the Information Industries Taskforce could point to an expansive and proactive legislative programme introduced by the Malaysian government.[20] However, with hindsight it does not appear that any great lead was taken over Australia. Specifically, the piece of Malaysian legislation most relevant to the present discussion, the *Digital Signatures Act* 1997, and also other legislation from its ASEAN neighbours[21] do not appear to have given those jurisdictions a great advantage. By pre-empting the UNCITRAL initiative, perhaps Malaysia has even denied itself the opportunity to be consistent with the rest of the world. Its *Digital Signatures Act* was based on the Utah legislation, and could be criticized in much the same way as the Utah Act.[22] Its scope is limited to digital signatures, the regulation of such signatures, and the establishment of the necessary certification authorities, and so it leaves a number of contractual issues open to question.

In contrast, although Singapore's *Electronic Transactions Act* 1998 contains much in common with the Malaysian legislation, it also makes clear the benefits of not acting in haste. Much of it is based on the UNCITRAL Model Law. It further incorporates many of the features of the Utah legislation pertaining to the issuing of certificates to regulate electronic signatures. Of course, the Singapore legislation is open to criticism, although here the strongest criticism must be reserved for the electronic signatures regime. In this respect, it is worth recalling why Australia did not adopt a signature regulation regime. As the Australian Electronic Commerce Expert Group reported:

> There is a growing assumption that existing electronic signature laws will need to be revised as the use of certification and electronic signatures expands and electronic commerce evolves, supplanted in some areas and streamlined in others. In addition, significant redrafting may be necessary if uniform laws are to be promulgated among different jurisdictions.[23]

Such considerations could explain why other nations in the region are following the Australian lead. Vanuatu's *Electronic Transactions Act* 2000[24] is clearly based on the Australian model, and across the Tasman Sea, New Zealand is adopting the same scheme – prompted perhaps by some criticism that the government was dragging its feet on the question of legislation for electronic transactions.[25]

In the light of the above, it appears that the legislative programme in Australia and the gradual introduction of the electronic transaction legislation would place Australia on a footing comparable with its trading partners. If only because the Australian legislation has been adopted by many other jurisdictions, or is comparable to other jurisdictions, Australia lies at the forefront of a global legislative movement tending towards consistency in the area of an electronic commerce framework. Consistency of electronic commerce legislation around the globe, therefore, should not be a matter for concern. What should concern us is the legal position regarding the 'gaps' in the framework.

5 Enforcing contracts made online, and the 'grey' areas

Developments in the United States tend to show that giving the messages exchanged over the Internet their plain and ordinary meaning could alter basic tenets of the law of contract, and have the effect of turning contract law 'on its head'. The fascination that such questions hold for legal scholars arises especially because very few cases of contract formation have been litigated in common law jurisdictions. Presently, the flaws or omissions in the regime are unexposed because of the dearth of electronic contract disputes before the courts. The legal issues have not been argued in a systematic and adversarial manner.

Under the legislation, it is specifically provided that a contract can be formed as effectively through the exchange of e-mails as through the exchange of paper correspondence. This is consistent so far with case law, which recognizes other forms of electronic communication as sufficient for contract formation.[26] As a matter of enforcing such a contract, therefore, the rules that govern the paper equivalents should apply. Accordingly, between businesses based in different jurisdictions, the creation of an electronic contract in which terms are included dealing with choice of law, method and forum of dispute resolution, should appear as familiar matters.

However, there has been an increase in electronic commerce by retail businesses selling or licensing goods or services, on websites that trade not by way of an exchange of e-mails, but rather by way of providing information via electronic 'shop fronts'. Frequently, such electronic vendors will set out various terms for such matters as payment, delivery and so on, and the consumer clicks on an icon labelled variously 'I agree' or 'I accept' or 'submit', hence the phrase 'clickwrap agreement'.[27]

From the point of view of contract law, a good question to ask is when 'I accept' effectually means 'I accept'. Does clicking on the 'I accept' icon constitute acceptance of an offer (as appearances would suggest), or is it merely an offer to the electronic vendor (consistent with the established principle of contract law that the vendor, by displaying its wares, is generally only making an invitation to treat[28])? In other words, can the offer of sale in a website constitute a contractual offer, be it to a specified group or even to the world at large?[29] The answer to the question could be of some significance to the location of formation of the contract; it could affect choice of law and forum.

Under the general position at common law, it is the purchaser clicking on 'I accept' who is actually making the offer. However, in a series of interlocutory decisions in the United States – possibly the only jurisdiction in which such matters have been litigated to date, albeit rarely to trial stage – it was held that clicking on the 'I accept' icon on a computer screen indicates more than a mere willingness to be legally bound, but actually constitutes acceptance of a contractual offer.

In *Compuserve Inc* v. *Patterson,*[30] a case concerning a trademark dispute over software, the United States Court of Appeals found that the defendant's typing of the words 'I agree' at various points in a standard licence agreement constituted assent to it. Similarly, in *Caspi* v. *Microsoft,*[31] when the defendant sought to enforce a choice of forum clause in an online agreement, the Superior Court of New Jersey determined that the plaintiff's clicking on the words 'I agree' at regular stages through the agreement was to be viewed as assent to the terms. The interlocutory judgment of the United States District Court in *Hotmail* v. *Van Money Pie*[32] also indicates that clicking on the 'I agree' box constituted the entry into a valid contract.

The 2000 decision of the Supreme Court of Washington in *Mortenson* v. *Timberline Software Corp*[33] should also be noted. Although, on the facts, this case dealt with the purchase of software offline in the form of discs, the formation of the agreement appears to be indistinguishable from situations involving online clickwrap agreements, since the terms in dispute were contained in electronic format on the discs.

In this case, owing to a fault in the software, the plaintiff underestimated a tender by $1.5 million and sought damages from the licensor of the software. However, the court found that a limitation of liability term in the licensing agreement which appeared on the computer screen – and to which the plaintiff signified his agreement by proceeding to use the software – excluded the defendant's liability. It is significant to note that after the plaintiff had signified his agreement, the defendant was required to do no more to complete the contract, meaning that the vendor's statement which appeared on the screen constituted the offer and the plaintiff's clicking constituted the acceptance that formed a contract. This finding of the court appears to contradict the established notion that a display in a shop window – or a virtual shop window – is no more than an 'invitation to treat'. Indeed, the dissenting minority judgment noted that the majority decision marked an abandonment of traditional contractual principles. To quote Sanders J:

> Although the majority states 'this is a case about contract formation, not contract alteration,' the majority abandons the traditional contract principles governing offer and acceptance and relies on distinguishable cases with blind deference to software manufacturers' preferred method of conducting business.[34]

However, this decision gives the expression 'I accept', as it is used in so many software agreements, the literal meaning of contractual acceptance.

Whether Australian courts will interpret 'I accept' as acceptance or merely an offer is a matter for speculation. It is suggested that the American approaches noted above will not be influential. Some Australian judges are on record as believing that Australian courts should not take any guidance from American judgments, regardless of their persuasive merits. However, in the land of the blind, the man with one functional eye is king, and in Australia at present there is no other judicial guidance offered on the question of contract formation.

Of course, time and location of contract formation are not frequently at the core of the dispute between litigating parties and, taken in isolation, where and when formation occurs is only one factor relevant to determining choice of law and forum. However, the judgment in *Mortensen* serves as a useful warning that contract law is perhaps on the verge of vast change from previously accepted principles. Accordingly, as a matter of prudence, it is advisable for any party seeking to trade over the internet to include terms dealing with such matters as choice of law, forum and so on at as early a time as possible and as prominently as possible. Indeed, it is advisable to consider terms beyond the usual warranties, including such matters as:

(a) choice of law and jurisdiction;
(b) limitation of target markets;

(c) limitation of contracts to those which comply with the law;
(d) where and when risk in the subject of the contract passes;
(e) a right for the seller to terminate the contract.

The terms, of course, should not be designed to unduly advantage or disadvantage either party to a transaction. Their inclusion should be viewed as no more than an attempt to introduce some certainty in an uncertain environment.

6 Conclusion

A number of conclusions can be drawn from the matters raised in this chapter. It would appear that Australian legislators, despite strong recommendations, found the introduction of electronic commerce legislation – if only to ensure the legal recognition of electronic communications – to be a protracted process. Some state governments are still undergoing this process, their legislation merely being a flicker in the draftsman's eye. However, compared with the progress of governments around the world, Australia appears able to make some claim to leadership. Australia was not the first country to introduce electronic commerce legislation, but it was one of the first to introduce legislation based upon a scheme recommended for global adoption. By not rushing in, Australia has avoided the potential pitfalls of having a regime that is out of step with the rest of the world. As noted above, this is presumably why other jurisdictions have sought to emulate the Australian legislation.

However, as we have also noted, Australia's legislation is threadbare. It is not a weighty statute, and it does not answer all of the questions that will inevitably arise. One of those matters has been raised in this chapter: the question of where formation of a contract occurs, and whether the established rules of contract will apply. The case of *Mortensen* v. *Timberline* runs contrary to the common law and so appears illogical, and yet it gives effect to the plain meaning of the words used in communications between parties to an electronic contract. What the Australian position will be is a matter for speculation. However, it should open the eyes of those with business dealings over the Internet to the uncertainties which still exist in the virtual world.

Notes

1 'O brave new world, that has such people in it', William Shakespeare, *The Tempest*, Act V, Scene 1, Line 183; adopted by Aldous Huxley as the title of his novel, *Brave New World* (1932), a disturbing prophetic tale of a future human society.

2 *http://www.netlondon.com/news/1999–46/2E764CE51813ED85802.html* (accessed 22 June 2001).
3 Parliament of Australia Joint Committee of Public Accounts and Audit, *Report 36, Internet Commerce: To Buy or Not to Buy?* (1998), 41.
4 *Hansard*, Legislative Assembly (Vic), 6 April 2000, 788 (*Electronic Transactions (Victoria) Bill*, second reading speech).
5 Andrew Field, 'Electronic Commerce and the Internet: Which Government is Doing What?', (1999) 73(4) *Law Institute Journal* 56 at 58.
6 This chapter addresses some of the positive developments. Some negative suggestions have been floated elsewhere. For example, the Australian Tax Office made a first attempt to address the challenge of electronic commerce and prevent the erosion of the national tax base in *Tax and the Internet* (Discussion paper, August 1997), which included a recommendation for a substantial licensing scheme for webshops, organizations that operate webshops, and hosts of webshops. In response, Telstra said such a scheme would impose 'unreasonable compliance costs in industry participants and will inhibit the growth of internet commerce' (see *Report 360, Internet Commerce*, supra n. 3, 56). In other words, rather than promoting e-commerce, the ATO's scheme would smother it at birth.
7 Information Industries Taskforce, *The Global Information Economy: the Way Ahead* (1997), pp. 71–3.
8 'The law already recognises contracts formed using facsimile, telex and other similar technology. It is unlikely that recognition would not be accorded to contract formed by way of offer and/or acceptance communicated electronically, provided the requisite elements are present. The principles are the same in the case of both paper and electronic communications.' See the report of the Electronic Commerce Expert Group, *Electronic Commerce: Building the Legal Framework* (31 March 1998), para 2.11.11.
9 UNCITRAL's mission is essentially to assist in the harmonization of commercial law around the world. Its usual devices for achieving this have been either through the adoption by member states of treaties or conventions, or through the promulgation of 'model' laws, legislative templates which are then adopted either wholly or in part by states into their domestic systems. Notable UNCITRAL successes in the last twenty years include the *Convention on Contracts in the International Sale of Goods* 1980.
10 Second reading speech, *Hansard*, House of Representatives, 30 June 1999, 7851.
11 Surprisingly, however, as it has not been referred to and excluded in the Regulations, it would appear that pursuant to the rule in *Walsh* v. *Lonsdale* (1882) 21 Ch 9 – which held that an equitable interest in land can be created by a contract in writing for the transfer of land which can justify an order for specific performance – an interest in land can be created via an electronic contract.
12 This summary is derived from the summary contained in the Report of the Electronic Commerce Expert Group, *Electronic Commerce: Building the Legal Framework*, para. 2.0.2; see n. 8 above.
13 A copy of the *Uniform Electronic Transactions Act* can be found at *http://www.law.upenn.edu/bll/ulc/fnact99/1990s/ueta99.htm* (accessed 2 July 2001). This document also contains background to the drafting of the Act. Information regarding progress towards the adoption of the Act can be found at http://www. uetaonline.com.
14 *http://www.law.upenn.edu/bll/ulc/fnact99/1990s/ueta99.htm* (accessed 2 July 2001).

15 Adrian McCullagh, 'Legal Aspects of electronic contracts and digital signatures', in Anne Fitzgerald (ed.), *Going Digital: Legal Issues for E-commerce, Software and the Internet* (St Leonards, NSW: Prospect Media, 2000), 191 at 203.
16 *Directive 2000/31/EC of the European Parliament and of the Council of 8 June 2000 on certain legal aspects of information society services, in particular electronic commerce, in the Internal Market*, Art. 9(1).
17 *Electronic Communications Act 2000* (UK), s. 8. A copy of the Act may be obtained at *http://www.hmso.gov.uk/acts/acts2000/200000007.htm* (accessed 21 June 2001).
18 PriceWaterhouseCoopers, 'Electronic Transactions Act 2000', obtained at *http://www.pwcglobal.com/im/eng/ins-sol/spec-int/elct_transation_act.html* (accessed 19 June 2001). A copy of the Act may be obtained at http://www.gov.im/infocentre/docs/etbill2000.html.
19 The *Electronic Commerce Act* 2000 (Ireland) may be obtained at http://www.entemp.ie/ecd/ebus1.htm.
20 See n. 7 above, p. 72.
21 A comparative table is set out at http://www.aseansec.org/ec/ec_legis.htm.
22 A discussion of the Malaysian *Digital Signature Bill 1997* (which became the *Digital Signature Act*) can be found at http://www.lawnet.com.sg/freeaccess/ech/Annex_B.htm.
23 See n. 8 above, para. 3.3.6.
24 Available at http://www.vanuatu.usp.ac.fj.
25 Adam Creed, 'New Zealand unhappy with national e-readiness ranking', 11 June 2001, *http://www.ecommercereport.com.au/story12.htm*, accessed 21 June 2001.
26 See, for example, *Brinkibon Ltd* v. *Stahag Stahl und Stahlwarenhandelsgesellschaft mbH* [1992] 1 All ER 293; *Entores Ltd* v. *Miles Far East Corporation* [1955] 2 QB 327; *Leach Nominees Pty Ltd* v. *Walter Wright Pty Ltd* [1996] WAR 244 (cases concerning telex communications).
27 The notion of a 'clickwrap' agreement is an extension of another form of agreement which is ubiquitous in the software industry, the 'shrinkwrap' agreement. As stated by the US Court of Appeal in *ProCD* v. *Zeidenberg* 86 F3d 1447 (7th Cir 1996): 'The "shrinkwrap" license gets it name from the fact that retail software packages are covered in plastic or cellophane "shrinkwrap", and some vendors ... have written licenses that become effective as soon as the customer tears the wrapping from the package.' The case may be obtained at http://www.law.emory.edu/7circuit/text/june96/96-1139.txt.
28 See, for example, *Boots Cash Chemists* v. *Pharmaceutical Society of Great Britain* [1953] 1 QB 401.
29 This was a matter adverted to by the Attorney-General's Electronic Commerce Expert Group but not really discussed beyond noting the issue. See n. 7 above, para 2.11.12.
30 89 F3d 1257 (6th Cir 1996), available at http://www.jmls.edu/cyber/cases/patter.html.
31 323 NJ Super 118 (1999), available at http://lawlibrary.rutgers.edu/courts/appellate/a2182-97.opn.html.
32 (1998) WL 388389 (ND Cal), available at http://eon.law.harvard.edu/h2o/property/alternatives/hotmail.html.
33 140 Wn.2d; 2000 Wash.LEXIS 287 (Supreme Court of Washington, Court of Appeal, 5 May 2000).
34 Ibid.

8

E-Commerce in China: Problems and Potential

John Wong and Wong Chee Kong

1 E-commerce[1] at the crossroads?

China has experienced spectacular growth in the information technology (IT) sector in recent years. Its IT sector is poised to overtake Australia to become the largest in the Asia-Pacific region, excluding Japan.[2] It has even become the world's largest mobile phone market, having 207 million subscribers in 2002, compared to the United States' 123 million.[3] Internet usage has also increased rapidly, from 8.9 million users in 1999 to almost 60 million in 2002, and with an estimated 200 million users by 2005 (see Figure 8.1).[4] Such development of the IT industry has set the background for the rapid growth of e-commerce in China. With entry into the World Trade Organization (WTO) on 10 November 2001, e-commerce will play a significant role in building up its new economy.

Since its inception in 1997, e-commerce as part of the emerging new economy has experienced an upsurge recently despite having started from a low base.[5] In April 2001, China had 238,249 Internet websites, which was about 3.5 per cent of the total number of websites in the world, according to the first Internet resources survey by the State Council's Information Application Promotion Office. It also revealed that China had registered 692,490 domain names and set up 45,598 online databases by April 2001.[6]

In 1999, China's B2B and B2C e-commerce revenue increased more than fivefold, from US$8 million in 1998 to over US$40 million in 1999.[7] For B2C e-commerce, or online shopping alone, the total turnover in 1999 amounted to 55 million yuan (US$6.6 million).[8] China's online sales are projected to hit 10 billion yuan (US$1.2 billion) by 2002, and leap further to 40 billion yuan (US$4.8 billion) by 2004.[9] B2B e-commerce revenue is also predicted to hit one trillion yuan (or US$125 billion) by 2005.[10]

However, these e-commerce figures do not reflect the true amount of all e-commerce transactions. Many 'e-commerce' transactions in China typically involve selecting a product online but paying offline, usually via cash

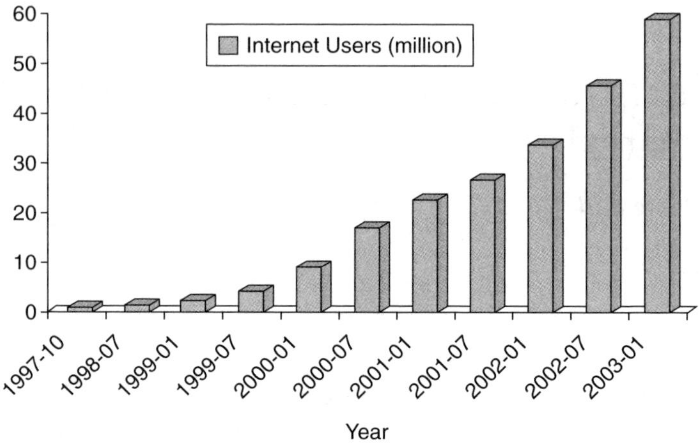

Figure 8.1 China's internet users, 1997–2002
Source: China Internet Network Information Center (CNNIC) website, 'Survey on China's Internet Development,' October 1997–January 2003, *http://www.cnnic. net.cn*.

on delivery.[11] In fact, China's actual e-commerce volume in 2000 totalled 77.2 billion yuan (US$9.3 billion), or 4.7 per cent of the world's total volume, with B2B transactions accounting for more than 99 per cent – amounting to 76.8 billion yuan (US$9.29 billion) – and B2C transactions volume of 390 million yuan (US$47.2 million), more than double the formal 'online shopping figures'. B2B and B2C transaction volumes are also predicted to hit 94.2 billion yuan (US$11.4 billion) and 1.3 billion yuan (US$157.3 million) in 2001 respectively.[12]

Despite the strong growth registered by the IT industry, in particular the telecom and Internet sectors, China still lags behind other countries in terms of market size and scope. For instance, it was estimated that China accounted for only 2.1 per cent of Asia's total online revenue in 2000.[13] In absolute terms, the size of e-commerce in China today is still very small, accounting for only 0.0018 per cent of its total retail sales, as compared to the US$33 billion turnover or 1.4 per cent of total retail sales in the US.[14] It was reported by the United Nations Conference on Trade and Development (UNCTAD) that e-commerce transactions in China represent only 0.87 per cent of its gross domestic product (GDP), whereas in comparison, those in the US represent 2.4 per cent of its GDP.[15] According to US investment bank Goldman Sachs, China's B2B e-commerce will not mature until 2003 or 2004.[16] Besides the 'online purchase offline payment' practice mentioned earlier, another reason for the small figure is because credit cards have only recently become relatively widespread in urban China, and few credit card holders feel comfortable enough to use them online.[17]

According to the survey conducted by the China Internet Network Information Centre (CNNIC) in July 2001, out of China's 26.5 million Internet users, about 31.9 per cent are reported to have tried online shopping, compared to about 40 per cent internationally.[18] Furthermore, only 29.6 per cent of these e-shoppers were satisfied with online trading.[19] While 46.7 per cent of Internet users chose to shop online because of the time saved compared to traditional shopping, 44.2 per cent shopped online due to convenience, 33.4 per cent in order to save expenditure and 32.6 per cent due to curiosity (see Table 8.1).[20] The majority of e-shoppers in China are young middle-class males with better education and higher incomes, mainly from Beijing, Guangdong and Shanghai (see Tables 8.2 and 8.3).

As for the reasons Internet users were reluctant to use e-commerce, 33.4 per cent felt insecure about online transactions, 33.0 per cent were concerned about the quality of goods and felt that after-sales services might not be provided, 11.5 per cent regarded online payment as inconvenient, 8.7 per cent feared that goods and services ordered online might not be delivered on time, 6.6 per cent did not find the price attractive enough, and 6.0 per cent doubted the information posted on the Internet (Table 8.4).[21]

It was reported that businesses in China lack expertise in information technology. For example, about 70 per cent of businesses considered investment

Table 8.1 Reasons for online shopping among internet users in China, 2002 (multiple choice)

	January 2002 (%)	*July 2002 (%)*
Save time	48.3	48.5
Convenient to use	41.7	42.4
Save money	38.8	43.7
Out of curiosity	31.5	25.5
Look for rare goods	28.9	33.5

Source: CNNIC, 'Survey on China's Internet Development', January and July 2002, *http://www.cnnic.net.cn*

Table 8.2 Internet users in China by age, 2002 (%)

Age	*18 below*	*18–24*	*25–30*	*31–5*	*36–40*	*41–50*	*51–60*	*61 & above*
January 2002	15.3	36.2	16.3	12.1	8.2	7.6	3.2	1.1
July 2002	16.3	37.2	16.9	11.6	7.2	6.8	3.1	0.9

Source: CNNIC, 'Survey on China's Internet Development', January and July 2002, *http://www.cnnic.net.cn*.

Table 8.3 Internet users in China by education, 2002 (%)

	Below high school	*High school*	*College*	*Bachelor's degree*	*Master's degree*	*Doctorate degree*
January 2002	10.2	30.0	26.9	30.4	2.1	0.4
July 2002	11.5	30.5	26.3	29.2	2.1	0.4

Source: CNNIC, 'Survey on China's Internet Development', January and July 2002, *http://www.cnnic.net.cn*.

Table 8.4 The biggest problem with online trading in China, 2002

	January 2002 (%)	*July 2002 (%)*
No guarantee for security	31.0	22.1
No guarantee for the quality of goods, post-sales service and manufacturer's credit	30.2	36.9
Inconvenient payment	11.8	13.0
Late delivery	13.9	10.2
Unattractive price	6.3	11.1
Unreliable information provided by the Internet	6.3	5.9
Others	0.5	0.8

Source: CNNIC, 'Survey on China's Internet Development', January and July 2002, *http://www.cnnic.net.cn*.

in information technology inadequate, accounting for merely 0.3 per cent of their total assets, far below the 8 per cent to 10 per cent investments by large enterprises in developed countries. Another 62 per cent of businesses lacked IT professionals. Although 74 per cent of key state enterprises have Internet access or launched their own home pages, only 28 per cent had satisfactory e-commerce services.[22] They merely set up a homepage and list their e-mail addresses, mainly for the purpose of advertisement; some do not even bother to update their websites. Moreover, about half of small and medium enterprises (SMEs), which constitute 99 per cent of the country's total industrial and commercial enterprises, have no computers.[23]

2 Driving forces of growth

E-commerce in China has been driven primarily by three forces of growth – namely, telecommunications, the Golden Projects and electronic banking. These are the three major wings of China's informatization drive in propelling national economic growth. According to Vice Premier Wu Bangguo, 'e-commerce development is key for the informatization of the national economy.'

2.1 Telecommunications

The rapid growth of the telecoms industry has spurred the rise of e-commerce, in at least two ways. First, China's Internet sector has exploded, with telecoms service providers such as China Mobile and China Unicom offering Internet services such as Wireless Application Protocol (WAP) networks. Second, the convergence of the telecoms industry with the IT industry has in turn resulted in greater demand for e-commerce services in the country.

China's telecoms service providers have jumped on the bandwagon to grasp the opportunities brought about by e-commerce. China Telecom, for example, has 1.5 million e-commerce users with revenue exceeding 80 million yuan (US$9.7 million). It has established 15 categories of e-commerce application services which include online telecom service hall, e-payment settlement, e-customs declaration, e-stock, secure commercial mail system, online mart and online ticket booking.[24]

Since the mid-1990s, China's telecoms growth has been driven by the expansion of mobile telephony, with mobile subscription consistently increasing by more than 80 to 90 per cent annually. The sharp increase has been made possible by China's booming economy and greater intensified competition in the telecoms market as a result of industrial restructuring.[25] Along with the introduction of WAP services, many Chinese users are enabled to directly access a variety of Internet services via their mobile phones. An online survey carried out in March 2000 on China's internet issues and the use of wireless internet access equipment found two-thirds (65.4 per cent) of survey respondents using mobile telephones to achieve wireless Internet access.[26] The number of Chinese mobile phone users is projected to hit 300 million in 2005, and by then, more people are expected to access the Internet through their mobile phones than through their computers.

WAP enables users without computers to conduct transactions such as shopping or online trading, known also as mobile commerce (m-commerce). For instance, WAP phone users can access various stock-related services for online stock trading. According to Hai Ling of e-business consultant firm SinoFusion, about 5.8 per cent of China's mobile subscribers have WAP phones, and more than 22 per cent of WAP-phone owners have expressed interest in mobile trading.[27] China is also predicted to have 21 million online trading accounts by 2005, up from 250,000 in 1999 and 3.1 million in 2001, and will have the largest number of online stock traders in Asia.[28]

2.2 The Golden Projects

China's rapid progress in financial reform and the modernization of its financial services in recent years have inadvertently paved the way for the subsequent development of e-commerce. The case in point are the

'Golden Projects' which have been particularly conducive to the growth of e-commerce. To promote the application of IT in China's economic development, the three Golden Projects (*Sanjin gongcheng*) – Golden Bridge (*Jinqiao*), Golden Customs (*Jinguan*), and Golden Card (*Jinka*) – were proposed in 1993 and launched in 1994, the purpose being to construct a nationwide information network.[29]

The Golden Bridge Project, announced in March 1993, served as a 'state public economic information network' which provided Internet access, e-mail, electronic data interchange (EDI) and communication services to government offices, enterprises and the public in major cities throughout the country.[30] The Golden Customs Project was intended as a specialized foreign trade information network connecting the information systems of foreign trade companies with China's banks, customs and tax offices. It was necessitated by China's rapid growth in foreign trade and the need to improve control over foreign trade activities by the government agencies.[31] The Golden Card Project, which began in 1995, was aimed at promoting and developing an electronic banking and credit card system, linking banks, businesses and consumers with adequate financial networks.[32] The project targeted to deliver 300 million credit or cash cards to 300 million people in 400 urban areas by the year 2005.

China's construction of its information superhighway gained momentum in March 1995 when several new golden projects were added (see Table 8.5). For example, Golden Taxation (*Jinshui*) was initiated by the Ministry of Finance and the People's Bank of China to computerize the tax collection system.[33] The others include Golden Agriculture (*Jinnong*) which would provide information about commodities and prices; Golden Enterprises (*Jinqi*) which would network the supply and demand information between China's larger enterprises and government; Golden Intelligence (*Jinzhi*) which would connect academic and research institutions; and Golden Macro-Economic Supporting System (*Jin Hong*) which would provide strategic information for central planners.[34]

China had basically fulfilled the targets set for the Golden Projects by 1997. By 1999, the Golden Bridge had its first phase completed with the installation of a nationwide Internet control centre and an information network connecting 30 provincial cities, hundreds of VSAT satellite stations, e-mail/EDI value-added service centre and the Golden Bridge internet information centre.[35]

2.3 Electronic banking

After the launch of the Golden Card Project, e-commerce development in China took a major step forward with the establishment of online banking in 1997, when China Merchants Bank, a major commercial bank, started its internet payment business.[36] Online banking is defined to be financial

Table 8.5 China's Golden Projects

Name	*Full title*	*Ministries, departments and enterprises involved*
Golden Bridge (*Jin Qiao*)	National Public Economic Information Communication Network	Ministry of Electronics (now Ministry of Information Industry), State Information Centre, Jitong Corp.
Golden Customs (*Jin Guan*)	National Foreign Economic Trade Information Network Project	Ministry of Foreign Trade, Customs Department, Jitong Corp.
Golden Card (*Jin Ka*)	Electronic Money Project	PBOC, Ministry of Electronics, Ministry of Internal Trade, Great Wall Computer Co.
Golden Sea (*Jin Hai*)	Secret project provides China's leaders with immediate access to reference data	State Statistical Bureau, PBOC, State Information Centre
Golden Macro (*Jin Hong*)	National Economic Macro-Policy Technology System	China Ex-Im Bank, Ministry of Finance, State Information Centre
Golden Tax (*Jin Shui*)	Computerised Tax Return & Invoice System Project	Ministry of Finance, Ministry of Electronics, National Taxation Bureau, Great Wall Computer Co.
Golden Intelligence (*Jin Zhi*)	China Education & Research Network	State Education Commission
Golden Enterprise (*Jin Qi*)	Industrial Production and Information Distribution System	State Economic and Trade Commission
Golden Agriculture (*Jin Nong*)	Overall Agriculture Administration & Information Distribution System	Ministry of Agriculture
Golden Health (*Jin Wei*)	National Health Information Network	Ministry of Health
Golden Info (*Jin Xin*)	State Statistical Information Project	State Statistical Bureau
Golden Cellular (*Jin Feng*)	Mobile Communications Production & Marketing Project	Ministry of Electronics Industry
Golden Switch (*Jin Kai*)	Digital 2000 Switch Systems Production Project	Ministry of Electronics Industry, Ministry of Posts & Telecommunications (now MII)

Source: EIU, 'China's Golden Projects', *Business China* (31 August 1998).

services provided by banks through the Internet and telephone.[37] It includes 24-hour customer bank account access, and allows transactions between accounts, personal financing consultation, fee payments, online shopping and online stock trading. The major banks in China, namely the People's Bank of China (PBOC), the Industrial and Commercial Bank of China (ICBC), the China Agricultural Bank, the China Construction Bank, the Bank of China and the China Merchants Bank have established an 'online banking research group' and started their electronic banking (or e-banking) services.[38] At the end of June 2001, China's national banks had issued 330 million bankcards in total, of which about 7.6 per cent or 25 million were credit cards.[39] China is expected to become the largest online banking market in Asia.[40]

China's largest commercial bank, the Industrial and Commercial Bank of China (ICBC), which started its e-banking services in 1998, expanded its online banking business to enterprises throughout China in February 2000.[41] It has planned to further extend its e-banking business this year by establishing telephone banking service centres and enhancing its co-operation with various dotcom companies to stimulate the development of e-commerce in China. The ICBC is projected to increase its e-banking transaction volume from 1.9 trillion yuan (US$229 billion) in 2000 to 3 trillion yuan (US$361 billion) this year, making up 5 per cent of its traditional business volume.[42]

China's major banks have also jointly provided e-banking services in alliance with the telecoms operators. Since April 2000, the ICBC has started providing banking services to mobile phone users using a subscriber identity module (SIM) card.[43] Currently, almost half a million subscribers of China Mobile can access their bank accounts via mobile phones for banking services such as checking bank balances, transferring funds between accounts and paying phone bills.[44]

China Telecom has signed an agreement on total e-commerce cooperation with China Agricultural Bank, Bank of China and China Merchants Bank. It has also come to an agreement with the ICBC on the joint construction of a unified payment platform for payment settlement of e-commerce, which was expected to be completed by July 2001. Such co-operation with China Telecom enables e-commerce service providers to accept all major bankcards for online transactions.[45]

In May 2000, China's central bank, the People's Bank of China (PBOC), established administrative procedures to approve online banking. It further considered amendments to current financial laws governing online banking, as China's banking law did not cover online banks and payments.[46] In July 2001, the PBOC launched a provisional guideline for regulating online banking, which aims to standardize and guide the future development of China's online banking business, prevent banking business risks and protect clients' legal rights and interests.[47]

3 Problems and weaknesses

Given the astonishing pace at which China has developed its information infrastructure, e-commerce, with its already promising start, is poised to be a major force for growth in the IT industry. However, China's fledgling e-commerce industry was dealt a severe blow when one of its most well-known online stores, my8848.net, closed down in October 2001. This dented Chinese consumers' faith in e-commerce.[48] Consequently, the Beijing authorities, which had already received numerous complaints from angry customers about the non-delivery of goods purchased online, issued a warning to their citizens about making online payments to e-commerce sites.[49] Such an incident actually highlights the problems and difficulties faced by China's e-commerce firms, already made worse off in the wake of the recent global economic downturn.

3.1 Business-to-business (B2B)

One of the weakest links, often cited, in China's e-commerce industry is the embryonic state of its B2B development. This means that B2B lags behind B2C in the number of transactions, despite the fact that B2B dominates total e-commerce turnover as mentioned earlier. China will have to develop a strong B2B market in order to break the deadlock of e-commerce activities focusing mainly on B2C transactions. With China's future economic development increasingly dependent on international linkages for investment and information, particularly now that it has become a member of the WTO, the country can ill afford to remain outside of the global B2B networks.[50] In addition, given that exports will greatly increase with China's entry into the WTO, investment banking giant Goldman Sachs has estimated that the adoption of B2B strategies could generate 5 to 10 per cent initial cost savings for the country's export sector.[51]

China's underdeveloped B2B market has been attributed to its peculiar features of national institutions and industrial organization, in this instance, having a state-controlled or command economy, which has created 'a system of hierarchical firm organizations and centralized management structures incompatible with the requirements of web design and management'.[52]

The situation is compounded by the dominance of SMEs, which lack the necessary resources and technical personnel for the adoption of B2B solutions. The backwardness of local businesses poses a problem because e-commerce development requires large companies for B2B adoption throughout the economy, but the ailing and inefficient state-owned enterprises (SOE), now accounting for less than 30 per cent of industrial production, are unlikely to adopt new technology. Furthermore, in an economy based on cheap labour, firms would rather hire local workers than adopt a technology solution.[53]

Besides its organizational structure, China's business culture is based on the development of informal social networks through which problems can be sorted out by means of personal, face-to-face contact, known as *guanxi*. The pervasiveness of such *guanxi* networks is a hindrance to the development of formalized internet-based B2B networks.[54] Most companies are more comfortable with agreements made face-to-face, between parties well known to one another, even without the transparency that B2B will afford them. *Guanxi* also entails the payment of monetary rewards or gifts in kind to customers with well-established connections, something that would be far more difficult, if not impossible, to conduct online.[55]

Chinese companies also face other constraints and obstacles in adopting e-commerce strategies. E-commerce will supposedly provide a more convenient service and offer lower prices than traditional commerce.[56] However, the cost of maintaining a website can be astronomical, ranging from US$500,000 to US$2 million, while a high-end e-commerce platform may cost as much as US$20 million.[57] Hence, a large volume of business is required to support logistic and overhead costs. Following the fall in stock prices of NASDAQ-listed Chinese dotcom companies (such as Chinadotcom, Netease.com and Sohu.com) in 2000, and the recent collapse of my8848.net, there are doubts over the future survival of Chinese internet companies. Lack of funding for such companies, partly due to excessive competition in the internet sector, which in turn led to increased marketing costs in the form of advertisement spending, has reduced their profitability.[58] Minister of Information Industry, Wu Jichuan, had predicted that more than 70–80 per cent of Chinese internet companies would face bankruptcy in the absence of new funding from banks.[59]

3.2 Business-to-consumer (B2C)

According to the CNNIC survey of July 2001, 0.3 per cent of Internet users (see Table 8.6) identified online shopping as the primary reason for going online, thus implying that B2C is unlikely to become a major force for development of e-commerce in China in the foreseeable future. Why have Chinese consumers at large shunned away from online shopping? The main obstacles have been the lack of credit cards and a credible delivery system, compounded by poor infrastructure and inefficient services.

For B2C to take off requires, unquestionably, an efficient online payment system and an improvement in the quality of goods purchased online. Online payment in China is hampered by low credit card penetration, which was only about 2 per cent in mid-2001. Many Chinese consumers have little faith in the price and quality of online products, on account of being unable to visually and manually try out the products prior to purchase. Online purchasing can only complement, but not displace, traditional retailing as China's existing traditional retail network such as corner shops, wet and dry markets, and hawkers, has served its resident consumers very well.[60] According to the CNNIC survey, the majority of consumers (about 38 per cent) prefer to pay by cash, such as payment on delivery, compared with 15 per cent who make online payment and 14 per cent who pay with the credit card (see Table 8.7).[61] This contrasts sharply with those from the US where 75 per cent of consumers use credit cards.[62] Furthermore, 16 per cent of users complained that they never received the goods they ordered and paid for online.[63]

Growth of B2C e-commerce in China is stifled by an underdeveloped and inadequate infrastructure and transportation network, poor delivery

Table 8.6 Main objectives for internet use in China, 2001

	January 2001 (%)[1]	*July 2001 (%)*
Acquire information (including news)	68.8	42.9
Recreation and entertainment	51.4	34.4
Work-related needs	11.3	5.8
Learn computer technology	13.3	4.3
Contact with the outside world (e-mail, SMS, fax, etc)	12.2	4.1
Stock trading	6.4	4.1
Acquire various free resources (e.g. free mailbox, personal homepage, various free downloads, etc)	9.9	3.1
Follow the trends and out of curiosity	2.7	0.5
Online shopping	*0.9*	*0.3*
Others	3.3	0.5

Note: 1. Survey in January 2001 allowed for multiple choices.
Source: CNNIC, 'Survey on China's Internet Development', January and July 2001, *http://www.cnnic.net.cn*.

Table 8.7 Method of payment in China, 2001

	January 2001 (%)	*July 2001 (%)*
Payment on delivery (cash settlement)	42.0	37.7
Credit card (or savings card)	12.7	16.4
Online payment	13.1	7.7
Postal remittance	23.7	5.4
Bank remittance	4.1	4.8
EMS or express delivery	2.7	4.3
Bank deposits account transfer	1.6	3.6

Source: CNNIC, 'Survey on China's Internet Development', January and July 2001, *http://www.cnnic.net.cn*.

system, and an inefficient distribution sector. A comparison with the US could shed some light on the problems facing China. The US developed a good IT infrastructure before e-commerce became popular. But the situation is just the opposite in China, where increasing demand for e-commerce is driving the upgrading and expansion of IT infrastructure.[64]

China's transportation network has been described as inefficient, with the railway system overloaded, expressways often congested, and the postal system slow in its deliveries. A report listed delivery as the biggest obstacle to e-commerce development in China.[65] It hampers payments through its Express Mailing Services (EMS) or express delivery services. Whereas in the US, where private delivery companies such as Federal Express and United Parcel Service (UPS) offer not only B2B linkages, but also door-to-door B2C services, China still relies on a mixture of online shopping and labour delivery systems, which would be inadequate for the expansion of e-commerce.[66] Such slow and uncertain services inevitably lower the credibility of e-commerce companies (websites).

It was reported that two-thirds of Chinese consumers preferred delivery within 24 hours, yet only 14.6 per cent of goods reach them on time, while 40.4 per cent arrived within 1–3 days, 30.5 per cent within 3–7 days and 14.6 per cent took longer than 7 days to arrive.[67] Many consumers would rather pay higher prices than wait long periods for delivery. Furthermore, given the requirement of advance payment, the lack of face-to-face contact and the 'invisibility' of the transaction site, B2C has to depend heavily on consumer trust and the credibility of the e-businesses and websites. Slow delivery will only undermine such credibility as consumers become impatient with the poor services.[68]

Finally, services provided by e-commerce companies (websites) in China are inefficient and slow by international standards. Unlike those in the US, many Chinese websites do not provide '24/7 service' (24 hours a day for 7 days a week).[69] Some websites can only confirm orders on business days – a working week in China has only 5 days. Many e-commerce companies (websites) have to resort to traditional forms of communication like the telephone to sort out problems with their suppliers and distributors.[70]

4 Potential after WTO

Despite all these institutional and technological setbacks, China's e-commerce still holds great future growth potential in the eyes of many foreign and Chinese observers alike. China's official entry into the WTO on 11 December 2001 will spur further growth of e-commerce through its commitments to liberalize the telecom and financial services sectors under WTO rules.[71]

How does WTO accession improve China's overall e-commerce environment? First, its entry into the WTO will open the market for foreign investment and create a competitive environment which will facilitate China's closer integration with the global e-commerce community.[72] Under the terms of the WTO agreement, China will allow global Internet companies to own 49–100 per cent of the shares of Chinese internet companies.[73] As competition in China's post-WTO economy heats up, and survivors focus on increasing profitability and expanding global markets, demand for technology will increase.[74] Competition will bring in global internet content providers (ICPs) with the most advanced interactive technologies which ensure that websites provide the best content.[75]

Second, China's commitment to lift its restrictions on both the banking and financial sectors, upon WTO entry, is expected to bring about an increase in credit card usage due to rising consumerism and the entry of foreign banks and financial institutions. Both local and foreign banks, shipping companies and insurance companies will have a wider scope for their e-business operations. More foreign online e-stores will be attracted to the China market on the promise of millions of potential Chinese online shoppers.[76] The Chinese side will also count on the rapid growth in the potential global demand for China's labour-intensive products via the e-commerce channel.

The pursuit of e-commerce is also seen as vital to China's foreign trade. To promote the use of e-commerce, the Chinese government will build up a network of administration of foreign trade and speed up the establishment of the most authoritative trade information network.[77] According to Gao Hucheng, an Assistant Minister of Foreign Trade and Economic Co-operation (MOFTEC), WTO entry will push China towards greater transparency in its foreign trade system with the help of information technology.[78] It is still uncertain what proportion of China's international trade will be handled via online trading. But foreign participation will certainly speed up the technical upgrading of China's IT infrastructure and the eventual standardization and modernization of China's e-commerce system, including the much-needed reform of China's online payment system, offline delivery, and Internet platforms.[79]

Finally, with increasing international linkages facilitated by WTO membership, China's e-commerce operators can play a greater role in empowering Asia's economy by updating Asian businesses about the market trends in China. The Chinese online trade services may also seek alliances with the more mature and experienced offline services in Asian economies such as Japan, Hong Kong and Singapore in order to improve its entire service industry.[80]

In conclusion, China's problems are unlikely to prevent it from emerging as one of the world's largest e-commerce markets. In fact, China is likely to become the largest e-commerce market in Asia after Japan.[81] Entry into the WTO will bring challenges as well as great prospects for the development of e-commerce in China. With the doubling or tripling of Chinese netizens every year, B2C e-commerce will flourish and an e-commerce culture will develop. According to the CNNIC survey, half of the respondents were optimistic that large scale e-commerce could be realized in China within two to five years time.[82]

Notes

1 E-commerce is known in Chinese as *Dianzi Shangwu*, and can be broadly classified into business-to-business (B2B), business-to-consumer (B2C), consumer-to-consumer (C2C), business-to-business-to-consumer (B2B2C) and business-to-consumer-to-business (B2C2B). In China, e-commerce is officially defined as profit-making activities on the Internet by commercial dealers and organizations. See J. Wong and S. L. Nah (2001), *China's Emerging New Economy: The Internet and E-Commerce* (Singapore: Singapore University Press).

2 'China to become Asia-Pacific region's second-largest IT market, study says', *China Online News* (22 June 2000).

3 See Ministry of Information Industry (MII) website, *http://www.mii.gov.cn* and Cellular Telecommunications & Internet Association website, *http://www.wow-com.com/internet/*.

4 '200 million online by 2005', *South China Morning Post* (6 November 2001).

5 E-commerce in China commenced in 1997 when the Electronic Information System Promotion Office of the State Council and eight government ministries jointly formed the China Electronic Data Interchange Technology Committee. See 'China's E-commerce: Today and Tomorrow', *China Telecommunications Construction* (September 2001).

6 'China has 3.5pc of world's Web sites', *South China Morning Post* (11 September 2001).

7 'China E-commerce Turnover Leaps 400 per cent in 1999', *China Online News* (11 January 2000), http://www.chinaonline.com.

8 'Beijing Website Serves Elderly Shoppers', *China Daily Business Weekly* (2–8 July 2000).

9 'China e-commerce sales projected to top US$1.2B in 2002', *China Online News* (13 July 2000).

10 'China B2B to drive Asian e-business', *South China Morning Post* (12 March 2001).

11 'China E-commerce Turnover Leaps 400 per cent in 1999', *China Online News* (11 January 2000), http://www.chinaonline.com.

12 'B-to-b transactions dominated China's e-commerce in '00, survey says', *China Online News* (21 February 2001), *http://www.chinaonline.com*.

13 'Efficiency gains', *China Economic Review* (June 2001).

14 S. P. Deng (2001) (in Chinese), 'Woguo dianzi shangwu de fazhan jiqi zouxiang' (The Development and Future Direction of China's E-Commerce), *Zhongguo keji chanye* (Science & Technology Industry of China), vol. 3, no. 141, pp. 24–7.

15 'China poised to be key player in e-commerce, says UN report', *The Straits Times* (21 November 2001).

16 'Goldman Sachs: China's e-commerce immature, won't grow up until 2003–04', *China Online News* (3 July 2000).

17 There are eight methods of payment in China: (1) Online payment by credit cards; (2) Online payment by bank cards issued by Chinese banks; (3) Payment upon delivery; (4) Payment by bank transfer; (5) Payment via the post office; (6) Payment

upon delivery collected by carriers such as EMS; (7) Payment by electronic wallets issued by some commercial banks; and (8) Offline payment. See 'E-Commerce With Chinese Characteristics', *Chinaonline, http://www.chinaonline.com.*

18 Zhongguo Hulian Wangluo Xinxi Zhongxin (China Internet Network Information Centre), 'Zhongguo Hulian Wangluo Fazhan Zhuangkuang Tongji' (Survey on China's Internet Development), Beijing (July 2001), *http://www.cnnic.net.cn.* This is a slight increase from a figure of 31.6 per cent in January 2001.

19 Ibid. Increased from 27.7 per cent in January 2001.

20 Ibid.

21 Ibid.

22 'It's a long road to e-commerce, says SETC official', *China Online News* (2 October 2000).

23 Ibid.

24 Huang, W. (2001), 'China Telecom Constructs for E-Commerce', *China Telecommunications Construction* (July 2001).

25 'China to be World's Largest Mobile Communication Market', *China Economic News* (25 December 2000), Beijing.

26 The survey was conducted by the Xenow and China Consumer Research companies, and reported by *Sina.com.* See '8.7 per cent China Net Users Have Wireless Access – Survey', *China Online News* (19 April 2000).

27 EIU, 'Dial-a-trade', *Business China* (23 April 2001).

28 'Experts predict online trading boom', *South China Morning Post* (8 November 2001).

29 Jeff Zhang and Y. Wang (1995), *The Emerging Market of China's Computer Industry* (London: Quorum Books), p. 85.

30 'Golden Projects', *CNET News.Com* (27 June 1997), *http://news.cnet.com/news/.*

31 Ibid.

32 M. Muller and Z.X. Tan (1997) *China in the Information Age: Telecommunications and the Dilemmas of Reform* (Washington, DC: The Center for Strategic and International Studies), p. 52.

33 'Golden Projects', *CNET News.Com* (27 June 1997), *http://news.cnet.com/news/.*

34 M. Mueller and Z.X. Tan (1997), *China in the Information Age,* p. 53.

35 Ibid, p. 200.

36 'PBOC revises online banking laws', *South China Morning Post* (15 September 2000).

37 'Online Banking', *China Legal Change,* 2001, Issue 13, *http://www.chinalegalchange.com/.*

38 'PBOC revises online banking laws', *South China Morning Post* (15 September 2000).

39 'WTO entry trigger for plastic avalanche', *South China Morning Post* (3 October 2001). By October 2001, credit card companies MasterCard International had issued 56 million cards in total, comprising 40 million debit cards and 16 million credit cards, while VISA International has issued more than 11.4 million bank cards in total. See also 'VISA, China to co-operate in payment system', *China Economic News* (29 October 2001).

40 While China will in top online banking users by 2004, it will fall behind in the amount of online trading due to low Internet penetration and with only 10 per cent of Chinese Internet users engaging in online stock trading, in contrast to South Korea which has more than half of its Internet subscribers trading online. See 'China to be top online banking market by 2004', *Hong Kong Computerworld* (18 April 2000), http://www.cw.com.hk/Analysis/a20000418001.htm.

41 'Bank Boosts Online Services', *China Daily* (22 June 2000).
42 'ICBC to expand its e-banking business', *China Daily* (2 March 2001).
43 'Motorola Partnership in Push for Mobile Banking', *South China Morning Post* (7 September 2000).
44 Collaborating with three leading banks in China, namely, the Bank of China, the Industrial and Commercial Bank of China and China Merchants Bank, China Mobile Communications Corp., China's largest mobile network operator, recently began offering mobile banking services throughout 17 provinces and municipalities to its half million subscribers in the initial phase. See J. Wong and S. L. Nah (2001) *China's Emerging New Economy: the Internet and E-Commerce* (Singapore: Singapore University Press).
45 Based on the 163/169 prepaid card platform, China Telecom will construct a secure payment settlement channel between the banks and the enterprises, offering one-stop payment service to Internet Content Providers, such as Ourgame.com, Netease.com and 800Buy.com, as well as online telecom service halls. See W. Huang (2001) 'China Telecom Constructs for E-Commerce', *China Telecommunications Construction* (July 2001).
46 'PBOC revises online banking laws', *South China Morning Post* (15 September 2000).
47 Under this guideline, all banking institutions have to obtain the central bank's permission before conducting online business. According to a PBOC's spokesman, policy-oriented banks, domestic commercial banks, joint-venture banks, foreign-funded banks and branches of foreign banks must apply to the central bank's headquarters before opening online banking businesses, while city commercial banks need to be approved by local branches of the bank. See 'First online rules issued', *South China Morning Post* (10 July 2001).
48 'Website collapse rocks China's faith in e-commerce', *The Straits Times* (5 November 2001). My8848.net was a result of a split from the original 8848.net, set up in May 1999 as a B2B operator, following a rift among its top management in late 2000. As a result, 8848.net became solely a B2B and my8848.net became the B2C operator. My8848.net was set up by Wang Juntao, one of the founders of 8848.net who believed that B2C was the future of China's e-commerce business. See 'my8848.net disappears leaving behind a trail of debt', *South China Morning Post* (30 October 2001); and 'E-commerce merger puts 8848.net on new path', *South China Morning Post* (20 September 2001).
49 'Store collapse blow to online trade', *South China Morning Post* (17 November 2001).
50 'E-commerce eclipse', *China Online* (17 November 2000).
51 EIU, 'B2B: Perpetual friction', *Business China* (9 April 2001).
52 East–West Center, 'The Future of E-Commerce in China', *Asia Pacific Issues*, no. 46, October 2000.
53 'Efficiency gains', *China Economic Review*, June 2001.
54 Ibid.
55 EIU, 'B2B: Perpetual friction', *Business China* (9 April 2001).
56 Wong and Nah, *China's Emerging New Economy*.
57 EIU, 'B2B: Perpetual friction', *Business China* (9 April 2001).
58 EIU, 'Nasty, brutish and short', *Business China* (23 October 2000).
59 'Grim forecast for bulk of cash-strapped online firms', *South China Morning Post* (23 June 2000).
60 Wong and Nah, *China's Emerging New Economy*.
61 Zhongguo Hulian Wangluo Fazhan Zhuangkuang Tongji, *Zhongguo Hulian Wangluo Xinxi Zhongxin* (Beijing, July 2001), *http://www.cnnic.net.cn*.

62 S. P. Deng (2001) (in Chinese), 'Woguo dianzi shangwu de fazhan jiqi zouxiang' (The Development and Future Direction of China's E-Commerce), *Zhongguo keji chanye* (Science & Technology Industry of China) vol. 3, no. 141, pp. 24–7.
63 However, this figure was a drop as compared to the 22 per cent found in a survey conducted in mid-2000. See Zhongguo Hulian Wangluo Fazhan Zhuangkuang Tongji, *Zhongguo Hulian Wangluo Xinxi Zhongxin* (Beijing, July 2000), http:// www.cnnic.net.cn.
64 Wong and Nah, *China's Emerging New Economy*.
65 'Delivery, Not Payment, Hindering E-commerce in China', *China Online News* (29 October 1999).
66 East–West Center, 'The Future of E-Commerce in China', *Asia Pacific Issues*, no. 46, October 2000.
67 'China Internet Users Hesitate To Shop Online', *China Online News* (29 March 2000).
68 Ibid.
69 S. P. Deng (2001) (in Chinese), 'Woguo dianzi shangwu de fazhan jiqi zouxiang' (The Development and Future Direction of China's E-Commerce), *Zhongguo keji chanye* (Science & Technology Industry of China), vol. 3, no. 141, pp. 24–7.
70 Wong and Nah, *China's Emerging New Economy*.
71 'China poised to be key player in e-commerce', *The Straits Times* (21 November 2001).
72 V. Bath (2000), 'E-commerce in China – Is China ready to do E-business?', Hong Kong: British Chamber of Commerce, May/June 2000.
73 However, China's WTO accession will allow foreign companies to own only 49–50 per cent of shares of Chinese telecommunications companies. See 'WTO Entry To Open China's E-commerce Market', *Chinaonline* (23 November 1999), http://www.chinaonline.com.
74 EIU, 'A tricky transplant', *Business China* (9 April 2001).
75 'WTO Entry To Open China's E-commerce Market', *China Online News* (23 November 1999), http://www.chinaonline.com.
76 Ibid.
77 'China to Upgrade E-Commerce in Foreign Trade', *CCTV.com News* (29 September 2001), *http://www.cctv.com/english/news/20010929/63120.html*
78 'E-commerce vital to trade strategy', *China Daily* (28 September 2001).
79 Wong and Nah (2001), *China's Emerging New Economy*.
80 'Online trade to empower Asia's economy', *China Daily* (6 November 2001).
81 The Economist Intelligence Unit (EIU), *Business China* (9 April 2001).
82 Zhongguo Hulian Wangluo Fazhan Zhuangkuang Tongji, *Zhongguo Hulian Wangluo Xinxi Zhongxin* (Beijing, January 2001), *http://www.cnnic.net.cn*.

Part III
Impersonal Networking and Endogenous Specialization: Theory and Applications

9
Towards a Theory of Impersonal Networking Decisions and Endogenous Structure of the Division of Labour

Guang-Zhen Sun, Xiaokai Yang and Shuntian Yao[1]

1 Introduction

The purpose of this chapter is to prove the existence theorem and the first welfare theorem for a general class of equilibrium models with endogenous network structure of the division of labour, which is based on impersonal networking decisions. The importance of networking decisions is not difficult to understand in our era of e-commerce. In this chapter, we first draw the distinction between strategic networking decisions and impersonal networking decisions and examine why the theory of impersonal networking decisions has not received its deserved attention in the literature. We shall then examine why the proof of the two theorems is essential for a theoretical foundation of studies of impersonal networking decisions.

The literature of networking decisions has been focusing on the strategic networking decision (see, for example, Katz and Shapiro, 1986; Jackson and Wolinsky, 1996; and Dutta and Mutuswami, 1997). The strategic networking decision implies that each decision-maker pays attention to other players' networking decisions or that prices can be manipulated by a player. But for the impersonal networking decision, the decision-maker does not care about whom she has trade connection with and no one person can manipulate prices. In response to impersonal prices (rather than to others' decisions) based on the Walrasian pricing mechanism, she chooses the number of goods she trades and the number of goods she self-provides. This determines the number of types of her trade partners and her network size and pattern of trade. If all individuals choose to self-provide all goods, then there is no network connection between individuals. If each person produces only one good and buys all other goods that she does not produce, then there are many trade connections among individuals. Hence, the network size and pattern of division of labour for society as a whole is endogenously determined by all individuals' impersonal networking decisions.

In macroeconomics, the network effects of such impersonal networking decisions are described as a circular causation: if each person buys more, then all individuals can sell more, which generates a higher aggregate productivity and a higher income, which in turn encourages all individuals to buy more. In so-called high development economies (see Krugman, 1995), this circular causation is considered a network effect of interdependent industrial linkage decisions in different sectors. The Young Theorem (1928) is an insightful observation of the network effects of impersonal networking decisions. It states that 'not only division of labour depends on the extent of the market, but also the extent of the market is determined by the level of division of labour.' In other words, the level of division of labour depends on all individuals' decisions of their levels of specialization, which depend on the network size of the market, which is in turn dependent on the number of participants in the network of division of labour, which are also determined by all individuals' participation decisions in the network of division of labour. Of course, we know now that the notions of fixed point and general equilibrium are powerful vehicles for formalizing the feedback mechanism that simultaneously determines all interdependent endogenous variables.

In a conventional Walrasian equilibrium model, interdependent variables in the circular causation are prices and quantities: each individual's decision about quantities produced, traded, and consumed is dependent on prices, while the equilibrium prices are determined by all individuals' decisions of quantities. But the more important explanatory power of the fixed point theorem and general equilibrium models relates to the following circular causation: not only does each individual's participation decision depend on the number of participants within a trade network, but the equilibrium number of participants is also determined by all individuals' participation decisions.

In many conventional markets for goods and factors, impersonal networking decisions are common. When we buy groceries and furniture, we do not care about who the seller is and what other buyers' decisions are, as a rule. Usually, the sellers do not know who are the buyers of their produce. In this framework, nobody can manipulate prices. The impersonal networking decision characterizes a large part of recent internet commerce as well. We do not care much if we get e-mail services from web mail services such as USAnet, Hotmail, or Yahoo! There are more than a thousand providers of such services and no one person can manipulate prices even if the network size is endogenously determined. But we do care between doing an internet search on our own or using a professional search engine provider. Such impersonal networking decisions will determine the extent of the market for professional email and search engine services and the network size of division of labour between the providers and other sectors.

If the impersonal networking decision is not a new economic phenomenon, and nor is it unique to e-commerce, why then did economists not pay attention to it earlier? The answer to the question relates to 'Smith's failure' noted by George Stigler on the 200th anniversary of the publication of *The Wealth of Nations*, 'there is no standard, operable theory to describe what Smith argued to be the mainspring of economic progress. Smith gave the division of labour an immensely convincing presentation – it seems to me as persuasive a case for the power of specialization today as it appeared to Smith. Yet there is no evidence, so far as I know, of any serious advance in the theory of the subject since his time, and specialization is not an integral part of the modern theory of production' (Stigler 1976, pp. 1209–10). According to Yang and Ng (1998), Smith's failure, technically, was due to the fact that the formalization of classical ideas about implications for economic development of the division of labour involves corner solutions, with which marginal analysis does not work. In order to apply marginal analysis of interior solutions, thereby avoiding corner solutions, Alfred Marshall (1890) assumed a dichotomy between pure consumers and pure producers (firms), which was then, unfortunately, taken as the rule by his followers. Consequently, in the neoclassical framework each consumer is not allowed to choose her level of self-sufficiency (or its reciprocal – her level of specialization) and she must buy all goods from the market. Also, productivity of a firm is dependent on its size (total input levels of labour and capital) and independent of each employee's level of specialization. Each consumer's pattern of labour allocation between firms employing her labour or between different production activities within the firm hiring her has no effect on productivity, which is determined by the size of labour pooled in the firm. For instance, in the Dixit–Stiglitz (DS) model (1977) with economies of scale, each consumer may allocate all of her labour to a firm producing a single good, or she may sell her labour to two or more firms. The individual's pattern of specialization is indeterminate in equilibrium since many different patterns of labour allocation of individuals may be associated with the same equilibrium prices and quantities of goods produced and consumed. Each person's pattern of labour allocation is associated with her network pattern of trade of goods and factors. Hence, each person's equilibrium network pattern cannot be well defined in the DS model. In other words, an equilibrium network of trade in the DS model cannot be well defined as a directed graph (or digraph). This is true for all Walrasian equilibrium models with a dichotomy between consumers and firms, including all Arrow–Debreu models with or without economies of scale. Because of the difficulty in accurately defining an equilibrium network of trade in the Walrasian models, economists did not pay much attention to impersonal networking decisions that generate a trade network for society as a whole until the late 1970s.

In the 1980s and 1990s, a growing literature on specialization and division of labour has emerged (see Yang and Ng, 1998 and Yang, 2001 for a survey of the literature, pioneered by Becker, 1981; Rosen, 1978, 1983; and Becker and Murphy, 1992). In this literature, the dichotomy between consumers and firms is abandoned and each individual is assumed to be a consumer-producer. Hence, her optimum decision is always a corner solution that determines her labour allocation, occupation, and her trade network pattern which is characterized by the number of types of her partners and the number of goods she buys or self-provides, subject to impersonal prices. All individuals' impersonal networking decisions jointly determine a network pattern of division of labour in equilibrium. Therefore, an equilibrium network can be well defined as a digraph. However, the models in the literature are very specific, and no general existence theorem of equilibrium had been established until the paper of Sun, Yang, and Zhou (1999). With the general existence theorem, Sun et al. (1999) then easily proved the two fundamental welfare theorems for a class of models with endogenous network structure of division of labour.[2]

However, Sun et al. have not satisfactorily defined an equilibrium network when they use Hildenbrand's approach (1974) of convexifying a large economy. One weakness of Hildenbrand's approach is that, while the idea of convexification plays a critical role in the existence proof, the issue of how convexification is realized in practice is ignored. As a result, the existence theorems derived from Hildenbrand's approach cannot be applied to equilibrium computation or equilibrium network construction. Our proof of the existence theorem for economies with *ex ante* identical consumer-producers is constructive. For the realization of convexification, the whole population of *ex ante* identical individuals are divided into several groups, each being characterized by the single good sold by its members. With the help of the generalized Wen Theorem, we can establish the existence of a general equilibrium in which all individuals in the same group choose the same decision plan. The significance of our existence theorem is that it can be directly applied to equilibrium computation and equilibrium network construction.

Our purpose in examining economies with *ex ante* identical consumer-producers is twofold. On the one hand, this formalizes Smith's notion of endogenous comparative advantage which implies that differences in productivity between individuals are the outcome rather than the cause of the division of labour (Smith, 1776, Chapter 2, p. 28). On the other, it also provides a simple and constructive way for computing an equilibrium and for defining the equilibrium network of the division of labour. Hence, our approach makes it possible to investigate equilibrium network patterns of division of labour based on impersonal networking decisions.

Once the existence theorem is proved, it is easy to prove the first welfare theorem. The first welfare theorem in a model of impersonal networking decision implies not only that the equilibrium resource allocation is Pareto optimal, but also that positive network effects of division of labour on aggregate productivity can be fully exploited when such network effects outweigh transaction costs. Such effects cannot be exploited if they are outweighed by transaction costs. This is in sharp contrast to the existing literature on strategic networking decisions, which shows that the equilibrium or stable network is not Pareto efficient. One possible explanation of the difference is that the literature of strategic networking decisions ignores interactions between prices, quantities and networking decisions, and does not pay due attention to impersonal networking decisions and the role of the price system in coordinating networking decisions.[3]

We consider an economy with many *ex ante* identical agents, each agent being both a consumer *and* a producer: she can use her labour to produce various goods for herself and for sale and she can also choose between self-provision and purchase of each good. There are transaction costs when agents purchase goods from the markets. Production functions are individual-specific and economies of labour specialization do not extend beyond an individual's limited working time. Increasing returns to labour are local since each agent's labour endowment is fixed, assumed to be one unit. For each agent, the optimal decision involves two parts – what goods and how much of each good to produce, and what and how much to trade. But she does not *ex ante* know who her potential trade partners might be. What she can do is follow the impersonal signals of prices to make her production and trade networking plan. Since the number of traded goods is endogenously chosen, so is the number of types of each person's trade partners. Hence, the network size of each person's trade partners is endogenized, though she does not care about whom she trades with. A price vector together with a utility-maximizing production–trade plan for each and every individual is a general equilibrium if the aggregate trades of all agents under this price vector are balanced. At the same time, a competitive equilibrium also determines an impersonal network of the division of labour endogenously (for a detailed definition, see subsection 3.2).

Our model bridges the recent literature involving strategic network (Jackson and Wolinsky, 1996 and Dutta and Mutuswami, 1997), which does not consider interactions between network size, quantities of goods produced, traded, and consumed, and prices, and the mainstream literature of Walrasian equilibrium, which focuses on the interactions between quantities and prices, ignoring networking decisions. We use a weighted digraph to describe a general equilibrium based on impersonal networking decisions, where a digraph represents a structure of network of division of labour and a system of weights represents resource allocation for a given network pattern of division of labour. In this sense, our model introduces resource allocation and price mechanism into the recent literature of equilibrium models of network and introduces network structure to the conventional literature of the Walrasian equilibrium model. We shall show that the notion of Walrasian equilibrium might be more powerful than the notion of the strategic networking decision for figuring out the interactions between networking decisions, quantities of goods produced, traded and consumed, and prices. It will be shown that prices carry not only abstract information on resource allocation, but also information of network of division of labour.

This chapter proceeds as follows. Section 2 is devoted to a description of the model. The existence and efficiency theorems of the general equilibrium are established in Section 3. To further illustrate that the decentralized pricing mechanism sorts out the efficient structure of the social division of labour, a network of the division of labour based on the general equilibrium is defined and briefly discussed. In Section 4 two examples of the model are considered and our model is compared with similar models in the literature. The final section concludes the paper.

2 The model

Since it is well understood that the competitive equilibrium may fail to exist for a finite economy with increasing returns to specialization (see, for example, Sun et al. 1999), we consider an economy $E = [I, L, M, f, g, u]$ with a continuum set of *ex ante* identical consumer-producers, I. That is, for any agent $i \in I$, she is both a consumer and a producer, maximizing her utility. $L = \{L^i: i \in I\}$ is the set of labour endowments. We assume that each individual in I is endowed with one unit of labour, i.e., $L_i = 1$, $i \in I$. $M = \{1, \ldots, m\}$ is a set of consumer goods and it is assumed that $2 \leq m < \infty$. Each individual can produce each good if she allocates some amount of labour to its production. $f = (f_1, \ldots, f_m)$ is a set of production functions for each individual in I, where $q_j = f_j(L_j)$ is the quantity of good j produced by an individual who allocates amount L_j of labour to the production of this good. L_j is called a person's *level of specialization* in producing good j. $g = (g_1, \ldots, g_m)$ is a set of transaction functions with $g_j(y_j)$ being the quantity of good j any individual actually receives when she buys amount y_j of good j from the market and $g_j(y_j) \leq y_j$ is assumed, due to transaction costs.[4] Finally u: $R^m_+ \rightarrow R$ is the utility function for any individual.

In addition, we make the following assumptions.

Assumption 1 For every $j = 1, \ldots, m$, f_j: $[0,1] \rightarrow \mathbf{R}_+$ is continuous, weakly increasing and convex with $f_j(0) = 0$ or linear with some positive fixed cost,

$$f_j(l_j) = Max\ \{0, b_j l_j - a_j\},\ b_j,\ a_j > 0.$$

Assumption 2 For every $j = 1, \ldots, m$, g_j: $R_+ \rightarrow R_+$ is continuous, weakly increasing, satisfying $0 \leq g_j(y_j) \leq y_j$, and $g_j(y_j) \rightarrow \infty$ as $y_j \rightarrow \infty$.

Assumption 3 u: $R^m_+ \rightarrow R$ is continuous and strictly increasing in each variable.

Since each individual can produce each good and production functions and the endowment constraint are specified for each individual, increasing returns to specialization in economy E are individual-specific and localized.[5] Therefore, increasing returns are compatible with a Walrasian regime in the economy. Assume that a price vector of the consumer goods $p = (p_1, \ldots, p_m)$ is announced by the Walrasian auctioneer. Each individual $i \in I$ chooses a plan for production and trade:

$$(L^i_1, \ldots, L^i_m; x^i_1, \ldots, x^i_m; y^i_1, \ldots, y^i_m)$$

where L^i_j is person i's amount of labour allocated to the production of good j. x^i_j is the amount of good j individual i sells, and y^i_j is the amount of good j she buys. Because of the endowment and budget constraints, these quantities must satisfy

$$L^i_j \geq 0, \ \Sigma^m_{j=1} L^i_j \leq 1 \qquad (9.1)$$
$$0 \leq x^i_j \leq f_j\,(L^i_j) \qquad (9.2)$$
$$y^i_j \geq, \ \Sigma^m_{j=1} p_j y^i_j \leq \Sigma^m_{j=1} p_j x^i_j \qquad (9.3)$$

If the plan of this individual i is realized, then her consumption vector of goods $z^i = (z^i_1, \ldots, z^i_m)$ will be given by

$$z^i_j = f_j\,(L^i_j) - x^i_j + g_j\,(y^i_j) \qquad (9.4)$$

The decision problem for this individual is then

$$\text{Max: } u(z^i_1, \ldots, z^i_m) \qquad (9.5)$$

with respect to $(L^i_1, \ldots, L^i_m; x^i_1, \ldots, x^i_m; y^i_1, \ldots, y^i_m)$ subject to the constraints (9.1)–(9.4).

Definition 1 Given the economy E as described above, a general equilibrium of E consists of a price vector p^* and a profile of individuals' production and trade plans $\{(L^{*i}_1, \ldots, L^{*i}_m; x^{*i}_1, \ldots, x^{*i}_m; y^{*i}_1, \ldots, y^{*i}_m): i \in I\}$ such that (i). for every $i \in I$, $(L^{*i}_1, \ldots, L^{*i}_m; x^{*i}_1, \ldots, x^{*i}_m; y^{*i}_1, \ldots, y^{*i}_m)$ solves the maximization problem (9.5) subject to the constraints (9.1)–(9.4) with p being replaced by p^*; and (ii). $\int_I y^{*i}_j \leq \int_I x^{*i}_j, \ \forall_j = 1, \ldots, m$.

If such a general equilibrium exists, we will denote it by

$$G = [p^*; \{(L^{*i}_1, \ldots, L^{*i}_m; x^{*i}_1, \ldots, x^{*i}_m; y^{*i}_1, \ldots, y^{*i}_m): i \in I\}].$$

Interestingly, as will be shown by some examples below, although all the individuals in our model are assumed to be *ex ante* identical, at the general equilibrium different individuals may choose different production and trade plans. In general the whole population is divided into a number of different types such that individuals of the same type choose the same decision plan. The following result allows us to characterize each type of individuals by the good they sell.

Wen Theorem[6] Under Assumptions 1–3 as stated in Section 2, as a price taker, any consumer-producer can achieve her maximal utility by selling at most one of her produce and not simultaneously selling and buying the same good.

Definition 2 A configuration chosen by a consumer-producer in her decision plan specifies the goods she is going to produce, that good she is going to sell and the goods she is going to buy, assuming her decision plan is in accordance with the Wen Theorem.

3 General equilibrium network of the division of labour: existence and efficiency

In this section, we first prove the existence theorem of the general equilibrium for large economies. A network of the division of labour, based on the general equilibrium, is then defined. Finally, the general equilibrium structure of the division of labour is shown to be efficient.

3.1 The existence of the general equilibrium

As generally understood, the general equilibrium solution is compatible with localized increasing returns for large economies due to the convexifying effect of Lyapunov's Theorem (see Hildenbrand, 1974, p. 45). Even for the case in which both transaction costs and increasing returns to specialization are allowed, it is also shown that the typical general equilibrium argument for large economies suffices to establish the existence and efficiency theorems for a quite general model, of which what is considered in this chapter turns out to be a special case (Sun et al., 1999). Thus, from the technical point of view, the existence problem to be addressed in this section is certainly not a challenging one. Nevertheless, the method we employ to establish the existence result is of interest in its own right. First, as is made clear below, for the particular model presented in this chapter it is sufficient to make use of relatively elementary mathematics without resorting to complex measure theory.

More importantly, our method is 'constructive' in the sense that for a large class of models of endogenous specialization with *ex ante* identical consumer-producers our method can be used to solve for the equilibrium quite easily, and our approach explains how a structure with different types of occupations characterized by what goods or services are traded might emerge from the population of *ex ante* identical individuals. In short, our approach makes it possible to construct an impersonal production–trade network in equilibrium.

In the following proof we assume that every individual chooses her decision in accordance with the Wen Theorem. We will refer to an individual selling good i as a good i seller. We first divide the population into m types, each selling one different good with a quantity greater than or equal to 0. In all the following arguments in this subsection, the superscript i represents the type of a consumer-producer. To establish the existence of the general equilibrium, we first prove the existence of a maximal utility equalization price vector, defined as follows:

Definition 3 (Maximal Utility Equalization Price Vector, MUEPV hereafter). A price vector is called a MUEPV if agents selling different goods (or of different configurations) achieve the same level of maximal utility under this price.

With $p \in \mathbf{R}_{++}^m$ given, the decision set for an individual i selling good i is $\Omega \equiv \{L^i_1, \ldots, L^i_m, x^i_i, y^i_1, \ldots, y^i_m$: (1)–(3)$\}$. Clearly, for any given $p \in \mathbf{R}_{++}^m$, $\Omega^i(p)$ is a compact subset in $\mathbf{R}_+^{2m+1}$. But the continuity of both the utility function and the map from $\Omega^i(p)$ to the consumption vector [see equation (9.4)] imply the following lemma.

Lemma 1: Given a price vector $p \in \mathbf{R}_{++}^m$. Then any good i seller can achieve her maximum utility $u^i(p)$ somewhere in her decision set $\Omega^i(p)$.

Note that $u^i(p)$ may be achieved at more than one point in $\Omega^i(p)$, but the maximal value of $u^i(p)$ is unique, still denoted by $u^i(p)$. It is easy to see that the utility function $u^i(p)$ is continuous with respect to the price vector as well as the decision variables. Thus Lemma 2 follows immediately from the compactness of $\Omega^i(p)$ by Berge's Theorem (Hildenbrand, 1974, p. 30),

Lemma 2: For any i, the indirect utility function $p \to u^i(p)$ is continuous at every point $p \in \mathbf{R}_{++}^m$.

To establish the existence of a strictly positive MUEPV, technically, we deal with a series of perturbed economies in the following way. For any given price vector $p \in P = \{p = (p_1, \ldots, p_m)\text{: } p_j \geq 0, \Sigma_j\, p_j = 1\}$, consider a family of perturbed economy E_ϵ, $\epsilon \in (0,1)$, of E such that in determining the allocation in E_ϵ, instead of the price vector p, the price vector $p^\epsilon \in \mathbf{R}_{++}{}^m$ is used, where the jth component of p^ϵ is $p_j^\epsilon = p_j + \epsilon$, j = 1, ..., m. Correspondingly, the indirect utility function for any individual selling good i in the perturbed economy E_ϵ is $u^i(p^\epsilon)$. According to lemma 2, for any given $\epsilon > 0$, $p \to u^i(p^\epsilon)$ is continuous in P. Consider the mapping $\psi_\epsilon: P \to P$ defined by

$$[\psi_\epsilon(p)]_j = [p_j + \max\{0, U(p^\epsilon) - u^j(p^\epsilon)\}]/[1 + \Sigma_l \max\{0, u(p^\epsilon) - u^l(p^\epsilon)\}],\quad j = 1, 2, \ldots, m \tag{9.6}$$

where $u(p^\epsilon) = \Sigma_i u^i(p^\epsilon)/m$. As $u^i(p)$ is a continuous function from $\mathbf{R}_{++}{}^m$ to R as shown above, it is straightforward to see that for any given ϵ, $\psi_\epsilon(p)$ is a continuous mapping from the convex compact set P into itself. By Brouwer's fixed point theorem (see, for instance, Border, 1985) there exists a $p^*(\epsilon) \in P$ such that $\psi_\epsilon(p^*(\epsilon)) = p^*(\epsilon)$, i.e.

$$p^*(\epsilon)_j = [\, p^*(\epsilon)_j + \max\{0, u([p^*(\epsilon)]^\epsilon - u^j([p^*(\epsilon)]^\epsilon)\}/[1 + \Sigma_l \max\{0, u([p^*(\epsilon)]^\epsilon) - u^l([p^*(\epsilon)]^\epsilon))\} \tag{9.7}$$
where $[p^*(\epsilon)]^\epsilon = [p^*(\epsilon)] + \epsilon$.

To prove that this price vector is indeed a MUEPV for the economy E_ϵ we claim (the proof is found in the Appendix to this chapter) the following.

Lemma 3: There exists a real number $r > 0$ such that for every $\epsilon \in (0, 1)$ and every j, it holds that $p^*(\epsilon)_j \geq r$.

By the continuity of $p \to u^i(p^\epsilon)$ in $\mathbf{R}_{++}{}^m$, both sides of (9.7) are continuous functions of ϵ. Let $\epsilon \to 0$; we obtain

$$p_j^* = [p_j^* + \mathrm{Max}\{0, u(p^*) - u^j(p^*)\}]/[1 + \Sigma_l \max\{0, u(p^*) - u^l(p^*)\}] \tag{9.8}$$
where $p_j^* = \lim_{\epsilon \to 0} p^*(\epsilon)_j$. Obviously, we have
$$p^* \in P, \qquad p_j^* \geq r, \ \forall j.$$

Now suppose that p^* is not an MUEPV. Without loss of generality we assume that $u^1(p^*)$ is the largest among the $u^i(p^*)$. Then, $\mathrm{Max}\{0, u(p^*) - u^1(p^*)\} = 0$, $\Sigma_l \mathrm{Max}\{0, u(p^*) - u^l(p^*)\} > 0$, contradicting (9.8). Thus we have the following lemma.

Lemma 4: The price vector $p^* \in P$ given in (9.8) is an MUEPV for economy E.

We now turn to determining a weight vector $d^* = (d_1^*, \ldots, d_m^*)$ such that p^* is market clearing when the measure of the subset of individuals selling good i equals to d_i^* for $i = 1, \ldots, m$.

Suppose that the optimal decision for every individual who chooses selling good i under p^* is[7]

$$\omega^{*i}(p^*) \equiv (L^i{}_1{}^*, \ldots, L^i{}_m{}^*, x^i{}_i{}^*, y^i{}_1{}^*, \ldots, y^i{}_m{}^*, p^*) \in \Omega^i(p^*).$$

A trivial case occurs when for a particular i_0 we have $x_{i0}{}^* = 0$. In this case every individual in that configuration chooses autarky. As a result we can choose

$$d_{i0}{}^* = 1,\ d_i{}^* = 0\ \forall i \neq i_0.$$

Assume now that $x^i{}_i{}^* > 0$ for every $i = 1, \ldots, m$. Consider the trading matrix

$$T \equiv \begin{pmatrix} -x_1^{1*} & y_1^{2*} & \cdots & y_1^{m*} \\ y_2^{1*} & -x_2^{2*} & \cdots & y_2^{m*} \\ \cdots & \cdots & \cdots & \cdots \\ y_m^{1*} & y_m^{2*} & \cdots & -x_m^{m*} \end{pmatrix}$$

Lemma 5: For any trade matrix T corresponding to a MUEPV p^*, there exists a vector $d^* \geq 0$ such that $Td^* = \mathbf{0}$, where $\mathbf{0}$ is the m-dimensional zero column vector.

A simple proof of Lemma 5 is given in the Appendix to this chapter.

We may normalize d by defining $d_i{}^* = d_i/\Sigma_j d_j$, which is the measure of the set of agents who sell good i on the market. Combining Lemmas 4–5 actually establishes the existence theorem.

Theorem 1: Any economy as described in section 2 that satisfies Assumptions 1–3 has at least one general equilibrium.

3.2 A network of the division of labour: definition and discussion

As stated in the Wen Theorem and mentioned in the last subsection, each individual is characterized by the good she sells, and the equilibrium decisions of all individuals of the same type i are all the same. We can therefore categorize all individuals in equilibrium in such a way, $V_i \equiv \{\omega \mid x_i^{\omega*} > 0\}$, $\forall i \in M$ and $V_0 \equiv \{\omega \mid x_i^{\omega*} = 0, \forall i \in M\}$, i.e., all the agents selling the same goods form a category and those who choose autarky in the equilibrium form a separate one. Clearly, this classification is both exclusive and exhaustive. We can then construct a weighted digraph with $(n + 1)$ vertices. Define $\phi_{ij} = y_i^{j*} d^*{}_j$, $\forall i \neq j$ and $\phi_{ii} = [f_i(L_i^{i*}) - x_i^{i*}]\, d_i^*$, $\forall i \in M$. If $\phi_{ij} \neq 0$, we draw a directed arc ij from vertex i to j and endow the arc ij a weight ϕ_{ij}, $i, j \in M$. Any vertex $i \in \{0,1, \ldots, n\}$ is given a weight equalling the measure share of V_i, i.e., $d_i \equiv \mu(V_i)$. Denote by A the arc set and by V the vertex set. We call the weighted digraph $G(V, A, \phi, d, p)$ the network of division of labour corresponding to the general equilibrium $(p, (l(\omega))_{\omega\in I}, (x(\omega))_{\omega\in I}, (y(\omega))_{\omega\in I})$. Clearly, $\sum_{s\in M} p_s\phi_{si} = \sum_{s\in M} p_r\phi_{ir} \forall i \in M$. The equilibrium uniquely determines a network defined as above.

It might appear curious to define what results from the interplay of decentralized individuals' decisions in an anonymous market, as a network, and it seems particularly so given that the networking strategy is usually specified as *pair-wise* links between agents or nodes in the contemporary network literature, no matter whether the themes under consideration are equilibrium networks (see, for example, Dutta and Mutuswami, 1997; Jackson and Wolinsky, 1996) or evolutionary networks (see, for example, Banks and Carley (1996) among others appearing in the special issue on 'evolution of social networks' of the *Journal of Mathematical Sociology*, 21(1–2) 1996). It is therefore worthwhile to pause in order to elaborate upon the very notion of the network of the division of labour defined as above before we proceed to explore what insights one might be able to gain by doing so. First of all, the general equilibrium network of the division of labour in our conception is indeed anonymous in the sense that it is indeterminate who sells a good to or buys a good from whom. The agent is simply guided by the abstract signal of prices without knowing who her potential trade partners might be. Needless to say, the anonymity is precisely the nature of the decentralized Walrasian pricing mechanism. But note that in our model there exists another kind of anonymity: in equilibrium it is indeterminate who is specialized in which activity. This kind of anonymity of trading connections is due to the assumption of *ex ante* identical individuals and the Walrasian regime prevailing in our model. But this point has some important implications which go far beyond the fact that the *ex ante* identity of agents could be used to justify Smith's notion of the endogenous comparative advantage resulting from the division of labour as is shown so far. A more interesting point is that even if individual elements are *ex ante* exactly identical, one still observes some complex order of specialization and the division of labour emerging from the decentralized individual decisions, in which the agent simply responds to the rather abstract environmental signals (prices in our context) without knowing or caring who might be at which particular point of the order. In this sense, we call the emergent order of the division of labour an *impersonal* network structure. The extent to which agents of different occupations are interdependent in the complicated structure of the division of labour, among other things, could be characterized more straightforwardly, seen from the network viewpoint (more discussion to follow later). Admittedly, the mechanism by which the network is formed in our model presented here is different from the fashionable one.

Once we establish the network of division of labour from general equilibrium, the concepts of component, spectrum, and connectedness of a network of division of labour could be defined in the same way as in graph theory (see, for instance, Dondran and Minoux, 1984). By doing so, we may get some new perspectives on the division of labour and economic development. For example, the concept of connectedness in graph theory could be used to describe the extent of market integration in the economy Furthermore, the implication of transaction condition for the structure and complexity of the division of labour could be spelt out by focusing on the structural change of the network of division of labour (when studying the comparative statics with respect to transaction condition). This is exemplified by Example 2 in Section 4.

The existence theorem in this chapter provides a theoretical foundation for a shift in the focus of mainstream microeconomics from resource allocation problems (interactions between prices and quantities) to impersonal networking decisions, which generate a network of division of labour for society as a whole. This shift echoes Coase's criticism (1937) of the theory of production in standard microeconomic texts which focuses on the interactions between quantities and prices and ignores properties of networking decisions in choosing between the labour market which is associated with the institution of the firm, and the market for goods. As Sun (1999) and Yang and Ng (1995) have shown, when intermediate goods and labour trade are introduced into the model given here, the relationship between the emergence of the firm from the division of labour and individuals' networking decisions can be investigated. Hence, the implications of structure of asymmetric residual rights and authorities for the expansion of the network of division of labour can be explored. A research project is expected to establish the existence theorem for an extended model with intermediate goods and labour market.

3.3 Efficiency of the general equilibrium network of the division of labour

Given an economy E, we now compare a general equilibrium network structure S with any possible network structure S′ for the same economy E. Assume that in S′ there are $m' \leq m$ goods being traded. By relabelling these goods in case it is necessary we may assume that these are goods 1, ..., m′. Assume that under the price vector $p'^* = (p'^*_1, \ldots, p'^*_{m'})$, every individual in S′ attains the same maximal utility through production and trade and the market is cleared. As a result we say that p'^* together with the production and trade profile in S′ forms a possible structure of E. According to the Wen Theorem, at this structure, every individual sells at most one good. We again refer the individuals selling good j as individuals of type j. Now we claim,

Theorem 2 The maximal utility for every individual in S is greater than or equal to the maximal utility for every individual in S′.

Proof.[8] Assume that the equilibrium price vector in S is $p^* = (p^*_1, \ldots, p^*_m)$. Without loss of generality we may assume that
$p^*_1/p'^*_1 = \max\{p^*_j/p'^*_j : j = 1, \ldots, m'\}$ which implies that, for all $j = 1, \ldots, m'$: $p_1^*/p^*_j \geq p'^*_1/p'^*_j$ thus under p^* any individual of type 1 in S can do at least as well as those individuals of type 1 under p'^* in S′.

We thus have $U(p^*) = U^1(p^*) \geq U^1(p'^*) = U(p'^*)$. ***Q.E.D.***

4 Two simple examples

Two numerical examples are considered in this section to explore the implications of the emergent structure of the division of labour.

Example 1 $I = [0, 1]$, $m = 2$, $f^i(L_j) = \max\{0, L_j - 0.4\}$, $g_j(y_j) = 0.1y_j$, $u(x_1,x_2) = 2\ln(1+0.01x_1) + \ln(1+0.01x_2)$.

It is easy to see that $p^* = (1, 10)$ is a MUEPV. Given p^*, the optimal decision of any individual of type 1 is to allocate all her labour to the production of good 1 and not to trade with any good 2 producer, ending up with a utility of 2ln1.006. On the other hand, the optimal strategy of any good 2 producer is to allocate all her labour to the production of good 2, exchanging all his produce for good 1. His amount of good 1 consumed is then $g_2[(0.6)(10)] = 0.6$, ending up with the same utility of 2ln1.006.

It is interesting to note that the trade required by the individuals of type 2 *is actually not possible*. However, this is automatically taken care of by our weight vector d^*. Since the trading matrix $T = \begin{bmatrix} 0 & 6 \\ 0 & -0.6 \end{bmatrix}$ we have $d^* = (1,0)$. Thus at the general equilibrium, every individual chooses autarky and produces good 1 only.

Example 2. The second example is adopted from Yang (1996). Linear production functions with fixed learning costs are assumed,

$y_i = \text{Max}\{L_i - a, 0\}$, $i = 1, 2, \ldots, m$ with $\Sigma^m_{i=1} L_i = 1$, $L_i \in [0, 1]$ and $a \in [0, 1]$

The labour share for producing good i, L_i, is called her specialization level in producing good i. Each agent's preference is represented by a CES utility function,

$$u = (1 - cm)v,\ v = (\Sigma^m_{i=1} z_i^\rho)^{1/\rho},\ \rho \in (0,1),\ c > 0$$

where z_i is the amount of good i consumed. The management cost of consumption variety is specified as $cm\,.\,v$ in terms of loss of a fraction of utility from consumption of m goods, to capture the fact that the calculation cost of the optimum decision increases with the number of goods consumed. The transaction function is specified as $g_j = ky_j$ where y_j is the quantity of good j that is purchased.

As there are increasing returns to specialization in production technology, according to the Wen Theorem (1998), any agent sells at most one type of good and does not purchase any good that she self-provides for consumption. Then, it can be shown that the interaction of the decentralized individual decisions gives rise to the general equilibrium structure of division of labour, specialization levels, the number of occupations and the extent of market integration (see Yang, 1996, for more details), which are given by:

$$\underset{n=1,\ldots m,\ m=1,2,\ldots}{Max:}\ u = (1 - cm)ak/[1 - A(m - n + 1)][n - 1 + K(m - n + 1)]^{(1-\rho)/\rho}$$

$$L_i = \{(n - 1)[1 - a(m - n)] + K\}/[n - 1 + K(m - n + 1)]$$
$$x_i = (n - 1)[1 - a(m - n + 1)]/[n - 1 + K(m - n + 1)]$$

where $K \equiv k^{\frac{\rho}{\rho-1}}$, n is the number of traded goods (also representing the number of different occupations and the size of the network of division of labour), L_i is the specialization level of each individual selling good, and i, and x_i is the amount of good i sold by every producer of good i, representing individuals' trade dependence and the extent of market of the economy as a whole due to the symmetry of the model.

It could be shown by comparative statics that all of the equilibrium variables above, n, m, L_i, y_i for any i increase with k and $1/c$, and n increases more quickly than m does. That is, as division of labour evolves (driven by improvements in transaction efficiency), not only do the number of consumption goods, the diversity of various occupations, trade dependence, the extent of the market, and each person's level of specialization increase, but all goods that are produced are eventually involved in exchange through market exchange. Furthermore, as demonstrated in Yang (1996), the difference in productivity of a traded good between a specialist seller and a novice buyer (what Yang and Borland (1991) call 'the extent of endogenous comparative advantage'), and the equilibrium number of markets for different goods also increase as the division of labour evolves.

Figure 9.1 gives an intuitive illustration of the evolution of the network structure of the division of labour driven by improvements in transaction conditions. Circles represent vertices, numbers in the circles represent goods sold by individuals choosing those vertices (configurations), directed lines represent arcs, and numbers beside lines represent goods delivered. Large arrows represent the direction of evolution. Figure 9.1. gives a vivid picture as to how division of labour evolves from primitive structures to more and more complex ones. The comparative statics of the general

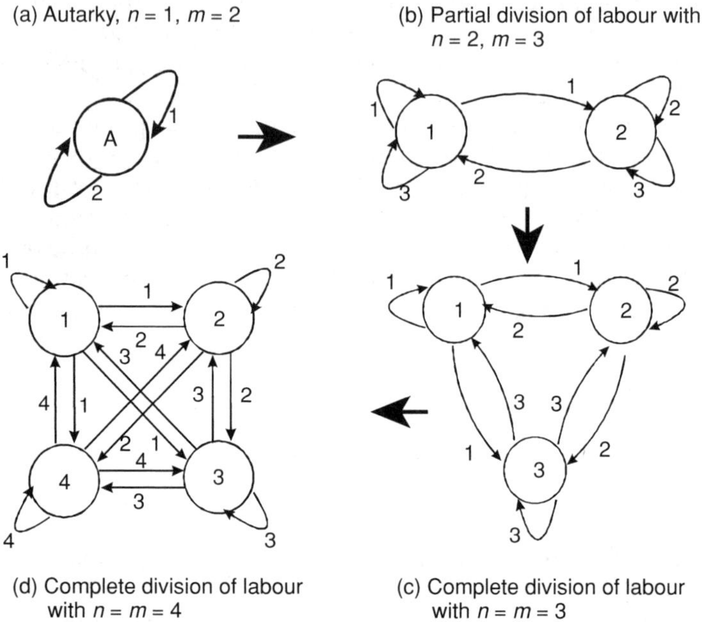

Figure 9.1 Evolution of equilibrium network structure of division of labour

equilibrium model suggest that in this symmetrical model with *ex ante* identical individuals, resource allocation problems that relate to relative prices and relative quantities of goods produced and consumed are too trivial to be of interest. The relative prices and relative quantities are 1 for all goods and for different levels of division of labour represented by n. However, the most important story in this model is the effects of changes in parameters on topological properties of the network of division of labour, which can be represented by a directed graph in which vertices denote individuals choosing different occupation configurations and edges denote flow of goods.

As shown in Yang (1996), a marginal cost pricing rule no longer holds in equilibrium and the equilibrium and the Pareto optimum may not coincide with the PPF because of the tradeoff between economies of specialization and transaction costs. But as transaction conditions are improved, the equilibrium and the Pareto optimum become closer to the PPF. This highlights greater implications of transaction conditions for the network size of the division of labour.

As far as we know, our model is not covered in the existing literature on general equilibrium. It is more general than the Arrow–Debreu pure exchange model in two ways. First, in our model each agent has a general production possibility set whereas in the Arrow–Debreu (AD) pure exchange model each agent is endowed with a fixed bundle of goods only. This feature enables us to discuss labour specialization of agents when production functions exhibit increasing returns to specialization. Second, our model also allows for transaction costs. Of course, in the past two decades, there have been many contributions on increasing returns to scale (see Quinzii, 1992 and Villar, 1996, for two rather extensive surveys) in the general equilibrium literature. In addition many authors have shown how transaction costs can be incorporated in the standard Arrow–Debreu general equilibrium model (for example, Hahn, 1971; Ulph and Ulph, 1975). Nevertheless, there has been virtually no formal analysis of general equilibrium models that allow for both increasing returns and transaction costs.[9] More importantly, no analysis has been done with regard to the endogenization of specialization of labour in the standard AD model.

The individual optimization problem in our model is different from that in the standard AD model with production. In our model an agent is *both* a consumer *and* a producer, and she chooses some utility-maximizing bundle among all bundles that can be achieved through production and trading. In the AD model an agent is *either* a consumer *or* a producer, and the optimization process is dichotomized. First, each firm chooses a production plan (or a plan that follows other 'pricing rules') that maximizes profit which is subsequently distributed among the shareholders of the firm. Second, after receiving her share of profits from all firms in which she holds stocks, each consumer chooses a utility-maximizing bundle that she can afford. In our model, if each consumer-producer first maximizes returns to production, then maximizes utility by choosing a consumption bundle and a trade plan, the optimum decision is usually different from the optimum production and trade networking plan that maximizes utility in one step (see a rigorous proof of this claim in Wen (1998)). As a result, the concept of equilibrium in our model may differ from the one in the AD model.

Our model is different from the AD models with local increasing returns to scale, not only because each individual's equilibrium labour allocation is not well defined in the AD model, but also because our focus is on network effect of division of labour rather than on economies of scale.[10] As pointed out by both Young (1928) and Stigler (1976), the notion of scale economies can hardly capture what should be termed as network effects of the division of labour.[11] If there are economies of specialization, each individual's decision of her level of specialization and her network of trade not only determines her productivity, but also the extent of the market for goods produced by another individual and therefore the latter's productivity and her decision in choosing her level of specialization and her network of trade. The notion of general equilibrium is a powerful vehicle for analysing the feedback mechanism that simultaneously determines all interdependent endogenous variables.[12]

5 Concluding remarks

We have used a framework with consumer-producers, network effects of the division of labour, and transaction costs to formalize the idea that a rather complicated structure of division of labour may emerge from *ex ante* identical agents whose conduct is guided by the 'invisible hand' of the decentralized price mechanism. Such a structure, viewed as one sort of emergent order, can be defined as an impersonal network induced and maintained only by the abstract price signals. Seen from this perspective, the most important function of the market is to coordinate individuals' decisions in choosing their patterns of specialization in order to fully exploit positive network effects of division of labour net of transaction costs.

The idea that the invisible hand of the price system not only efficiently coordinates resource allocation but also sorts out the efficient order of the division of labour, to the best of our knowledge, has not yet been formally dealt with in the literature, despite its long-held tradition in economics and despite the fact that the idea itself is far from new to those who have ever tried to elaborate upon Adam Ferguson's and Adam Smith's notion of spontaneous order. As Hayek remarks on Smith's contribution in the same year as Stigler (1976), 'The great achievement of his famous discussion about the division of labour was the recognition that men who were governed in their efforts, not by the known concrete needs and capacities of their intimate fellows, but by the abstract signals of the prices at which things were demanded and offered on the market, were thereby enabled to serve the enormous field of the "great society" that "no human wisdom and knowledge could ever be sufficient" to survey' (Hayek, 1976/1978, p. 268).[13]

Our chapter has shown that the fixed point theorem is a powerful vehicle for investigating impersonal networking decisions. In our model, though individuals' networking decisions are impersonal rather than strategic, each individual's decision on her trade network pattern is dependent on prices, which is in turn determined by the network structure of the division of labour for society as a whole. In other words, each person's decision on participating in a network depends indirectly on the number of participants in the network, while the equilibrium number (measure) of participants of the network is determined by all individuals' impersonal networking decisions. We have two arguments to justify our focus on impersonal networking decisions rather than on strategic networking decisions. First, in a model with many players, it is prohibitively expensive to figure out all direct interactions among all individuals' networking decisions. This high cost of strategic calculation prohibits sensible strategic articulation. If uncertainties are introduced, it is prohibitively expensive for a person to know all other players' utility and production functions, as well as distribution functions of others' characteristics, which is necessary for the strategic calculation of effects of information asymmetry about realized states of such characteristics.

In the models of strategic networking decisions, the equilibrium network is not Pareto efficient. This is because the models ignore interactions between prices, quantities, and all individuals' networking decisions, which include consumer-producers' decisions in choosing their occupations. All the interactions among a large number of players not only nullify – via interactions between prices and free choices of occupations efforts of strategic manipulation of prices, but also nullify efforts of strategic manipulation of relative numbers of different specialists. Hence, as the circular causation (or a feedback mechanism) among prices, quantities, the number of different specialists, and networking decisions is formalized in a fixed point theorem, it can be convincingly proven that for a large class of general models, the equilibrium network of division of labour (represented by a digraph) and the equilibrium resource allocation (represented by a system of weights) are Pareto optimal.[14]

Our proof of the existence theorem and the first welfare theorem for a class of models with endogenous network structure of the division of labour based on impersonal networking decisions has thus resurrected the spirit of classical economics in a modern body of mathematical formalism. It might be a starting point toward the theoretical foundation of the studies of impersonal networking decisions in our current era of an e-commerce-driven economy.

Notes

1 Acknowledgements: We are grateful for comments and criticisms from Guoqiang Tian, Bob Rice, Sherwin Rosen, Lin Zhou and participants in the seminars at Harvard University and Texas A&M University and of the International Symposium of 'Economics of E-Commerce and Networking Decisions' held at Monash University, Australia, 6–7 July 2001. Sun gratefully acknowledges the research support from Research Committee of the University of Macau. The remaining errors are solely ours.

2 Although Koopman (1957) and Arrow, Enthoven, Hurwicz, and Uzawa (1958) incorporate nonlinear programming, labelled inframarginal analysis by Buchanan and Stubblebine (1962), into the Walrasian equilibrium model, general equilibrium implication of inframarginal analysis cannot be fully explored in a model with dichotomy between consumers and firms since the corner solution is exceptional and marginal analysis of interior solutions is still the rule. As proved by Wen (1998), in a model of endogenous specialization, the interior solution is never optimal and the optimum decision is always a corner solution. Hence, marginal analysis does not work and implications of inframarginal analysis for investigating equilibrium network of division of labor can be fully explored in a model with endogenous specialization.

3 In most models of strategic networking decisions, prices of goods and services are not specified.

4 The transaction costs are assumed to be borne by buyers alone throughout this chapter in order to simplify the technical analysis.

5 This specification does not disallow cooperation of individuals by combining their production functions via the market to achieve a higher aggregate productivity. As shown in Yang and Ng (1995), if labour trade is allowed in such a model, individuals can combine their production functions to generate a production function for a firm. Hence, the production function for the firm can endogenously emerge from the division of labor as a result of individuals' decisions of specialization and structure of transactions which are essential for the division of labour. But if transaction conditions are the same between labour and goods, the institution of the firm will not emerge in equilibrium (Coase, 1937). Hence, the absence of the firm in the current chapter is equivalent to the assumption of the same transaction condition for labour and goods. We disallow all individuals to pool their labour together in a production function. If this is allowed, ad hoc economies of scale of a firm will miss the phenomenon of economies of specialization and division of labor (Young, 1928, p. 539).

6 What we state here is actually the generalized form of the Wen Theorem proved by Yao (2002). The Wen Theorem does not mean that each person produces only one good since she may self-provide many goods for her own consumption even if she sells only one good in exchange for other goods that she does not produce.

7 Note that $U^i(p)$ may be achieved at more than one point in $\Omega^i(p)$. For simplicity, we assume that all individuals selling the same good choose the same maximum point.

8 Indeed, the efficiency of the equilibrium follows from the fact that the standard revealed preference argument applies. Sun et al. (1999) proves the efficiency of the equilibrium for a more general model of endogenous specialization. We contend that a simple argument as below suffices for the particular model considered in this chapter.

9 A paper by Jouini and Kallal (1993) is the only one we find that considers models which allow for both increasing returns and transaction costs. But they did not directly attack the existence problem. Instead they assume that firms follow a pricing rule that, 'is an upper-semi-continuous convex compact value correspondence' (p. 258), which immediately leads to existence. Moreover, their paper does not address the issue of specialization of labour.

10 Our model differs from the DS model, not only because each consumer's level of specialization in the DS model with monopolistic competition is not endogenized, but also because the equilibrium level of specialization of each firm is always a constant and the equilibrium degree of market integration is not endogenized in the DS model. These variables are endogenized in our model.

11 Young (1928, p. 539) expressed this as follows. 'The mechanism of increasing returns is not to be discerned adequately by observing the effects of variations in the size of an individual firm or of a particular industry, for the progressive division of labor and specialisation of industries is an essential part of the process by which increasing returns are realized. What is required is that industrial operations be seen as an interrelated whole.'

12 As reviewed in Yang and Ng (1998), in a model of endogenous specialization, the equilibrium and Pareto optimum utility frontier may not coincide with the production possibility frontier (PPF), the interior solution is never optimal for an individual's decision, and marginal cost pricing may not hold.

13 Hayek's emphasis, as is well known, is certainly put on the 'order' based on his sociology of knowledge. To claim that Hayek endorses the classical spirit of the emergent structure of the division of labour does in no way mean to claim that he is happy with the general equilibrium approach as such taken in this chapter.

14 Gale (1986) has proved that a Walrasian equilibrium is equivalent to a bargaining equilibrium in a model similar to the one shown in our chapter.

References

Arrow, K., Enthoven, A., Hurwicz, L. and Uzawa, H. (eds) (1958) *Studies in Linear and Nonlinear Programming* (Stanford: Stanford University Press).

Banks, D. L. and Carley, K. M. (1996) 'Models of network evolution', *Journal of Mathematical Sociology*, 21, 1–2, 173–96.

Becker, G. (1981) *A Treatise on the Family* (Cambridge, MA: Harvard University Press).

Becker, G. and Murphy, K. (1992) 'The Division of Labor, Coordination Costs, and Knowledge', *Quarterly Journal of Economics*, 107, 1137–60.

Border, K. C. (1985) *Fixed Point Theorems with Applications to Economics and Game Theory* (Cambridge: Cambridge University Press).

Buchanan, J. M. and Stubblebine, W. C. (1962) 'Externality', *Economica*, 29, 371–84.

Coase, R. (1937) 'The Nature of the Firm', *Economica*, 4, 386–405.

Dondran, M. and Minoux, M. (1984) *Graphs and Algorithms* (New York: John Wiley & Sons).

Dutta, B. and Mutuswami, S. (1997) 'Stable Networks', *Journal of Economic Theory*, 76, 322–44.

Gale, D. (1986) 'Bargaining and Competition. Part I: Characterization and Part II: Existence', *Econometrica*, 54, 785–818.

Hahn, F. (1971) 'Equilibrium with transaction costs', *Econometrica*, 39, 417–39.

Hayek. F. (1976/1978) 'Adam Smith's message in today's language', in *New Studies in Philosophy, Politics, Economics and the History of Ideas* (London: Routledge, 1978), 267–69.

Hayek, F. (1983) *Knowledge, Evolution and Society* (London: Adam Smith Institute).

Hildenbrand, W. (1974) *Core and Equilibria of a Large Economy* (Princeton, NJ: Princeton University Press).

Jackson, M. and Wolinsky, A. (1996) 'A Strategic Model of Social and Economic Networks', *Journal of Economics Theory*, 71, 44–74.

Jouini, E. and Kallal, H. (1993) 'General Equilibrium with Producers and Brokers', *Economics Letters*, 41, 257–63.

Katz, M. and Shapiro, C. (1986) 'Technology Adoption in the Presence of Network Externalities', *Journal of Political Economy*, 94, 822–41.

Koopman, T. R. (1957) *Three Essays on the State of Economic Science* (New York: McGraw-Hill).

Krugman, P. (1995) *Development, Geography, and Economic Theory* (Cambridge, MA: MIT Press).

Marshall, A. (1890) *Principles of Economics*, 8th edition (New York: Macmillan, 1948).

Quinzii, M. (1992) *Increasing Returns and Efficiency* (New York: Oxford University Press).

Rosen, S. (1978) 'Substitution and the Division of Labor', *Economica*, 45, 235–50.

Rosen, S. (1983) 'Specialization and Human Capital', *Journal of Labor Economics*, 1, 43–9.

Smith, A. (1776) *An Inquiry into the Nature and Causes of the Wealth of Nations*. Reprint, edited by E. Cannan (Chicago: University of Chicago Press, 1976).

Stigler, G. (1976) 'The Successes and Failures of Professor Smith', *Journal of Political Economy*, 84, 1199–1213.

Sun, G.-Z. (1999) 'Increasing Returns, Roundabout Production and Urbanization: A General Equilibrium Analysis of the Division of Labor', PhD Dissertation, Department of Economics, Monash University.

Sun, G.-Z., Yang, X, and Yao, S. (1999) 'Theoretical Foundation of Economic Development Based on Networking Decisions in the Competitive Market', Harvard Center for International Development Working Paper No. 17.

Sun, G.-Z., Yang. X. and Zhou, L. (1999) 'General equilibrium in large economies with transaction costs and specialization', Working paper, Department of Economics, Monash University.

Takayama, A. (1974) *Mathematical Economics* (Hinsdale, IL: The Dryden Press).

Ulph, A.M. and Ulph, D. T. (1975) 'Transaction Costs in General Equilibrium Theory – A Survey', *Economica*, November, 355–72.

Villar, A. (1996) *General Equilibrium with Increasing Returns*, Lecture Notes in Economics and Mathematical Systems, vol. 438 (Heidelberg and New York: Springer).

Wen, M. (1998) 'An Analytical Framework of Consumer-Producers, Economies of Specialization and Transaction Costs', in K. Arrow, Y.-K. Ng, and X. Yang (eds), *Increasing Returns and Economic Analysis* (London: Macmillan).

Yang, X. (1996) 'A New Theory of Demand and the Emergence of International Trade from Domestic Trade', *Pacific Economic Review*, 1, 215–17.

Yang, X. (2001) *Economics: New Classical Versus Neoclassical Frameworks* (Cambridge, MA: Blackwell).

Yang, X. and Borland, J. (1991) 'A Microeconomic Mechanism for Economic Growth', *Journal of Political Economy*, 99, 460–82.

Yang, X. and Ng, S. (1998) 'Specialization and Division of Labor: a Survey', in K. Arrow *et al.* (eds), *Increasing Returns and Economic Analysis* (London: Macmillan).

Yang, X. and Ng, Y.-K. (1995) 'Theory of the Firm and Structure of Residual Rights', *Journal of Economic Behavior and Organization*, 26, 107–28.

Yao, Shuntian (2002) 'Walrasian Equilibrium Computation, Network Formation and the Wen Theorem', *Review of Development Economics*, 6, 415–27.

Young, Allyn (1928) 'Increasing Returns and Economic Progress', *Economic Journal*, 38, 527–42.

Appendix

Proof of Lemma 3. Assume the conclusion is not true. Then there exists a sequence $\{\epsilon_n\}_{n=1}^{\infty}$, which tends to zero such that

$$\text{Lim}_n \min_j \{[p^*(\varepsilon_n)]_j^{\varepsilon n}\} = 0$$

By considering some subsequence if necessary, we assume that $\{p^*(\epsilon_n)\}$ converges. Define $I = \{i|\lim_n p^*(\varepsilon_n)_i > 0$, $J = \{j|p^*(\varepsilon_n)_j \to 0$. Assume, w.l.o.g., $1 \in I$ and individuals selling good 1 have the highest maximal utility among occupations selling I-type goods for every ϵ_n when n is large enough. Assume further, w.l.o.g., $p^*(\epsilon_n)_{\underline{j}} \to 0$ is one of the smallest components of $p^*(\varepsilon_n)$ when n is large enough. Then, either (i) the optimal amount of good i persons selling good $\underline{j}$ consumed, $\{z^{\underline{j}*}(\varepsilon_n)\}_i \to 0$ as $n \to \infty$, $\forall i \in I$, or (ii) $\exists \tilde{i} \in I$, $\{z^{\underline{j}*}(\varepsilon_n)\}_{\tilde{i}} \to z^{\underline{j}}_{\tilde{i}} > 0$. In the case (i), it is easy to verify that there exists $\delta > 0$ such that $U^1(p^*(\varepsilon)_n) > U^{\underline{j}}(p^*(\varepsilon_n)) + \delta$ when n is sufficiently large. But that in turn means there exists $\sigma > 0$ such that $\Sigma_l \max\{0, U(p^*(\varepsilon)) - U^1(p^*(\varepsilon))\} \geq \sigma$ as n is large enough. Letting $j = 1$ in (9.7) yields, $p^*(\varepsilon_n)_1 \to 0$, a contradiction. In the case of (ii), clearly $\{z^{\underline{j}*}(\varepsilon_n)\}_{\underline{j}} < f_j(1) + f_{\underline{j}}(1)$ for any $j \in j$. Suppose, $z^{\underline{j}*}(\epsilon_n) \to z^{\underline{j}}$ as $n \to \infty$. Let

$$\{z^{\tilde{i}'}\}_h = \begin{cases} z^{\underline{j}}_h - \delta', h = \tilde{i} \\ z^{\underline{j}}_h, h \in I/\{\tilde{i}\} \\ 2[f_{\underline{j}}(1) + f_h(1)], h \in J \end{cases} \quad \text{and} \quad \{z^{\underline{j}'}\}_h = \begin{cases} z^{\underline{j}}_h, h \in I \\ f_{\underline{j}}(1) + f_h(1), h \in J \end{cases}$$

as u is continuous and strictly increasing, we can choose δ' so small as to make $u(z^{\tilde{i}'}) > u(z^{\underline{j}'})$ hold. Similarly, we construct

$$\{z^{\tilde{i}'}(\varepsilon_n)\}_h = \begin{cases} \{z^{\underline{j}*}(\varepsilon_n)\}_h - \delta', h = \tilde{i} \\ \{z^{\underline{j}*}(\varepsilon_n)\}_h, h \in I/\{\tilde{i}\} \\ 2[f_{\underline{j}}(1) + f_h(1)], h \in J \end{cases} \quad \text{and}$$

$$\{z^{\underline{j}}(\varepsilon_n)\}_h = \begin{cases} \{z^{\underline{j}*}(\varepsilon_n)\}_h, h \in I \\ f_{\underline{j}}(1) + f_h(1), h \in J \end{cases}$$

It is trivial to show that $\{z^{\tilde{i}}(\epsilon_n)$ becomes feasible for individuals selling good $\tilde{i}$ when n is sufficiently large, and hence $U^{\tilde{i}}(p^*(\varepsilon_n)) \geq u(\{z^{\tilde{i}}(\varepsilon_n\})$. Since $z^{\tilde{i}}(\varepsilon_n) \to z^{\tilde{i}}$ and $z^{\underline{j}}(\varepsilon_n) \to z^{\underline{j}'}$, one obtains $u(z^{\tilde{i}'}(\varepsilon_n)) - u(z^{\underline{j}}(\epsilon_n)) > 0$ for all large n. But $w(z^{\underline{j}}_{h'}, h \in I) \equiv u(z^{\tilde{i}'}) - u(z^{\underline{j}'}) > 0$ could be formally seen as a function of $(z^{\underline{j}}_{h'}, h \in I)$. Thus, there exists a very small closed neighbourhood of $(z^{\underline{j}}_{h'}, h \in I)$ in $R^{|I|}_+$, denoted as $\bar{B}_\tau \equiv \bar{B}((z^{\underline{j}}_{h'}, h \in I), \tau)$ such that for any $v \in \bar{B}_\tau$, $w(v) > 0$ holds. Clearly $w(v)$ is continuous, which in turn means that there exists a positive number, μ, such that $w(v) \geq \mu$ for any $v \in \bar{B}_\tau$. On the other hand, $(\{z^{\underline{j}*}(\varepsilon_n)\}_h, h \in I)$ falls into $\bar{B}((z^{\underline{j}}_h, h \in I), \tau)$ as n is large enough and hence $u(\{z^{\tilde{i}}(\varepsilon_n)\}) - (\{z^{\underline{j}}(\varepsilon_n)\}) \geq \mu$. But $U^1(p^*(\varepsilon_n)) \geq U^{\tilde{i}}(p^*(\varepsilon_n)) \geq u(\{z^{\underline{j}}(\varepsilon_n)\})$, and $U(\{z^{\underline{j}}(\varepsilon_n\}) \geq U^{\underline{j}}(p^*(\varepsilon_n))$ as n is sufficiently large. Therefore, $U^1(p^*(\varepsilon_n)) \geq U^{\underline{j}}(p^*(\epsilon_n)) + \mu$. By the same argument as for case (1), one obtains $p^*(\varepsilon_n)_1 \to 0$, a contradiction. Lemma 3 is thus established.

Q.E.D.

Proof of Lemma 5. Define $X \equiv (\max_i \{x_i^{i*}\}$ and $B \equiv T + XI$. Thus B is a non-negative matrix. Denote by λ B's Frobenius engenvalue and by d* the associated engenvector (see, for instance, Theorem 4B.2 in Takayama 1974, p. 375), $Bd^* = \lambda d^*$. Then from $P^*T = 0$ due to the budget constraint for each individual (Walras' Law), one obtains $0 = p^*Td^* = p^*(Bd^* - Xd^*) = (\lambda - X)p^*d^*$, and hence $\lambda = X$. But $Td^* = Bd^* - Xd^* = 0$, we are done.

Q.E.D

10

Identification of Equilibrium Structures of Endogenous Specialization: a Unified Approach Exemplified

*Guang-Zhen Sun**

1 A brief review of the existing literature

In the rapidly growing literature on endogenous specialization, of which the modern pioneering studies are Rosen (1978), Becker (1981) and Yang (1988) among others, a technically challenging problem is that many interesting models with intra-firm and inter-firm division of labour among *ex ante* heterogeneous agents, are not tractable by the existing toolkit, and therefore an obstacle to further progress needs to be overcome. This chapter develops a new apparatus to fill the void.

We review some of the existing analytical tools before introducing the new method. To solve for the equilibrium of economies with *ex ante* identical agents (largely for addressing the Smithian specialization, rather than the more discussed Ricardian specialization based on *ex ante* comparative advantages among people/countries), Yang (1988) proposes what may be referred to as a two-step approach to identify the general equilibrium structure of the division of labour (as well as the associated equilibrium prices) among all possible structures. In the first step, for each structure, the 'equilibrium' prices and utilities are calculated by equalizing utilities across all specialization patterns in the said structure. Secondly, the structure with the highest utility is selected as the general equilibrium structure of specialization, in which no agent has an incentive to deviate from her specialization pattern. Years later, in their ambitious monograph, Yang and Ng (1993) cover and apply the two-step algorithm to many specific models. Sun, Yang and Yao (1999) further argue that the two-step approach applies to a much larger class of models. It is clear that the two-step approach has proved quite powerful in solving many endogenous specialization models (for a recent survey, see Yang, 2003). The assumption of *ex ante* identical

* I thank, but in no way implicate, Yew-Kwang Ng, Xiaokai Yang and Dingsheng Zhang for helpful comments and discussions. Research support from the Research Committee of the University of Macau is gratefully acknowledged.

agents, however, is a severe limitation to its application to many interesting economic issues (say, Yang's (2001) model on foreign direct investment between two countries, to mention only one example). Moreover, the two-step approach may miss some equilibrium prices even for quite simple models of *ex ante* identical agents, as shown in Examples 1 and 3 in Section 3.

To deal with a model of *ex ante* two-type agents, Sun, Yang and Zhou (1999) elaborate on the two-step approach and develop what may be termed a 'benchmark price' analytical method. Similar to the two-step approach, in the first step market-clearing prices are worked out for each structure. But differing from the two-step approach, individuals' utilities are then compared among constituent specialization patterns (occupations) in this structure and occupations in other structures *under these market clearance prices* to identify the parameter subspace within which this structure occurs in general equilibrium (agents have no incentive to deviate from this structure).[1] The benchmark method has been employed successfully to analyse important phenomena such as globalization and dual structures emerging from international trade (see Sachs, Yang and Zhang 2000). Yet this approach does not apply to models with possible substitution between markets (for intermediate products and that for labour, for instance), as in Li's (2001) multiple national enterprise model, for the simple reason that the markets for some products or services are absent in some structures and hence no price for them could be used to compare utilities across occupations occurring in different structures of the division of labour.

A much better known approach to equilibrium computation is of course the conventional simplex triangulation (see, for instance, Scarf and Hansen, 1973; van der Laan and Talman, 1987). But this approach, as an algorithm, requires well-framed excess demand functions in order to start the fixed point searching process in the price simplex. Yet in most models of endogenous specialization as surveyed in Yang (2003), it is rather difficult to construct the excess demand across different structures of the division of labour with different goods or services actually traded in the markets. In addition, the algorithm, at best, converges to a (locally unique) equilibrium price vector from the starting point, while in models of endogenous specialization, there may exist a continuum of equilibrium prices (refer to examples in Section 3). Most importantly, the simple triangulation algorithm, complicated and time-consuming as it is, does not convey information about the structure of the division of labour, which is a major concern in this literature.

2 Brief introduction to a unified approach

The key idea of our unified approach could be summarized as follows: For any price vector (p, w) where p is the non-labour commodity price vector and w the wage vector, the agent maximizes utility u (p, w) across specialization patterns. The market-clearing condition (and utility equalization condition among *ex ante* identical agents) *directly* leads to the general equilibrium structure and prices. As such, a complete characterization of parameter subspaces, in which different structures of the division of labour occur in equilibrium, is obtained.

Put in a few more details, the approach proceeds as follows. For any given prices (p, w) where the price vector $p = (p_1,\ldots, p_m)$ and wage vector $w = (w_1,\ldots, w_n)$, each *possible* kind of expert maximizes utility for his/her potential occupation(s). For simplicity (no loss of generality), consider the situation in which there is only one type of expert who buys units of labour from the market, and agents of all the other occupations sell either some type of product or his/her own labour only. Due to the increasing returns to specialization, agents may specialize in producing some products while trading for other products, provided that the transaction cost is not too high. For any person, the maximized utility under (p, w) if she chooses to sell product i is denoted as u_i (p, w), $i = 1,2,\ldots, m$, while the indirect utility if she chooses to sell labour in labour market j is denoted as u_{Lj} (p, w), $j = 1,2,\ldots, n$, and the indirect utility if she buys labour is denoted as u_0 (p, w). The said agent derives the highest real income among u_i (p, w), $i = 1,2,\ldots, m$; u_{Lj} (p, w), $j = 1,2,\ldots, n$, and u_0 (p, w), under a given price signal (p, w) by choosing the corresponding specialization pattern. However, which pattern brings about the highest real income apparently depends on the relative prices. By means of partitioning the price space into several subspaces (in each of which some particular specialization pattern(s) brings about the highest real income), and by the market clearance condition (and utility equalization among agents who are *ex ante* identical but may be *ex post* different in specialization), we can identify the subspace of parameters, in which some particular structure of specialization occurs in equilibrium. In short, we partition the price space first, based on which we then partition the parameter space to identify the condition under which the equilibrium specialization structures and prices occur.

It should be emphasized that this approach identifies, in one step, subspaces of parameters in which different structures of endogenous specialization occur and in which all equilibrium prices are computed. In other words, this approach also applies to comparative statics and in fact constitutes a complete characterization of the subspaces of parameters for different structures of labour specialization. Note in some parameter subspaces, the equilibrium prices may be shadow prices and some occupations and markets may actually not occur. Indeed, it is often the case, as shown below by some typical models in the literature of endogenous specialization.

Compared to existing methods solving for the equilibrium structure of the division of labour (for all the situations to which the benchmark price approach and/or the two-step approach apply), our method not only works but also simplifies the algebraic manipulation significantly in many cases. Some equilibrium prices (shadow prices) might be missed by the above two approaches, as shown by examples in the next section. Furthermore, our unified approach applies to a more general class of models than does the benchmark price one or the two-step one, particularly to models with substitution between markets and with *ex ante* heterogeneous agents.

3 Examples

We illustrate the new method by discussing four examples, which are typical of the models in the literature of endogenous labour specialization. Price-taking behaviour is assumed throughout. Example 1 is a basic model in which agents are *ex ante* identical and all the goods are consumption ones. Example 2 incorporates producer goods and a labour market, hence firms are allowed, but agents are still assumed to be *ex ante* identical. Example 3 considers an economy with consumption goods only but in which *ex ante* differences among agents are allowed. Example 4 allows both (*ex ante*) heterogeneous agents and producer goods, and the emergence of multinational firms from the expansion of trade, and the division of labour is made endogenous.

Example 1. *Ex ante* identical agents with only consumption goods

Consider a simple economy with a continuum of *ex ante* identical agents and two consumption goods, X and Y. Each agent is endowed with one unit of labour. The production functions for X and Y are $f(l_X) = l_X - \alpha$ and $f(l_Y) = l_Y - \beta$ respectively, where l_X (l_Y) is the labour input in the production of good X (Y). Labour is assumed the only input for production. Utility is a Cobb–Douglas function, $u(x, y) = xy$ and the transaction function is specified as $g(z) = kz$, $Z \in \{X, Y\}$, where $k \in (0,1)$ characterizes the trading efficiency.

For any given price of X (in terms of Y), $p \equiv p_X/p_Y$, the agent's production–trade choice is made among (1) producing only good X, selling X and buying Y; (2) producing only good Y, selling Y and buying X; and (3) producing both but selling neither (autarky). For a relative price p, the indirect utility of agents choosing trading X [Y] for Y [X] is $u_x = \frac{(1-\alpha)^2}{4}kp$ $[u_y = \frac{(1-\alpha)^2}{4p}k]$ and she trades $\frac{1-\alpha}{2}[\frac{1-\beta}{2}]$ amount of X [Y] for $\frac{(1-\alpha)p}{2}[\frac{1-\beta}{2p}]$ of Y [X], but she can only receive $\frac{(1-\alpha)kp}{2}[\frac{(1-\beta)k}{2p}]$ of Y [X] due to the transaction costs incurred. Values in boxed brackets represent cases for agents trading good Y for X. Denoting the maximized utility under autarky as $u_A, u_A = \frac{(1-\alpha-\beta)^2}{4}$.

Under the equilibrium price, either (i) some trade occurs and thus there exists the division of labour; or (ii) no trade occurs, hence everyone is in autarky. In the case of (i), it is required that $u_X = u_Y > u_A$. It follows that the equilibrium price $p = p^* \equiv \frac{1-\beta}{1-\alpha}$ and the trading efficiency has to be high enough to support the division of labour, $k > k^* \equiv \frac{(1-\alpha-\beta)^2}{(1-\alpha)(1-\beta)}$. In case (ii), $u_A > u_X$ and $u_A > u_Y$, hence, $\frac{(1-\alpha-\beta)^2}{4} > \frac{(1-\alpha)^2}{4}kp$ and $\frac{(1-\alpha-\beta)^2}{4} > \frac{(1-\alpha)^2}{4p}k$.

Thus,

$$\frac{k}{k^*}p^* < p < \frac{k^*}{k}p^* \tag{10.1}$$

For the price set satisfying (10.1) to be non-empty, it follows that $k < k^*$. Any price $p \in (\frac{k}{k^*}p^*, \frac{k^*}{k}p^*)$ is an equilibrium price that clears the market (demand equals supply, both being equal to zero). Table 10.1 summarizes the above analyses.

Table 10.1 Parameter subspaces and equilibria for Example 1

	$k < k^*$	$k > k^*$
Equilibrium prices	$(\frac{k}{k^*}p^*, \frac{k^*}{k}p^*)$ (shadow equilibrium price set)	p^*
Structure of the division of labour	Autarky (no trade)	Division of labour (half population specialize in producing X(Y))

Note: p^* is referred to as a MUEPV (Maximal Utility Equalization Price Vector) in Sun, Yang and Yao (1999), under which the utility is the same across experts producing and selling different goods or services. It can be seen that for any values of parameters, p^* is an equilibrium. What's especially interesting, however, is that when transaction costs are too high to allow for trade and the division of labour ($k < k^*$), the equilibrium (shadow) price still exists. But the two-step approach taken in Sun, Yang and Yao (1999) yields only one equilibrium price, namely, p^*, among infinitely many others in this case. (refer to Example 1 considered in Sun, Yang and Yao (1999) wherein only one equilibrium price is identified). The approach we develop in this chapter identifies all the equilibrium prices and structures for *any* possible values of parameters. In other words, the equilibrium analysis and comparative statics could be done in one step, as shown by Table 10.1.

Example 2. *Ex ante* identical agents with producer goods and possibly with firms

In this example we consider an economy with one intermediate product X and one final product Y. Each agent is endowed with one unit of labour.

For each agent, the production function of X is $f(l_X) = Max\{l_X - b, 0\}$ and that of Y is $h(x_Y, l_Y) = x_Y^{\alpha} l_Y^{\beta}$, $\alpha, \beta \in (0,1)$, $\alpha + \beta > 1$, where l_X (l_Y) is the labour input in the production of good X (Y) and x_Y is the amount of X used in the production of Y. Note that $\alpha + \beta > 1$ implies increasing returns to scale in the production of Y. The utility function is taken as $u(y) = y$ for simplicity, where y is the amount consumed of Y. As in Example 1, the transaction function for goods X and Y is specified as $g(z) = kz$, $Z \in \{X, Y\}$, where $k \in (0,1)$ characterizes the trading efficiency in the product market. Differing from Example 1, there is intermediate product in this model. By the indirect pricing theory of the firm (Yang and Ng, 1995), there may exist trade of labour and hence firms, which could replace the market exchange of intermediate products. The firm owner may hire some agents, called workers, direct their labour effort to produce goods, part of which she may sell in the market, and claim residual rights. The worker sells his labour for a salary (in terms of consumption good Y in this example). But note what is really traded in the labour market is the worker's production function (rather than labour per se) since the labour of heterogeneity by its nature cannot be aggregated (and put into anyone's or the firm's *ex ante* 'production function' (for more on this point, refer to Sun, 2000). The transaction function of labour is assumed as $g_L(l) = sl$, where $s \in (0,1)$ characterizes the trading efficiency of the labour market.

For any given price of good X, p, and the wage rate w, both in terms of good Y, it is clear that any agent may choose among (i) selling nothing (in autarky); (ii) producing and selling X (and buying Y); (iii) selling Y; or (iv) selling labour and buying Y (being an employee). No rational person would sell two or three among X, Y and labour (refer to Appendix 1 for analysis). We denote by u_A (u_X or u_L) the maximum utility if the agent makes choice (i) (choice (ii) or (iv)). It is easy to see that $u_A = \dfrac{\alpha^{\alpha}\beta^{\beta}(1-b)^{\alpha+\beta}}{(\alpha+\beta)^{\alpha+\beta}}$, $u_x = kp(1-b)$, and $u_L = kw$.

What's intriguing is the decision problem if the agent chooses option (iii). She may buy part or all of the intermediate inputs used to produce Y from the markets, produce Y and sell Y. In this case, no labour is traded. However, she may also hire some workers and direct their labour to producing part or all intermediate goods that she uses to produce Y.[2] In general, the decision problem could be stated as

$$u_Y = \underset{l,x,N}{Max}\{[Max\{l-b,0\} + kx + N(s.1-b)]^{\alpha}(1-l)^{\beta} - px\} - wN \tag{10.2}$$

where decision variables l is the labour input to producing intermediate product X, x is the amount purchased of X from the market and N the number of employees hired to produce X. Due to transaction costs in both labour market and product markets, only $s \cdot 1$ units of labour will be actually put into production of X by each worker and kx of X is actually received. The last two terms in equation (10.2) refer to the balanced budget. The integer problem for N is ignored throughout to simplify the analysis. One could show that if $p < \frac{k}{s-b}w$, then $N = 0$, $l = 0$ and that if $p \geq \frac{k}{s-b}w$, then $x = 0$, $l = 0$ by noting that in any case ($p < \frac{k}{s-b}w$ or $p \geq \frac{k}{s-b}w$), the first-order conditions of interior solutions of x and N and cannot both hold and that the interior solution for l and x (or l and N), if any, is a saddle point, as could be seen from the negative-ness of determinants of the Hessian matrix (to save space, we omit the calculation details), and hence $l = 0$ as l cannot be 1. It follows that for any (p, w) satisfying $p < \frac{k}{s-b}w$, problem (2) turns out to be $\underset{x}{Max}(kx)^\alpha - px$, of which the solution is $x^* = (\alpha k^\alpha / p)^{\frac{1}{1-\alpha}}$ and the indirect utility, denoted as u_{YX}, $u_{YX}(p, w) = [(1-\alpha)^{1-\alpha}\alpha^\alpha(\frac{k}{p})^\alpha]^{\frac{1}{1-\alpha}}$. For any (p, w) satisfying $p \geq \frac{k}{s-b}w$, problem (2) turns out to be $\underset{N}{Max}(s-b)^\alpha N^\alpha - wN$, of which the solution is $N^* = [\alpha(s-b)^\alpha / w]^{\frac{1}{1-\alpha}}$ and the indirect utility, denoted as u_{YL}, $u_{YL}(p, w) = [(1-\alpha)^{1-\alpha}\alpha^\alpha(\frac{s-b}{w})^\alpha]^{\frac{1}{1-\alpha}}$.

We are now ready to identify the subspaces of parameters, in which different structures of the division of labour are in equilibrium. Should u_{YX} be achieved in equilibrium, there must be some other agents selling X for the demand for X to be met. In addition, the utilities of the buyers and sellers of X are equalized in equilibrium because the agents are *ex ante* identical and freely enter and exit any profession. It is required that $p < \frac{k}{s-b}w$, $u_{YX}(p, w) = u_X(p, w)$, $u_{YX}(p, w) > u_L(p, w)$ and $u_{YX}(p, w) > u_A(p, w)$, from which we can obtain, after some algebraic manipulation, that $k > \frac{s-b}{1-b}$ and $k > k^* \equiv [\frac{\beta^\beta(1-b)^\beta}{(\alpha+\beta)^{\alpha+\beta}(1-\alpha)^{1-\alpha}}]^{\frac{1}{2\alpha}}$, with $p^* = k^{2\alpha-1}(1-b)^{\alpha-1}(1-\alpha)^{1-\alpha}\alpha^\alpha$, with the shadow wage rate set at $(\frac{s-b}{k}p^*, (1-b)p^*)$ and utility given by $u_{YX} \equiv u_{YX}(p^*, w) = k^{2\alpha}(1-b)^\alpha(1-\alpha)^{1-\alpha}\alpha^\alpha$. Should u_{YL} be obtained in equilibrium, there must be some potential employees in the labour market (for the demand of labour to be met). In addition, the utilities of both buyers and sellers of labour are equalized in equilibrium. It is required that $p > \frac{k}{s-b}w$, $u_{YL}(p, w) = u_L(p, w)$, $u_{YL}(p, w) > u_X(p, w)$ and $u_{YL}(p, w) > u_A(p, w)$. It then follows that $k < \frac{s-b}{1-b}$ and $k(s-b) > KS \equiv [\frac{\beta^\beta(1-b)^{\alpha+\beta}}{(\alpha+\beta)^{\alpha+\beta}(1-\alpha)^{1-\alpha}}]^{\frac{1}{\alpha}}$ with $w^* = k^{\alpha-1}(s-b)^\alpha(1-\alpha)^{1-\alpha}\alpha^\alpha$, shadow price set at $(\frac{k}{s-b}w^*, \frac{1}{1-b}w^*)$ and $u_{YL} \equiv u_{YL}(p, w^*) = k^\alpha(s-b)^\alpha(1-\alpha)^{1-\alpha}\alpha^\alpha$. If neither u_{YX} nor u_{YL} is the utility in equilibrium, the equilibrium utility cannot be greater than in autarky, thus we should have $u_A(p, w) > u_Y(p, w) \equiv Max\{u_{YX}(p, w), u_{YL}(p, w)\}$, $u_A(p, w) > u_X$

(p, w) and $u_A(p, w) > u_L(p, w)$. It is in turn required that $k < k^*$ and $k > \frac{s-b}{1-b}$ or $k(s-b) < KS$ and $k < \frac{s-b}{1-b}$.

A complete characterization of equilibria and the corresponding parameter subspaces is summarized in Table 10.2.

Indeed, Table 10.2 may be even more neatly summarized, as Table 10.2′.

Example 3. *Ex ante* heterogeneous agents with only consumption goods

We reconsider Example 3.2 in Sun, Yang and Zhou (1999) in which there are an infinite number of agents of two distinct types and the population

Table 10.2 Parameter subspaces and equilibria for Example 2

$k > \frac{s-b}{1-b}$	**When** $k < k^*$: Equilibrium prices and wage rates (both being shadow prices): Any $p \in (\alpha k(\frac{1-\alpha}{u_A})^{\frac{1}{\alpha}-1}, \frac{u_A}{k(1-b)})$, any $w \in (\alpha(s-b)(\frac{1-\alpha}{u_A})^{\frac{1}{\alpha}-1}, \frac{u_A}{k})$ results in autarky (no trade) **When** $k > k^*$: Equilibrium price: $p^* = k^{2\alpha-1}(1-b)^{\alpha-1}(1-\alpha)^{1-\alpha}\alpha^\alpha$ Equilibrium wage rates (shadow prices): any $w \in (\frac{s-b}{k}p^*, (1-b)p^*)$ results in division of labour between experts producing X and experts producing Y (without firm), with the population ratio of X experts and Y experts being $\frac{\alpha}{1-\alpha}k^{\frac{1}{1-\alpha}}$
$k < \frac{s-b}{1-b}$	**When** $k(s-b) < KS$: Equilibrium prices and wage rates (both being shadow prices): any $p \in (\alpha k(\frac{1-\alpha}{u_A})^{\frac{1}{\alpha}-1}, \frac{u_A}{k(1-b)})$ any $w \in (\alpha(s-b)(\frac{1-\alpha}{u_A})^{\frac{1}{\alpha}-1}, \frac{u_A}{k})$ results in autarky (no trade) **When** $k(s-b) > KS$: Equilibrium wage rate: $w^* = k^{\alpha-1}(s-b)^\alpha(1-\alpha)^{1-\alpha}\alpha^\alpha$ Equilibrium prices (shadow prices): any $p \in (\frac{k}{s-b}w^*, \frac{1}{1-b}w^*)$ results in division of labour with firms, the population ratio of employees (hired to produce X) and employers (producing and selling Y) being $\frac{\alpha}{1-\alpha}k$.

Table 10.2′ A simplified Table 10.2

$k > \frac{s-b}{1-b}$	$k < k^*$: Shadow p and w; Autarky. $k > k^*$: Equilibrium p^* and shadow w; Division of labour, no firm
$k < \frac{s-b}{1-b}$	$k\ (s-b) < KS$: Shadow p and w; Autarky. $k\ (s-b) > KS$: Equilibrium w^* and shadow p; Division of labour with firms

ratio between the two types is 1:1. Each agent is endowed with one unit of labour, which can be used to produce two consumption goods, X_1 and X_2. The utility function of both Type 1 and Type 2 agents is $u\ (x_1, x_2) = x_1\ x_2$, where $x_1\ (x_2)$ is the amount consumed of $X_1\ (X_2)$. The production functions are $f_{1x_1}\ (l_{1x_1}) = (l_{1x_1})^2$ and $f_{1x_2}\ (l_{1x_2}) = l_{1x_2}$ for Type 1 agents and $f_{2x_1}\ (l_{2x_1}) = al_{2x_1}$, $a < 1$ and $f_{2x_2}\ (l_{2x_2}) = (l_{2x_2})^2$ for Type 2 agents. Type 1 agents have a Ricardian advantage in producing X_1 while Type 2 agents have a comparative advantage in producing X_2. The transaction technologies are $g_{1x_i}\ (x_i = k_1\ x_i$ and $g_{2xi}\ (x_i) = k_{2xi}\ (i = 1,2)$ for Type 1 and Type 2 agents respectively. Sun, Yang and Zhou (1999) solved this model by the benchmark price method. We re-solve the same model by our new method, which not only simplifies the algebra but, more importantly, also identifies more equilibrium (shadow) prices for some structures of the division of labour.

Obviously, for any price p, $p \equiv p_{x_2}/p_{x_1}$, each agent chooses one of the following: (i) autarky, with utility $u_A = 4/27$ for both types of agents; (ii) producing and selling X_1 and buying X_2, the indirect utilities denoted as u_{1x_1} (p) and $u_{2x_1}\ (p)$ for Type 1 and Type 2 agents respectively; and (iii) producing and selling X_2 and buying X_1, the indirect utility denoted as $u_{1x_2}\ (p)$ and $u_{2x_1}\ (p)$ for Type 1 and Type 2 agents respectively. In choosing (ii), a Type 1 agent trades 1/2 amount of X_1 for 1/(2p) of X_2, $u_{1X_1}(p) = \frac{k_1}{4p}$, while a Type 2 agent trades a/2 amount of X_1 for a/(2p) of X_2, $u_{2X_1}(p) = \frac{k_2 a^2}{4p}$. In choosing (iii), both a Type 1 agent and a Type 2 agent trade 1/2 amount of X_2 for $p/2$ of X_1, $u_{1X_2}(p) = \frac{k_1 p}{4}$, $u_{2X_2}(p) = \frac{k_2 p}{4}$. Note in each of (ii) and (iii), the agent can only receive a fraction of what she purchases from the market due to the transaction costs. We begin by analysing the decision made by the Type 1 agent. Given a price signal p, it is required, for (i) to be actually chosen, that $u_A\ (p) > u_{1x_1}\ (p)$ and $u_A\ (p) > u_{1x_2}\ (p)$, i.e., $\frac{16}{27k_1} < p < \frac{27k_1}{16}$, from which it follows $k_1 < k_0 \equiv \frac{16}{27}$. For (ii) to be chosen, $u_{1X_1}\ (p) > u_A\ (p)$ and $u_{1X_1}\ (p) > u_{1X_2}$ (p), i.e. $p < 1$ and $p < \frac{k_1}{k_0}$. For (iii) to be chosen, $u_{1x_1}\ (p) > u_A\ (p)$ and u_{1X_2}

$(p) > u_{1x_1}(p)$, i.e., $p > 1$ and $p > \frac{k_0}{k_1}$. Similar analyses could made with regard to the decision problem that Type 2 agents face: autarky is chosen when $\frac{ak_2}{k_0} < p < \frac{ak_0}{k_2}$ (from which it follows $k_2 < k_0$); choice (ii) is made when $p < a$ and $p < \frac{ak_2}{k_0}$; and choice (iii) is made when $p > a$ and $p > \frac{ak_0}{k_2}$. Since for some subspaces of parameters, it may be that trade occurs between the two types of agents, it is necessary to simultaneously take account of the decisions made by Type 1 agents and those by Type 2 agents. It might be thought that an analysis of all possible combinations of choices by two types of agents is an algebraically complicated one. Actually, it could be rather straightforward as shown in the following analysis. If no trade occurs for price p, autarky (choice (i)) must be preferred by both types of agents, or, $\frac{k_0}{k_1} < p < \frac{k_1}{k_0}$ and $\frac{ak_2}{k_0} < p < \frac{ak_0}{k_2}$, from which it follows $k_1 < k_0$, $k_2 < k_0$, $k_1k_2 < ak_0^2$ and the equilibrium (shadow) price set is $(Max\{k_1/k_0, ak_2/k_0\}, Min\{k_0/k_1, ak_0/k_2\})$. If trade occurs under a price p, the sellers of X_1 are types 1 agents and/or Type 2 agents. We first consider the situation in which some or all agents of Type 1 choose to be X_1 sellers and no Type 2 agent sells X_1. It follows that $p \leq 1$ and $p \leq k_1/k_0$. In this case, for the market to clear, some (or all) agents of Type 2 or some other Type 1 agents buy X_1 and sell X_2. Namely,

> Either (A) (some or all) Type 2 agents supply X_2; or (B) no Type 2 agents supply X_2 (X_2 is supplied only by Type 1 agents).

Case (A) requires that $Max\{a, ak_0/k_2\} \leq p \leq Min\{1, k_1/k_0\}$, hence, $k_1 \geq ak_0$, $k_2 \geq ak_0$ and $k_1k_2 \geq ak_0^2$. Each X_1 seller from Type 1 agents supplies half a unit of X_1 and each X_2 seller from Type 2 agents demands (p/2) unit of X_1. But note the population ratio between the two types is 1:1. Therefore, when $k_1 < k_0$, which implies $p \leq k_1/k_0 < 1$, there are only a fraction of the population of Type 1 supplying X_1 in equilibrium. But the price cannot be strictly less than k_1/k_0, since otherwise every agent of Type 1 would prefer to be a X_1 supplier. Thus, the equilibrium price, $p = k_1/k_0$, $(\frac{k_1}{k_0})100\%$ of Type 1 agents supply X_1 and $(1-\frac{k_1}{k_0})100\%$ of Type 1 agents in autarky, and all agents of Type 2 supply X_2. That is, Type 2 agents reap all the benefits from the division of labour. When $k_1 \geq k_0$, $p = 1$ (note each Type 1 agent would sell half unit of X_1 and the demand of X_1 by Type 2 agents would be less than the total supply if $p < 1$) and all agents of Type 1 (2) supply (demand) X_1. Case (B) requires $p = 1$, $k_1 \geq k_0$ and $k_2 < ak_0$. The half population of Type 1 supply (demand) X_1 and demand (supply) X_2, and no agent of Type 2 gets involved in the division of labour and trade. We now consider the situation in which some or all agents of Type 2 choose to be X_1 suppliers. It follows that $p \le a$ and $p \le \frac{ak_2}{k_0}$. For the market to clear, some agents of Type 1 or Type 2 must demand X_1. But it is impossible for Type 1 agents to do so in equilibrium, otherwise, we have $p \ge 1$, contradicting $p \le a$. Therefore, the demanders of X_1 must be of Type 2. It follows that $p \ge a$ and $p \ge \frac{ak_0}{k_2}$. Hence, $p = a$ and $k_2 \ge k_0$. But note that for agents of Type 1 not to be X_1 suppliers, it requires that $p \ge 1$ or $p \ge \frac{k_1}{k_0}$, that is, $k_1 \le ak_0$ (due to $p = a$). Thus, when $k_2 \ge k_0$ and $k_1 \ge ak_0$, half population of Type 2 supply (demand) X_1 and demand (supply) X_2 at price $p = a$ and no agent of Type 1 gets involved in the trade. We summarize the above analysis in Table 10.3.[3]

Table 10.3 Parameter subspaces and equilibria of Example 3

	$k_1 < k_0$	$k_1 > k_0$
$k_2 < k_0$	**When** $k_1k_2 < ak_0^2$ Equilibrium (shadow) price set $(Max\{k_1/k_0, ak_2/k_0\}, Min\{k_0/k_1, ak_0/k_2\})$ Structure: all agents in autarky. **When** $k_1k_2 > ak_0^2$ Equilibrium price $p = k_1/k_0$ Structure Type 1: $(\frac{k_1}{k_0})100\%$ sell X_1 $(1-\frac{k_1}{k_0})100\%$ in autarky Type 2: all sell X_2	**When** $k_2 < ak_0$ Equilibrium price p = 1 Structure Type 1: half sell X_1 and half sell X_2 Type 2: autarky **When** $k_2 > ak_0$ Equilibrium p = 1 Structure Type 1: all sell X_1 Type 2: all sell X_2
$k_2 > k_0$	**When** $k_1 < ak_0$ Equilibrium price p = a Structure Type 1: autarky Type 2: half sell X_1, half sell X_2 **When** $k_1 > ak_0$ Equilibrium price $p = k_1/k_0$ Structure Type 1: $(\frac{k_1}{k_0})100\%$ sell X_1 $(1-\frac{k_1}{k_0})100\%$ in autarky Type 2: all sell X_2	Equilibrium price $p = 1$ Structure Type 1: all sell X_1 Type 2: all sell X_2

When transaction technologies are less effective, autarky is the only equilibrium. As transaction technologies improve, labour specialization starts to emerge. Eventually, the more effective transaction technologies will lead to the division of labour, in which all Type 1 agents produce X_1 and all Type 2 agents produce X_2. As discussed in more detail in Sun, Yang and Zhou (1999), this example could be interpreted as a Ricardian story of two regions with Type 1(2) agents from Region 1(2). Note that continuous changes in transaction conditions cause discontinuous shift in the trade structure and levels of labour specialization. If the transaction condition for both regions is high enough, the inter-regional trade will emerge from domestic trade. What's intriguing is the endogenous dual structure in one region for some range of the trading efficiency parameters. If the trading efficiency for Region 1 (characterized by k_1) is not that high, there will emerge two distinct sub-regions in that region, one sub-region producing X_1 and trading with Region 2 for X_2 and the other one autarkic, though the per capita real income is the same across the two sub-regions. But the gains from inter-regional trade are distributed between the two regions quite asymmetrically such that all the gains from trade go to Region 2. The income inequality between regions would be enlarged as the trading efficiency in Region 2 improves provided that the dual structure in Region 1 remains qualitatively unchanged. It may be worthwhile to emphasize that the existence of a dual structure within the region is robust to parameter changes in some subspaces of parameters (k_1, k_2).

Example 4. *Ex ante* heterogeneous agents with producer goods and possibly with firms

In this example we consider an economy with two types of agents and one intermediate good X and one final good Y. This example is the same as Example 2 except that the trading efficiencies in the labour market for the two types of agents are allowed to be different. Namely, it is allowed that $s_1 \neq s_2$, where s_1 (s_2) is the trading efficiency coefficient in the labour market for Type 1 (2) agents. Without loss of generality, we assume $s_1 > s_2 > 0$ (the case $s_1 = s_2$ is precisely Example 2). As is done in the analysis of Example 2, we exclude the possibility that the agent may hire some workers to produce Y to simplify the algebra. Thus, for a given price signal (p, w) where p is the price of good X and w the wage rate both in terms of good Y, the agent of each type may choose from (i) selling nothing (in autarky); (ii) producing and selling X (and buying Y); (iii) selling Y; or (iv) selling labour and buying Y (being an employee). As analysed earlier, no rational person would sell two or three among X, Y and labour, and no Y seller will both buy X and hire workers to produce X. We denote by u_A (u_{iX} or u_{iL} for Type i agents, $i = 1,2$) the maximum utility if the agent makes a choice of (i) (choice (ii) or (iv)), and by u_{iYX} (u_{iYL}) for a Type i agent ($i = 1,2$) the maximum utility if she chooses option (iii) such that she buys intermediate good X from the market (hires workers to produce X in the firm).

We have $u_A(p,w) = \frac{\alpha^{\alpha}\beta^{\beta}(1-b)^{\alpha+\beta}}{(\alpha+\beta)^{\alpha+\beta}}$, $u_{iX}(p, w) = kp(1-b)$, $u_{iL}(p, w) = kw$,

$u_{iYX}(p,w) = [(1-\alpha)^{1-\alpha}\alpha^{\alpha}(\frac{k}{p})^{\alpha}]^{\frac{1}{1-\alpha}}$ and $u_{iYX}(p,w) = [(1-\alpha)^{1-\alpha}\alpha^{\alpha}(\frac{s_i-b}{w})^{\alpha}]^{\frac{1}{1-\alpha}}$, $i = 1,2$.

For any given (p, w), every agent of each type chooses her specialization pattern among the above five options to obtain the highest utility.

If no trade occurs under prices p and w, then $u_A > Max\{u_{iX}, u_{iL}, u_{iYX}, u_{iYL}\}$, $i = 1,2$ (we suppress p and w in the indirect utilities throughout this paragraph), from which we obtain $k < k^* \equiv [\frac{\beta^{\beta}(1-b)^{\beta}}{(\alpha+\beta)^{\alpha+\beta}(1-\alpha)^{1-\alpha}}]^{\frac{1}{2\alpha}}$, $k(s_1-b) >$ $KS \equiv [\frac{\beta^{\beta}(1-b)^{\alpha+\beta}}{(\alpha+\beta)^{\alpha+\beta}(1-\alpha)^{1-\alpha}}]^{\frac{1}{\alpha}}$ and the equilibrium (shadow) prices are any

$p \in (\alpha k(\frac{1-\alpha}{u_A})^{\frac{1}{\alpha}-1}, \frac{u_A}{k(1-b)})$ and any

$$w \in (\alpha(s_1-b)(\frac{1-\alpha}{u_A})^{\frac{1}{\alpha}-1}, \frac{u_A}{k}).$$

If only products are traded (no labour trade) in equilibrium, the utility level for both X sellers and Y sellers must be the same across agents of the same type, $u_{iX} = u_{iYX} > Max\{u_A, u_{iL}, u_{iYL})$, $i = 1,2$, which in turn implies $k > k^*$, $k > \frac{s_1-b}{1-b}$ and the equilibrium price $p = p^* \equiv k^{2\alpha-1}(s_1-b)^{\alpha}(1-b)^{-1}(1-$ $\alpha)^{1-\alpha}\alpha^{\alpha}$ and the (shadow) price set of the wage rate is $(\frac{s_1-b}{k}p^*, (1-b)p^*)$.

All agents in the economy freely choose between X sellers and Y sellers, but the number of agents from each type who are X (or Y) sellers is indeterminate. If X is not traded but both labour and final good Y are traded in equilibrium, then at least some Type 1 agents are Y suppliers. Note that the real income of a Type 1 agent who sells labour cannot be higher than that of the Type 2 agent who sells Y, but the Type 1 agent (who is a Y seller) hiring workers to produce X can always have a higher income level than a Type 2 agent doing the same thing. This is due to the fact that the Type 1 agent has an advantage over a Type 2 agent in trading labour. There may or may not exist Y sellers who are Type 2 agents. In the case of coexistence of Type 1 and Type 2 Y sellers, the workers can only be Type 2 agents. Thus, $u_{1YL} > Max\{u_A, u_{1L}, u_{1YX}, u_{1X})$ and $u_{2L} = u_{2YL} > Max\{u_A, u_{2X}, u_{2YX})$, from which follows $k < \frac{s_2-b}{1-b}$, $k(s_2-b) > KS$ and the equilibrium wage rate $w = w_2^* \equiv k^{\alpha-1}$ $(s_2-b)^{\alpha}(1-\alpha)^{1-\alpha}\alpha^{\alpha}$ and the equilibrium (shadow) price set is

$(\frac{k}{s_2 - b}w_2^*, \frac{1}{1-b}w_2^*)$. A careful reader may be concerned by the fact that the labour market might not clear since the population ratio between Type 1 and Type 2 is 1:1 and all Type 1 agents choose to hire workers but only some Type 2 agents choose to be workers. It is indeed problematic for a finite economy. But note that the existence of equilibrium usually requires the economy to be a large one (Sun, Yang and Zhou, 1999), and that the population ratio is not a problem for the equilibrium if the population of each type is a continuum, as is assumed in this example. In the case that there are only Type 1 Y sellers, both Type 1 and Type 2 agents might be workers. Hence, $u_{1YL} > Max\{u_A, u_{1YX}, u_{1X}), u_{1YL} \geq u_{1L}$ and $u_{2L} > Max\{u_A, u_{2X}, u_{2YX}, u_{2YL})$, from which follows $k < \frac{s_1 - b}{1-b}$, $k(s_1 - b) > KS$ and the equilibrium wage rates are a continuum $(Max\{w_2^*, u_A/k, k^{2\alpha-1}(1-b)^\alpha (1-\alpha)^{1-\alpha}\alpha^\alpha\}, w_1^*]$ and the (shadow) price set (for any equilibrium wage rate w) is $(\frac{k}{s_1 - b}w, \frac{1}{1-b}w)$. In particular, when $w = w_1^*$, some Type 1 agents might be workers while all Type 2 agents are workers. But for any equilibrium $w < w_1^*$, only (all) Type 2 agents are workers. That there are infinitely many equilibrium wage rates and (shadow) prices is dependent on the assumption of continuum agents of both agents. If the population is finite, then the labour market clearing condition leads to a unique wage rate which is determined by the population ratio of the two types, provided that the integer problem (of employee numbers) that the Y seller faces does not result in the non-existence of equilibrium.

If both good X and labour (as well as Y) are traded in equilibrium, all Type 1 agents are Y sellers who hire workers to produce X. The Y sellers who buy X from the market, the workers, as well as X suppliers are all of Type 2: $u_{1YL} > Max\{u_A, u_{1YX}, u_{1X}, u_{1L}\}$, and $u_{2YX} = u_{2Y} = u_{2L} > Max\{u_A, u_{2YL}\}$, from which it follows that $k > k^*$, $\frac{s_2 - b}{1-b} < k < \frac{s_1 - b}{1-b}$, and the equilibrium price $p = p^*$ and wage rate $w = (1-b)p^*$. Note $w_2^* < w < w_1^*$. Should this example be interpreted as a two-region (country) model with Type 1(2) agents from Region 1(2) with different trading conditions in the factor markets, the workers from Region 2 (of the poorer factor market) enjoy a higher wage from the inter-regional(-national) division of labour than in the absence of inter-regional division of labour even if they work in the firms owned by Type 2 agents. Agents from Region 1 also benefit from a lower wage than if the wage was paid to workers from Region 1. Thus, this model, once elaborated, can be well developed into a story of endogenous emergence of multiple national firms and FDI.

Table 10.4 summarizes the above analyses.

Table 10.4 Parameter subspaces and equilibria for Example 4

	$k(s_1 - b) < KS$	$k(s_1 - b) < KS$
$k < k^*$	Equilibrium prices and wage rates (both being shadow prices) any $p \in (\alpha k(\frac{1-\alpha}{u_A})^{\frac{1}{\alpha}-1}, \frac{u_A}{k(1-b)})$ any $w \in (\alpha(s_1 - b)(\frac{1-\alpha}{u_A})^{\frac{1}{\alpha}-1}, \frac{u_A}{k})$ Autarky (no trade)	Equilibrium wage rates: any $w \in (Max\{w_2^*, u_A/k, k^{2\alpha} - 1$ $(1-b)^{\alpha}(1-\alpha)^{1-\alpha}\alpha^{\alpha}\}, w_1^*]$ Shadow prices (for any equilibrium w) $(\frac{k}{s_1 - b}w, \frac{1}{1-b}w)$. Labour and Y are traded (firms exist). Type 1: firm owners and workers (for $w = w_1^*$, some firm owners some workers; for $w < w_1^*$, all firm owners) Type 2: workers
$k > k^*$	Equilibrium price $p = p^*$ Shadow price of wage rate; any $w \in (\frac{s_1 - b}{k}p^*, (1-b)p^*)$ X and Y are traded (no firms). Agents of both types freely choose between X sellers and Y sellers, but how many agents from each type are X (or Y) sellers is indeterminate.	**When** $k > \frac{s_1 - b}{1-b}, p = p^*$ (shadow) wages $(\frac{s_1 - b}{k}p^*, (1-b)p^*)$ X and Y are traded (no firms). Agents of both types freely choose between X sellers and Y sellers, but how many agents from each type are X (or Y) sellers is indeterminate. **When** $\frac{s_2 - b}{1-b} > k > \frac{s_1 - b}{1-b}$, $p = p^*, w = (1-b)p^*$ X, Y and labour are traded (firms exist). Type 1: Firm owners (labour buyers, Y sellers) Type 2: Y suppliers (no employment), X suppliers and workers. **When** $k < \frac{s_2 - b}{1-b}$ Shadow prices $(\frac{k}{s_2 - b}w_2^*, \frac{1}{1-b}w_2^*)$ wage rate $w = w_2^*$ Labour and Y are traded (firms exist). Type 1: firm owners. Type 2: firm owners and workers.

We may simplify Table 10.4 highlighting the structures of specialization, as in Table 10.4′.

Table 10.4′ A simplified Table 10.4

	$k\,(s_1 - b) < KS$	$k\,(s_1 - b) < KS$
$k < k^*$	Shadow p and shadow w Autarky	Shadow p (dependent on wage w). A continuum of equilibrium w. Division of labour (with firms, no intermediate goods traded)
$k > k^*$	Equilibrium p and shadow w. Division of labour (no firms).	**When** $k > \frac{s_1 - b}{1 - b}$, Equilibrium p and shadow w Division of labour (no firms). **When** $\frac{s_2 - b}{1 - b} > k > \frac{s_1 - b}{1 - b}$, Equilibrium p and equilibrium w Division of labour (firms exist, X traded). **When** $k < \frac{s_2 - b}{1 - b}$, Shadow p and equilibrium w Division of labour (with firms).

4 Concluding remarks

The new approach introduced in this chapter is in some senses an elaboration on both the two-step approach and the benchmark price approach. The major breakthrough, however, is that the new approach starts by partitioning the price space and then goes on to a corresponding partition of the parameter space. By doing so, the equilibrium computation and comparative statics is integrated together in a natural manner. As such, models involving possible substitution between markets across different structures of the division of labour, *ex ante* heterogeneous agents, and intra- and inter-firm division of labour can be rather easily solved, without overlooking any equilibrium price or structures.

While the major motivation for developing this analytical tool is mainly of technical interest, it may nonetheless help to clarify some theoretical issues, particularly those regarding the efficiency of the 'invisible hand' price system in coordinating the division of labour, and the characterization of equilibrium with firms. For instance, some may be concerned to know, after reading papers based on the two-step analyses, how agents coordinate with each other to switch from one 'bad' structure to a 'good' one. The role played by the Walrasian price system in coordinating the decentralized decisions of many price-takers in our approach is much more transparent: agents simply don't bother, nor do they need to care about structures, as their decisions on labour–trade plans are guided only by the price signal.[4] In addition, the new approach may help to analyse some theoretical issues in the new classical microeconomic framework such as the conditions under which the equilibrium is (locally) unique, comparative statics is monotonic, the general equilibrium with firms exists for a general class of models and so on. Some extensions to this approach may offer some progress in this direction.

Notes

1 Strictly speaking, the subset of parameters identified as such is often not a (sub-) space. But we rather loosely refer to them as subspaces throughout this chapter.
2 We purposely ignore the possibility that the agent may hire some workers to produce Y, mainly to simplify the algebra which would otherwise be much more complicated. We do this for the sake of illustrating how the new method can be used to solve models that necessitate the substitution between the market of labor and the market of the (intermediate) product.
3 It may be noted that Table 10.3 is slightly different from the results in Sun, Yang and Zhou (1999) in that we ignore the equilibrium analysis for the very 'threshold' values of parameters k_1 and k_2 to keep Table 10.3 less complicated, though it is rather easy to incorporate these cases into our analysis by the new method.
4 Note that the process of how a new market and/or the equilibrium price is created/discovered (presumably by entrepreneurs) goes beyond the scope of this essay. As is well known, this topic has long been a major concern of the Austrian School (see, for example, Kirzner, 1997). Also note the coordination in a non-traditional Walrasian price system (say, with information asymmetry) is rather a *conceptually different* problem, which should be dealt with elsewhere as well.

References

Becker, G. (1981) *A Treatise on the Family* (Cambridge, MA: Harvard University Press).

Kirzner, I. M. (1997) 'Entrepreneurial discovery and the competitive market process: an Austrian approach', *Journal of Economic Literature*, XXXV, 60–85.

Li, G. (2001) 'The emergence of the multinational enterprise: a model formalizing Dunning's eclectic paradigm', presented at the International Symposium of Economics of e-Commerce and Networking Decisions at Melbourne, 6–7 July.

Rosen, S. (1978) 'Substitution and the division of labor', *Economica*, 45, 235–50.

Sachs, J., Yang, X. and Zhang, D. (2000) 'Globalization, dual economy and economic development', *China Economic Review*, 11, 2, 189–209.

Scarf, H. (with the collaboration of T. Hansen) (1973) *The Computation of Economic Equilibria* (New Haven: Yale University Press).

Sun, G.-Z. (2000) 'The size of the firm and social division of labor', *Australian Economic Papers*, 39, 263–77.

Sun, G.-Z., Yang, X., and Yao, S. (1999) 'Theoretical foundation of economic development based on networking decisions in the competitive market', Harvard Center for International Development Working Paper No. 17.

Sun, G.-Z., Yang, X. and Zhou, L. (1999) 'General equilibria in large economies with endogenous structure of the division of labor', working paper, Department of Economics, Monash University.

van der Laan, G. and Talman, A. J. J. (1987) 'Adjustment processes for finding economic equilibria', in A. J. J. Talman and G. van der Laan (eds), *The Computation and Modeling of Economic Equilibria* (Amsterdam: North-Holland), 85–123.

Yang, D. (2001) 'Division of labor and the emergence of international trade and foreign direct investment', presented at the International Symposium of Economics of e-Commerce and Networking Decisions at Melbourne, 6–7 July.

Yang, X. (1988) 'A Microeconomic Approach to Modeling the Division of Labor Based on Increasing Returns to Specialisation', PhD Dissertation, Princeton University.

Yang, X. (2002) 'A review of the literature of inframarginal analysis of network of the division of labor', in Y.-K. Ng, H. Shi and G.-Z. Sun (eds), *The Economics of e-Commerce and Networking Decisions: Applications and Extensions of Inframarginal Analysis* (London: Macmillan).

Yang, X. and Ng, Y.-K. (1993) *Specialization and Economic Organization: a New Classical Microeconomic Framework* (Amsterdam: North-Holland).

Yang, X. and Ng, Y.-K. (1995) 'Theory of the firm and structure of residual rights', *Journal of Economic Behavior and Organization*, 26, 107–28.

Appendix 1

We establish in this appendix that in Example 2 no rational person would sell two or three 'goods' among X, Y and labour. The increasing returns to specialization in producing X immediately imply that no one sells X and labour simultaneously. Suppose someone sells both Y and labour (or X), then the MVP (marginal value product) of labour in producing Y equals the wage w (or marginal productivity in producing X in terms of good Y, namely, p). But the diminishing marginal productivity of labour in Y and the given w and p implies that it will pay better if she puts a bit less (more) labour into the production of Y (sold labour or production of X). Thus, no one sells more than one among X, Y and labour.

11

Transaction Efficiency, Division of Labour and Foreign Direct Investment: a Unified Model

*Dexin Yang**

1 Introduction

The purpose of this chapter is to develop a general equilibrium model incorporating foreign direct investment (FDI). Inframarginal analysis is used to capture the mechanisms for the emergence and development of FDI. (Motives for such an effort come from our observation of the gaps in the literature of mainstream economics and FDI.)

Mainstream economic theory has extensively explored economic organization under two sets of conception, namely, price and hierarchy, and the market and the firm (see Coase, 1937; Williamson, 1975). It is basically held that the market uses the price system to organize transactions between firms and the firm organizes internal activities via hierarchy. However, there is relatively little exploration of how location affects economic activity, another crucial feature of economic organization. For various reasons, the market is not universal and homogenous, but consists of different markets at different locations for different factors and products, and economic activity can take place in different regions, whether at home or abroad. In addition, the firm is not deemed to be a single-plant production unit where all firm activities take place in a single location. The multinational enterprise (MNE), the main subject of FDI and a direct consequence of such investment, illustrates this feature.

From the perspective of economic organization, the institution of the MNE involves not only the classical question of the boundary between the administrative allocation of resources within the firm and the market allocation of resources between firms, but also the question of the geographical setting of the boundary between firm and market as well as the question of the hierarchical form. It is an important question in economic organization why multinationals expand their administrative boundaries internationally

* The author is grateful to Xiaokai Yang, Yew-Kwang Ng, Guang-Zhen Sun, Dietrich Fausten, Meng-Chun Liu, and Dingsheng Zhang for their helpful comments and critics. The remaining errors are mine.

rather than domestically. A related issue is why some firms expand their administrative boundaries internationally while others do not. In principle it is natural that, in a market economy, entrepreneurs are free to reduce market transactions by increasing the scope of allocations made administratively within their firms, and in the end the most profitable pattern of enterprise organization should prevail. Where more profitable results can be obtained from placing plants under common administrative control, ultimately multi-plant enterprises will predominate and single-plant firms will merge or go out of business. But it is not clear from the existing literature why multi-plant firms prevail. Furthermore, there is little understanding in the literature about the prevalence of the multi-plant transnational enterprises (multinational enterprises), which involves more than one economy and market conditions varying between economies. Buckley and Casson (1976) argue that MNEs exist because the transaction cost of doing business through an internalized network of wholly owned subsidiaries is in many cases lower than that of 'arm's-length' relationships. However their theory falls short of explaining why firms have to invest abroad to bypass the external market rather than investing at home for the same purpose. In addition, research in this vein 'was often (at best) partial equilibrium in nature and focused on individual firms rather than on explaining the pattern of direct investment in relation to country and industry characteristics' (Markusen and Maskus, 1999, p. 2).

The division of labour is a focus in classical economics (see, for example, Smith, 1776). For centuries international division of labour was essentially carried out through arm's-length trade. The classical division of labour through trade implied that the developing countries almost exclusively exported raw materials to the industrialized countries. In exchange they received the processed goods which were manufactured in the industrialized countries. However, the situation has been changing since the late nineteenth century when FDI began to play an ever-increasing role in the world economy (Dunning, 1997, pp. 17–18). The relocation and establishment of industry by MNEs from developed countries implied a considerable change in the international division of labour, as some developing countries began to export industrial goods (Martinussen, 1997, p. 115). In addition, when created assets become more important in determining national comparative advantages, FDI aimed at exploiting firm-specific assets and acquiring strategic resources can find a suitable investment environment in developed countries. As a consequence, North America, the EU and Japan are not only the main investors, but also the main destinations for FDI. More than 80 per cent of FDI is directed to industrialized countries (Graham and Krugman, 1991; Markusen, 1995).

A notable feature of FDI's role in the division of labour is the MNE internalized international division of labour via FDI. Here the hierarchy of the MNE replaces the market in the organization of division of labour. In contrast to the division of labour by arm's-length trade, the internalized international division of labour depends on the extent of the intra-firm 'market', which essentially depends on technical progress determined by the division of labour. As a result of rapidly growing FDI and MNE activity, MNEs' internal trade, which mainly reflects the intra-firm international division of labour, is impressive in volume. MNE's internal trade alone accounts for about one-third of world trade and their combined internal trade and related public market trade account for about two thirds of world trade (UNCTAD, 1999).

Internalized international division of labour forms cross-border specialization within the firm. The contemporary concentration of FDI in developed countries reflects the fact that the division of labour in its advanced state has now extended to what Casson calls a 'division of thought' (Casson, 1988). This represents a form of advanced intellectual specialisation, which can easily find the technical base in developed countries.

Nevertheless, as Yang indicates that division of labour has been essentially ignored since Walras and Marshall (Yang, 2001, pp. 10–11). The interdependence between division of labour and FDI attracts little attention in mainstream economics. Correspondingly, FDI has been approached without considering its associated division of labour in the literature of FDI. Except for a few odd scraps describing multinational activities, the question of division of labour is excluded from the existing models and theorems of FDI and MNEs, no matter whether they are general equilibrium models or partial equilibrium models.

Motivatd by the intention to fill these gaps in the literature, this chapter develops a Walrasian general equilibrium model to investigate the mechanisms for the emergence and development of international direct investment. It yields rich findings regarding the organization of FDI and other international activities. FDI is a form of organizing international activity and division of labour. Through FDI, the investing firm indirectly prices intangible intermediate goods in the context of international economy by expanding the firm's governance boundary to the host country. When other factors are given, high transaction efficiency for ordinary labour (or all factors other than the indirect pricing related ones) in the host country and high transaction and transfer efficiencies for professionals (including all factors related to the indirect pricing) from the home country encourage FDI between the two countries. The relationships between FDI and the trade of final goods and trade of intermediate goods (for instance, foreign licensing) are determined and shaped by the transaction efficiencies for goods and factors within and between countries.

This chapter proceeds as follows. Section 2 describes the model. Section 3 identifies the general equilibrium results and its comparative statics and explains the main findings. The final section concludes the essay.

2 The basic model

Consider a world economy consisting of country i and country j, each with a continuum number of *ex ante* identical consumer-producers of mass M_i and M_j respectively. This assumption implies that the population size is very large. It therefore avoids the integer problem for numbers of different specialists, which may lead to the non-existence of equilibria with the division of labour. In order to avoid unnecessarily complex patterns of economic structures, we assume that $\frac{M_j}{M_i}$ is neither too large nor to small.

There is one consumer good y and one intangible intermediate good x, which is an essential input for the production of good y. Each individual consumes the consumer good and produces at least one of the two goods. Both goods can either be self-provided or be purchased in the markets. We use x to represent the quantity of self-provided good x and y the self-provided good y. In a similar way, we use x^s and y^s to represent the quantities of good x and good y supplied in the markets respectively, and x^d and y^d the quantities of good x and good y purchased in the markets respectively. Market transactions absorb resources. This fact is captured by 'iceberg' costs in the transaction cost model such that a fraction $(1 - k)$ of the good sold disappears in the domestic transaction.[1] Conversely, k $(0 \leq k \leq 1)$ represents the transaction efficiency as the proportion of the purchased good that is left after each transaction. Larger values of k indicate better transaction conditions. Subscripts x and y identify the good concerned. Therefore k_x and k_y are the transaction efficiency coefficients for good x and good y in the markets respectively. Accordingly, $k_x x^d$ and $k_y y^d$ represent the respective quantities of x and y that an individual obtains from purchasing x y. Similarly, s denotes the transaction efficiency (TE) coefficient for labour in the domestic market, where $0 < s < 1$. Particularly, s_x and s_y are the transaction efficiency coefficients for specialists producing x and specialists producing y in the market respectively.

We further use subscripts i and j to identify the country in which an activity takes place. For example, in country i, the self-provided quantities of goods x and y are x_i and y_i, the quantities sold in the markets are $x^s{}_i$ and $y^s{}_i$ the quantities purchased in the markets are x_i^d and y_i^d respectively. Where both good-denoting subscripts (i.e., x and y) and country-denoting subscripts (i.e., i and j) are applicable, the latter become sub-subscripts. So the quantities of good x and good y and individual in country i obtains from purchasing them locally are $k_{x_i} x_i^d$ and $k_{y_i} y^d{}_i$ respectively. So as in country j.

The utility function of each individual in country i is represented by:

$$U_i = y_i + k_{y_i} y_i^d + \theta k_{y_j} y_j^d \qquad 0 < \theta < 1 \qquad (11.2.1)$$

where θ is the international transaction efficiency coefficient for goods, capturing an iceberg-type international transaction cost. In the case of international purchase, besides of loss of $1 - k$ due to domestic transaction cost in the sourcing country, a further fraction of $1 - \theta$ is lost in international transit for each unit of a good purchased from the other country. In the meantime, we assume that all goods of the same 'type' (x or y), no matter whether self-supplied or purchased from the market, are perfect substitutes.

We assume that both goods, x and y, are freely tradable domestically and internationally. However, while labour producing good x is internationally mobile, labour producing good y is internationally immobile. The assumption of the international immobility of y producers is intended to simplify the analysis. It also captures the economic reality that, compared to the high mobility of professionals and managerial personnel, the international movement of the ordinary workforce incurs a much higher relative cost (cost divided by value-added per head) due to national barriers. The international movement of x producers incurs international personnel movement costs, take for instance, transport cost, adaptation cost for setting down to the local environment, and so on. These costs are all together captured by an international transaction cost coefficient $1 - \delta$, where $0 < \delta < 1$. δ is the international transaction efficiency coefficient for labour, and has the similar feature as θ for goods.

An individual's production function for the intermediate good in country i is:

$$x_i + x_i^s = Max\left\{0, 1_{x_i} - b_{x_i}\right\} \tag{11.2.2}$$

where $x_i + x_i^s$ is the output of good x, and l_{x_i} is an individual's level of specialization in as well as his amount of labour allocated to the production of good x ($0 < l < 1$). Parameter b_{x_i} is the fixed learning cost in producing good x in country i. It exhibits the degree of economies of specialization, and its value is positive but less than each individual's time endowment, such that, $b_{x_i} \in (0,1)$ This indicates that each individual can save on repeated learning costs by specializing in producing the intermediate good which has higher technological content.

An individual's production function for the consumer good in country i is:

$$y_i + y_i^s = \left(x_i + k_{x_i} x_i^d + \theta k_{x_j} x_j^d\right)^a l_{y_i} \qquad a \in (0,1) \tag{11.2.3}$$

where x_i^d is the amount of the intermediate good purchased from the domestic market and x_j^d is the amount of the intermediate good purchased from abroad. The value of $x_i + k_{x_i} x_i^d + \theta k_{x_j} x_j^d$ is the total amount of intermediate good which is employed by a y producer in the production of the consumer good y in country i. l_{y_i} is an individual's level of specialization in as well as his amount of labour allocated to the production of good y. The sum of $y_i + y_i^s$ is the output of the consumer good. The parameter a represents the degree of economies of specialization in producing the consumer good.

The time endowment constraint for each individual in country i is given as follows:

$$l_{x_i} + l_{y_i} = 1 \tag{11.2.4}$$

The above equations are applicable to country j when the country denoting subscript i is replaced by j and j is replaced by i.

3 Configuration and economic structure

Each individual makes decisions concerning his production and consumption. In other words, he makes decisions about which good to produce as well as his demand for and supply of any traded good to maximize his utility. A given profile of production and trade activities for an individual is defined as a *configuration*, and the combination of configurations of the M individuals in a country is defined as a market structure, or *structure* in short. Each configuration has a corner equilibrium. In order to derive an individual's optimum decision, the Kuhn–Tucker theorem can be used to rule out the interior solutions. So does the market structure.

Yang (2000) re-establishes and refines Wen's Theorem based on Kuhn–Tucker conditions for the model with intermediate goods as follows:

> **Lemma**: An individual sells at most one good and does not buy and self-provide the same good. He self-provides the consumer good if he sells it. If $a \in (0.5,1)$, he does not self-provide the intermediate good unless he produces the final good.

3.1 Structures and corner equilibriums

3.1.1 *Closed economy*

In a closed economy, no individuals carry out overseas production or cross-border trade. There are four possible structures for a closed economy, namely: autarky, simple domestic division of labour (*SD*), firm owned and run by the producer of good y (*FY*), and firm owned and run by the producer of good x (*FX*) (Yang and Ng, 1995). Their respective features are shown in Figure 11.1.

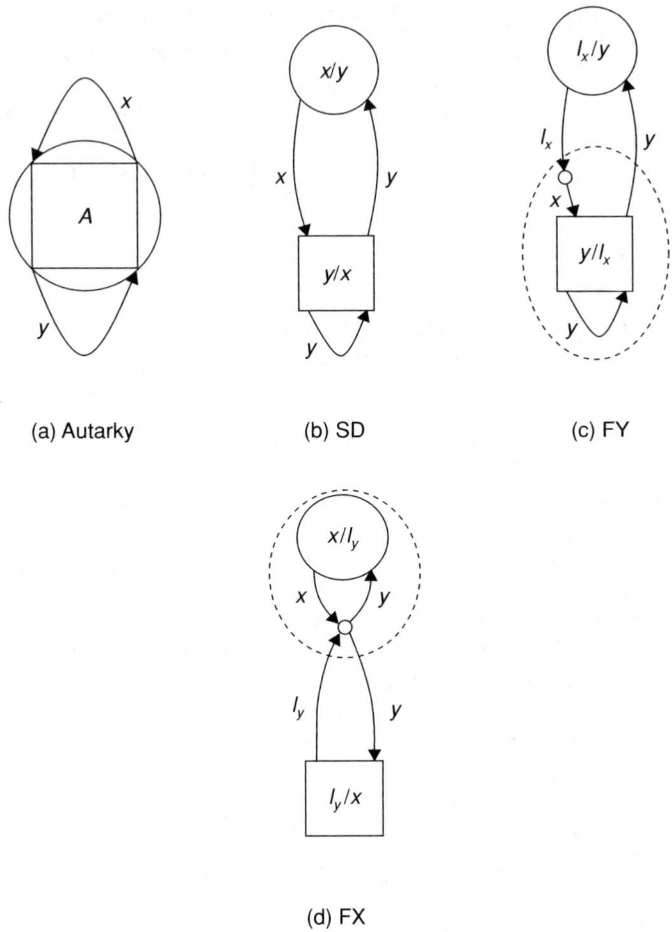

Figure 11.1 Structures in a closed economy
Note: The arrowheads indicate the flow of goods or factors, and dotted lines indicate the boundary of the firm.

- Structure A: Autarky

In the structure of autarky, each individual chooses a configuration with $x^s = y^s = x^d = y^d = 0$ The decision problem for each individual in this structure is:

$$\begin{aligned} \text{Max} \quad & U = y \\ \text{s.t.} \quad & y = x^a\, l_y; \quad x = l_x - b_x;\ l_x + l_y = 1 \end{aligned} \tag{11.3.1a}$$

The solution for this structure is:

$$l_x = \frac{a+b_x}{a+1}; \quad l_y = \frac{1-b_x}{a+1} \tag{11.3.1b}$$

$$U_A = a^a \left(\frac{1-b_x}{a+1} \right)^{a+1} \tag{11.3.1b}$$

- Structure *SD*: Simple Domestic Division of Labour

The structure comprises configuration (*x*/*y*) and configuration (*y*/*x*) in a country. There is no asymmetric distribution of residual rights in this structure. Individuals exchange goods for goods in a condition where no institution of the firm and a related labour market exist.

The decision problem for each individual choosing configuration (*x*/*y*) in this structure is

$$\begin{aligned} &\text{Max} \quad U_x = k_y y^d && (11.3.2a) \\ &\text{s.t.} \quad x^s = l_x - b_x; \quad l_x = 1; \quad P_x x^s = P_y y^d \end{aligned}$$

where P_x and P_y are the prices of good *x* and good *y* respectively.

The decision problem for each individual choosing configuration (*y*/*x*) in this structure is

$$\begin{aligned} &\text{Max} \quad U_y = y && (11.3.2b) \\ &\text{s.t.} \quad y + y^s = (k_x x^d)^a l_y; \; l_y = 1; \; P_x x^d = P_y y^s \end{aligned}$$

Having considered the market-clearing and utility equalization conditions and the number of individuals in the structure, the corner equilibrium can be derived as follows:

$$U_{SD} = a^a (1-a)^{1-a} [k_x k_y (1-b_x)]^a \tag{11.3.2c}$$

$$\frac{P_x}{P_y} = \left[\frac{k_y(1-b_x)}{1-a} \right]^{a-1} (ak_x)^a \tag{11.3.2d}$$

$$M_x = \frac{ak_y M}{1-a+ak_y}; \quad M_y = \frac{(1-a)M}{1-a+ak_y} \tag{11.3.2e}$$

where U_{SD} is the per capita income and $\frac{P_x}{P_y}$ the relative price of the two goods in structure *SD*. M_x is the number of individuals selling good *x* and M_y the number of individuals selling dood *y*, the total number of individuals in the two groups is $M = M_x + M_y$

- Structure *FY*: Y's Firm

This structure comprises configuration (l_x/y) and configuration (y/l_x) in a country. (y/l_x) is a specialist producer of y who hires workers and directs them to specialize in producing intermediate good x within his firm. And (l_x/y) denotes a worker who is hired to produce the intermediate good x within his boss's firm and buys the final good with his wage.

This decision problem for the individual choosing configuration $(y/(l_x)$ in this structure is:

$$\begin{aligned} \text{Max:} \quad & U_y = y \qquad (11.3.3a) \\ \text{s.t.} \quad & y + y^s = (x^d)^a\, l_y; \quad x^s = s_x l_x - b_x; \quad l_x = 1;\ l_y = 1; \\ & x^d = Nx^s \\ & P_y y^s = W_x N l_x = W_x N \end{aligned}$$

Where s_x is the transaction efficiency (TE) coefficient for each unit of labour hired, W_x is the wage rate, and N the number of workers hired by the employer.

The decision problem for the individual choosing configuration (l_x/y) in this structure is:

$$\begin{aligned} \text{Max:} \quad & U_x = k_y y^d \qquad (11.3.3b) \\ \text{s.t.} \quad & P_y y^d = W_x l_x{}^s; \quad y^d = \frac{W_x}{P_y} \end{aligned}$$

Having considered the market-clearing and utility equalization conditions and the number of individuals in the structure, the corner equilibrium can be derived as follows:

$$U_{FY} = a^a(1-a)^{1-a}[k_y(s_x - b_x)]^a \qquad (11.3.3c)$$

$$\frac{W_x}{P_y} = \left(\frac{k_y}{1-a}\right)^{a-1} \left[a(s_x - b_x)\right]^a \qquad (11.3.3d)$$

$$M_x = \frac{ak_y M}{1-a+ak_y}; \quad M_y = \frac{(1-a)M}{1-a+ak_y} \qquad (11.3.3e)$$

- Structure *FX*: X's Firm

This structure comprises configuration (l_y/x) and configuration (x/l_y) in a country. (x/l_y) is a specialist producer of x who hires workers and directs them to specialize in producing the final good y by using his produce x within his firm. And (l_y/x) denotes a worker who is hired to produce the final good y by using the intermediate good within his boss's firm and buys the final good with his wage.

The decision problem for the individual choosing configuration (x/l_y) in this structure is:

$$\text{Max:} \quad U_x = Y \tag{11.3.4a}$$

$$\text{s.t.} \quad Y + Y^s = Ny^s;\ y^s = (x^d)^a s_y l_y; \quad l_x = 1; \quad l_y = 1;$$

$$x^d = \frac{x^s}{N}$$

$$x^s = l_x - b_x; \quad P_y Y^s = Wl_y N = WN$$

The decision problem for the individual choosing configuration (l_y/x) in this

$$\text{Max:} \quad U_y = k_y y^d \tag{11.3.4b}$$

$$\text{s.t.} \quad P_y y^d = Wl_y = W;\ U_y = k_y \frac{W}{P_y}$$

Having considered the market-clearing and utility equalization conditions and the number of individuals in the structure, the corner equilibrium can be derived as follows:

$$U_{FX} = a^a(1-a)^{1-a} s_y k_y^{1-a}(1-b_x)^a \tag{11.3.4c}$$

$$\frac{W}{P_y} = \left[\frac{(1-b_x)a}{k_y}\right]^a s_y(1-a)^{1-a} \tag{11.3.4d}$$

$$M_x = \frac{aM}{a+(1-a)k_y}; \quad M_y = \frac{(1-a)k_y M}{a+(1-a)k_y} \tag{11.3.4e}$$

3.1.2 *Open economy*

We define an open economy as one that involves some kind of complete division of labour with the rest of the world. In other words, in our assumed open economy, individuals in one country only produce the same goods and their production and consumption depend on exchanges with individuals of the other country for other goods. Such division of labour can be realized through trade of goods or by involving he international movement of factors. After taking into consideration the assumed international division of labour the location of production, and the owner of the firm, there are three possible structures for an open economy, namely: simple international division of labour (*SI*), export of intermediate good (*FL*), and international firm (*MS*). Each type of structure has two symmetrical variants. While *SI* denotes the structure in which country *I*(*j*) exports *x*(*y*) and imports *y*(*x*), *SI** does the other way around. *FL* denotes the structure in which the *x* specialist of country *i* is employed in country *j* and country *i* imports *y*, and *FL** the other way around. Here the owner of the firm is local specialist of *y*. *MS* denotes specialist of *x* from country *i* undertaking FDI and importing y, and MS^* denotes specialist of x from country j undertaking FDI and importing y. Their distribution and composition are shown in Figure 11.2 and their features are shown in Figure 11.3.

In the following section we examine the structures without superscript*, for example, *SI*, *FL* and *MS*. Due to the symmetrical nature between each pair of structures, the specifications and results for one structure without* are equivalent to those for another structure which has superscript* in the pair when country-denoting subscript i is changed to j and j is changed to i.

- Structure *SI*: simple international division

This structure comprises configuration (x_i/y_j in country i and configuration (y_j/x_t) in country j. There is no asymmetric distribution of residual right in this structure. Individuals exchange goods for goods in an environment where no institution of the firm or a related labour market exists.

The decision problem for each individual in country i choosing configuration (x_i/y_j) in this structure is:

$$\text{Max} \qquad U_{x_i} = \theta k_{y_j} y_j^{\ d} \tag{11.3.5a}$$

		Configuration in Country *j*							
		○	□	●	■	○̲	□̲	●̲	■̲
Configuration in Country *i*	○	–	○–□	–	○–■	–		–	○–■̲
	□	□–○	–		–		–		–
	●	–		–	~	–	●–□̲	–	~
	■	■–○	–	~	–		–	~	–
	○̲	–		–		–		–	
	□̲		–	□̲–●	–		–		–
	●̲	–		–	~	–		–	~
	■̲	■̲–○	–	~	–		–	~	–

Figure 11.2 Distribution and composition of structures for an open economy

Note:

1. ○——x; □——y; Dark——Owner of the firm; Underlined——Location of the firm.
2. ■–○ and ■̲–○ are the same structures that y specialist from Country i imports x from Country j (employing x specialist from Country j) Similarly, ○–■ and ○–■̲ are the same structures that y specialist from Country j imports x from Country i (employing x specialist from Country i). Therefore there are six possible structures for international division of labour.
3. Main reasons for the non-exist of a structure:

■——Immobility of labour producing y.

–——No division of labour to sustain the production of good x or good y.

~——No employees to form a firm.

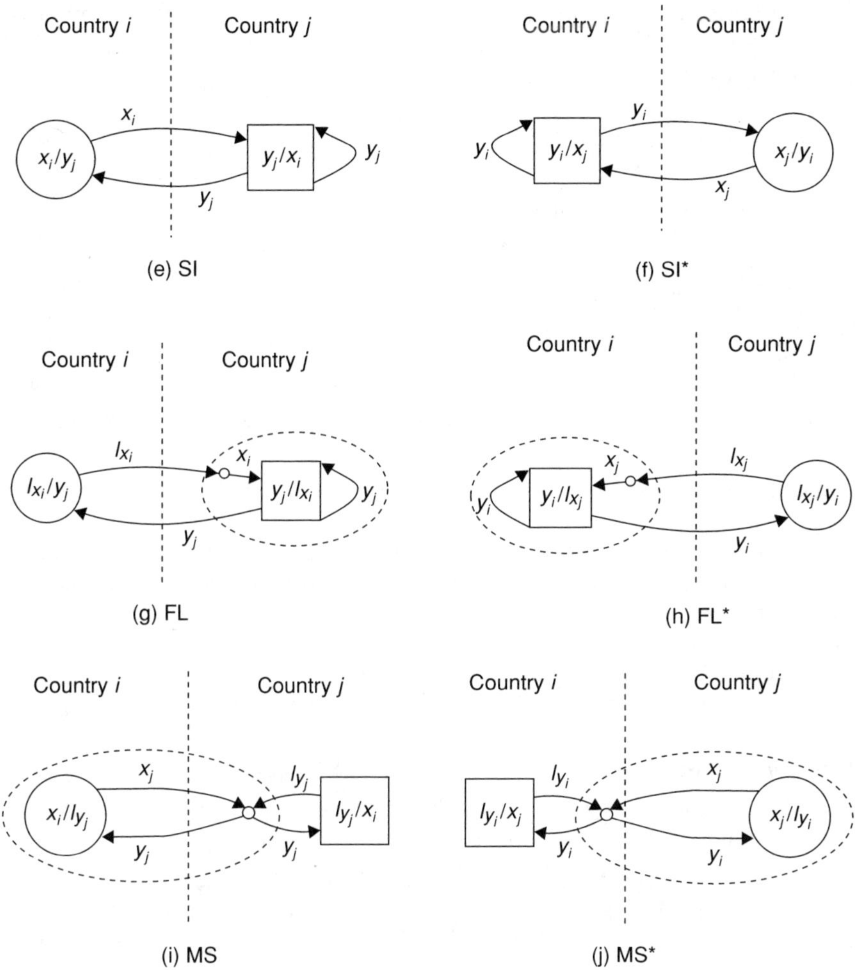

Figure 11.3 Structures in an open economy

s.t. $\quad x_i^s = l_{x_i} - b_{x_i};\ l_{x_i} = 1;\ P_{xi}x_i^s = P_{y_j}y_j^d$

where P_{x_i} and P_{y_j} are the price of goods *x* and *y* respectively.

The decision problem for each individual in country *j* choosing configuration (y_j/x_i) in this structure is

$$\text{Max} \quad U_{y_j} = y_j \qquad (11.3.5b)$$

$$\text{s.t.} \quad y_j + y_j^s = \left(\theta k_{x_i} x_i^d\right)^a l_{y_j};\ l_{y_j} = 1;\ P_{x_i}x_i^d = P_{y_j}y_j$$

Having considered the market-clearing requirements and the number of individuals in each country in the structure, the corner equilibrium can be derived as follows:

$$U_{SI_i} = a\theta^{1+a} k_{x_i}{}^{a} k_{y_j} \left(1 - b_{x_i}\right)^a \left(\frac{M_i}{M_j}\right)^{a-1} \tag{11.3.5c}$$

$$U_{SI_j} = (1-a)\left[\theta k_{x_i}\left(1-b_{x_i}\right)\right]^a \left(\frac{M_i}{M_j}\right)^a \tag{11.3.5d}$$

$$\frac{P_{x_i}}{P_{y_j}} = a\left(\theta k_{x_i}\right)^a \left[\left(1-b_{x_i}\right)\frac{M_i}{M_j}\right]^{a-1} \tag{11.3.5e}$$

where U_{SI_i} and U_{SI_j} are the per capita income in country *i* and country *j*, respectively, and $\frac{P_{x_i}}{P_{y_j}}$ the relative price of the two goods. M_i is the number of individuals selling good *x* as well as the total population in country *i* and M_j the number of individuals selling good *y* as well as the total population in country *j*.

- Structure *FL*: export of intermediate goods

This structure comprises configuration $\left(l_{x_i} / y_j\right)$ in country *i* and configuration $\left(y_j / l_{x_i}\right)$ in country *j*. $\left(y_j / l_{x_i}\right)$ is a specialist producer of *y* who hires and directs another country's producers of *x* to specialize in producing intermediate good *x* within his firm. $\left(l_{x_i} / y_j\right)$ denoted a producer of *x* who is hired by a foreign boss to produce the intermediate good *x* within his boss's firm in the boss's home country and imports the final good to his native country.

The decision problem for the individual choosing configuration (y_j/l_{xi}) in this structure is:

$$\text{Max:} \quad U_y = y_j \tag{11.3.6a}$$

$$\text{s.t.} \quad y_j + y_j{}^s = \left(x_i{}^d\right)^a l_{y_j}; \quad l_{x_i} = 1; \quad l_{y_j} = 1; \quad x_i{}^s = \delta s_{x_i} l_{x_i} - b_{x_i};$$

$$x_i{}^d = N x_i{}^s$$

$$P_{y_j} y_j{}^s = W_j N l_{x_i} = W_j N$$

The decision problem for the individual choosing configuration $\left(l_{x_i} / y_j\right)$ in this structure is:

$$\text{Max:} \quad U_x = \theta k_{y_j} y_i^{\,d} \tag{11.3.6b}$$

$$\text{s.t.} \quad P_{y_j} y_i^{\,d} = W_j l_{x_i}$$

Having considered the market-clearing conditions and the number of individuals in the structure, the corner equilibrium can be derived as follows:

$$U_{FL_i} = \theta a \left(\frac{M_j}{M_i}\right)^{1-a} k_{y_j}\left(\delta s_{x_i} - b_{x_i}\right)^a; \tag{11.3.6c}$$

$$U_{FL_i} = (1-a)\left(\frac{M_i}{M_j}\right)^a \left(\delta s_{x_i} - b_{x_i}\right)^a \tag{11.3.6d}$$

$$\frac{W_j}{P_{y_j}} = \left(\frac{M_j}{M_i}\right)^{1-a} a\left(\delta s_{x_i} - b_{x_i}\right)^a \tag{11.3.6e}$$

- Structure *MS*: international firm

This structure stretches across two countries and comprises configuration $\left(l_{y_j}/x_i\right)$ and configuration $\left(x_i/l_{y_j}\right)$. $\left(x_i/l_{y_j}\right)$ is a specialist producer of *x* from country *i* who sets up a firm in the foreign country (country *j*) where he hires local workers and directs them to specialize in producing final good *y* by using his output of *x* within his firm. And $\left(l_{y_j}/x_i\right)$ denotes a worker who is hired to produce final good *y* by using the intermediate good within his foreign boss's firm and buys the final good with his wage.

The decision problem for the individual choosing configuration $\left(x_i/l_{y_j}\right)$ in this structure is:

$$\text{Max:} \quad U_{x_i} = \theta Y_j \tag{11.3.7a}$$

$$\text{s.t.} \quad Y_j + Y_j^{\,s} = Ny_j^{\,s};\ l_{x_i} = 1;\ l_{y_j} = 1;\ y_j^{\,s} = \left(x_i^{\,d}\right)^a s_{y_j} l_{y_j};$$

$$x_i^{\,d} = \frac{x_i^{\,x}}{N};$$

$$x_i^{\,s} = \delta l_{x_i} - b_{x_i};\ P_{y_j} Y_j^{\,s} = W_j l_{y_j} N = W_j N$$

The decision problem for the individual choosing configuration $\left(l_{y_j}/x_i\right)$ in this structure is:

$$\text{Max:} \quad U_{y_j} = k_{y_j} y_j^{\,d} \tag{11.3.7b}$$

$$\text{s.t.} \quad P_{y_j} y_j^{\,d} = W_j l_{y_j} = W_j$$

Having considered the market-clearing and the number of individuals in the structure, the corner equilibrium can be derived as follows:

$$U_{MS_i} = \theta a \left(\frac{M_j}{M_i}\right)^{1-a} s_{y_j}\left(\delta - b_{x_i}\right)^a \tag{11.3.7c}$$

$$U_{MS_j} = (1-a)\left(\frac{M_i}{M_j}\right)^a k_{y_j} s_{y_j}\left(\delta - b_{x_i}\right)^a \tag{11.3.7d}$$

$$\frac{W_j}{P_{y_j}} = \left(\frac{M_i}{M_j}\right)^a (1-a) s_{y_j}\left(\delta - b_{x_i}\right)^a \tag{11.3.7e}$$

The structures of all configurations and their utilities in both a closed economy and an open economy are shown in Table 11.1. The relative prices of the two goods and wages in various structures are shown in Table 11.2. The numbers of specialists in each structure in the closed economy in specified in Table 11.3.

3.2 General equilibrium and evolution of structures

This section partitions the parameter space into subspaces. A particular structure occurs in each equilibrium. As indicated in Sun (1999), for a large economy consisting of *ex ante* heterogeneous agents and intermediate goods, the Walrasian general equilibrium not only exists but is also Pareto optimal. Thus, only the efficient structure(s) could occur in equilibrium. We let per capita real incomes in each pair of structures be equal and then obtain equations which partition the parameter space of 14 dimensions set by 14 parameters (a, θ, δ, b_{x_i}, b_{x_j}, k_{x_i}, k_{x_j}, k_{y_i}, k_{y_j}, s_{x_i}, s_{x_j}, s_{y_i}, s_{y_j}, $\frac{M_i}{M_j}$) into subspaces. Then we identify which structure is the general equilibrium structure within each subspace. Part I in Table 11.1 contains close economy configurations; any two configurations in the same row are identical. Parts II and III contain configurations involving complete international division of labour between the two countries, and any two configurations in the same row constitute an inseparable pair of structures for the two countries. As the pairs *SI* and *SI**, *FL* and *FL**, and *MS* and *MS** are each symmetrical, the result of analysis for SI_i, FL_i, and MS_i is applicable for SI_j^*, FL_j^* and MS_j^* and that for SI_j, FL_j, and MS_j is applicable for SI_i^*, FL_i^* and MS_i^*. Therefore, we only need to analyse configurations in Part I and in Part II. The results of the analysis of Part II are applicable to Part III if we make some appropriate changes.

Comparisons between per capita real incomes in each pair of structures in Part I and Part II for the parameter subspaces yield the results of the general equilibrium and its inframarginal comparative statics, which are summarized in Table 11.4.

Table 11.1 Configurations and utilities

Part	Structure	Form	Utility in country i	Utility in Country j
	A	A	$a^a\left(\frac{1-b_{x_i}}{1+a}\right)^{1+a}$	$a^a\left(\frac{1-b_{x_j}}{1+a}\right)^{1+a}$
I	SD	○ □	$a^a(1-a)^{1-a}[k_{x_i}k_{y_i}(1-b_{x_i})]^a$	$a^a(1-a)^{1-a}[k_{x_j}k_{y_j}(1-b_{x_j})]^a$
	FY	○ ■	$a^a(1-a)^{1-a}[k_{y_i}(s_{x_i}-b_{x_i})]^a$	$a^a(1-a)^{1-a}[k_{y_j}(s_{x_j}-b_{x_j})]^a$
	FX	● □	$a^a(1-a)^{1-a}s_{y_i}k_{y_i}{}^{1-a}(1-b_{x_i})^a$	$a^a(1-a)^{1-a}s_{y_j}k_{y_j}{}^{1-a}(1-b_{x_j})^a$
II	SI	○—□	$a\theta^{1+a}k_{x_i}{}^a k_{y_j}(1-b_{x_j})^a\left(\frac{M_j}{M_i}\right)^{1-a}$	$(1-a)[\theta k_{x_i}(1-b_{x_i})]^a\left(\frac{M_i}{M_j}\right)^a$
	FL	○—■	$\theta a\left(\frac{M_j}{M_i}\right)^{1-a}k_{y_j}\left(\delta s_{x_i}-b_{x_i}\right)^a$	$(1-a)\left(\frac{M_i}{M_j}\right)^a(\delta s_{x_i}-b_{x_i})^a$
	MS	●—□	$\theta a\left(\frac{M_j}{M_i}\right)^{1-a}s_{y_j}\left(\delta-b_{x_i}\right)^a$	$(1-a)\left(\frac{M_i}{M_j}\right)^a k_{y_j}s_{y_j}(\delta-b_{x_i})^a$
III	SI*	□—○	$(1-a)\left[\theta k_{x_j}\left(1-b_{x_j}\right)\right]^a\left(\frac{M_j}{M_i}\right)^a$	$a\theta^{1+a}k_{x_j}{}^a k_{y_i}(1-b_{x_j})^a\left(\frac{M_i}{M_j}\right)^{1-a}$
	FL*	■—○	$(1-a)\left(\frac{M_j}{M_i}\right)^a\left(\delta s_{x_j}-b_{x_j}\right)^a$	$\theta a\left(\frac{M_i}{M_j}\right)^{1-a}k_{y_i}\left(\delta s_{x_j}-b_{x_j}\right)^a$
	MS*	□—●	$(1-a)\left(\frac{M_j}{M_i}\right)^a k_{y_i}s_{y_i}\left(\delta-b_{x_j}\right)^a$	$\theta a\left(\frac{M_i}{M_j}\right)^{1-a}s_{y_i}(\delta-b_{x_j})^a$

Note: ○——*x*; □——*y*; Shadowed——Boss; Underlined——Location of the firm.

In the following sections we interpret the results of Table 11.4. For simplicity, we assume the value of a is close to 0.5 but does not equal 0.5 in the analysis.

3.2.1 *The range of the division of labour*

A close examination of Table 11.1 and Table 11.4 generates the terms for the range of division of labour.

For the international division of labour to exist, a necessary precondition is that the coefficient θ, which represents the international transaction efficiency for final goods, and the coefficient δ, which represents international transfer efficiency for cross-border movement of professionals, are not close to zero. Otherwise, utilities specified in SI_i, FL_i, MS_i tend towards

Table 11.2 Relative price

Part	*Structure*	*Country i*	*Country j*
	A	N/A	N/A
	SD	$\frac{P_{x_i}}{P_{y_i}} = \left[\frac{k_{y_i}(1-b_{x_i})}{1-a}\right]^{a-1}(ak_{x_i})^a$	$\frac{P_{x_j}}{P_{y_j}} = \left[\frac{k_{y_j}(1-b_{x_j})}{1-a}\right]^{a-1}(ak_{x_j})^a$
I	*FY*	$\frac{W_{x_i}}{P_{y_i}} = \left(\frac{k_{y_i}}{1-a}\right)^{a-1}\left[a\left(s_{x_i}-b_{x_i}\right)\right]^a$	$\frac{W_{x_j}}{P_{y_j}} = \left(\frac{k_{y_j}}{1-a}\right)^{a-1}\left[a\left(s_{x_j}-b_{x_j}\right)\right]^a$
	FX	$\frac{W_{y_i}}{P_{y_i}} = \left[\frac{(1-b_{x_i})^a}{k_{y_i}}\right]^a s_{y_i}(1-a)^{1-a}$	$\frac{W_{y_j}}{P_{y_j}} = \left[\frac{(1-b_{x_j})^a}{k_{y_j}}\right]^a s_{y_j}(1-a)^{1-a}$
	SI	$\frac{P_{x_i}}{P_{y_j}} = a(\theta k_{x_i})^a\left[(1-b_{x_i})\frac{M_i}{M_j}\right]^{a-1}$	
II	*FL*	$\frac{W_j}{P_{y_j}} = \left(\frac{M_j}{M_i}\right)^{1-a} a\left(\delta s_{x_i}-b_{x_i}\right)^a$	
	MS	$\frac{W_j}{P_{y_j}} = \left(\frac{M_i}{M_j}\right)^a (1-a)s_{y_j}\left(\delta-b_{x_i}\right)^a$	
	*SI**	$\frac{P_{x_j}}{P_{y_i}} = a\left(\theta k_{x_j}\right)^a\left[(1-b_{x_j})\frac{M_j}{M_i}\right]^{a-1}$	
III	*FL**	$\frac{W_i}{P_{y_i}} = \left(\frac{M_i}{M_j}\right)^{1-a} a\left(\delta s_{x_j}-b_{x_j}\right)^a$	
	*MS**	$\frac{W_i}{P_{y_i}} = \left(\frac{M_j}{M_i}\right)^a (1-a)s_{y_i}\left(\delta-b_{x_j}\right)^a$	

zero, which would in turn result in the non-existence of solutions of SI_j, FL_j, MS_j due to the inseparability condition of SI_i and SI_j, FL_i and FL_j, and MS_i and MS_j.

Given this precondition, the occurrence of the international division of labour in general equilibrium models depends on the transaction conditions for both labour and goods in the two countries. There are two scenarios where a structure with international division of labour might result in a general equilibrium.

Table 11.3 Number of specialists in the closed economy

Structure	*Country i*	*Country j*
A	N/A	N/A
SD	$\frac{M_{x_i}}{M_{y_i}} = \frac{ak_{y_i}}{1-a}$	$\frac{M_{x_j}}{M_{y_j}} = \frac{ak_{y_j}}{1-a}$
FY	$\frac{M_{x_i}}{M_{y_i}} = \frac{ak_{y_i}}{1-a}$	$\frac{M_{x_j}}{M_{y_j}} = \frac{ak_{y_j}}{1-a}$
FX	$\frac{M_{x_i}}{M_{y_i}} = \frac{a}{(1-a)k_{y_i}}$	$\frac{M_{x_j}}{M_{y_j}} = \frac{a}{(1-a)k_{y_j}}$

Scenario 1: $k_{yi} < v_{i14}$ and $k_{yj} < v_{j14}$ when $k_{xi} < r_i$ and $k_{xj} < r_j$
When each country's domestic transaction efficiency (TE) coefficient for intermediate goods is smaller than each country's value of $\frac{s_x - b_x}{1-b_x}$, the general equilibrium would lead to a structure with international division of labour, provided that each country's transaction efficiency for final goods is lower than $s_y^{\frac{1}{2a-1}}\left(\frac{1-b_x}{s_x-b_x}\right)^{\frac{a}{2a-1}}$. Term $k_x < \frac{s_x - b_x}{1-b_x}$ means that TE for specialists of x is sufficiently high in relation to TE for x goods that the output of a specialist of x employed in another firm is larger than the net quantity of his produce received by a buyer under a self-employe.d condition. Under such a condition, a structure with international division of labour could be the general equilibrium if TE for producers of final goods is also relatively high in relation to TE for final goods (in this case, $k_y < \left(\frac{s_y}{k_x{}^a}\right)^{\frac{1}{2a-1}}$) in both countries.

When a is slightly larger than 0.5, the slightly higher TE for producers of good y compared with the TE for intermediate goods will increase the possibility that structures with international division of labour become general equilibria. When a is slightly smaller than 0.5, we see the opposite result.

Scenario 2: $k_{yj} < \min\{v_{i1}, v_{j1}\}$ when $k_{xi} > r_i$ and $k_{xj} > r_j$
When the TE coefficient for intermediate goods is larger than the value of $\frac{s_x - b_x}{1-b_x}$ in both countries, the general equilibrium will be one of the structures with international division of labour provided the TE coefficient for final goods in the host country is lower than the minimum of either of these two values: $s_{y_j}\left(\frac{\delta - b_{x_i}}{\delta s_{x_i} - b_{x_i}}\right)^a$ or $\frac{1}{s_{y_j}}\left(\frac{\delta s_{x_i} - b_{x_i}}{\delta - b_{x_i}}\right)^a$. Here the magnitude of

Table 11.4 The general equilibrium and its inframarginal comparative statics

Values of k_{x_i} *and* k_{x_j}	$k_{xi} < r_i$ $k_{xj} < r_j$											
Values of k_{y_i} and k_{y_j}	$k_{yi} < v_{i14}$ $k_{yj} < v_{j14}$						$k_{yi} > y_{i14}$ $k_{yj} > y_{j14}$					
Values of $\frac{M_j}{M_i}$, k_{y_i} and k_{y_j}	$\frac{M_j}{M_i} < v_{ia}$ $\frac{M_i}{M_j} < v_{ja}$	$\frac{M_j}{M_i} > v_{ia}$ $\frac{M_i}{M_j} > v_{ja}$	$\frac{M_j}{M_i} < v_{ib}$ $\frac{M_i}{M_j} < v_{jb}$	$\frac{M_j}{M_i} > v_{ib}$ $\frac{M_i}{M_j} > v_{jb}$	$\frac{M_j}{M_i} < v_{if}$ $\frac{M_i}{M_j} < v_{if}$	$\frac{M_j}{M_i} > v_{if}$ $\frac{M_i}{M_j} > v_{if}$	$k_{y_i} < v_{id}$ $k_{y_j} < v_{jd}$	$k_{y_i} > v_{id}$ $k_{y_j} < v_{jd}$	$k_{y_i} < v_{ic}$ $k_{y_j} < v_{jc}$	$k_{y_i} > v_{ic}$ $k_{y_j} > v_{jc}$	$k_{y_i} < v_{ie}$ $k_{y_j} < v_{je}$	$k_{y_i} > v_{ie}$ $k_{yj} > v_{je}$
Equilibrium structure	*A*	*MS*	*A*	*FL*	*A*	*SI*	*A*	*FY*	*A*	*FX*	*A*	*SD*
Values of k_{x_i} and k_{x_j}	$k_{xi} > r_i$ $k_{xj} > r_j$											
Values of k_{y_i} and k_{y_j}	$k_{yj} < v_{il}$ $k_{yj} < v_{jl}$									$k_{yj} > v_{il}$ $k_{yj} > v_{il}$		
Values of $\frac{M_j}{M_i}$, k_{yi} and k_{y_j} and k_{y_j}	$\frac{M_j}{M_i} < v_{ia}$ $\frac{M_i}{M_j} < v_{ja}$	$\frac{M_j}{M_i} > v_{ia}$ $\frac{M_i}{M_j} > v_{ja}$	$\frac{M_j}{M_i} < v_{ib}$ $\frac{M_i}{M_j} < v_{jb}$	$\frac{M_j}{M_i} > v_{ib}$ $\frac{M_i}{M_j} > v_{jb}$	$\frac{M_j}{M_i} < v_{if}$ $\frac{M_i}{M_j} < v_{if}$	$\frac{M_j}{M_i} > v_{jf}$ $\frac{M_i}{M_j} > v_{if}$	$k_{yi} < v_{ic}$ $k_{yj} < v_{jc}$	$k_{yi} > v_{ic}$ $k_{yj} > v_{jc}$	$k_{yi} < v_{ie}$ $k_{yj} < v_{je}$	$k_{yi} > v_{ie}$ $k_{yj} > v_{je}$	$k_{yi} < v_{id}$ $k_{yj} < v_{jd}$	$k_{yi} > v_{id}$ $k_{yj} > v_{jd}$
Equilibrium structure	*A*	*MS*	*A*	*FL*	*A*	*SI*	*A*	*FX*	*A*	*SD*	*A*	*FY*

Table 11.4 The general equilibrium and its inframarginal comparative statics (*Continued*)

where the values of the variables are listed in the following table.

$r_i \equiv \frac{S_{x_i} - b_{x_i}}{1 - b_{x_i}}$	$v_{j_i} \equiv \tilde{k}_{y_j} \equiv s_{y_j}\left(\frac{\delta - b_{x_i}}{\delta s_{x_i} - b_{x_i}}\right)^a$	$v_{j14} \equiv \tilde{k}_{y_i} \equiv S_{y_i}^{\frac{1}{2a-1}}\left(\frac{1 - b_{x_i}}{s_{x_i} - b_{x_i}}\right)^{\frac{a}{2a-1}}$
$r_j \equiv \frac{S_{x_j - b_{x_j}}}{1 - b_{x_j}}$	$v_{j_i} \equiv \tilde{k}_{y_j} \equiv \frac{1}{s_{y_j}}\left(\frac{\delta s_{x_i} - b_{x_i}}{\delta - b_{x_i}}\right)^a$	$v_{j14} \equiv \tilde{k}_{y_j} \equiv S_{y_j}^{\frac{1}{2a-1}}\left(\frac{1 - b_{x_j}}{S_{x_j} - b_{x_j}}\right)^{\frac{a}{2a-1}}$
$v_{i_a} \equiv \frac{\tilde{M}_j}{M_i} \equiv \frac{(1 - b_{x_i})^{\frac{1+a}{1-a}}}{a(1+a)^{\frac{1+a}{1-a}}(\theta s_{y_j})^{\frac{1}{1-a}}(\delta - b_{x_i})^{\frac{a}{1-a}}}$	$v_{i_b} \equiv \frac{\tilde{M}_j}{M_i} \equiv \frac{1}{a(\theta k_{y_j})^{\frac{1}{1-a}}(1+a)^{\frac{1+a}{1-a}}}\left[\frac{(1 - b_{x_j})^{1+a}}{(\delta s_{x_i} - b_{x_i})^a}\right]^{\frac{1}{1-a}}$	$v_{i_c} \equiv \tilde{k}_{y_i} \equiv \frac{(1+a)^{\frac{a+1}{a-1}}}{1-a}\left(\frac{1 - b_{x_i}}{s_{y_i}}\right)^{\frac{1}{1-a}}$
$v_{j_a} \equiv \frac{\tilde{M}_i}{M_j} \equiv \frac{a}{(\delta - b_{x_i})[(1-a)k_{y_j}s_{y_j}]^{\frac{1}{a}}}\left(\frac{1 - b_{x_j}}{1+a}\right)^{\frac{1+a}{a}}$	$v_{j_b} \equiv \frac{\tilde{M}_i}{M_j} \equiv \frac{a}{(1+a)^{\frac{1+a}{a}}(1-a)^{\frac{1}{a}}}\frac{(1 - b_{x_j})^{\frac{1+a}{a}}}{(\delta s_{x_i} - b_{x_i})}$	$v_{j_c} \equiv \tilde{k}_{y_j} \equiv \frac{(1+a)^{\frac{a+1}{a-1}}}{1-a}\left(\frac{1 - b_{x_j}}{s_{y_j}}\right)^{\frac{1}{1-a}}$
$v_{i_d} \equiv \tilde{k}_{y_i} \equiv \left[\frac{1}{(1+a)^{1+a}(1-a)^{1-a}}\right]^{\frac{1}{a}}\frac{(1 - b_{x_i})^{\frac{1+a}{a}}}{s_{x_i} - b_{x_i}}$	$v_{i_e} \equiv \tilde{k}_{y_i} \equiv \frac{1}{k_{x_j}}\left[\frac{1 - b_{x_j}}{(1+a)^{1+a}(1-a)^{1-a}}\right]^{\frac{1}{a}}$	$v_{i_f} \equiv \frac{\tilde{M}_j}{M_i} \equiv \frac{1}{a}\left[\frac{1}{\theta(1+a)}\right]^{\frac{1+a}{1-a}}\left(\frac{1 - b_{x_i}}{k_{x_i}{}^a k_{y_j}}\right)^{\frac{1}{1-a}}$
$v_{j_d} \equiv \tilde{k}_{y_j} \equiv \left[\frac{1}{(1+a)^{1+a}(1-a)^{1-a}}\right]^{\frac{1}{a}}\frac{(1 - b_{x_j})^{\frac{1+a}{a}}}{s_{x_j} - b_{xj}}$	$v_{j_e} \equiv \tilde{k}_{y_j} \equiv \frac{1}{k_{x_j}}\left[\frac{1 - b_{x_j}}{(1+a)^{1+a}(1-a)^{1-a}}\right]^{\frac{1}{a}}$	$v_{j_f} \equiv \frac{\tilde{M}_i}{Mj} \equiv \frac{a}{[(1-a)(1+a)^{1+a}]^{\frac{1}{a}}}\frac{(1 - b_{x_j})^{\frac{1+a}{a}}}{\theta k_{x_i}(1 - b_{x_i})}$

*See Appendix for calculations.

the coefficient representing international transfer efficiency for cross-border movement of professionals, δ, is critical. When $s_{y_j}\left(\frac{\delta - b_{x_i}}{\delta s_{x_i} - b_{x_i}}\right)^a$ is smaller than $\frac{1}{s_{y_j}}\left(\frac{\delta s_{x_i} - b_{x_i}}{\delta - b_{x_i}}\right)^a$, whether international division of labour prevails to a large extent depends upon whether the value of δ is sufficiently large in relation to the value of b_{x_i}. When $s_{y_j}\left(\frac{\delta - b_{x_i}}{\delta s_{x_i} - b_{x_i}}\right)^a$ is larger than $\frac{1}{s_{y_j}}\left(\frac{\delta s_{x_i} - b_{x_i}}{\delta - b_{x_i}}\right)^a$, we see the reverse.

Correspondingly, there are two cases where the general equilibrium would lead to structures without the international division of labour. One is that when both countries' TE coefficient for intermediate goods is smaller than $\frac{s_x - b_x}{1 - b_x}$, but their respective TE for final goods is larger than $s_y^{\frac{1}{2a-1}}\left(\frac{1 - b_x}{s_x - b_x}\right)^{\frac{a}{2a-1}}$. Another is that when the TE coefficient for intermediate goods in both countries is larger than $\frac{s_x - b_x}{1 - b_x}$ and the TE coefficient for final goods in the host country is also higher than the maximum of either of these two values: $s_{y_j}\left(\frac{\delta - b_{x_i}}{\delta s_{x_i} - b_{x_i}}\right)^a$ or $\frac{1}{s_{y_j}}\left(\frac{\delta s_{x_i} - b_{x_i}}{\delta - b_{x_i}}\right)^a$. The impacts of the relevant variables in determining the general equilibrium structure are in the opposite direction to the situation with international division of labour.

The results of the above analysis lead to Proposition 1. As general equilibrium analysis for closed economies is not the intention of this Chapter, we briefly address the findings about domestic structures in Proposition 1.

Proposition 1: The range of division of labour is essentially dependent on transaction efficiencies (TE) for labour and goods in and between the two countries.

Closed economy: If both international TE for goods (θ) and international transfer efficiency for professionals (δ) are extremely low, opportunities for international division of labour do not exist. *Under such a condition,*
(1) If TE for goods and labour in both countries are also sufficiently close to zero, utilities in all structures with domestic or international trade and division of labour tend to zero. Hence, the corner equilibrium in autarky is the general equilibrium.

(2) If TE for goods and labour are sufficiently large, then a structure with domestic division of labour will occur in general equilibrium due to endogenous comparative advantage which is generated by the fixed learning cost in producing intermediate goods.

(2.1) If TE for intermediate goods and final goods are sufficiently larger than TE for the labour used in producing these two kinds of goods, domestic division of labour will be organized by the markets themselves for intermediate and final goods in the absence of labour trade and the associated institution of the firm.
(2.2) If TE for final goods or TE for labour producing final goods or intermediate goods are sufficiently larger than TE for intermediate goods, then domestic division of labour will be organized by the markets for the final good and labour and associated with institution of the firm. The relative value of s_x to s_y determines which kind of specialists will be the owner of the firm. If s_x is sufficiently larger than s_y, the specialist of y is the owner. Otherwise, the specialist of x is the owner.

Open economy: If international TE for goods, θ, and international transfer efficiency for professionals, δ, are sufficiently high, international division of labour may occur in general equilibrium due to exogenous comparative advantage in technology $(b_{x_i} \neq b_{x_j})$ and transaction conditions for goods and labour.

Specifically, if both countries' transaction efficiencies for intermediate goods and final goods are sufficiently low in relation to the transaction efficiencies for their producers, a structure with international division of labour will be the general equilibrium. If both countries' transaction efficiencies for intermediate goods are relatively high in relation to transaction efficiencies for the two types of labour producing them, the emergence of the international division of labour depends upon whether the transaction efficiency coefficient for final goods in the host country is sufficiently small, relative to the values of transaction efficiency coefficient for labour and fixed learning cost in producing final goods in the home country, as well as the international transfer efficiency coefficient for professionals.

3.2.2 *Trade of final goods, trade of intermediate goods, or FDI*

When international division of labour prevails, which one of the three structures – *SI* (trade of final goods), *FL* (trade of intermediate goods) or *MS* (FDI) prevails in the general equilibrium depends upon the value of $\frac{M_j}{M_i}$ in terms of values of other variables in and between the two countries.

- Structure, *SI*, involving international trade of final goods, is the general equilibrium if $\frac{M_j}{M_i} \in (v_{if}, 1/v_{if})$, where

$$v_{i_f} \equiv \frac{1}{a}\left[\frac{1}{\theta(1+a)}\right]^{\frac{1+a}{1-a}}\left(\frac{1-b_{x_i}}{k_{x_i}{}^a k_{y_j}}\right)^{\frac{1}{1-a}}; \quad \frac{1}{v_{j_f}} \equiv \frac{\left[(1-a)(1+a)^{1+a}\right]^{\frac{1}{a}}}{a}\frac{\theta k_{x_i}(1-b_{x_i})}{(1-b_{x_j})^{\frac{1+a}{a}}}.$$

- Structure *FL*, involving international trade in intermediate goods, in the general equilibrium if $\frac{M_j}{M_i} \in (v_{ib}, 1/v_{jb})$, where

$$v_{i_b} \equiv \frac{1}{a(\theta k_{y_j})^{\frac{1}{1-a}}(1+a)^{\frac{1+a}{1-a}}}\left[\frac{(1-b_{x_i})^{1+a}}{(\delta s_{x_i}-b_{x_i})^a}\right]^{\frac{1}{1-a}};$$

$$\frac{1}{v_{j_b}} \equiv \frac{(1+a)^{\frac{1+a}{a}}(1-a)^{\frac{1}{a}}}{a}\frac{(\delta s_{x_i}-b_{x_i})}{(1-b_{xj})^{\frac{1+a}{a}}}$$

- Structure *MS*, with international direct investment, is the general equilibrium, if $\frac{M_j}{M_i} \in (v_{ia}, 1/v_{ja})$, where

$$v_{i_a} \equiv \frac{(1-b_{x_i})^{\frac{1+a}{1-a}}}{a(1+a)^{\frac{1+a}{1-a}}(\theta s_{y_j})^{\frac{1}{1-a}}(\delta-b_{x_i})^{\frac{a}{1-a}}};$$

$$\frac{1}{v_{j_a}} \equiv \frac{(\delta-b_{x_i})\left[(1-a)k_{y_j}s_{y_j}\right]^{\frac{1}{a}}}{a}\left(\frac{1+a}{1-b_{x_j}}\right)^{\frac{1+a}{a}}.$$

Where the population of the two countries, and therefore the value of M_j/M_i is known, by comparing the values of each pair of v_i and v_j of any two adjacent structures, we can generate the criteria for which the general equilibrium jumps from one structure to another.

For instance, comparing values of v_{if} and v_{ib}, $1/v_{if}$ $1/v_{jb}$ generates the term for the critical point between *SI* and *FL*: $\bar{k}_{x_{fi}} \equiv \frac{\delta s_{x_i}-b_{x_i}}{\theta(1-b_{x_i})}$. When $k_{x_i} > \bar{k}_{x_{fi}}$, structure *SI* is superior to structure *FL*. When the relative value of k_{xi} changes from $k_{x_i} > \bar{k}_{x_{fi}}$ to $k_{x_i} < \bar{k}_{x_{fi}}$, structure *FL* will take the place of *SI* to become the superior structure. This change can be a result of sufficient improvements in either international transfer efficiency for labour and/or home country's TE for professionals (x producers), or perhaps a sufficient reduction in international TE for final goods and/or in TE for intermediate goods at home. This leads to Proposition 2.

Proposition 2: International trade of final goods would be a superior outcome to that of trade of intermediate goods if international TE for final goods is sufficiently high but international transfer efficiency and home country's TE for producers of intermediate goods are sufficiently low. When international transfer efficiency for cross-border movement of labour and home country's TE for labour are sufficiently improved (or alternatively international TE for final goods and TE for intermediate goods at home are sufficiently reduced), international trade of final goods would become less profitable and therefore international trade of intermediate goods becomes the general equilibrium.

Comparing values of v_{ia} and v_{ib}, $1/v_{ja}$ and $1/v_{jb}$ generates the criteria for the critical point between *MS* and *FL*: $\bar{k}_{y_{ai}} \equiv s_{y_j}\left(\frac{\delta - b_{x_i}}{\delta s_{x_i} - b_{x_i}}\right)^a$ for country i and $\bar{k}_{y_{aj}} \equiv \frac{1}{s_{y_j}}\left(\frac{\delta s_{x_i} - b_{x_i}}{\delta - b_{x_i}}\right)^a$ for counry j. When $k_{y_j} > \bar{k}_{y_{ai}}$ and $k_{y_j} < \bar{k}_{y_{aj}}$, or $s_{y_j}^{\frac{1}{a}}\left(\frac{\delta - b_{x_i}}{\delta s_{x_i} - b_{x_i}}\right) < 1$, structure *FL* is superior to structure *MS*. When the relative values of k_{y_j} change from $k_{y_j} > \bar{k}_{y_{ai}}$ and $k_{y_j} < \bar{k}_{y_{aj}}$ to $k_{y_j} < \bar{k}_{y_{ai}}$ and $k_{y_j} > \bar{k}_{y_{aj}}$, or from $s_{y_j}^{\frac{1}{a}}\left(\frac{\delta - b_{x_i}}{\delta s_{x_i} - b_{x_i}}\right) < 1$ to $s_{y_j}^{\frac{1}{a}}\left(\frac{\delta - b_{x_i}}{\delta s_{x_i} - b_{x_i}}\right) > 1$, structure *MS* will take the place of *FL* to become the superior structure. This change is mainly a result of sufficient improvement in the host country's transaction efficiencies for ordinary labour (y producers). In addition, improvements in home country's transaction efficiency and international transfer efficiency for professionals (x producers) would also help bring about such changes since the improvements lead overseas transaction efficiency coefficient for professionals, δs_{x_i}, closer to b_{x_i} rather than δ to b_{x_i}.

This leads to Proposition 3.

Proposition 3: International trade of intermediate goods would be a superior outcome to FDI if the host country's transaction efficiency for ordinary labour is sufficiently low. When there are sufficient improvements

in the host country's transaction efficiency for ordinary labour and a certain degree of improvement in the home country's transaction efficiency and international transfer efficiency for professionals, international trade of intermediate goods would become less profitable and FDI becomes the superior structure.

Comparing values of v_{ia} and v_{if}, $1/v_{ja}$ and $1/v_{jf}$ can generate the criteria for the critical point between *MS* and *SI*: $\bar{k}_{y_{fi}} \equiv s_{y_j}\left[\frac{\delta - b_{x_i}}{\theta k_{x_i}(1-b_{x_i})}\right]^a$ for country *i* and $\bar{k}_{y_{fi}} \equiv \frac{1}{s_{y_j}}\left[\frac{\theta k_{x_i}(1-b_{x_i})}{\delta - b_{x_i}}\right]^a$ for country *j*. When $k_{y_j} > \bar{k}_{y_{fi}}$ and $k_{y_j} < \bar{k}_{y_{fi}}$, or $s_{y_j}^{\frac{1}{a}}\left[\frac{\delta - b_{x_i}}{\theta k_{x_i}(1-b_{x_i})}\right] < 1$, structure *SI* is superior to *MS*. When the relative values of k_{y_j} change from $k_{y_j} > \bar{k}_{y_{fi}}$ and $k_{y_j} < \bar{k}_{y_{fi}}$ to $k_{y_j} < \bar{k}_{y_{fi}}$ and $k_{y_j} > \bar{k}_{y_{fi}}$, or from $s_{y_j}^{\frac{1}{a}}\left[\frac{\delta - b_{x_i}}{\theta k_{x_i}(1-b_{x_i})}\right] < 1$ to $s_{y_j}^{\frac{1}{a}}\left[\frac{\delta - b_{x_i}}{\theta k_{x_i}(1-b_{x_i})}\right] > 1$, structure *MS* will take the place of *SI* as the superior structure. This change could be a result of sufficient improvement in both the host country's transaction efficiency for ordinary labour (*y* producers) and the international transfer efficiency for the cross-border movement of professionals. This change could also be a result of reduction in international transaction efficiency for final goods as well as the home country's transaction efficiency for professionals (*x* producers).

This leads to Proposition 4.

Proposition 4: International trade of final goods is superior to FDI if international TE for final goods and home country's TE for intermediate goods are sufficiently high while the host country's TE for ordinary labour and international transfer efficiency for professionals are sufficiently low. Sufficient improvements in either the host country's TE for ordinary labour and international transfer efficiency for professionals and/or sufficient reduction in international TE for final gods and the home country's TE for intermediate goods would result in FDI becoming the superior structure.

The core ideas of the above three propositions can be illustrated in Figure 11.4.

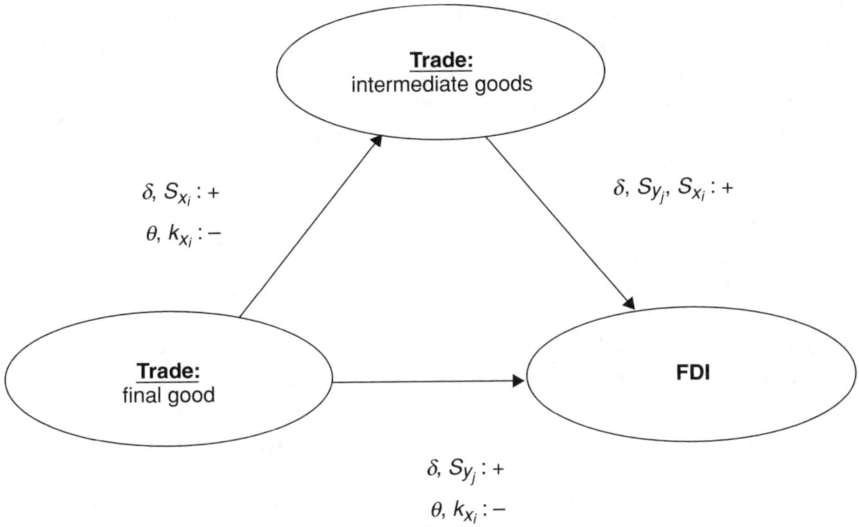

Figure 11.4 General equilibrium structure and its determining factors
Note: +: Positive impacts; –: Negative impacts
→ Direction of change of general equilibrium structure

Synthesizing Propositions 2, 3 and 4 leads to Proposition 5 about the general equilibrium structure for organizing international activities.

Proposition 5: The general equilibrium in the form of organizing international activity depends on the TE for goods relative to TE for labour within and between the two countries.

(5.1) If international transfer efficiency for professionals δ, home country's TE for professionals s_{x_i} and host country's TE for ordinary labour s_{y_j} are sufficiently low, but international TE θ and host country's TE for final goods k_{y_j} and home country's TE for intermediate goods k_{x_i} are sufficiently high, international division of labour is organized via markets for final goods and intermediate goods in the absence of FDI and MNEs.
(5.2) If international transfer efficiency and home country's TE for professionals (δ, – s_{x_i} respectively) and the host country's TE for ordinary labour s_{y_j} are sufficiently high, but home country's TE for intermediate goods k_{x_i} is sufficiently low, the international division of labour will be organized via FDI and MNEs.

From Proposition 5.2 we have the following corollary:

Corollary: *International direct investment is a method to price indirectly intangible intermediate goods in the context of the international economy by expanding* *the firm's governance boundary to the host country, so as to reduce or avoid the high transaction costs for direct pricing and marketing the goods and the high transaction costs that are caused by the low transaction efficiency for the goods. The transaction efficiency for factors other than those related to the indirect pricing in relevant countries is a critical factor for determining the volume and direction of international direct investment.*

3.2.3 Brief discussion

The advanced Walrasian general equilibrium model yields rich findings regarding the organization of FDI and other international activities.

First of all, international transaction efficiency for final goods and international transfer efficiency for professionals, more than any other factors, determine the potential of the international division of labour. This finding is consistent with the history of the international division of labour. International trade is the oldest form of the international division of labour. The emergence and development of international trade were dependent on the cross-border movement of merchants. The establishment of free trade zones as the starting point for increasing regionalization reflects the basic requirement of the international division of labour for a certain level of transaction efficiency for goods.

FDI is a form of organizing international activity and the international division of labour. Via FDI the investing firm indirectly prices intangible intermediate goods in the context of the international economy by expanding the firm's governance boundary to the host country. When other factors are given, high transaction efficiency for ordinary labour (or all factors other than the indirect pricing related ones) in the host country and high transaction and transfer efficiencies for professionals from the home country (including all factors related to the indirect pricing) encourage FDI between the two countries. The finding is especially important for explaining FDI from less developed countries to more developed countries, a phenomenon which has puzzled the academic community for many years. Following our finding, it is perhaps understandable why the United States, the world's most developed country, is also the world's largest recipient of FDI. Its free market policies and high transaction efficiency contribute to the huge inflow of FDI.

The relationships between FDI and other forms of international division of labour – for example, trade of final or intermediate goods – are neither simply complementary nor simply supplementary. As the general equilibrium structure is dependent on the specific transaction efficiencies for goods and factors within and between countries, it is meaningless to talk about which relationship should be maintained for a country without considering the prevailing transaction conditions in the relevant countries.

One of the policy implications of our findings is that a country should make its foreign economic policies in the light of its technological advantage and transaction efficiencies for goods and factors, relative to that of other countries.

For developing countries, the improvement in transaction efficiency for both professional labour and ordinary labour is crucially important in attracting FDI.

Concluding remarks

This chapter develops a Walrasian general equilibrium model to investigate the forces that drive the emergence and development of international direct investment. It yields rich findings regarding the organization of FDI and other international activities. The approach of inframarginal analysis adopted in developing this model makes it different from the mainstream theorems in the current literature of FDI. Due to various reasons so far, there is a lack of general equilibrium models in the existing theories of FDI. The awkwardness of partial equilibrium approaches and descriptions has greatly affected the expressions of some original ideas. This in turn has affected the exploration of the changing pattern of FDI in the era of globalization and the transition to a knowledge-based economy. Our model contributes originally in methodology and theory to address this ever-changing situation.

On the other hand, this model incorporates various structures ranging from individual autarky in a closed economy to those involving widespread international division of labour in an open economy. This enables current research on FDI to incorporate a wider perspective and more integrated view. We hope this could be helpful whilst incorporating some existing original ideas while reducing their limitations.

Some promising extensions of our model can be made without much difficulty in order to trace more specific relationships between selected structures for specific purposes of analysis, for example, the integrated relationships between FDI and trade and the validity of empirical studies under such a framework. In addition, this model can incorporate hybrids of structures into its analysis when a few such structures are added to the candidates of choice.

Notes

1 The specification of such iceberg transaction cost is a common practice in modelling issues involving transactions in the market (Krugman, 1995). It enables the analyses to rid of formidable index sets of destinations and origin of trade flows.

References

Andersen, P. H., Blenker, P. and Christensen, P. R. (1993) 'Generic Routes to Subcontractors' Internationalisation', paper presented at the Rent IX Conference on Entrepreneurship and SMEs in Milan, Italy, November.

Benito, G. R. G. and Gripsrup, G. 'The Internationalisation Process Approach to the Location of Foreign Direct Investments: an Empirical Analysis', in M. B. Green and R. B. McNaughton (eds), *The Location of Foreign Direct Investment: Geographic and Business Approaches* (Aldershot: Avebury)

Blomström, Magnus and Kokko, Ari (1994) 'Home Country Effects of Foreign Direct Investment: Evidence from Sweden', NBER Working Paper Series, No. 4639.

Blomström, Magnus and Kokko, Ari (1997) 'How Foreign Investment Affect Host Countries', *Policy Research Paper 1745* (Washington, DC: World Bank).

Brush, C. G. (1992) *Factors Motivating Small Companies to Internationalise: the Effect of Firm Age* (Boston: Boston University Press).

Buckley, Peter, J. (1997) 'Trends in International Business Research: the Next 25 Years', in Iyanatul Islam and William Shepherd (eds), *Current Issues in international Business* (Cheltenham: Edward Elgar).

Buckley, Peter, J. and Casson, Mark (1976) *The Future of the Multinational Enterprise* (London: Macmillan).

Casson, Mark (1979) *Alternatives to the Multinational Enterprises* (London: Macmillan).

Casson, Mark (1988) 'Recent Trends in International Business: a New Analysis', University of Reading Economics Department Discussion Paper, No. 112.

Caves, Richard E. (1996) *Multinational Enterprise and Economic Analysis* (New York and Melbourne: Cambridge University Press).

Caves, Richard E. (1998) 'Research in International Business: Problems and Prospects', *The Journal of International Business Studies*, 29(1), 5–20.

Chen, E. K. Y. and Drysdale, Peter (1995) *Corporate Links and Foreign Direct Investment in Asia and the Pacific* (Pymble: Harper Educational).

Cheung, S. N. S. (1983) 'The Contractual Nature of the Firm', *Journal of Law and Economics*, 26, 386–405.

Coase, R. H. (1937) 'The Nature of the Firm', *Economica*, 4 (November), 386–405. Reprinted in G. J. Stigler and K. Boulding (eds), *Readings in Price Theory (Homewood, IL: Irwin, 1952)*, 331–51.

Contractor, F. J. (1990) 'Contractual and Cooperative Forms of International Business: Towards a Unified Theory of Modal Choice', *Management International Review*, 30 (1).

Dunning, John H. (1977) 'Trade, Location of Economic Activity and the MNE: a Search for an Eclectic Approach', in B. Olin, P.-O. Hesselborn and P. M. Wijkman (eds), *The International Allocation of Economic Activity: Proceedings of a Nobel Symposium Held of Stockholm* (London: Macmillan), 395–418

Dunning, John H. (1997) 'The Advent of Alliance Capitalism', in John H. Dunning and Khallil A. Hamdani (eds), *The New Globalism and Developing Countries* (New York: United Nations University Press), 12–50.

Dunning, John H. and Rajneesh Narula (1996) 'The Investment Development Path Revisited: Some Emerging Issues', in John H. Dunning and Rajneesh Narula (eds), *Foreign Direct Investment and Governments: Catalysts for Economic Restructuring* (London: Routledge), 1–41.

Graham, E. M. (1978) 'Transatlantic Investment by Multinational Firms: a Rivalistic Phenomenon?', *Journal of Post-Keynesian Economics*, vol. 1.

Graham, E. M. (1997) 'The (Not Wholly Satisfactory) State of the Theory of Foreign Direct Investment and the Multinational Enterprise', in J. L. Stein (eds), *The*

Globalization of Markets: Capital Flows, Exchange Rates and Trade Regimes (Heidelberg: Physica-Verlag).

Hennart, J.-F. (1993) 'Control in Multinational Firms: the Role of Price and Hierarchy', in Sumantra Ghoshal and D. Eleanor Westney (eds), *Organisation Theory and the Multinational Corporation* (New York: St Martin's Press), 157–81.

Hirsch, S. (1976) 'An International Trade and Investment Theory of the Firm', *Oxford Economic Papers*, 28 (July, 258–69.

Kogut, Bruce (1993) 'Foreign Direct Investment as a Sequential Process', in Benjamin Gomes-Casseress and David B. Yoffice (eds), *The International Political Economy of Direct Foreign Investment* (Aldershot: Edward Elgar), 273–91. Originally in C. P. Kindleberger and D. B. Audretsch (eds), *The Multinational Corporation in the 1980s* (Cambridge, MA: MIT Press), 38–56.

Kojima, Kiyoshi (1978) *Direct Foreign Investment: a Japanese Model of Multinational Business Operations* (London: Croom Helm).

Krugman, P. (1995) *Development, Geography, and Economic Theory* (Cambridge, MA: MIT Press).

Macneil, I. R. (1974) 'The Many Futures of Contracts', *Southern California Law Review*, 47.

Markusen, James R. (1995) 'The Boundaries of Multinational Enterprises and the Theory of International Trade', *Journal of Economic Perspectives*, 9, 2.

Martinussen, John (1997) *Society, State and Market: a Guide to Competing Theories of Development* (London: Zed Books).

Mundell, R. A. (1957) 'International Trade and Factor Mobility', *American Economic Review*, 47, 3.

Narula, Rajneesh (1996) *Multinational Investment and Economic Structure* (London: Routledge).

Riemens, P. J. H. (1989) *On the Foreign Operations of Third World Firms* (Amsterdam: Koninklijk Nederlands Aardrijkskundig Genootschap, Insituut voor Sociale Geografie, Faculteit Ruimtelijke Wetenschappen, Universiteit van Amsterdam).

Smith, Adam (1776) *An Inquiry into the Nature and Causes of the Wealth of Nations* (Reprinted: Chicago: University of Chicago Press, 1976).

Sun, Guang-Zhen (1999) 'Increasing Returns, Roundabout Production and Urbanization: A General Equilibrium Analysis of the Division of Labour', PhD Dissertation, Department of Economics, Monash University.

Teece, David (1981) 'The Multinational Enterprise, Market Failure and Market Power Consideration', *Sloan Management Review*, Spring.

Teece, David (1985) 'Multinational Enterprise, Internal Governance and Industrial Organization', *American Economic Review*, 75 2, 233–7.

Tolentino, P. E. (1993) *Technological Innovation and Third World Multinationals* (London: Routledge).

UNCTAD (1999) *World Investment Report* (New York and Geneva: United Nations).

Vernon, Raymond (1966) 'International Investment and International Trade in the Product Cycle', *Quarterly Journal of Economics*, 80.

Wen, Mei (1997) 'Division of Labour in Economic Development', PhD Dissertation, Department of Economics, Monash University.

Williamson, Oliver E. (1975) *Markets and Hierarchies: Analysis and Anti-trust Implications* (New York: Free Press)

Williamson Oliver E. (1985) *The Economic Institutions of Capitalism* (New York: Free Press).

Yang, Xiaokai (2001) *Economics: New Classical versus Neoclassical Frameworks* (Cambridge, MA: Blackwell Publishers).

Yang, Xiaokai and Ng, Yew-Kwang (1993) *Specialization and Economic Organization: a New Classical Microeconomic Framework* (Amsterdam: North-Holland).
Yang, Xiaokai and Ng, Yew-Kwang (1995) 'Theory of the Firm and Structure of Residual Rights', *Journal of Economic Behavior and Organization*, 26, 107–28.
Young, Allyn (1928) 'Increasing Returns and Economic Progress', *The Economic Journal* 38, 152, 275–42.

Appendix: parameters partitioning space

	Parameters for country i	*Conditions*		*Parameters for country* i	*Conditions*
V_{i1}	$k_{y_j} = s_{y_j}\left(\frac{\delta - b_{x_i}}{\delta s_{x_i} - b_{x_i}}\right)^a$	$U_{FL} = U_{MSi}$	V_{j1}	$k_{y_j} = \frac{1}{s_{y_j}}\left(\frac{\delta s_{x_i} - b_{x_i}}{\delta - b_{x_i}}\right)^a$	$U_{FL} = U_{MSj}$
V_{i2}	$k_{y_j} = s_{y_j}\left[\frac{\delta - b_{x_i}}{\theta k_{x_i}(1 - b_{x_i})}\right]^a$	$U_{SIi} = U_{MSi}$	V_{j2}	$k_{y_j} = \frac{1}{s_{y_j}}\left[\frac{\theta k_{x_i}(1 - b_{x_i})}{\delta - b_{x_i}}\right]^a$	$U_{SIj} = U_{MSj}$
V_{i3}	$k_{x_i} = \frac{\delta s_{x_i} - b_{x_i}}{\theta(1 - b_{x_i})}$	$U_{SIi} = U_{FLi}$	V_{j3}	$k_{x_i} = \frac{\delta s_{x_i} - b_{x_i}}{\theta(1 - b_{x_i})}$	$U_{SIj} = U_{FLj}$
V_{i4}	$k_{y_i} = \left(\frac{a}{1-a}\frac{M_j}{M_i}\right)\left(\frac{\theta s_{y_j}}{s_{y_i}}\right)^{\frac{1}{1-a}}\left(\frac{\delta - b_{x_i}}{1 - b_{x_i}}\right)^{\frac{a}{1-a}}$	$U_{FXi} = U_{MSi}$	V_{j4}	$k_{y_j} = \frac{a}{1-a}\frac{M_j}{M_i}\frac{1 - b_{x_j}}{\delta - b_{x_i}}$	$U_{FXj} = U_{MSj}$
V_{i5}	$k_{y_i} = \left(\frac{a}{1-a}\frac{M_j}{M_i}\right)\left(\frac{\theta k_{y_j}}{s_{y_i}}\right)^{\frac{1}{1-a}}\left(\frac{\delta s_{x_i} - b_{x_i}}{1 - b_{x_i}}\right)^{\frac{a}{1-a}}$	$U_{FXi} = U_{FLi}$	V_{j5}	$k_{y_j} = \left[\frac{1-a}{a}\frac{M_i}{M_j}\frac{\delta s_{x_i} - bx_i}{1 - b_{x_j}}\right]^{\frac{a}{1-a}} s_{y_j}^{\frac{1}{a-1}}$	$U_{FXj} = U_{FLj}$
V_{i6}	$k_{y_i} = \frac{a}{1-a}\frac{M_j}{M_i}\theta^{\frac{1+a}{1-a}} k_{x_i}^{\frac{a}{1-a}} k_{y_j}^{\frac{1}{1-a}}$	$U_{FXi} = U_{SIi}$	V_{j6}	$k_{y_j} = \left[\frac{1-a}{a}\frac{M_i}{M_j}\frac{\theta k_{x_i}(1 - b_{x_i})}{1 - b_{x_j}}\right]^{\frac{a}{1-a}} s_{y_j}^{\frac{1}{a-1}}$	$U_{FXj} = U_{SIj}$
V_{i7}	$k_{y_i} = \left(\frac{a}{1-a}\frac{M_j}{M_i}\right)^{\frac{1-a}{a}}(\theta s_{y_j})^{\frac{1}{a}}\frac{\delta - b_{x_i}}{k_{x_i}(1 - b_{x_i})}$	$U_{SDi} = U_{MSi}$	V_{j7}	$k_{y_j} = \left[\frac{1-a}{a}\frac{M_i}{M_j}\frac{\delta - b_{x_i}}{(1 - b_{x_j})k_{y_j}}\right]^{\frac{a}{a-1}} s_{y_j}^{\frac{1}{a-1}}$	$U_{SDj} = U_{MSj}$
V_{i8}	$k_{y_i} = \left(\frac{a}{1-a}\frac{M_j}{M_i}\right)^{\frac{1-a}{a}}(\theta k_{y_j})^{\frac{1}{a}}\frac{\delta s_{x_i} - b_{x_i}}{k_{x_i}(1 - b_{x_i})}$	$U_{SDi} = U_{FL_i}$	V_{j8}	$k_{y_j} = \frac{1-a}{a}\frac{M_i}{M_j}\frac{\delta s_{x_j} - b_{x_i}}{k_{x_j}(1 - b_{x_j})}$	$U_{SDj} = U_{FLj}$

	Parameters for country i	*Conditions*		*Parameters for country* i	*Conditions*
V_{i9}	$k_{y_i} = \left(\frac{a}{1-a}\frac{M_j}{M_i}\right)^{\frac{1-a}{a}} \theta^{\frac{1+a}{a}} k_{y_j}^{\frac{1}{a}}$	$U_{SDi} = U_{SIi}$	V_{j9}	$k_{y_j} = \frac{1-a}{a}\frac{M_i}{M_j}\frac{\theta k_{x_i}(1-b_{x_i})}{k_{x_j}(1-b_{x_j})}$	$U_{SDj} = U_{SIj}$
V_{i10}	$k_{y_i} = \left(\frac{s_{y_i}}{k_{x_i}^{a}}\right)^{\frac{1}{2a-1}}$	$U_{SDi} = U_{FXi}$	V_{j10}	$k_{y_j} = \left(\frac{s_{y_j}}{k_{x_j}^{a}}\right)^{\frac{1}{2a-1}}$	$U_{SDj} = U_{FXj}$
V_{i11}	$k_{y_i} = \left[\left(\frac{a}{1-a}\right)\frac{M_j}{M_i}\right]^{\frac{1-a}{a}} (\theta s_{y_j})^{\frac{1}{a}} \frac{\delta - b_{x_i}}{s_{x_i} - b_{x_i}}$	$U_{FYi} = U_{MSi}$	V_{j11}	$k_{y_j} = \left[\frac{1-a}{a}\frac{M_i}{M_j}\frac{\delta - b_{x_i}}{s_{x_j} - b_{x_j}}\right]^{\frac{a}{a-1}} s_{y_j}^{\frac{1}{a-1}}$	$U_{FYj} = U_{MSj}$
V_{i12}	$k_{y_i} = \left[\left(\frac{a}{1-a}\right)\frac{M_j}{M_i}\right]^{\frac{1-a}{a}} (\theta k_{y_j})^{\frac{1}{a}} \frac{\delta s_{x_i} - b_{x_i}}{s_{x_i} - b_{x_i}}$	$U_{FYi} = U_{FLi}$	V_{j12}	$k_{y_j} = \frac{1-a}{a}\frac{M_i}{M_j}\frac{\delta(s_{x_i} - b_{x_i})}{s_{x_j} - b_{x_j}}$	$U_{FYj} = U_{FLj}$
V_{i13}	$k_{y_i} = \left(\frac{a}{1-a}\frac{M_j}{M_i}\right)^{\frac{1-a}{a}} \theta^{\frac{1+a}{a}} k_{y_j}^{\frac{1}{a}} \frac{k_{x_i}(1-b_{x_i})}{s_{x_i} - b_{x_i}}$	$U_{FYi} = U_{SIi}$	V_{j13}	$k_{y_j} = \frac{1-a}{a}\frac{M_i}{M_j}\frac{\theta k_{x_i}(1-b_{x_i})}{s_{x_j} - b_{b_j}}$	$U_{FYj} = U_{SIj}$
V_{i14}	$k_{y_i} = s_{y_i}^{\frac{1}{2a-1}} \left(\frac{1-b_{x_i}}{s_{x_i} - b_{x_i}}\right)^{\frac{a}{2a-1}}$	$U_{FYi} = U_{FXi}$	V_{j14}	$k_{y_j} = s_{y_j}^{\frac{1}{2a-1}} \left(\frac{1-b_{x_j}}{s_{x_j} - b_{x_j}}\right)^{\frac{a}{2a-1}}$	$U_{FXj} = U_{FYj}$
r_i	$k_{x_i} = \frac{s_{x_i} - b_{x_i}}{1-b_{x_i}}$	$U_{SDi} = U_{FYi}$	r_j	$k_{x_j} = \frac{s_{x_j} - b_{x_j}}{1-b_{x_j}}$	$U_{SDj} = U_{FYj}$
V_{ia}	$\frac{M_j}{M_i} = \frac{(1-b_{x_i})^{\frac{1+a}{1-a}}}{a(1+a)^{\frac{1+a}{1-a}} (\theta s_{y_j})^{\frac{1}{1-a}} (\delta - b_{x_i})^{\frac{a}{1-a}}}$	$U_{Ai} = U_{MSi}$	V_{ja}	$\frac{M_i}{M_j} = \frac{a}{(\delta - b_{x_i})[(1-a)k_{y_j}s_{y_j}]^{\frac{1}{a}}} \left(\frac{1-b_{x_i}}{1+a}\right)^{\frac{1+a}{a}}$	$U_{Aj} = U_{MSj}$

	Parameters for country i	*Conditions*		*Parameters for country* i	*Conditions*
V_{ib}	$\frac{M_j}{M_i}=\frac{1}{a\left(\theta k_{y_j}\right)^{\frac{1}{1-a}}(1+a)^{\frac{1+a}{1-a}}}\left[\frac{\left(1-b_{x_i}\right)^{1+a}}{\left(\delta s_{x_i}-b_{x_i}\right)^{a}}\right]^{\frac{1}{1-a}}$	$U_{Ai}=U_{FLi}$	V_{jb}	$\frac{M_i}{M_j}=\frac{a}{(1-a)^{\frac{1}{a}}\left(\delta s_{x_i}-b_{x_i}\right)}\left(\frac{1-b_{x_j}}{1+a}\right)^{\frac{1+a}{a}}$	$U_{Aj}=U_{FLj}$
V_{ic}	$k_{y_i}=\frac{(1+a)^{\frac{a+1}{a-1}}}{1-a}\left(\frac{1-b_{x_i}}{s_{y_i}}\right)^{\frac{1}{1-a}}$	$U_{Ai}=U_{FXi}$	V_{jc}	$k_{y_j}=\frac{(1+a)^{\frac{a+1}{a-1}}}{1-a}\left(\frac{1-b_{x_j}}{s_{y_j}}\right)^{\frac{1}{1-a}}$	$U_{Aj}=U_{FXj}$
V_{id}	$k_{y_i}=\left[\frac{1}{(1+a)^{1+a}(1-a)^{1-a}}\right]^{\frac{1}{a}}\frac{\left(1-b_{x_i}\right)^{\frac{1+a}{a}}}{\left(s_{x_i}-b_{x_i}\right)}$	$U_{Ai}=U_{FYi}$	V_{jd}	$k_{y_j}=\left[\frac{1}{(1+a)^{1+a}(1-a)^{1-a}}\right]^{\frac{1}{a}}\frac{\left(1-b_{x_j}\right)^{\frac{1+a}{a}}}{\left(s_{x_j}-b_{x_j}\right)}$	$U_{Aj}=U_{FYj}$
V_{ie}	$k_{y_i}=\frac{1}{k_{x_i}}\left[\frac{1-b_{x_i}}{(1+a)^{1+a}(1-a)^{1-a}}\right]^{\frac{1}{a}}$	$U_{Ai}=U_{SDi}$	V_{je}	$k_{y_j}=\frac{1}{k_{x_j}}\left[\frac{1-b_{x_j}}{(1+a)^{1+a}(1-a)^{1-a}}\right]^{\frac{1}{a}}$	$U_{Aj}=U_{SDj}$
V_{if}	$\frac{M_j}{M_i}=\frac{1}{a}\left[\frac{1}{\theta(1+a)}\right]^{\frac{1+a}{1-a}}\left(\frac{1-b_{x_i}}{k_{x_i}{}^{a}k_{y_j}}\right)^{\frac{1}{1-a}}$	$U_{Ai}=U_{SIi}$	V_{jf}	$\frac{M_i}{M_j}=\left[\frac{1}{(1-a)(1+a)^{1+a}}\right]^{\frac{1}{a}}\frac{a\left(1-b_{x_j}\right)^{\frac{1+a}{a}}}{\theta k_{x_i}\left(1-b_{x_i}\right)}$	$U_{Aj}=U_{SIj}$

12

The Division of Labour and the Allocation of Time

*Monchi Lio**

1 Introduction

Compared to a typical family several decades ago, a contemporary family spends significantly less time on work, has more time for leisure, and consumes a wider variety of goods and services of better quality and in larger quantities. Most conventional theories explaining this phenomenon emphasize that improvements in technology and the accumulation of capital are the most important factors for this prominent feature in economic development. In this chapter, we will provide a supplemental explanation by focusing on how changes in economic organization affect time allocation and productivity, with special attention being paid to the extent of the market and the level of division of labour.

According to Gronau's (1977) trichotomy, a typical family allocates its time between work in the market, work at home, and leisure. Compared to its counterpart several decades ago, a modern family not only uses more advanced techniques and employs more capital in production, but it also engages in a far more sophisticated network of division of labour. A much higher level of division of labour greatly increases the modern family's level of specialization, and enables it to exploit economies of specialization by increasing returns. As Locay (1990) and Reynolds (1983) have pointed out, an important characteristic of economic development is how changes in the level of division of labour would shift production as well as time spent on production from self-sufficient activities to market activities. Therefore, both productivity and the allocation of time should have a strong correlation with the extent of the market and the level of division of labour.

This correlation is supported by recent empirical findings. First, Juster and Stafford (1991) report that more time spent on market work and higher wages are strongly associated with more 'meals out', which imply a higher level of division of labour. Secondly, according to the data provided by

* Corresponding Address: Department of Political Economy, National Sun Yat-Sen University, 70 Lien-hai Rd. Kaohsiung 804, Taiwan. E-mail: mclio@mail.nsysu.edu.tw.

Juster and Stafford (1991, p. 477), in both the US and Norway, women's total work time and housework time decline as their market work time and leisure rise significantly between 1965 and the 1980s, as shown in Table 12.1.

To investigate how improvement in transaction efficiency affects the level of division of labour and the allocation of time, this chapter formulates a model with transaction costs and endogenous specialization. In this model there are increasing returns due to learning costs, thus *ex ante* identical households can enhance productivity significantly by specialization through a division of labour associated with the extension of the market. The extent of the market and the level of division of labour, however, are limited by transaction costs. The optimal level of division of labour is thus determined by the tradeoff between transaction costs and economies of specialization.

A household allocates a part of their time to self-sufficient activities if, at some point, transaction costs outweigh the benefit from specialization. As transaction efficiency is improved, the level of division of labour increases and the household purchases some previously self-provided goods in the extended market, at the same time reallocating time from the production of these self-provided goods and services to other production and consumption activities. The increase in productivity and reduction of time spent on the production of a given set of goods explain the concurrent increase in the variety of available goods, the amount of each good consumed, and the time spent on leisure observed in economic development. Therefore, our model simultaneously endogenizes consumption variety and time allocation, and demonstrates that consumption variety and leisure concurrently increase with transaction efficiency.

An interesting question to ask about time allocation is how changes in people's desire for leisure would affect productivity. According to

Table 12.1 Changes in Time Allocation of Females in US and Norway, 1965–1980s[1] (Hours per Week)

	US			*Norway*		
Activity	*1965*	*1981*	*Changes*	*1971*	*1980*	*Changes*
(1) Total work	60.9	54.4	–6.5	54.6	50.6	–4.0
(2) Market work	18.9	23.9	+5.0	13.3	17.6	+4.3
(3) Housework	41.8	30.5	–11.3	41.3	33.0	–8.3
(4) Leisure	35.4	41.9	+6.5	39.2	45.2	+6.0
(5) Personal care	71.9	71.6	–0.3	74.2	72.1	–2.1
Total = (1) + (4) + (5)	168.0	168.0	–0.3	168.0	168.0	–0.1

Source: Juster and Stafford (1991, p. 477, Table 3).[2]
Note: (1) = (2) + (3).

conventional wisdom, a stronger desire for leisure negatively affects productivity. It is argued by Buchanan (1994) that since labour supply limits the level of division of labour, productivity must necessarily be hurt by a stronger desire for time-intensive consumption, which negatively affects labour supply. This chapter investigates how the desire for time-intensive consumption affects productivity. Somewhat surprisingly, the results show that the effects are not necessarily negative.

In Section 2 of this chapter, our model is specified and the general equilibrium is solved. Section 3 discusses the comparative statics from the model and the economic implications arising. In Section 4 the conclusion of our investigation will be delivered.

2 The model

Consider an economy with M *ex ante* identical consumer-producer households and m goods or services. Following Gronau (1977), it is assumed that the goods can be either purchased in the market or self-provided. For a household, the self-provided quantity of good i is x_i. The quantity of good i sold in the market is x_i^s. The quantity of good i purchased in the market is x_i^d. The transaction cost coefficient is $1 - k$ for each unit of good i purchased, and thus only kx_i^d is received from purchasing x_i^d, and the total quantity of good i consumed is $x_i + kx_i^d$. Following Becker (1965), it is assumed that the household combines time and goods to produce 'basic goods' that enter its utility function directly. A basic good i is denoted as Z_i. It is further assumed that the quantity of Z_i is determined by the quantity of good i consumed, and the time spent on consuming good i given by

$$Z_i = (x_i + kx_i^d)t_i^\beta \tag{12.1}$$

where t_i is the time spent on consuming good i. The basic good can be viewed as a final product, and it is produced by a Cobb–Douglas production function which characterizes the 'consumption technology' with good i and time t_i as inputs. Term β represents the degree of time-intensity in producing this basic good, with higher β denoting a stronger desire for time-intensive consumption.

Following Yang and Shi (1992), it is assumed that the more basic goods a household consumes, the greater the utility cost of calculating optimal consumption, production, and trade becomes. Suppose that c is the cost coefficient for a household to manage one basic good, and cm is a proportion of utility that is lost due to the management of m basic goods. The utility of a household is given by the CES utility function

$$u = (1 - cm)V,\ V = (\sum_{i=1}^{m} Z_i^{-\rho})^{-1/\rho},\ c \in (0,1),\ \rho \in (-1,0) \tag{12.2}$$

where *cm* represents the total management cost of consumption variety, and V represents the preference for diverse consumption. Note that V increases monotonically with the number of basic goods. The elasticity of substitution between input varieties is $1/(1 + \rho)$. The degree of economies of complementarity between each pair of basic goods is represented by $-1/\rho$.

The production functions and endowment constraints for a household are further given by

$$x_i + x_i^s = l_i - \alpha, \ \alpha \in (0,1) \tag{12.3}$$
$$\sum_{i=1}^{m}(l_i + t_i) = 1, \ \ l_i \in [0,1), \ \ t_i \in (0,1), \ \ i$$

where $x_i + x_i^s$ is the output level of good i. Term l_i is the time spent on producing good i and represents the household's level of specialization in producing this good, while α is a fixed learning or training cost coefficient and represents the degree of economies of specialization.[3] Term $\sum_{i=1}^{m} l_i$ is the total time a household spends on work, and $\sum_{i=1}^{m} t_i$ is the total time spent on consumption.

This system of production characterizes economies of specialization since the productivity increases with the level of specialization. Note that in our model economies of specialization are household-specific, and thus increasing returns are localized. Three tradeoffs have been formalized within this model: the tradeoff between the time allocated on market and non-market production activities and the time spent on consumption activities, following Becker (1965) and Gronau (1977); the tradeoff between economies of specialization and economies of complementarity, following the Dixit–Stiglitz model (1977); and the tradeoff between economies of specialization and transaction costs, which is the basic feature of the Yang–Shi model (1992).

The budget constraint is given by

$$\sum_{i=1}^{m}(p_i x_i^s) = \sum_{i=1}^{m}(p_i x_i^d) \tag{12.4}$$

where p_i is the price of good i.

As in Yang and Shi (1992), a Walrasian regime or a multilateral bargaining game is assumed. The following lemma has been established by Yang and Shi (1992) and Wen (1998):

LEMMA 1. *According to Kuhn–Tucker conditions, for a household's optimum decision, a household sells at most one good. It does not buy and sell the same good, neither does it buy and self-provide the same good.*

With Lemma 1, we may specify the decision problem for a household selling good i as

$$\text{Max:}\quad u_i = (1-cm)[(x_i t_i^{\beta})^{-\rho} + \sum_{r\in R} (kx_r^d t_r^{\beta})^{-\rho} + \sum_{j\in J} (x_j t_j^{\beta})^{-\rho}]^{-1/\rho} \tag{12.5}$$

$$\begin{aligned} \text{s.t}\quad & x_i + x_i^s = \max\{l_i - \alpha, 0\} \\ & x_j = \max\{l_j - \alpha, 0\}, \quad \forall j \in J \qquad \text{(production function)} \\ & l_i + \sum_{j\in J} l_j + t_i + \sum_{r\in R} t_r + \sum_{j\in J} t_j = \qquad \text{(endowment constraint)} \\ & p_i x_i^s = \sum_{r\in R} (p_r x_r^d) \qquad \text{(budget constraint)} \end{aligned}$$

where u_i is the utility of a household selling good i. Term R is the set of goods the household purchases in the market and consists of $n-1$ elements. Term J is the set of goods the household self-provides at home and consists of $m-n$ elements, and n is the number of goods traded by the household.

Decision variables for this maximization problem are l_i, l_j, t_i, t_j, t_r, x_i, x_i^s, x_r, x_r^d, n, and m, where $n \in (1, m)$ and $m \in (1, \infty)$. The first-order conditions yield the optimal l_i, l_j, t_i, t_j, t_r, x_i, x_r^s, x_r, x_r^d, n, and m as functions of relative prices. The optimal x_i^s and x_r^d are a household's demand and supply, respectively, of good i. Inserting the optimal decision variables into u_i yields the indirect utility function.

The $n-1$ utility equalization conditions for the $n-1$ types of households selling different goods determine the $n-1$ relative prices of n traded goods. The $n-1$ market-clearing conditions determine the $n-1$ relative numbers of households selling n traded goods. The relative prices and the relative numbers of households selling different goods are given by

$$p_i/p = 1, \quad M_i/M_r = 1 \tag{12.6}$$

where M_s is the number of households selling good S, $s = i, r$. The other market-clearing condition is not independent of (12.6) due to Walras' Law.

Inserting the equilibrium relative prices into the first-order conditions yields the equilibrium values for all decision variables, given by

$$\begin{aligned} \beta x_i = \beta x_j = t_i = t_j &= \beta[1-\alpha(m-n+1)]/ \\ &\quad \{(1+\beta)[K(n-1)+m-n+1]\} \\ &= -\rho\alpha\beta/[(1-K)(1+(1+\beta)\rho)], \quad \forall j \in J, \quad i = 1, \ldots, n \\ \beta x_r^d = t_r &= \beta K[1-\alpha(m-n+1)]/\{(1+\beta)[K(n-1)+m-n+1]\} \\ &= -\rho\alpha\beta K/\{(1-K)[1+(1+\beta)\rho]\} \\ x_i^s &= (n-1)x_r^d, \quad \forall r \in R, \quad i = 1, \ldots, n \end{aligned} \tag{12.7}$$

$$\begin{aligned} l_i &= \{-\rho\alpha[1+K(n-1)]/\{(1-K)[1+(1+\beta)\rho]\}\} + \alpha, \quad i = 1, \ldots, n \\ l_j &= \{-\rho\alpha/\{(1-K)[1+(1+\beta)\rho]\}\} + \alpha, \quad \forall j \in J \end{aligned} \tag{12.8}$$

$$
\begin{aligned}
m &= [\rho(1 - K)/(\alpha K) + 1/c]/(1 - \rho) \qquad (12.9)\\
n &= \{1 - K[1 + (1 + \beta)\rho]\}m/(1 - K)\} - [1 + (1 + \beta)\rho]/\alpha + 1\\
&= 1 + [1/(1 - \rho)]\{\rho/(K\alpha) + \{1 - K[1 + (1 + \beta)\rho]\}/[c(1 - K)]\}\\
&\quad - [1 + (1 + \beta)\rho]/\alpha
\end{aligned}
$$

$$
\begin{aligned}
u &= \beta^{\beta} (1 + \beta)^{-(1 + \beta)} (1 - cm) \qquad (12.10)\\
&[1 - \alpha(m - n + 1)]^{1 + \beta} [K(n - 1) + (m - n + 1)]^{-[1 + (1 + \beta)\rho]/\rho}\\
&= \beta^{\beta} (- \rho)^{2 + \beta} (1 - \rho)^{(1 - \rho)/\rho} \alpha^{(1 + \beta\rho)/\rho} c^{1/\rho} K^{-1} (1 - K)^{-(1 + \beta)}\\
&[c(1 - K) + \alpha K]^{1 - 1/\rho} [1 + (1 + \beta)\rho]^{-[1 + (1 + \beta)\rho]/\rho}
\end{aligned}
$$

where $K = k^{-\rho/[1 + (1 + \beta)\rho]}$. Note that $-1/\rho > 1 + \beta$ is necessary for the number of goods to be positive, since $\partial u/\partial m < 0$ if $-1/\rho < 1 + \beta$ holds. This means that economies of complementarity must be sufficiently large. The second-order conditions for the maximum point of n and m to be interior are also satisfied if $-1/\rho > 1 + \beta$. Due to symmetry, the optimal values of m, n, and other decision variables are the same for all households. Therefore n is not only a household's number of traded goods but also the number of traded goods in the whole economy. This implies that the value of n can be used to represent the level of division of labour.

3 Comparative statics and related economic implications

Given $-1/\rho > 1 + \beta$, comparative statics of our model are given by

$$
\begin{aligned}
&dn/dk > 0, \quad dn/dc < 0, \quad dn/d\alpha > 0, \quad dm/dk > 0, \qquad (12.11)\\
&dm/dc < 0, \quad dm/d\alpha > 0,\\
&d(m - n)/dk < 0, \quad d[(m - n)/m]/dk < 0
\end{aligned}
$$

$$
\begin{aligned}
&dx_i^s/dk > 0, \quad dx_i^s/d\alpha > 0, \quad dx_r^d/dk > 0, \quad dx_r^d/d\alpha > 0, \qquad (12.12)\\
&d(Mx_i^s)/dk = d[M\,(n - 1)x_r^d]/dk > 0
\end{aligned}
$$

$$
\begin{aligned}
&dt_s/dk > 0, \quad dt_s/d\alpha > 0, \quad s = i, j, r, \qquad (12.13)\\
&dl_i/dk > 0, \quad dl_i/d\alpha > 0,\\
&d(m - n)l_j/dk < 0, \quad d(m - n)l_j/d\alpha < 0
\end{aligned}
$$

where n is the number of traded goods and represents the level of division of labour. Term m is the number of all goods produced and consumed in this economy, which represents the degree of diversity of goods. Term $m - n$ is the number of self-provided goods, and $(m - n)/m$ represents the degree of self-sufficiency. Note that an interior solution of n is greater than 1, and no goods are traded at the corner solution if n is equal to unity. Term k is the transaction efficiency coefficient, c is the variety management cost coefficient, $1/c$ is the efficiency in managing a variety of goods, and α is the degree of economies of specialization. Term x_i^s is the per-household value of production sold in the market and is equal to per-household total demand for all traded goods, $(n-1)x_r^d$. Term Mx_i^s is the equilibrium aggregate supply and is equal to the equilibrium aggregate demand, which can be defined as the extent of the market. Term l_i is the time spent on producing the traded good, which represents the level of specialization and the degree of commercialization. Term l_j is the time spent on producing non-traded good j, $\forall j \in J$. Term t_s is the time spent on consuming good s, $s = i, j, r, r \in R$.

Defining L as the total time spent on producing goods and services and H as the total time spent on consumption activities or leisure, we have

$$H = \sum_{s=1}^{m} t_s = [-\rho/(1-\rho)]\{1+\alpha K/[c(1-K)]\} \tag{12.14}$$

$$L = 1 - H = l_i + \sum_{j \in J} l_j$$

The comparative statics of H and L are

$$dH/dk > 0, \quad dH/dc < 0, \quad dH/d\alpha > 0, \qquad (12.15)$$
$$dL/dk < 0, \quad dL/dc > 0, \quad dL/d\alpha < 0.$$

From equations (12.11) to (12.15) we derive the following propositions:

PROPOSITION 1. *The number of traded goods, the extent of the market, and the level of division of labour increase as transaction efficiency is improved, or as the degree of economies of specialization increases. The degree of self-sufficiency decreases as transaction efficiency is improved.*

PROPOSITION 2. *For each household, the time spent on producing the traded good, the level of specialization, the time spent on each consumption activity, the time spent on all consumption activities, the number of goods consumed, the labour productivity, and real income concurrently increase with improvement in transaction efficiency. The time spent on producing non-traded goods and the time spent on all production activities decrease as transaction efficiency is improved.*

PROPOSITION 3. *For each household, the number of traded goods, the time spent on producing the traded good, and the time spent on consumption activities increase as the degree of economies of specialization increases. The time spent on producing non-traded goods and the time spent on production activities both decrease as the degree of economies of specialization decreases.*

PROPOSITION 4. *An increase in the household's management efficiency of consumption variety would increase the number of all available goods, the number of traded goods, the time spent on each consumption activity, and the time spent on all consumption activities.*

The four propositions predict that the time spent on leisure and the time spent on work for the market increases simultaneously, while the time spent on total work and the time spent on housework decreases simultaneously, as an economy develops through the extension of the network of division of labour. This predication is consistent with the changes in females' time allocation in the US and Norway between 1965 and the 1980s, as shown in Table 12.1.

The propositions also explain the average time use of Israeli married women, shown in Table 12.2. Here the time spent on leisure and the time spent on work for the market increase simultaneously as the years of schooling increase, and the time spent on total work and the time spent on housework decrease simultaneously as years of schooling increase. There are two ways to interpret this data. Firstly, more years of schooling represent higher fixed learning investments and related higher degrees of economies of specialization. According to Proposition 3, when the degree of economies of specialization increases, the time spent on leisure and the time spent on work for the market both increase, and the time spent on total work and the time spent on housework both decrease. Secondly, it is reasonable to assume that transaction efficiency improves with higher education levels. According to Proposition 2, when transaction efficiency is improved, the time spent on leisure and the time spent on work for the market both increase, and the time spent on total work and the time spent on housework both decrease.

The supply of labour

We have shown that the improvement in transaction efficiency shifts time from non-market production activities to market production activities.

Table 12.2 Average time use of Israeli Married Women (1968) (hours per day)

	Years of schooling			*Changes (hours)*		
Activities	(1) 0–8	(2) 9–12	(3) 13+	(2)–(1)	(3)–(2)	(3)–(1)
a. Total work	8.15	7.55	7.32	–0.60	–0.23	–0.83
b. Work at home	6.94	5.84	4.75	–1.10	–1.09	–2.19
c. Market work	1.21	1.71	2.57	+0.50	+0.86	+1.36
d. Leisure	5.10	5.78	6.08	+0.68	+0.30	+0.98
e. Physiological needs	10.21	10.04	10.06	–0.17	+0.02	–0.15

Note: a = b + c, a + d + e = 24 (the latter may not always be satisfied because of missing data).
Source: Gronau (1977, p. 1103, Table 2).

Therefore, an improvement in transaction efficiency increases the labour supply for the market. In other words, our model treats the topic of labour supply according to the classic concept of Young (1928): demand and supply are two sides of the division of labour.

Our model explains the empirical finding reported by Juster and Stafford (1991) that the increase in time spent on market work, the higher wages, and the rising share of total female work time in the labour market are strongly associated with 'meals out'. Improvements in the transaction efficiency of dining services motivate households to substitute meals at home with meals out. Some households, therefore, will specialize in providing meals, while other households take the food service from the market and thereby save time for other production activities and for leisure. The increase in the time spent on market work will increase the level of specialization and thus increase the labour productivity, which implies higher wages. Since women provide the major part of housework, the substitution of meals out for preparing food at home will strongly coincide with the rising share of total female work time in the labour market.

An important implication of our model is the tax effect on labour supply. Aside from the negative effect of tax on the marginal wage rate and income, our model suggests that the negative correlation between tax and transaction efficiency should be noted, since this would generate negative impact on the extent of the market and thus on the supply of labour for market work.[4] Our model also suggests that a high level of self-sufficiency is related to low transaction efficiency. Considering the high tax rates in Sweden in 1984, it is therefore hardly surprising that Swedish men are the leader in home improvement time, averaging over four hours per week in 1984, compared to 2.8 hours in the US and less than one hour in Japan.[5]

According to (12.11), the number of traded goods eventually reaches the number of all goods if transaction efficiency is sufficiently improved, because $d(m - n)/dk < 0$. If n reaches m, the comparative statics of n and m in (12.11) are no longer relevant. Letting $m = n$, $l_j = x_j = t_{ij} = 0$ and solving the general equilibrium for a complete division of labour yields

$$m = n = \{\rho(1 - K)/K + [1 + (1 + \beta)\rho]/c\}/(1 + \beta\rho), \quad (12.16)$$
$$dm/dk > 0, \quad dm/dc < 0$$

$$x_i = (1 - \alpha)/\{(1 + \beta)[1 + K(m - 1)]\}, \quad x_r^d = Kx_j \quad (12.17a)$$
$$t_i = \beta x_i, \; t_r = \beta K x_i$$

$$l_i = (1 + \alpha\beta)/(1 + \beta), \quad dl_i/d\alpha > 0, \quad dl_i/d\beta < 0 \quad (12.17b)$$

where the labour supply is a constant if the economy eventually reaches a complete division of labour. Although there is no labour market in our model, we can take the average wage rate as the value of goods a household receives from the market through an hour's work at producing the traded good. Denote w as the average wage rate. It can be shown that $w \approx k(n - 1)x_r^d/l_i \approx k(l_i - \alpha)/l_i$ given a sufficiently large n and $(n - 1)x_r^d = x_i^s >> x_i$. The wage rate w is a monotonically increasing function of l_i because of increasing returns. The relationship between the wage rate and labour supply is depicted in Figure 12.1. The wage rate and labour supply concurrently increase as the division of labour evolves. As soon as the economy reaches the complete division of labour, the labour supply will be a constant. Therefore, the supply of labour for the market will be rigid if the economy has exhausted the potential for further specialization and higher levels of division of labour.

The concurrent increases in leisure and consumption variety

According to Proposition 3, an increase in the level of division of labour is associated with an increasing leisure and consumption variety. An increase in consumption variety creates a new demand for time spent on consuming new goods, which can be satisfied only by decreasing the total work time. But producing a greater variety of goods creates a new demand for work time spent on producing the new goods. Since there is no exogenous technical progress in our model, only a higher level of specialization that shrinks the number of self-sufficient activities to exploit increasing returns can simultaneously provide the necessarily high productivity and satisfy the new demands for time spent on leisure and on producing new goods.

Figure 12.2 provides an intuitive illustration of how the division of labour may evolve. The lines in each panel of Figure 12.2 represent the flow of goods, with the arrows indicating the direction of flow. The numbers beside the lines denote the goods involved. A circle with the letter i represents a person selling good i.

Panel (a) represents autarky, in which each household self-provides three goods because of low transaction efficiency. As transaction efficiency improves slightly, the economy evolves to the state depicted in panel (b), in which each household sells one good, buys one good, trades two goods,

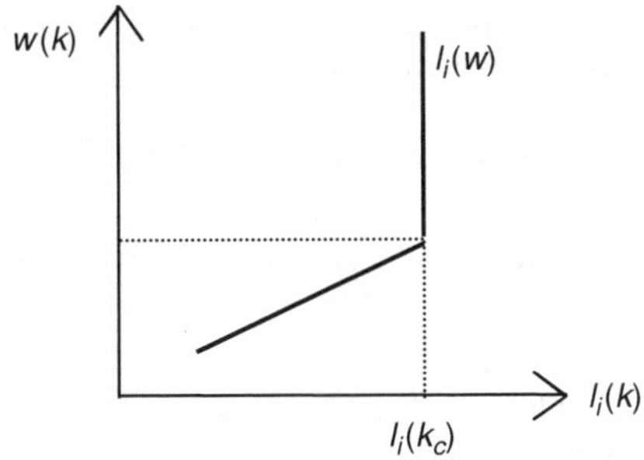

Figure 12.1 The relationship between labour supply and wage rate

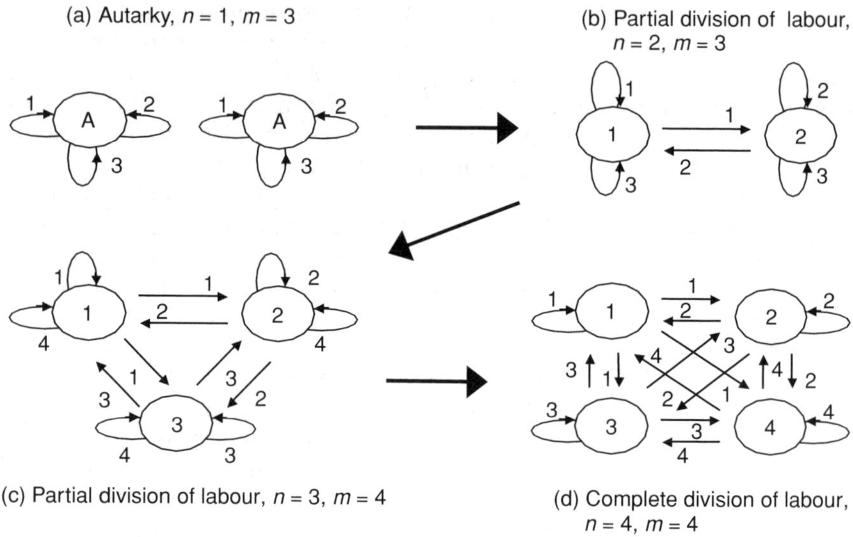

Figure 12.2 The evolution of division of labour

and engages in two production activities. The level of specialization, the time spent at market work, and the time spent at leisure increase from panel (a) to (b), since the number of production activities for each person is reduced from three to two.

When transaction efficiency improves further, the economy evolves to panel (c), in which each household sells one good, buys two goods, trades three goods, and engages in two production activities. The consumption variety increases as the number of goods increases from three to four. If transaction efficiency is sufficiently improved, the economy evolves to panel (d), in which each household sells one good, buys three goods, and engages in only one production activity. In panel (d), the level of specialization, the time spent on work for the market, and the time spent on leisure are higher compared to panel (c), as the number of production activities is reduced from two to one. In panels (c) and (d), the time spent on leisure and the consumption variety are noticeably higher compared to autarky.

The effect of changes in desire for time-intensive consumption on productivity

Differentiating m, n, x_i, x_j, and x_r^d with respect to β yields

$$dm/d\beta = \{-\rho/[\alpha K^2(1-\rho)]\}(dK/d\beta) < 0 \tag{12.18}$$

$$dn/d\beta = \{-\rho/[\alpha c(1-\rho)(1-K)]\}\{c(1-k)\{1+(1/K)(\rho^2 \ln k)/[1+(1+\beta)\rho]^2\} + \alpha K\{1+[(1+\beta)/(1-K)]\{(\rho^2 \ln k)/[1+(1+\beta)\rho]^2\}\} \tag{12.19}$$

$$dx_i/d\beta = dx_j/d\beta = \{(\alpha\rho^2)/\{(1-K)[1+(1+\beta)\rho^2\}\}$$
$$\{1-\{(\rho K \ln k)/\{(1-K)[1+(1+\beta)\rho]\}\}\} \quad (12.20)$$

$$dx_r^d/d\beta = \{(\alpha\rho^2 K)/\{(1-K)[1+(1+\beta)\rho]^2\}\}$$
$$\{1-\{(\rho \ln k)/\{(1-K)[1+(1+\beta)\rho]\}\}\} \quad (12.21)$$

From equations (12.19) to (12.21) we can show that $dx_i/d\beta = dx_j/d\beta > 0$, $dx_r^d\ d\beta > 0$ and $dn/d\beta > 0$ if ρ is sufficiently large, or if the degree of economies of complementarity between each pair of consumption activities $-1/\rho$ is sufficiently large (see the Appendix to this chapter). Moreover, we can show that $dx_i/d\beta = dx_j/d\beta < 0$, $dx_r^d/d\beta < 0$ and $dn/d\beta < 0$ if ρ is very small and satisfies $\rho > -1/(1+\beta)$.[6] Since $l_i = (n-1)x_r^d + x_i + \alpha$ and $l_j = x_j + \alpha$, we can show that $dl_i/d\beta > 0$ and $dl_j/d\beta > 0$ if ρ is sufficiently large, and that $dl_i/d\beta < 0$ and $dl_j/d\beta < 0$ if ρ is very small and satisfies $\rho > -1/(1+\beta)$. Observing that productivity increases with labour input, we arrive at our concluding proposition:

> PROPOSITION 5. *The number of all available goods decreases as the desire for time-intensive consumption becomes stronger. If the degree of economies of complementarity in consumption is sufficiently large, the number of traded goods, the level of division of labour, the level of specialization, and productivity all increase as the desire for time-intensive consumption increases.*

The proof of Proposition 5 is set out in the Appendix to this chapter. This proposition suggests that, far from reducing productivity, an increase in the desire for time-intensive consumption can be a source of productivity growth if the desire for diverse consumption is strong enough.

Proposition 5 is amenable to an intuitive explanation. If people place more value on the time spent on consumption, they have an incentive to withdraw time from some production activities in order to increase the time spent on consumption. This will decrease the consumption variety, as shown in (18). However, people can reduce either the time spent on work for the market, or the time spent on self-sufficient production activities. If people strongly prefer diverse consumption, their choice would be to shrink the number of self-sufficient activities through a higher level of specialization and division of labour, since this way, which exploits increasing returns to satisfy new demands for time, minimizes the negative impact on the consumption variety. A strong preference for time-intensive consumption in addition to a strong preference for diverse consumption generates greater demands on productivity, which can be achieved only through a higher level of specialization and division of labour. Hence, an increase in β for a given large value of ρ can raise the level of division of labour and productivity.

Proposition 5 raises several interesting implications. Firstly, the coexistence of high consumption diversity, abundant leisure, and high productivity in developed economies is linked to high levels of specialization and division of labour. Secondly, an increase in the preference for time-intensive consumption combined with an increase in the preference for diverse consumption could be the engine for productivity growth. Commercial advertisements in modern everyday life, therefore, may play an important role in stimulating economic development by changing people's preference toward more time-intensive and more diverse consumption. Thirdly, tighter restriction on endowments can generate higher levels of specialization and division of labour. A stronger preference for time-intensive consumption in addition to a strong preference for diverse consumption would tighten the endowment constraint of time. Specialization and the division of labour are the answer to this resource shortage. Fourthly, the conventional understanding that a stronger preference for time-intensive consumption tends to weaken productivity actually constitutes a special case in our model. It may hold only if the degree of economies of complementarity is not significant.

Note that $d(m - n)/d\beta < 0$ if ρ is sufficiently large. This implies that, if the degree of economies of complementarity is sufficiently large, the number of traded goods will eventually reach the number of all goods as the desire for time-intensive consumption increases. Combining (12.17b) with (12.19), (12.20), and (12.21) yields (12.22) $dl_i/d\beta = d[(n - 1)x_r^d + x_i + \alpha]/d\beta > 0$ for $m < n$ if ρ is sufficiently large.

$$dl_i/d\beta < 0 \text{ for } m = n$$

The explanation for equation (12.22) is straightforward. Since there are no self-sufficient production activities to withdraw time from, a stronger desire for time-intensive consumption will decrease the labour supply if the economy has reached a complete division of labour. Equation (12.22) implies a back-bending phenomenon in labour supply. If the economy does not reach the complete division of labour and the degree of economies of complementarity is sufficiently large, the level of division of labour and labour supply for the market will increase as the desire for time-intensive consumption increases. On the other hand, if the economy has reached the complete division of labour, labour supply for the market will fall as the desire for time-intensive consumption increases.

Figure 12.3 depicts the relationship between labour supply and the desire for leisure when ρ is sufficiently large. In Figure 12.3, the economy reaches the complete division of labour when $\beta > \beta_c$, where $l_i(\beta_c) = (1 + \alpha\beta)/(1 + \beta)$. The labour supply curve will bend backwards as the economy has exhausted the potential for a further division of labour.

4 Conclusion

We have formulated a model with three tradeoffs: the tradeoff between economies of specialization and transaction costs, the tradeoff between

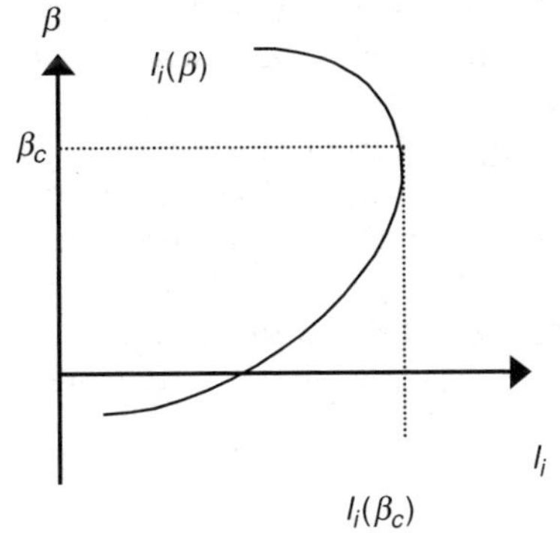

Figure 12.3 The relationship between l_i and β when ρ is sufficiently large

economies of specialization and economies of complementarity, and the tradeoff between time spent on production activities and time spent on consumption activities. These features are used together to investigate the relationship between the division of labour based on endogenous comparative advantage and the allocation of time. Our model demonstrates a process in which the productivity of time, the time spent on each consumption activity, the time spent on all consumption activities, the consumption variety, and per capita real income concurrently increase with increasing levels of division of labour, because of improvements in transaction efficiency. In this process, more and more non-market goods become commodities, the degree of self-sufficiency and the time spent on self-sufficient production activities decrease, and households allocate more time to producing the traded good while enjoying more leisure by exploiting increasing returns through specialization.

Our model shows that labour supply and wage rate concurrently increase with improvements to transaction efficiency. The labour supply will be rigid if the economy has exhausted its potential for any further division of labour. Our model also shows that a stronger desire for time-intensive consumption can increase productivity if the degree of economies of complementarity is sufficiently large. The labour supply will bend backwards as the desire for time-intensive consumption increases, if the economy has reached a complete division of labour.

What are the welfare implications of the division of labour? Buchanan (1994, p. 13) has pointed out:

> Imagine ... what it would be like to try to produce everything on your own, with no economic interaction with others. How much could a person produce in total independence from any exchange nexus? A person's life would indeed be solitary, nasty, brutish, and short, to use Thomas Hobbes's description in a different context. We might want to

> add the word '*tiring*,' since the valued output that would be secured from the maximal inputs of labour would scarcely ensure survival.

Aside from increasing per capita real income, productivity, and consumption variety, specialization and the division of labour free people from time spent on self-sufficient production activities. When non-market production activities are reduced, the time saved is added to consumption activities, and this directly increases the utility. Therefore, the reallocation of time constitutes an important part of the welfare from the division of labour.

Notes

1 It is obvious that during this period there are changes in the division of labour between men and women inside the household. For men, however, the time spent on housework increased only 2.3 hours per week in the US, and 1.4 hours per week in Norway, while for women the time spent on housework decreased 11.3 hours per week in the US, and 8.3 hours in Norway. In this chapter, we will focus on the division of labour between households, which is organized by the market.

2 In Norway, the increase in females' leisure time can be explained either by the decrease in the time spent on work or by the decrease in the time spent on personal care. However, the former can explain 66% of the change in leisure time. For the US female, the time spent on personal care does not change significantly between 1965 and 1981. Most of the increase in leisure can be explained by the decrease in total work time.

3 This specification of production functions follows Becker (1981) and Rosen (1983), who assume that the fixed learning or training costs generate economies of specialization through increasing the utilization rate of the investments in learning and training. According to Marshall (1948, pp. 250–1), the fixed learning costs in acquiring knowledge and skill are caused by a difficult learning process that needs intensive exertion of the central nervous system in coordinating local nerve centres, and reflex actions become routes which do not need much exertion of the central nervous system as the learning process has reached a threshold level.

4 North (1981) has examined the negative relationship between arbitrary tax extraction and transaction efficiency.

5 See Juster and Stafford (1991, p. 497).

6 Note that the conditions for $dx_i/d\beta = dx_j/d\beta < 0$, $dx_r^d/d\beta < 0$ and $dn/d\beta < 0$ may not hold, with the latter part of Proposition 5 also not holding, if the necessary upper threshold level of ρ is too small and $\rho > -1/(1 + \beta)$ is not satisfied: see the Appendix at the end of this chapter.

References

Becker, G. (1965) 'A Theory of the Allocation of Time', *Economic Journal*, 75, 493–517.

Becker, G. (1981) *A Treatise on the Family* (Cambridge, MA: Harvard University Press).
Borland, J. and Yang, X. (1992) 'Specialization and a New Approach to Economic Organization and Growth', *American Economic Review*, 82, 386–91.
Buchanan, J. (1994) *Ethics and Economic Progress* (Norman, OK: University of Oklahoma Press).
Coase, R. (1946) 'The Marginal Cost Controversy', *Economica*, 13, 169–82.
Coase, R. (1960) 'The Problem of Social Cost', *Journal of Law and Economics*, 3, 1–44.
Dixit, A. and Stiglitz, J. (1977) 'Monopolistic Competition and Optimum Product Diversity', *American Economic Review*, 67, 297–308.
Gronau, R. (1977) 'Leisure, Home Production, and Work – the Theory of the Allocation of Time Revisited', *Journal of Political Economy*, 85, 1099–1123.
Juster, F. T. and Stafford, F. P. (1991) 'The Allocation of Time: Empirical Findings, Behavioral Models, and Problems of Measurement', *Journal of Economic Literature*, 29, 471–522.
Locay, L. (1990) 'Economic Development and the Division of Production between Households and Markets', *Journal of Political Economy*, 98, 965–82.
Marshall, A. (1948) *Principles of Economics*, 8th edition (New York: Macmillan).
North, D. (1981) *Structure Changes in Economic History* (New York: Norton).
Reynolds, L. (1983) 'The Spread of Economic Growth to the Third World: 1850–1980', *Journal of Economic Literature*, 21, 941–80.
Rosen, S. (1983) 'Specialization and Human Capital', *Journal of Labour Economics*, 1, 43–9.
Wen, M. (1998) 'An Analytical Framework of Consumer-producers, Economies of Specialization, and Transaction Costs,' in K. Arrow, Y.-K. Ng and X. Yang (eds), *Increasing Returns and Economic Analysis* (London: Macmillan), 170–85.
Yang, X. and Ng, Y.-K. (1993) *Specialization and Economic Organization: a New Classical Microeconomic Framework* (Amsterdam: North-Holland).
Yang, X. and Shi, H. (1992) 'Specialization and Product Diversity', *American Economic Review*, 82, 392–98.
Young, A. (1928) 'Increasing Returns and Economic Progress', *Economic Journal*, 152, 527–42.

Appendix: proof of proposition 5

Proposition 5 is established if the two following claims are true:

claim 1: $dn/d\beta > 0$, $dx_i/d\beta > 0$, $dx_j/d\beta > 0$ and $dx_r^d/d\beta > 0$ hold if ρ is sufficiently large.

claim 2: $dn/d\beta < 0$, $dx_i/d\beta = dx_j/d\beta < 0$, and $dx_r^d/d\beta < 0$ may hold if ρ is very small and satisfies $\rho > -1/(1+\beta)$.

To establish claim 1 we prove that $dn/d\beta > 0$ holds if ρ is sufficiently large. To establish claim 2 we prove that $dn/d\beta < 0$ may hold if ρ is very small and satisfies $\rho > -1/(1+\beta)$. The remaining parts of the two claims can then be easily established.

We begin by denoting $F(k, \beta, \rho) \equiv 1 + (1+\beta)[\ln k/(1-K)]\,\{\rho/[1+(1+\beta)\,\rho]\}^2$ and $G(k, \beta, \rho) \equiv 1 + (\ln k/K)\,\{\rho/[1+(1+\beta)\,\rho]\}$.[2] From equation (12.19), we know that $dn/d\beta > 0$ if $F > 0$ and $G > 0$, and $dn/d\beta < 0$ if $F < 0$ and $G < 0$. It can be further shown that

$$
\begin{aligned}
&F > 0 \quad \text{iff} \quad \rho > f(\rho) \\
&G > 0 \quad \text{iff} \quad \rho > g(\rho) \\
&f(\rho) \equiv -1/\{(1+\beta) + [-\ln k(1+\beta)/(1-K)]^{1/2}\} \\
&g(\rho) = -1/[(1+\beta) + (-\ln k/K)^{1/2}]
\end{aligned}
\tag{A12.1}
$$

The claims can thus be established if it can be shown that $\rho > f(\rho)$ and $\rho > g(\rho)$ hold if ρ is sufficiently large, and that $\rho < f(\rho)$ and $\rho < g(\rho)$ hold if ρ is very small and satisfies $\rho > -1/(1+\beta)$.

Since $df/d\rho > 0$, $dg/d\rho < 0$ and $f, g \in (-1,0)$, the solutions for $\rho = f(\rho)$ and $\rho = g(\rho)$ must exist for $\rho \in (-1,0)$. Assume that $\rho_f = f(\rho_f)$ and $\rho_g = g(\rho_g)$, $\rho_f, \rho_g \in (-1,0)$, and we have $\rho > f(\rho)$ for $\rho > \rho_f$ and $\rho > g(\rho)$ for $\rho > \rho_g$, since $-1 < f(\rho \to -1) < f(\rho \to 0) < 0$ and $dg/d\rho < 0$. We know that $\rho > -1/(1+\beta)$ holds because the number of goods is positive. Assuming, $\rho_{min} = -1/(1+\beta)$, we then obtain Table A12.1. Note that $dn/d\beta > 0$ holds when $\rho > f(\rho)$ and $\rho > g(\rho)$, and $dn/d\beta < 0$ holds when $\rho < f(\rho)$ and $\rho < g(\rho)$. From Table A12.1, we conclude that $dn/d\beta > 0$ holds if $\rho > \max(\rho_f, \rho_g)$, and $dn/d\beta < 0$ holds if $\min(\rho_f, \rho_g) > \rho > \rho_{min}$. Proposition 5 is thus established. *Q.E.D.*

Table A12.1 The sign of $dn/d\beta$

The sign of $dn/d\beta$	$\rho_{min} > \max(\rho_f, \rho_g)$	$\max(\rho_f, \rho_g) > \rho_{min}$	$> \min(\rho_f, \rho_g)$
$\rho > \max(\rho_f, \rho_g)$	+	+	+
$\max(\rho_f, \rho_g) > \rho$	N.E.	?	?
$\min(\rho_f, \rho_g) > \rho$	N.E.	N.E.	–

Part IV

Transaction Costs and the Division of Labour: Measurement and Empirical Analysis

13

An Indirect Approach to the Identification and Measurement of Transaction Costs

George S. Rivers

1 Introduction to transaction costs

Nobel Laureate Ronald Coase had previously argued, in his paper titled 'The Nature of the Firm', that exchange was not *costless* and that 'the most obvious cost of organizing production through the price mechanism is that of discovering what the relevant prices are' (1937, p. 390). Coase identified the nature of such price discovery costs as being 'the cost of negotiating and concluding a separate contract for each exchange transaction' (1937, p. 390). Understanding the exact nature of such transaction costs becomes crucial for attaining transaction efficiency and thereby minimizing the cost of transactions. Moreover, transaction costs are seen to have deep implications for not only resource allocation but also the assignment of property rights and the structure of economic organization (Eggertsson, 1990). Put simply, *transaction costs* can be defined as being: 'the costs incurred to achieve the benefits of exchange and cooperation' (Denzau, 1992, p. 34).

The following quote provides an alternative definition:

> costs that arise when individuals exchange ownership rights to economic assets and enforce their exclusive rights... [and]... are in one way or another associated with the cost of acquiring information about exchange (Eggertsson, 1990, pp. 14–15).

The failure to find a rigorous discussion or theory on transaction costs has been due to the fundamental assumption made by most economic models of 'full information'. Traditionally, economists around the time of Marshall did away with the need to look at transaction costs because it did not fit neatly into the mathematics of geometry or algebra or calculus (Cheung, 1998). Early twentieth-century economists like Leon Walras deleted these price components by adopting the assumption that the auctioneer supplier provides services free of charge (Cheung, 1998). Indeed, transaction costs are 'infrequently noted as distinct line items in budgets, and are instead subsumed in supervisory, overhead, or administrative cost categories' (Stiles, 1996). In looking at the apparent lack of consideration for transaction costs, it is important to remember that in the 'modern world, it would be difficult to find a rich country where transaction costs sum to less than half of national income' (Cheung, 1998, p. 522).

Hobbs (1997, p. 1096) adds that 'one criticism of Transaction Cost Economics, is that its theoretical development has not been accompanied by successful measurement of transaction costs'. It has been argued that it is 'fruitless to study transaction costs, because it is frequently impossible to measure them' (Cheung, 1998, p. 522). This dilemma can be overcome by employing an indirect approach to measure transaction costs. Therefore, rather than measuring in strictly dollars and cents terms, it would be more constructive to compare types of transaction costs in hypothetical situation A as compared to situation B and specifying a ranking to distinguish between them (Cheung, 1998). Hobbs (1997) states that such analysis, which measures the significance of particular transaction costs, is a more fruitful approach in determining the vertical coordination outcomes.

Hence, the aim of this chapter is to identify and develop a more appropriate and detailed method of identifying and measuring transactions costs associated with the exchange of intermediate goods and services, as well as those associated with the exchange of labour. Hobbs (1997) suggests the construction of 'proxy' variables would appear to yield the best results.

The classification of transaction costs

Transaction costs rely on the important assumptions of both *bounded rationality* and *opportunism*. *Bounded rationality* is responsible for the computational limitations of organization man, while *opportunism* is responsible for the unreliable behaviour of at least *some* economic agents (Williamson, 1986) and (Hallwood, 1990). Stiles states that:

> the combined effect of bounded rationality and opportunism is that actors realize that their knowledge is limited, further realize that those with whom they transact are not to be trusted, and thus incur costs, 'transaction costs', as they try to mitigate those factors (1996, p. 1)

Eggertsson (1990) states that the activities commonly associated with the exchange of property rights which give rise to transaction costs are: the search for information, bargaining or negotiating, monitoring or policing contracts, enforcing contracts, external arbitration and protection against the misappropriation of rents. Furthermore, in a world of perfect information, such activities would not be required and hence there would be no transaction costs.

Moreover, in addition to the activities associated with the exchange, other factors like the *characteristics of partners to an exchange* and the *environment of exchange* are important in distinguishing between the various types of transaction costs (Stiles, 1996). Furthermore, because transaction costs are opportunity costs, they have both a fixed and a variable cost feature (Eggertsson, 1990).

For the purpose of discussion later, transaction costs have been broken down into two major categories: *ex ante* and *ex post* costs of market exchange. Matthews argues that 'the fundamental idea of transaction costs is that they consist of the cost of arranging a contract *ex ante* and monitoring and enforcing it *ex post*' (1986, p. 906). The next section will begin by looking at the *ex ante* transaction costs of market exchange. Each section is organized as a collection of observations and each subsection concludes with a summary table.

2 *Ex ante* transaction costs of market exchange

Such transaction costs are related directly to the actual costs of contracting as referred to by Coase (1937), and are classified as either search costs or information costs, negotiation costs or bargaining costs (Hallwood, 1990).

2.1 The search cost of information

The assumption of perfect information is seen as a useful starting point in economic analysis. However, this assumption fails to consider the real-world cost of obtaining information for both consumers and producers. Denzau (1992) states that information on the complete range of potential transaction possibilities available throughout the world is imprecise and only partial, due to the overwhelming cost involved in communicating such possibilities. The problem of imperfect information can best be understood by considering these search costs. Henceforth, search costs and the cost of information will be used interchangeably. Search costs are defined as:

> the costs involved in obtaining information about a product or particular service on issues relating to quantity, quality or price; and locating potential buyers or sellers with whom to negotiate trade with (Abdel-Latif and Nugent, 1996) and (Hobbs, 1997) and (North and Thomas, 1973).

Abdel-Latif and Nugent (1996) argue that the search costs in international marketing costs include:

I. The costs of acquiring information about quantities and qualities of commodities being traded, as well as the prevailing prices for each category;
II. The reciprocal costs for agents in foreign countries;

III. The costs of acquiring information about regulations and policies of the respective countries (such as environmental, health regulations and exchange rate, tariff or trade-barrier policies);
IV. The costs of identifying appropriate trading partners.

As mentioned above, search effort includes researching the costs borne by the other party to the transaction, in order to determine what that party would accept (Denzau, 1992 and Hobbs, 1997). Transactions involving large sums of money like the purchase of an oilrig, or the hiring of a new company chairman, are likely to induce the consumer or producer to expend a greater search effort, especially with regards to price because even a one-per cent variation in price is likely to be costly.

Observation 1: Search costs are positively related to the value of transactions.

Search costs involve a fixed cost of gathering information. Once gathered, any number of buyers or sellers can use the information. Hence, the larger the number of buyers or sellers using the information (the larger the volume of transactions) the larger the frequency of transactions – this would lower the per unit search cost since search costs are subject to economies of scale (North and Thomas, 1973). Liu and Yang (2000) argue that an increase in the number of firms in the economy increases competition, making it less costly to obtain intermediate inputs (i.e. lower search costs). Nam, Rajagopalan, Rao and Chaudhury (1996, p. 39) state that 'as the number of available vendors increases, the extent of competition among vendors increases... [and]... it is easier for firms to find alternative vendors without incurring high search costs.' Moreover, per-unit costs of disseminating information fall as markets are centralized and the geographical density of firms increase (North and Thomas, 1973 and Yang and Pak-Wai, 1994). Also, 'if firms interact with a certain vendor *frequently* for a certain specific information systems function, firms can outsource that function at a lower cost on a routine basis' (Nam et al., 1996, p. 41).

Observation 2: Search costs are inversely related to the volume of transactions (the number of buyers and sellers) and frequency of transactions.

Hence, the volume, the value and the frequency of transactions can each be used as proxy measures for the cost of information in both the labour market and the intermediate goods(services) markets. The determinants of search costs are each listed in Table 13.1.

Table 13.1 Determinants of search costs for all markets

Search costs are positively related to the:
• value of transactions;
Such costs are negatively related to the:
• volume of transactions; and the
• frequency of transactions.

2.2 The costs of contract negotiation

Coase (1937) argued that firms internalize production when it becomes less possible and less desirable for the person purchasing the commodity or service to stipulate what the other contracting party is expected to do (owing to the difficulty of measurement). An example of this is given by weavers at the beginning of the factory system and how inputs and the production process became organized within the firm (for example, the 'putting out' system was abandoned in the cloth industry) in order to reduce the cost of negotiating contracts, which specified the exchange of intermediate goods and services (Alchian and Demsetz, 1972).

While the aim of a market contract is to ensure the largest possible 'pie' available for all parties involved in a market exchange (be it for labour or intermediate inputs) – the division of such a pie (or surplus) will depend on costly negotiation processes. Negotiation costs of a contract are related to the determination of the terms of exchange (North and Thomas, 1973). The basic idea behind negotiation costs hence arises from the notion of *quid pro quo*, understood as 'something for something'. Notwithstanding that price is the key variable to an exchange, agreement must also be made as to the quality of the good or service, as well as the place and time that the exchange will occur and how payments will be made (North and Thomas, 1973). Consequently, negotiation costs involving trade in the market for labour and the intermediate goods (services) markets may be defined as:

> the amount of expenditure allocated by a party *ex ante* to negotiations over price, quality, time and place of exchange or mode of payment in the attempt to obtain the highest possible share of surplus *ex post* (Rivers, 2000).

To illustrate the idea behind this definition, the following simple example is constructed. Consider two periods 1 and 2, where period 1 represents the *ex ante* situation and period 2 represents the *ex post* exchange. Assuming that the value of the good, service or labour input purchased is equal to some value V and likewise, the production cost is equal to some value C, a total surplus or total gain from trade equal to $(v - C)$ is generated in period 2. Furthermore, assuming in this simple example, that price p is the only central variable to the exchange, then the buyer's surplus *ex post* is given by $(v - p)$, and the seller's surplus is given by $(p - C)$ (Tirole, 1989). Subsequently, it is in the interests of the buyer to minimize the price to maximize his/her share of surplus, while the seller would attempt to maximize the price in order to increase his/her surplus share. However, any investment made by either party in the negotiation over price *ex ante* to obtain the largest amount of *ex post* surplus, will be deemed as being a cost of negotiation.

Indeed, Hallwood (1990) points out that even with symmetrical information, there is a cost to affixing prices to the quantities being exchanged. The costs of affixing prices may involve the appointment of an auctioneer, broker or dealer who is compensated by some bid–offer spread and may also involve the expenditure on actuarial or cost accounting calculations. Even in a Bedouin *souk* (market), for example, where buyers and merchants may not speak the same language, interpreters are paid a commission by the merchant to help in the price negotiation process (Denzau, 1992). Abdel-Latif and Nugent (1996) also point to differences in language, culture and taste as adding to negotiation costs.

Goods or services exchanged only once will incur more severe price affixing costs as part of negotiation costs, whilst standardized goods and services involving multiple transactions lower the per-unit cost of affixing prices (Hallwood, 1990). Transaction costs occurring in the labour market or goods and services market increase with the irregularity of the transactions between trading parties (Abdel-Latif and Nugent, 1996). The determinants of negotiation costs for both the labour market and the intermediate goods (services) market are outlined in Tables 13.2 and 13.3.

Observation 3: Negotiation costs (price affixing costs) are inversely related to the degree of standardization of goods (services) and to the frequency of transactions, in both the labour market and the intermediate goods (services) market.

Furthermore, 'as the volume of trade increases, the non-price terms of trade also become standardized... [and]... less time and effort (or costs) are

Table 13.2 Determinants of negotiation costs (labour market)

Negotiation costs are negatively related to the:
- degree of labour service standardization;
- volume of transactions; and the
- frequency of transactions.

Negotiation costs are positively related to the:
- degree of information asymmetry; and
- degree of unionization.

Table 13.3 Determinants of negotiation costs (intermediate goods (services) market)

Negotiation costs are inversely related to the:
- degree of goods (services) standardization;
- volume of transactions; and the
- frequency of transactions.

Negotiation costs are positively related to the:
- degree of information asymmetry.

needed to negotiate a contract of sale' (Denzau, 1992, p. 39). By increasing the number of vendors, it is argued that contractibility and standardization of information system assets increases, thereby decreasing the need for centralized coordination of such assets within firms (Nam et al., 1996). In addition, North and Thomas (1973) argue that as the scale of transactions in the market increases, it becomes increasingly profitable as well as viable to set up a standard code of trade practices or terms, thereby reducing the costs of negotiation. In cattle marketing, price uncertainty is lowered if the number of buyers present at the auction sale is high (Hobbs, 1997). Liu and Yang (2000) note that an increase in the number of firms makes the price of the intermediate input more competitive, thereby lowering price negotiation costs.

Observation 4: Negotiation costs are inversely related to the volume of transactions (the number of buyers and sellers) in both the labour market and the intermediate goods (services) market.

In the symmetrical information case of exchange involving intermediate goods (services) or labour, it follows that the volume of transactions, frequency of transactions and the degree of standardization can be used as proxy measures for negotiation costs.

The impact of unionized labour on negotiation costs

In looking specifically at employer–employee negotiations in labour markets, Christensen (1980, p. 37) argues that 'whether in the public or the private sector, employer-employee conflicts are going to arise concerning compensation, advancement, discipline, supervision and a host of other issues affecting the work [contract]'. Tirole (1989) notes that while contracts are aimed at maximizing the size of the 'pie', its division will depend on the relative *ex ante* negotiation powers of each contracting party. To this effect, it can be seen that the negotiation power of employees is influenced fundamentally and directly by the degree of unionization. MacBeath (1979) argues that trade unions are organizations which exist for the sole purpose of endowing their members with power, thereby influencing the behaviour of other parties to the labour market contract. Taylor et al. (1977) note that collective bargaining:

> provides an orderly, peaceful setting for discussion; second, it constitutes a form of industrial democracy; third, unions that bargain collectively are also active in representing their workers politically; and, fourth, individual bargaining cannot provide the same benefits as collective bargaining (1977, p. 185).

In the case of labour contracts, a major negotiation cost that arises out of trade union power is the strike. Freeman and Medoff (1984) argue that during the 1980s, most of the strikes in the United States were related to contract negotiations and included 80 per cent of the total number of striking workers. Strikes typically involve the loss of services provided by participating members and can be loosely defined as any action by a group of employees which disrupts usual work activity. Ninety five per cent of the total time lost (because of strikes) during the 1980s in the United States was a direct result of *striking activity involving contract negotiations* (Freeman and Medoff, 1984). Hiller gives a more formal definition of a strike as follows:

> a strike... may be more specifically characterized as a concerted and temporary suspension of function, designed to exert pressure upon others within the same social unit – industrial, political or cultural... [and]... is not a mere cessation of work; it is a conflict in the form of a corporate refusal to participate (1969, p. 12).

It follows that the negotiation costs associated with the exchange of unionized labour should include the total financial losses incurred by the firm as a result of striking activity during the labour contract bargaining process. A concerted agreement by a group of employees can inflict severe financial losses on the firm and can arouse the attention and involvement by political action or public opinion (Hiller, 1969). Freeman and Medoff (1984) argue that strikes have a modest impact on an economy as a whole because of the build up of inventories by firms in advance of a strike or the substitution of goods by customers in the face of lost output. Instead, 'the major cost of a strike is on the direct participants... [in the form of]... lower profits and lost wages' (Freeman and Medoff, 1984, p. 219). The strike 'decreases production, interferes with trade connections and gives advantages to the competitors of the employer' (Hiller, 1969, p. 125).

Cortes et al. (1987) state that one of the reasons why labour might be cheaper in small firms where firm size is defined by 'the number of workers employed', is that small firms can often hire workers without being subject to union pressures. Subsequently, without union pressure small firms can keep wage and non-wage costs down (Cortes et al., 1987). Hiller adds (as shown in Table 13.4) that 'large firms are more frequently unionized and have more strikes than do smaller ones' (1969, p. 29). Miller and Mulvey (1996) note that for Australian firms with more than 500 workers, union density is 72 per cent. It is only fitting therefore that striking costs should also be included as part of the negotiation costs for labour market contracts.

Observation 5: Negotiation costs are positively related to the degree of unionization in the labour market.

Hence, the degree of unionization or the percentage of workers belonging to a union can be used as one of the proxy measures for negotiation costs in the labour market.

The impact of asymmetric information on negotiation costs

In general, at the bargaining table, asymmetric information results in problems of adverse selection and moral hazard. Where parties to a transaction do not have access to complete information concerning, for example, the buyer's value or the supplier's cost *ex ante*, inefficient pricing activity will arise *ex post* (Tirole, 1989). Information asymmetries create the potential for rents to be unduly appropriated – either by the buyer if the seller reveals too much, or by the seller if the buyer is not fully informed (Alston and Gillespie, 1986).

Hart argues that, in the case of labour contracts, 'there are potential incentives for each party to misinform the other as to its own true estimates in an attempt to increase its share of the quasi-rent to specific capital' (1983, p. 113). Workers may try to increase the perception of the employer of their true marginal productivity whilst the employer may try to underplay its assessment of the employee's marginal product (Hart,

Table 13.4 Percentage of striking firms according to size (Russia at the turn of the twentieth century)

Number of workers in firms	*Percentage of firms having strikes*
Less than 20	2.7
20–50	7.5
51–100	9.4
101–500	21.5
501–1,000	49.9
More than 1000	89.7

Source: E. T. Hiller (1969) *The Strike: a Study in Collective Action* (Arno & The New York Times), p. 29.

1983). The consequence will be that too little trade results from the negotiation process as parties to the exchange haggle over the price (wage) *ex ante*. Negotiation costs no longer equal the costs of affixing prices in a fixed-price contract but now also include investments in obtaining estimates for the values of other crucial variables pertaining to the exchange.

A mathematical model of negotiation costs with asymmetric information

To understand the costs of negotiation and specifying a contract in the case of information asymmetry, consider the following model discussed by Hart (1983). In this model there are two periods (i.e. investment and post-investment periods). Initially in the investment period the worker is endowed with human capital (k_g), which is a fixed value. Each unit of firm-specific human capital, k_s, provides a value to the firm of $(m + n)$ where m is a fixed value and that the employee's beliefs about n are represented by a density function $\theta(n)$ with $E(n) = 0$.

Moreover, in alternative employment, the value of each unit of k_s is identified by a random variable ϵ and the employer's beliefs about ϵ are represented by a density function $\psi(\epsilon)$ with $E(\epsilon) = 0$. Hence n and ϵ represent prediction errors and it is assumed for simplicity that $Cov(n,\epsilon) = 0$. In period 2 (the post-investment period), the value of the marginal product of each employee of the firm in question is given by:

$$v = k_g + (m + n)k_s$$

The value of the marginal product of each employee in alternative employment (the value of the best alternative or opportunity wage) is given by:

$$y = k_g + (\epsilon)k_s$$

The firm's quasi-rent is given by:

$$R = v - y = (m + n - \epsilon)k_s$$

The worker's fully *flexible wage*, also known as the 'opportunity wage plus a share of the difference between his/her marginal product and the opportunity wage', is given by:

$$\omega = y + \alpha(v - y) = k_g + (\epsilon)k_s + \alpha(m + n - \epsilon)k_s \; 0 \le \alpha \le 1$$

where α is the share of returns to firm-specific human capital. The share of quasi-rent represents the worker's net gain from the firm-specific human capital investment. Rosen (1985) argues that the observed continuity of employment can be explained by the existence of firm-specific human capital, whereby the wage is in part an installment payment on such specific investments. The firm's net gain from employing the worker is given by the difference between the worker's marginal product V, and the wage ω (Hart, 1983).

Tirole (1989) states that in the case of bilateral asymmetric information, both parties can agree to adopt a 'rigid norm' which fixes the amount of trade and price in advance, if and only if the size of the quasi-rent to firm-specific human capital is positive. In other words, there are gains from trade. While layoffs and resignations might occur despite the potential for positive quasi-rents, yet a 'a long term contract, pre-specifying the wage while allowing neither side to initiate separation, would overcome this type of resource loss or inefficient volume of trade' (Hart, 1983, p. 113). A fixed-wage contract (for example, tenure or indenture contracts) would be given by the following:

$$\varpi = k_g + \alpha m k_s$$

Under the fixed-wage contract regime, parties would only mutually agree to separate if $R < 0$:

$$m \leq \epsilon - n$$

Workers would quit if $\varpi - y \leq 0$ or $\alpha m \leq \epsilon$. Moreover, firms would fire employees if $v - \varpi \leq 0$ or $(1 - \alpha)m \leq - n$. The fixed wage contract incorporates the expected values of the random variables n and ϵ. Consequently, these aforementioned separation rules depend on such expected values. Hence optimal separation will only occur as an average in this fixed-wage strategy. Moreover, if separation occurs with positive quasi-rent losses will be incurred thereby creating the incentive for both parties to determine a sharing ratio, α, that minimizes such losses. Obtaining an appropriate sharing ratio will not be without cost and will be determined by the negotiating power of each party to the exchange.

Under the system of fully flexible wages, each party would be required to reach a costless agreement as to the value of n and ϵ (Hart, 1983). However in this regime parties would need to obtain estimates of n and ϵ, based on mutually acceptable economic indicators of post-investment productivity. The greater the disagreement of indicators the more the wage system approaches its fixed case. Efforts to secure acceptable economic indicators for n and ϵ by both parties to the exchange can be counted as part of the negotiation costs.

Observation 6: Negotiation costs are positively related to the degree of information asymmetry between parties to an exchange *ex ante* in both the labour market and the intermediate goods (services) market.

Where there is information asymmetry, negotiation costs regarding labour contracts and intermediate goods (services) contracts also include the level of expenditure incurred by parties to an exchange for securing estimates of contract-specific economic indicators.

Hence for the asymmetric information case, expenditures made by parties, for the estimation of contract-specific economic indicators, can be used as one of the proxy measures for negotiation costs in the intermediate goods (services) market or the labour market.

3 *Ex post* transaction costs of market exchange

These transaction costs are classified as either: policing (enforcement) costs, coordination costs, external arbitration costs, or holdup costs:

- the costs of policing a contract which consists of monitoring the quantity or quality of goods or services exchanged;
- the coordination costs of contracting in the labour market;
- the costs of dispute machinery used (for example, external arbitration); and
- the holdup costs of rent appropriation by the opportunistic party (also known as the loss of quasi-rent on transaction-specific assets) (Hallwood, 1990, p. 7).

3.1 The costs of policing (enforcing) a contract

Amongst the activities engaged by parties to a transaction, is the evaluation and monitoring of the quantity and/or quality of the good (service) being exchanged. Indeed, it is difficult to ascertain the quality of some commodities until they are consumed (Wang, 1999). Subsequently, the policing (enforcement) cost of a transaction involving a good or service is defined as: 'the expenditure of resources for the measurement of the activity... [or product]... for which one is paying' (McManus, 1975, p. 337).

While random variations and/or fear of cheating are given as reasons for incurring measurement costs for goods (services) of a simple nature – *product idiosyncrasy* is provided as an additional reason for increasing the cost of contract policing *ex post* (Hallwood, 1990). Hallwood (1990) defines the state of product idiosyncrasy as goods or services having multi-attributes or variable multi-attributes. Such a state complicates the process of product or service selection, thereby raising measurement costs (Hallwood, 1990). What determines the extent of policing costs are listed in Tables 13.5 and 13.6.

> **Observation 7: Policing (enforcement) costs, in both the intermediate goods (services) market and the labour market, are positively related to the extent of random variations in goods (services) being exchanged, as well as, the extent of its attributes.**

Table 13.5 Determinants of contract policing (enforcement) costs (labour market)

Supervision and management costs
Policing costs are positively related to the:
• probability of random variations;
• extent and variability of labour service attributes;
• probability of shirking; and the
• probability of perquisite over-consumption.
Policing costs are negatively related to the:
• volume of transactions; and
• frequency of transactions.

Table 13.6 Determinants of contract policing (enforcement) costs (intermediate goods (services) market)

Policing costs are positively related to the:
• probability of random variations;
• extent and variability of good/service attributes; and the
• probability of cheating.
Policing costs are negatively related to the:
• volume of transactions; and
• frequency of transactions

Subsequently, McManus (1975) recognizes that the cost of such policing is not only made up of the direct cost of measuring the quantity and/or quality of output, but also includes the foregone gains from trade which result from errors in the measurement itself. However, with an increase in the precision of measurement comes an increase in costs. Therefore, in the interests of efficiency, a certain amount of error in measurement will not be worthwhile for buyers and sellers to eliminate (McManus, 1975). Hallwood (1990) adds that rather than their eliminating measurement errors, the market compensates for such errors as illustrated by such mechanisms as product warranties (guarantees), brand names (trademarks) and share contracts like royalty agreements.

North and Thomas (1973) note that enforcement costs, as with search costs, have a fixed cost component and therefore are subject to economies of scale as the number of transactions increase. Subsequently, Wang (1999) states that reputation can work to protect consumers from fraudulent vendors; however, in order for this to work, the 'game' must have many players, must be played frequently and cheating behaviour must be detectable in a given round before the next one takes place.

Observation 8: Policing (enforcement) costs in both the labour and intermediate goods (services) markets are negatively related to the volume and frequency of transactions.

As highlighted, the volume and frequency of transactions can be used as a proxy measure for policing (enforcement) costs for both the labour and the intermediate goods (services) markets.

Cheung (1983) argues that the measurement costs of knowing about a product are reduced if it is a final one. However, in the case of intermediate goods and services – where the difficult arises in identifying in advance the good or service wanted – the exchange of such goods (services) is replaced by the market exchange of labour (Cheung, 1983). Moreover, wherein such goods and services are difficult to identify and are produced 'in-house', measurement costs are not eradicated. Indeed, since there is still a market exchange, the price mechanism still works. Cheung (1983) notes that the firm does not supersede the market, but, instead, replaces transactions in one market with transactions in another market. The main idea here is that measurement costs involving the exchange of goods and services are replaced by measurement costs involving the exchange of labour.

Shirking and policing (enforcement) costs

Measurement costs involving the market exchange of labour when team production is used, relate specifically to measuring the marginal productivity of each labour unit and providing the appropriate rewards (Alchian and Demsetz, 1972). In modern society as a direct consequence of technological factors, teamwork is seen to be the most efficient form of work as it deepens the level of specialization and the division of labour (Adam Smith, 1776). Hence in the case of teamwork, the productivity of each team member is greater compared to the individual productivity resulting from separate work. Team production is defined as any co-operative activity of production whereby several inputs are used and where the product is not a sum of the separable outputs created by each input (Alchian and Demsetz, 1972). The following simple example can help to better appreciate the concept of team production. Take a final output Z which requires the use of two labour inputs x_1 and x_2. With team production the production function of Z does not involve two separate functions (one function belonging to x_1 and the other belonging to x_2). Hence one cannot simply add up two separate functions to obtain a sum equal to Z.

Subsequently, because in team production relevant inputs do not yield identifiable separable products, the market can only identify the marginal productivity of the team and there will be measurement costs associated with identifying the marginal productivity of each team member (Alchian and Demsetz, 1972). This matter of policing team production is crucial as there will be a greater incentive for team members to shirk if their individual marginal productivity is not easily identifiable (Alchian and Demsetz, 1972). Within the firm, 'there is no immediate loss of pecuniary income from consumption on the job, and individuals therefore, tend to reduce the total output generated by the firm by shirking' (McManus, 1974, p. 345).

Alchian and Demsetz (1972) argue that a supervisor can be appointed to monitor the marginal productivity of each team member but because the supervisor has the same incentive to shirk, a residual reward should be used to control the behavior of the supervisor. Hence higher supervision which is required to reduce shirking and increase productivity, would necessitate higher residual rewards.

> **Observation 9: Policing (enforcement) costs in the labour market are positively related to the level of shirking.**

Hence, the measurement costs of team production relate to the costs of monitoring the quantity and/or quality of the labour service provided in the market exchange. Consequently, the policing costs of a transaction involving the exchange of labour specifically includes

> **the expenditure of resources on measuring the marginal productivity of labour.**

Gordon (1996) points to the 'bureaucratic burden' which relates to the extensive size and cost of the managerial and supervisory machine in US corporations and argues that it had grown larger during the 1990s. According to US statistics, in 1994 there were 17.3 million private non-farm workers employed in supervisory jobs, roughly equaling the entire population of Australia (Gordon, 1996).

Perquisite overconsumption and agency costs

An additional point regarding the monitoring and enforcement costs of contracting in the *managerial labour market* involves the separation of ownership and control within a firm. While managers can be paid a residual reward to give them the incentive to adequately supervise the productivity of team members. Such a residual also serves to reduce abuse by managers of the owners' capital thereby reducing agency costs. Jensen and Meckling (1976) argue that the separation of ownership from management leads to the principal–agent problem. The principal (owners of capital or shareholders) whose interest is maximum returns on investment of capital is at odds with the agents (managers) whose interest is more likely related to the growth of the firm or perhaps their own prestige.

Iaobucci and Trebilcock (1996) point out that managers may undertake *perquisite overconsumption*, in the form of using firm's resources for private benefit. Take, for example, the acquisition of lavish office furniture or a private jet. Vilasuso and Minkler (2001) argue that if a firm opts for equity finance then the owner/manager dilutes his/her control but would be persuaded to follow perquisite overconsumption because such a cost can be shared with new bondholders. Moreover, managers who are concerned about their future reputation in managerial labour markets and the way this is affected by the outcome of current investment decisions, may be less likely to undertake investment in a risk-neutral way. Hence, managers are less likely to pursue investments with the highest expected values and instead, are more likely to pursue the maximization of their own personal utility (Iaobucci and Trebilcock, 1996).

Subsequently, agency costs necessitate the need for the careful construction and implementation of an appropriate incentive system, which is designed by the principals to capture and reduce the abuse of their capital by managers. Indeed, supervision and management costs are not only positively associated with the measurement costs of the marginal productivity of team members but also reflect the extent of potential agency costs.

Observation 10: Policing (enforcement) costs in the labour market are positively related to the extent of perquisite overconsumption by managers.

In theory, the greater the difficulty of measuring the *potential* abuse of capital, the higher should be the residual rewards given to management. Indeed, greater management costs reflect greater measurement costs, involving the monitoring of the marginal productivity of managers themselves. The following schedule illustrates some of the escalating annual salaries of various corporate executives in the United States over a period of less than ten years:

1981	Rand Araskog (ITT)	$1.15 million
1986	Lee Iacocca (Chrysler)	$20.5 million
1987	Charles Lazarus (Toys 'R' Us)	$60 million
1990	Steven Ross (Time Warner)	$78.2 million
1990	Donald Pels (LIN Broadcasting)	$186.2 million
1993	Michael Eisner (Disney)	$203 million

Abbasi and Hollman (1998) state that the average salary of corporate executives has grown by 39 per cent and while top executives made 34 times more than the average worker did in 1974, by 1995 top executives were making, on average, 159 times more. Consequently, it is argued that the policing or enforcement costs of a transaction involving the exchange of (management) labour also includes

the amount of residual rewards given to managers to prevent their abuse of the owners' capital via perquisite overconsumption.

To further illustrate the agency costs of contracting, consider the model proposed by Diamond (1992). In the model there is the consideration of the firm and its shareholders on one hand, and management on the other – along with the corresponding assumptions. In regards to management, it is assumed that there are two choices for the level of effort: low or high. Effort is used in this model to capture the conflict of interests between management and their shareholders. Moreover, it is assumed that the utility of the manager is a function of both the manager's wealth, and effort level. Furthermore, it is assumed that management dislikes positive effort because it provides negative utility, and correspondingly is risk averse towards wealth which provides positive utility.

The key finding in Diamond's model is that there is a positive relationship between the effort level of management and the probability of earning a high return in the firm. Hence, the problem for shareholders is to design a salary package for the managers which will induce a high level of effort and yet increase the probability of the firm earning a high profit. Additionally, it is assumed that a manager can obtain alternative employment, which would provide him/her with an expected utility of one unit which we will count as a reservation wage. Therefore, shareholders need to provide a compensation package, which is worth at least one unit to the manager to keep him/her in their employ.

Where effort is completely observable and at zero cost to the shareholders, there is no agency problem because managers may be directed to provide a specific level of effort. All that is needed is a corresponding compensation package designed to yield the required expected probability outcome for profit. In such a case, a simple or 'pure' wage can be paid: a high wage for high effort and a low wage for low effort. In this way, it is in the direct interest of the shareholders once effort is completely observable, to pay the manager a high wage and direct him/her to provide a high level of effort.

However when management effort is not completely observable, the agency (incentive) issue becomes an matter of concern. In this imperfect information case, 'an optimal contract from the point of view of the stockholders is one which pays the manager just enough to get him/her to take the job, and still provide just enough risk (as an incentive) to get him/her to choose the proper level of effort' (Diamond, 1992, p. 6). Hence in summary, the optimal contract

- induces the manager to select a high level of effort;
- provides managers with an expected utility equal to 1; and
- leaves managers indifferent between expected utilities given high levels and low levels of effort.

This outcome is, of course, only 'second best' when effort is not directly observable. Under the full information 'pure' wage case, expected profit is going to be higher, yet due to high measurement costs or the bounded rationality of agents themselves, such a contract is seldom realized. The difference between the expected profits from the full information case and the imperfect information case is the so called *agency cost* of providing incentives (Diamond, 1992).

Hence, amount of policing costs of labour market contracts can be linked to the extent of investment in supervision or management costs. Such investment or costs are the direct result of the need by firms to measure the marginal productivity of lower tier employees and reduce the potential abuse of capital by managers through the provision of incentives.

Subsequently, in addition to the volume of transactions as mentioned in Table 13.5 and Table 13.6, supervision and management costs can also be used as proxy measures for policing (enforcement) costs of transactions involving labour inputs.

3.2 The costs of coordinating the inputs of a labour market contract

According to the viewpoint of some economists, there is an ideal equilibrium condition where only decreasing demand curves and increasing factor supply curves determine the static limitations of a firm's size (Kaldor, 1934). Indeed, in this state of the world, there are no coordination problems. However, such an 'ideal' equilibrium provides very limited insight to understanding variations in customer purchases, manufacturing disturbances, distribution problems and the vagaries of labour and materials procurement (Williamson, 1967).

As an extension, Williamson (1967) introduces the stochastic equilibrium in regards to understanding business behaviour and defines such equilibrium one where the firm responds to changing circumstances occurring with stochastic regularity and where knowledge of such circumstances in advances is limited or non-existent. Williamson adds that:

> There is a great deal of evidence that almost all organizational structures tend to produce false images in the decision-maker, and that the larger the more authoritarian the organization, the better the chance that its top decision makers will be operating tin purely imaginary worlds. This perhaps is the most fundamental reason for supporting that there are ultimately diminishing returns to scale. (1967, p. 123)

Indeed, when a firm gets larger, 'there may be decreasing returns to the entrepreneur function... due to the failure of the entrepreneur to make the best use of factors of production... [by not placing]... the factors in the uses where their value is the greatest' (Coase, 1937, pp. 394–5). The notion of the 'firm' involves the following characteristics:

- it is a set of contracts between an employer and employees;
- the contracts specify the payment for labour of employees;

- the employer claims the residual of the contracts; and
- the employer has the authority to decide on the allocation of labour use of its employees (Yang, 1993a).

Hence, any discussion of firm size will ultimately involve the number of labour contracts. As such, decreasing returns to the entrepreneurial function (or increasing coordination costs) can be linked to the number of labour contracts in the firm. Moreover, outsourcing, in particular, production processes can reduce such coordination costs of contracting in the labour market (Alston and Gillespie, 1986).

Williamson (1967) notes that these coordination costs can be explained by looking at what is commonly referred to as the 'control-loss phenomenon'. Control-loss is defined as the loss in the quality of data handed down to a coordinator and instructions handed down to the operating units of an organization. It turns out that a firm's hierarchical structure can be used to alleviate problems of control-loss resulting from increases in the size of the firm or increases in labour market contracts (Williamson, 1967). Ross writes, 'by appropriate measures of decentralization and control, the firm may expand without incurring costs of co-ordination' (1951–52, p. 154).

It follows, then, that the careful coordination for the process of production, as well as the flow of inputs from suppliers and outputs to final or intermediary users, cannot happen without the constant attention of a managerial team or hierarchy (Chandler, 1990). An important consideration here is that notwithstanding economies of roundabout production achieved by increasing the number of layers in a hierarchy, an increase in a firm's hierarchical structure also alleviates the control-loss phenomenon. This results in the reduction of the coordination costs of firm size as measured by the number of labour contracts. Hence an increase in the number of layers in the production process leads to greater economies of roundabout production and lower transaction costs for labour exchange.

Observation 11: Coordination costs involving labour contracts are inversely related to the number of layers in a production process as commonly referred to as 'the degree of roundaboutness'.

Upon examination, there remains an optimum hierarchy or optimum number of layers of production (constrained by the bounded rationality of human beings) which maximizes the difference of advantages and disadvantages of an increasing number of layers (Yang, 1994, p. 12). To illustrate the advantages and disadvantages of hierarchical organization, consider the following two examples of the division of labour between 100 workers as shown in Figures 13.1 and 13.2.

In the flat structure shown in Figure 13.1, there is the advantage of low management costs. Inherent in this structure, there is a disadvantage in

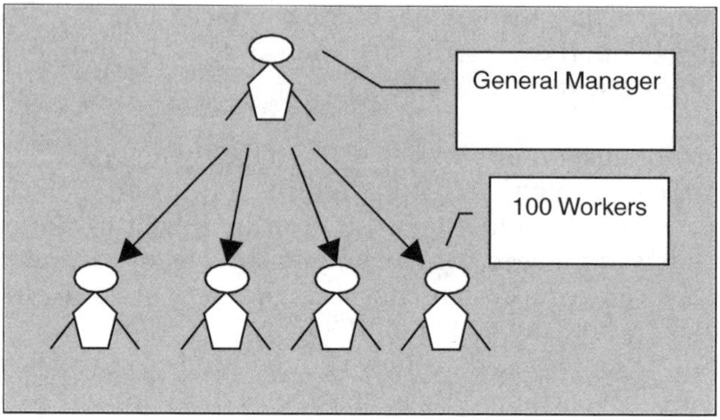

Figure 13.1 Flat organization of production

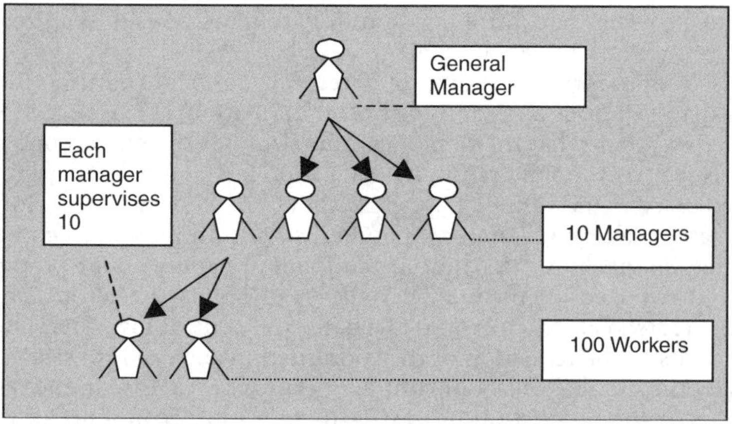

Figure 13.2 Hierarchical organization of production

terms of low quality supervision and the potential for control-loss increases, thereby increasing the coordination costs of labour.

In the hierarchical structure shown in Figure 13.2, adding a layer of middle management to the production process will result in the disadvantage of higher managerial costs, however, there is now the advantage of higher quality supervision. Consequently, the potential for control-loss has decreased (the coordination costs of labour decrease).

In Williamson's (1967) formal model of optimal hierarchy it is established that there is indeed an increase in control-loss (coordination costs) resulting from an increase in the number of employees. In his model, Williamson found that as the compliance with the supervisors' intention increases, so too does the optimal number of hierarchical tiers within the firm. Indeed, in optimal terms, an infinite number of tiers are associated with 100 per cent compliance with the supervisors' intentions. Indeed, there is no control-loss. Williamson (1967) states, however, that values for compliance are typically less than 100 per cent. Indeed Williamson has found that in the US, the degree of compliance has an implied value of 90 per cent and there remains some control-loss. The reasons for this are, firstly, that the ability to increase the number of tiers to improve control-loss is constrained by the amount of subordinates that each supervisor can monitor (i.e. span of control). The greater the span of control, then the more tiers can be adopted to improve co-ordination costs. Secondly, the wage multiple between hierarchical levels (or the amount of additional payment that supervisors are given over an above their subordinates) will also affect the number of tiers adopted. As more tiers are adopted with more supervisors then this will increase supervision costs.

Hence, as the span of control increases, so too does the number of optimal tiers, but when the wage multiple between levels increases the number of optimal tiers decreases. Ultimately, with more hierarchical levels and improved quality in supervision, there is a tradeoff between *improvements in control-loss* (a reduction in coordination costs of labour) and an *increase in supervision (management) costs.*

Therefore, the number of hierarchical layers in a firm can be used as a proxy measure for the coordination costs of labour inputs.

3.3 The costs of external arbitration

Arbitration is defined as 'a quasi-judicial process... [the sole purpose being] ... the adjudication of disputes by an impartial umpire akin to a judge in a legal action' (Baer, 1982, p. ix). Tirole (1989) argues that in the event of asymmetric information *ex ante*, parties to a transaction may resort to such a third party *ex post.*

Should disputes arise concerning the share of surplus *ex post*, buyers and sellers may agree to accept arbitration via court action, tribunal hearings, or other arbitration bodies (for example, Industrial Relations Commission or Basic Wage Commission) (Plowman, 1992). Hence third parties become involved when normal bargaining between employers and employees (or their representative trade union) fails to produce mutually beneficial solutions (Owen-Smith et al., 1989). The idea here is that the 'trusted' arbitrator would be able to independently arrive at decisions, which would be impartial and emulate the outcome of complete contracts. The extent of contract completeness will depend on the frequency and number of exchanges occurring in the market. However, in the absence of this occurring, Baer (1982) states that the provision for arbitration is the 'sole and exclusive' means for obtaining a final and binding decision on the interpretation of a contract or its application – necessary for sound contractual performance.

> **Observation 12: External arbitration costs are positively related to the extent of information asymmetry between parities and the incompleteness of labour market or intermediate goods (services) market contracts.**

However, 'external arbitration is likely to be costly' (Tirole, 1989, p. 30). The cost of external dispute machinery is defined as:

> the amount of expenditure allocated by a party to a market exchange on legal or other external arbitration grounds in order to rule out 'unfair practices' by the other party to such an exchange *ex post*. This may be with regards to price quality, time or place of exchange and/or form of payment.

Baer (1982) notes that labour arbitration has grown rapidly since the Second World War and is provided for practically all of labour contracts in the United States. However, external arbitration costs apply to intermediate goods (services) markets as well.

Subsequently, the costs of external arbitration will be used as one of the measures of the transaction costs involving labour and intermediate goods (services) contracts.

3.4 The costs of rent appropriation with asset-specific investment (holdup costs)

It has been argued that due to reasons of *location* or *characteristics* of transactions, there arises the need for asset-specific investments in order for exchange to take place between buyer and seller (Williamson, 1981). Investments become site-specific in nature if the location of transactions between buyer and seller is small enough so as to take advantage of reduced transportation costs (Tirole, 1989). With regards to the *characteristics* of transactions, it can be seen that one or both parties may need to initiate investments which are human-specific or physical-specific whereby such human or physical capital becomes specifically tailor-made or custom designed for the transaction in question (Joskow, 1988; Tirole, 1989). Generally speaking, a specific asset can be defined as an 'asset whose value for alternative uses is significantly lower than its value for its current use' (Nam et al., 1996, p. 36). In time, such transaction-specific investments, whether the result of location or characteristic purposes, lead to asset immobility (Joskow, 1988).

Normally, buyers would have the facility to select each other from a vast pool within a competitive environment. Lyons states that 'if the product being traded is very standard, so that there are many alternative buyers and sellers at all times, contracting between producers will be informal' (1996,

p. 33). However, the spot market fails *ex post* because idiosyncratic transactions between buyers and sellers quickly become relationships characterized by bilateral monopolies due to the transaction-specific nature of costs. The problem here is that with such idiosyncratic transactions of goods and services, the realized benefits of relationship-specific investment depend upon the successful execution of transactions (Williamson, 1986). Williamson (1986) argues, however, that the combination of idiosyncratic transactions and the incompleteness of an *ex ante* contract could entail hazards of '*ex post* opportunism'. Indeed where contracts fail to provide for all future contingencies, a change in circumstances favouring either buyer or seller allows one economic agent to behave opportunistically *ex post* and extract rents from the other agent. This is known as the problem of 'holdup' (Tirole, 1989). Nam et al. (1996, p. 36) argues that 'if the client firm has a tied-in relationship with a vendor, the vendor's opportunistic behaviour can result in a significant loss to the client'. Contracts are likely to be incomplete because of uncertainties, information asymmetries, and the incontractibility of intangibles such as entrepreneurial know-how (Yang, 1992). Denzau (1992) argues that the ability of markets to coordinate decentralized decisions by economic agents is hampered by agents' opportunistic behaviour. Losses occurring from such a failure to cooperate are strictly defined by economists as transaction costs.

It follows that unless buyers and sellers adopt a way to overcome the costs of writing a more complete *ex ante* spot contract, investment incentives in the economy will remain defective with inefficient amounts of *ex ante* investment being made (Grossman and Hart, 1986). Hallwood discusses the highly site-specific and physical-specific nature of oil platforms and states that 'with obvious risks of rent appropriation, it would be unlikely that investment platforms would be forthcoming, much less optimal, and oil companies would have to invest in their own platforms' (1990, p. 177). Nam et al. (1996) adds that since the return of such specific assets is also highly specific to the client firm, vendors are likely to be reluctant about investing in these assets, thereby requiring in-house provision.

Furthermore, if firm-specific investments are also relevant for the labour market, 'employment specificity implies that the worker is effectively a partner of the enterprise' (Rosen, 1985, p. 1148). However, this raises the problem that the return on specific capital inherent in employees is stochastic and its joint ownership raises the two problems of how this specific human capital is to be used and how its risks are to be shared (Rosen, 1985).

Avoiding the holdup problem (and the subsequent deficiency in *ex ante* investment) would require a reduction of the incentives for *ex post* opportunistic behaviour by simply making *ex ante* contracts more complete through accounting for greater future contingencies. Rosen (1985) argues that an *ex ante* agreement or contract resolves such issues as utilization of human capital and risk sharing. Rosen adds that in the case of labour market exchange:

> A contract is a voluntary *ex-ante* agreement that resolves the distribution and uncertainty about the value and utilization of shared investments between contracting parties. The contract specifies precisely the amount of labour to be utilized and the wages to be paid in each state of nature. (1985, p. 1145)

However, Lyons (1996, p. 34) notes that 'contracts are costly and should rely on only the necessary minimum of detail and contingencies'. Rosen (1985) agrees with this notion, stating that contracts do not contain all states of nature because many of these are unforeseen with so many possibilities. In addition, Milgrom and Roberts (1990) state that even if one was able to specify every contingency, the *limitations of language* may result in an ambiguous interpretation by a court seeking to enforce the contract. Indeed, evidence from US manufacturing shows that most contracts do not contain sophisticated terms and a survey on UK manufacturing shows that while most firms specify price, payment dates, and product specification, the formulation of prime duties and rewards is quite simplistic (Lyons, 1996). The reason for this simplicity of contracts can be seen as a direct result of both the frequency and number of exchanges occurring in the market. As with measurement costs, increasing the number of transactors on both sides of the market increases the mobility of the specific-attribute assets (reducing their specific nature) and hence the potential for rent appropriation (or holdup costs) declines (Hallwood, 1990). Therefore the environment for more simplistic contracts is created.

Observation 13: Holdup costs of idiosyncratic investment with asset specificity are inversely related to the volume and frequency of transactions in the imperfect information case.

By increasing the number and frequency of transactions of a particular market, in either the intermediate goods (services) market or labour market, it has the effect of reducing search costs, negotiation costs and enforcement costs and any potential holdup costs of such transactions (for example, rent appropriation).

Hence, the volume and frequency of transactions can both be used as proxy indicators of holdup costs in the labour market and intermediate goods (services) market.

Moreover, Alt et al. (1999) adopts a number of measures for assessing the mobility of physical and human capital. In terms of the degree of asset specificity of physical capital, Alt et al. (1999) use R&D intensity, whereby the higher the level of investment of R&D the higher the immobility of an asset and its associated 'holdup' costs. Firms that sell products or services with close substitutes are less likely to invest in R&D. Where there are 'learning-by-doing' effects, R&D leads to human capital specificity as well.

Observation 14: Holdup costs of idiosyncratic investment with asset specificity are positively related to the degree of R&D intensity in the presence of imperfect information.

Subsequently, R&D intensity, which indicates the degree of asset specificity, can be used as a proxy measure for the holdup costs in the labour market and intermediate goods (services) market.

In terms of human-capital specificity, Alt et al. (1999) utilizes a job mobility measure, which is calculated as annual gross increase plus annual gross decrease in jobs divided by total jobs, and argues that low job mobility implies higher human specificity.

Observation 15: Holdup costs of idiosyncratic investment with asset specificity are inversely related to the degree of job mobility in the presence of imperfect information.

Hence, the degree of job mobility can be used as a proxy measure for the degree of human capital specificity and, by implication, holdup costs in the labour market.

Vilasuso and Minkler (2001) argue that other appropriate proxies for asset specificity used in their analysis of agency costs and asset specificity on the capital structure of firms are the ratio of government sales to total sales and the ratio of advertising expenditure to total sales. Vilasuso and Minkler (2001, p. 64) argue that 'government procurement by its very nature, involves substantial recurring investment in relationship-specific assets, especially in the case of defense contracting'. The ratio of government sales to total sales is relevant particularly in the transportation equipment industry.

Observation 16: Holdup costs of idiosyncratic investment with asset specificity are positively related to the ratio of government sales to total sales of the organization in the presence of imperfect information.

For print and publishing industries, Vilasuso and Minkler (2001) argue that sunk costs like advertising are a firm-level strategic decision used to influence the consumer's willingess to pay for the firm's product or service. However, given that this sunk cost has no salvage value, advertising has no value outside the current transaction and due to this immobility, investment in advertising can be regarded as involving a high degree of asset specificity (Joskow, 1988; Nam et al., 1996). Since printing and publishing has a high degree of advertising to total sales, this ratio is used to measure the degree of asset specificity in these two industries (Vilasuso and Minkler, 2001). Conceivably this proxy measure for asset specificity would be relevant in other industries where the degree of advertising expenditure to sales is high (such as in tourism).

Observation 17: Holdup costs of idiosyncratic investment with asset specificity are positively related to the ratio of advertising expenditure to total sales of an organization in the presence of imperfect information.

The determinants of holdup costs are listed in Tables 13.7 and 13.8.

Finally, the proxy measures for each of the aforementioned transaction costs relating to the labour/intermediate goods (services) markets are summarized in Table 13.9. These proxy measures are inferred from the aforementioned observations (1–17).

According to Table 13.9, the entire range of transaction costs of dealing in the labour market will be measured by:

1: the number of buyers and sellers in the labour market, the value of transactions and the frequency of transactions;
2: the degree of labour contract standardization.
3: the degree of unionization;
4: the cost of estimating labour-contract-specific economic indicators;

Table 13.7 Determinants of holdup costs (labour market)

Holdup costs are positively related to the:
- degree of R&D intensity; and the
- degree of job mobility.

Holdup costs are negatively related to the:
- volume of transactions; and
- frequency of transactions.

Table 13.8 Determinants of holdup costs (intermediate goods (services) market)

Holdup costs are positively related to the:
- degree of R&D intensity;
- extent of government sales to total sales; and the
- extent of advertising to total sales.

Holdup costs are negatively related to the:
- volume of transactions; and
- frequency of transactions.

Table 13.9 A listing of proxy measures used for transaction costs in the labour and intermediate goods (services) markets

Proxy/actual measures	*Types of transaction cost*
Value of transactions	Search costs
Volume of transactions	Search costs (negotiation) costs/ Policing (enforcement) costs/holdup costs
Frequency of transactions	Search (negotiation) costs/ policing (enforcement) costs/holdup costs
Standardization of goods (services)	Negotiation costs
Degree of union membership	Negotiation costs
Expenditures on estimations for contract-specific economic indicators	Negotiation costs
External arbitration costs	External arbitration costs
Supervision and management costs	Policing and enforcement costs
Number of hierarchical layers of a firm	Coordination costs
Degree of R&D intensity	Holdup costs
Job mobility	Holdup costs
Government sales to total sales	Holdup costs
Advertising expenditure to total sales	Holdup costs

5: the cost of supervision and management;
6: the degree of roundabout production which refers to the number of hierarchical layers of production;
7: the cost of external arbitration to settle *ex post* disputes involving labour inputs over work conditions (requirements), wage payments;
8: the degree of R&D intensity; and
9: the degree of job mobility.

On the other hand, the transaction costs of dealing in the intermediate goods (services) market will be measured by:

1: the number of buyers and sellers of intermediate inputs in the market, the value of transactions and the frequency of transactions;
2: the degree of intermediate goods (services) contract standardization;
3: the cost of estimating specific economic indicators for intermediate good (service) contracts;
4: the cost of external arbitration; and
5: the degree of R&D intensity.
6: the degree of government sales to total sales
7: the degree of advertising to total sales

Upon observing the various transaction costs associated with exchanges in the market, it has been demonstrated that labour market contracts reveal additional types of costs not traditionally found in the exchange of intermediate goods (services). These additional types of costs relate to the negotiation costs of strikes and the coordination costs of hierarchical production, as well as the policing (enforcement) costs of shirking and abuse of an owner's capital by managers. Moreover, unlike with intermediate goods (services), simply increasing the level of competition in the market cannot reduce these additional types of costs.

4 Conclusion

It has been claimed that 'transaction costs theory contains no account of how or when novel organizational designs emerge' (Roberts and Greenwood, 1997, p. 349). Jones (1997, p. 26) states that 'the choice theoretic framework which focuses on transaction cost economizing under given circumstances ignores the way in which new choice sets evolve'. However, these aforementioned authors fail to consider two important factors.

Firstly, unlike the analysis of Williamson (1981) and Coase (1937), this chapter does not presume that 'market transaction costs' are only associated with the exchange of intermediate goods and services. That is, if the firm organizes production then this chapter does not assume that it is done primarily to reduce the transaction costs of using the market. According to the traditional transaction cost view, the mode of organizing resources will be the one which minimizes market transaction costs. Such a distinction of a firm/market boundary looks at transaction costs from a one-sided perspective. It should be re-stated here that the choice to exchange goods and services within the firm as opposed to the market *necessitates hiring labour through the market anyway*.

Secondly, since both institutions (the firm and the market) involve the use of markets, the key is not to see which institution minimizes 'market transaction costs' but rather to look at the relative market transaction costs for intermediate goods (services) and for labour. By seeing transaction costs in this way, it becomes possible, as Jones has stated, 'to comprehend the dynamic interaction between organization and technology so crucial to an understanding of strategic development and structural change' (1997, p. 26).

References

Abbasi, Sami M. and Hollman, Kenneth W. (1998) 'The Myth and Realities of Downsizing', *Records Management Quarterly*, April, 32, 2, 31–37.

Abdel-Latif, Abla M. and Nugent, Jeffrey B. (1996) 'Transaction Cost Impairments to International Trade: Lessons from Egypt', *Contemporary Economic Policy*, XIV, April, 1–14.

Alchian, A. and Demsetz, H. (1972) 'Production, Information Costs, and Economic Organization', *American Economic Review*, 62, 777–95.

Alston, L.J. and Gillespie, W. (1989) 'Resource Co-ordination and Transaction Costs: A Framework for Analysing the Firm/Market Boundary', *Journal of Economic Behavior and Organization*, 11, 2, 191–212.

Alt, J.E., Carlsen, F., Heum, P., and Johansen, K. (1999) 'Asset Specificity and the Political Behavior of Firms: Lobbying for Subsidies in Norway', *International Organization*, 53, 99–112.

Baer, W.E. (1982) *Winning in Labour Arbitration* (Chicago, IL: Crain Books).

Chandler, A. (1990) *Scale and Scope: the Dynamics of Industrial Capitalism* (Cambridge MA: Belknap Press).

Cheung, S. (1998) 'The Transaction Costs Paradigm', *Economic Inquiry*, October, 36, 4, 514–21.

Cheung, S. (1983) 'The Contractual Nature of the Firm', *Journal of Law and Economics*, XXVI, April, 2–12.

Christensen, S. (1980) *Unions and The Public Interest* (Vancouver: The Fraser Institute).

Coase, R.H. (1937) 'The Nature of the Firm', *Economica*, 4, 386–405.

Cortes, M., Berry, A. and Ishaq, A. (1987) *Success in Small and Medium-scale Enterprises: the Evidence from Colombia* (New York: Published for the World Bank [by] Oxford University Press).

Denzau, A.T. (1992) *Microeconomic Analysis: Markets and Dynamics* (Homewood, IL: Irwin Inc).

Diamond, D.W. (1992) 'Principal–Agent Model', University of Chicago, Class Notes.

Eggertsson, Thrainn (1990) 'The Cost of Transacting and Allocation of Resources', *Economic Behavior and Institutions* (New York: Cambridge University Press), 13–20.

Freeman, R.B. and Medoff, J.L. (1984) *What do Unions Do?* (New York: Basic Books, Inc).

Gordon, D.M. (1996) *Fat and Mean: the Corporate Squeeze of Working Americans and the Myth of Managerial Downsizing* (New York: Martin Kessler Books).

Grossman, Sanford and Hart, Oliver (1986) 'The Costs and Benefits of Ownership: a Theory of Vertical and Lateral Integration', *Journal of Political Economy*, 94, 691.

Hallwood, P.C. (1990) *Transaction Costs and Trade between Multinational Corporations: a Study of Offshore-Oil Production* (Boston: Unwin Hyman).

Hart, O. (1983) 'Optimal Labour Contracts under Asymmetric Information: an Introduction', *The Review of Economic Studies*, 50, 1, 3–35.

Hiller, E.T. (1969) *The Strike: a Study in Collective Action* (Arno & The New York Times).

Hobbs, J.E. (1997) 'Measuring the Importance of Transaction Costs in Cattle Marketing', *American Journal of Agricultural Economics*, 79, 4, 1083–93.

Iacobucci, E. and Trebilcock, M.J. (1996) *Value for Money, C.D.* (Toronto: Howe Institute).

Jensen, M.C. and Meckling, H.W. (1976) 'The Theory of the Firm: Managerial Behavior, Agency Costs and Ownership Structure', *Journal of Financial Economics*, 3, 305–60.

Jones, S.R.H. (1997) 'Transaction Costs and the theory of the firm: the scope and limitations of the new institutional approach', *Business History*, 39, 9–25.

Joskow, P.L. (1988) 'Asset Specificity and the Structure of Vertical Relationships', in O. Williamson and S. Winter (eds) (1993), *The Nature of the Firm* (New York: Oxford University Press).

Kaldor, N. (1934) 'The Equilibrium of the Firm', *Economic Journal*, 44, 173, 60–76.

Liu, Pak-Wai and Yang, Xiaokai (2000) 'Division of Labour, Transaction Cost, Evolution of the Firm and Firm Size', *Journal of Economic Behaviour and Organization*, 42, 145–65.

Lyons, B.R. (1996) 'Empirical Relevance of Efficient Contract Theory: Inter-Firm Contracts', *Oxford Review of Economic Policy*, 12, 4, 27–52.

Matthews, R.C.O. (1986) 'The Economics of Institutions and the Sources of Growth', *Economic Journal*, 96, 384, 903–19.

McBeath, I. (1979) *Votes, Virtues and Vices: Trade Union Power* (Associated Business Press).

McManus, J.C. (1975) 'The Costs of Alternative Economic Organization', *Canadian Journal of Economics*, 8, 3, 26.

Milgrom, P. and Roberts, J. (1990) 'Bargaining influence costs and the organization of economic activity', in J. Alt and K. Shepsle (eds), *Perspectives on Positive Political Economy* (Cambridge: Cambridge University Press).

Miller, P. and Mulvey, C. (1996) 'Unions, Firm Size and Wages', *The Economic Record*, 72, 217, 138–53.

Nam, K., Rajagopalan, S., Raghav Rao, H. and Chaudhury, A. (1996) 'A Two-Level Investigation of Information Systems Outsourcing', *Communications of the ACM*, 39, 7, 36(9).

North, D.C. and Thomas, R.P. (1973) *The Rise of the Western World: a New Economic History* (New York: Cambridge University Press).

Owen-Smith, E., Frick, B. and Griffiths, T. (1989) *Third Party Involvement In Industrial Disputes: a Comparative Study Of West Germany And Britain* (Aldershot: Avebury).

Plowman, D.H. (1992) 'Australian Wage Determination: Select Documents', UNSW Industrial Relations Resource Series, no. 9.

Roberts, P.W. and Greenwood, R. (1997) 'Integrating Transaction Cost and Institutional Theories: Toward a Constrained-Efficiency Framework for Understanding Organizational Design Adoption', *Academy of Management Review*, 22, 2, 346–73.

Rosen, S. (1985) 'Implicit Contracts: a Survey', *Journal of Economic Literature*, XXIII, September, 1144–1175.

Ross, N.S. (1951–52) 'Management and the Size of the Firm', *Review of Economic Studies*, 19, in O. Williamson (1967) 'Hierarchical Control and Optimum Firm Size', *Journal of Political Economics*, 75.

Stiles, Renee A. (1996) 'Controlling Overhead Expense with Transaction Cost Economics', http://dfca.larc.nasa.gov/dfc/trcst.html.

Taylor, W.J., Roger, J.A., and Lockwood, R.S. (1977) *Military Unions: U.S. Trends and Issues* (Beverly Hills, CA and London: Sage Publications).

Tirole, J. (1989) *The Theory of Industrial Organization* (Cambridge: The MIT Press).

Vilasuso, J. and Minkler, A. (2001) 'Agency Costs, Asset Specificity, and the Capital Structure of the Firm', *Journal of Economic Behavior and Organization*, 44, 55–69.

Wang, Ning (1999) 'Transaction Costs and the Structure of the Market: A Case Study', *The American Journal of Economics and Sociology*, 58, 4, October, 783–98.

Williamson, O.E. (1967) 'Hierarchical Control and Optimum Firm Size', *Journal of Political Economics*, 75.

Williamson, O.E. (1986) *Economic Organisation: Firms, Markets and Policy Control* (New York: New York University Press).

Williamson, O.E. (1981) 'The Modern Corporation: Origins, Evolution, Attributes', *Journal of Economic Literature*, XIX, 1537–68.

Yang, X. and Ng, S. (1994) 'Specialization and Division of Labour: a Survey', Department of Economics, Monash University, Seminar paper.

Yang, X. and Ng, Y.-K. (1993) *Specialization and Economic Organization* (Amsterdam: North-Holland).
Yang, X. (1992) 'A Reading List for New Developments of the Theory of the Firm', Department of Economics, Monash University.
Yang, Xiaokai (2001) *Economics: a New Classical Versus Neoclassical Framework* (Cambridge, MA: Blackwell).

14

An Empirical Study on the Division of Labour and Economic Structural Changes*

Monchi Lio[a] *and Meng-chun Liu*[b]

1 Introduction

It has long been recognized by economists that there is a systematic connection between the progress in economic productivity and the growth of cities. Yang and Rice (1994) develop a general equilibrium model to explain this intrinsic connection. Their model shows that in an economy, one of the functions of cities is to be able to improve transaction efficiency, and thus to expand the level of division of labour. People become more specialized as the division of labour evolves, and in this process labour productivity improves due to economies of specialization.

The purpose of this study is to empirically test the Yang–Rice model and to investigate the interrelationships between transaction efficiency, economic structural changes including urbanization and specialization, the division of labour, and productivity. The Yang–Rice model is outlined as follows. Suppose that the production of food is land-intensive, but the production of many manufactured goods is not. In the following example, take the manufacturing goods to be cloth, tools and furniture. If transaction efficiency is low, individuals will choose autarky in which there are no markets and no cities. As exogenous transaction efficiency slightly improves, the division of labour between partially specialized farmers and partially specialized cloth-weavers emerge. Since farming is land-intensive, farmers must live far away from each other. While the transaction efficiency is still relatively low, cloth-weavers will choose to live close to farmers to save the transaction costs caused by the division of labour. Hence, the level of division of labour between farmers and cloth-makers is low and cities have not yet emerged.

* We have benefited from the comments of referees and editors of this book. This research was funded by the NSF of Taiwan (grant 91–2451-H-110–001).

[a] Corresponding Address: Department of Political Economy, National Sun Yat-sen University, 70 Lien-hai Rd. Kaohsiung 804, Taiwan. E-mail: mclio@mail.nsysu.edu.tw.

[b] The International Division, Chung-Hua Institution for Economic Research, Taiwan.

As the transaction efficiency improves still further, a further division of labour between cloth-weavers, tool-makers, and furniture-makers emerges in addition to the existing division of labour between farmers and manufacturers. If the difference in transaction efficiencies of the urban and the rural sectors is sufficiently high, manufacturers prefer residing together in a city rather than residing near the farmers. This is because manufacturers' production technology is land-saving. Therefore, a city grows and the distinct dichotomy between urban and rural sectors emerges because of a high level of the division of labour between specialist manufacturers (urban residents) and between cottage manufacturers and farmers (rural residents).

According to the Yang–Rice model, the transaction efficiency plays a critical role in positively determining the per capita real income of an economy. The effects of transaction efficiency on per capita real income are mediated by the division of labour accompanied by economic structural changes in terms of urbanization and specialization. Employing a cross-country data set for 1996 released by the World Bank, this study tests the following hypotheses based on Yang and Rice's theoretical arguments: (1) the improvements in transaction efficiency enhance the level of urbanization, but reduce the share of agricultural labour force; (2) improved transaction efficiency yields a directly positive effect on per capita real income; and (3) both the increase in urbanization and the reduction in agricultural labour share, which are driven by the improvement in transaction efficiency, improve per capita real income.

This chapter is organized as follows. Section 2 provides a simplified version of the Yang–Rice model and specifies the research hypotheses. Section 3 introduces the empirical methodology used – principally the method of factor analysis, considering transaction efficiency as a theoretical latent variable. This chapter constructs two transaction efficiency factors: transportation efficiency (TE) and information/communication efficiency (ICE). Multiple Ordinary Least Squares (OLS) regression and a Three Stage Least Squares (3SLS) analysis are applied to test the research hypotheses specified in Section 2. The results are reported in Section 4. Section 5 gives some concluding remarks.

2 The model and hypotheses

Consider a simplified version of the Yang–Rice model (1994) that investigates the interrelationships between transaction efficiency, the division of labour, and urbanization (Yang, 2001). Assume that an economy produces only three goods: cloth (good 1), furniture (good 2), and food (good 3). Cloth and furniture are industrial goods requiring limited land for production, and the residences of producers of these two goods can either be dispersed over a large area or concentrated in a small area – the city. The production of food is land-intensive. The residences of farmers must be dispersed over a large area. There are M *ex ante* identical consumer-producers who can choose to specialize in producing any goods and may choose to live either close to their neighbours or at some distance. Those individuals who produce only industrial goods are labelled as C-type persons and those who produce agricultural goods are R-type persons.

The transaction cost coefficient for a unit of good purchased is $1 - K$, or, alternatively, the transaction efficiency coefficient is K. Assume that the degree of K differs from one type of person to another, and is dependent upon individuals' decisions concerning the geographical pattern of their residence. If C-type persons reside together within a small area, the transaction efficiency coefficient is $K = k$ between a pair of C-type persons. The transaction efficiency coefficient is $K = r$ between a pair of R-type persons and is $K = s$ between a C-type and an R-type person. We assume that $k > s > rk > s$. This is because the average distance between a pair of C-type persons residing together is less than the average distance between a C-type person and an R-type person occupying a large area of land. Moreover, we suppose that an R-type person resides at the centre of his/her farm, which has the shape of a circle with radius 1. Since a C-type person can minimize transaction costs by residing on the boundary of the farm if he/she trades with the farmer, the minimum distance between the R-type person and the C-type person is 1. But the distance between two R-type persons who reside at the respective centres of their farms with radius 1 is 2. Therefore, we place the implicit assumption that $s > r$.

The utility function for each consumer-producer is

$$u = \sum_{i=1}^{3} (x_i + Kx_i^d) \tag{14.1}$$

where superscript d stands for the quantity purchased (demanded). Each consumer-producer has the following production functions and endowment constraint for working time.

$$x_i + x_i^s = \text{Max}\ \{l_i - \alpha, 0\},\ l_1 + l_2 + l_3 = 1,\ \alpha \in (0,1),\ l_i \in [0, 1],\quad i = 1, 2, 3 \tag{14.2}$$

where α is a fixed learning or training cost in producing a good, l_i is an individual's level of specialization in producing good i, superscript s stands for the quantity sold (supplied), and superscript d stands for the quantity purchased (demanded). Each consumer-producer has the following budget constraint equation:

$$\sum_{i=1}^{3} p_i(x_i^s - x_i^d) = 0 \tag{14.3}$$

According to Yang (2001), there are three types of configurations: autarky, denoted by A, as shown in Figure 14.1(a); selling good i and buying good *j*, denoted as (*i*/*j*); and selling good *i* and buying goods *j* and *t*, denoted as (*i*/*jt*). There are six of the second type of configuration: (1/2), (2/1), (1/3), (3/1), (2/3), and (3/1), as shown in Figure 14.1(b). There are three of the third type of configurations: (1/23), (2/13), and (3/12), as shown in Figure 14.1(c).

Combinations of these configurations yield four structures. *M* individuals choosing configuration A constitute an autarky structure. The division of *M* individuals between configurations (1/2) and (2/1) constitutes a partial division of labour structure – P1. A division of the population between configurations (1/3) and (3/1) constitutes a partial division of labour structure – P2, as shown in Figure 14.1(b). Since a structure based on configurations (2/3) and (3/2) is symmetric to structure P2 and yields the same per capita real income as P2, it is omitted. A division of individuals between the other configurations – (1/23), (2/13), and (3/12) – constitutes the complete division of labour structure D, as shown in Figure 14.1(c).

In structure P2 the individual selling an industrial good does not produce the agricultural good. If her decision is to either reside far away from her farmer trade partner or reside on the boundary of the farm, obviously, she

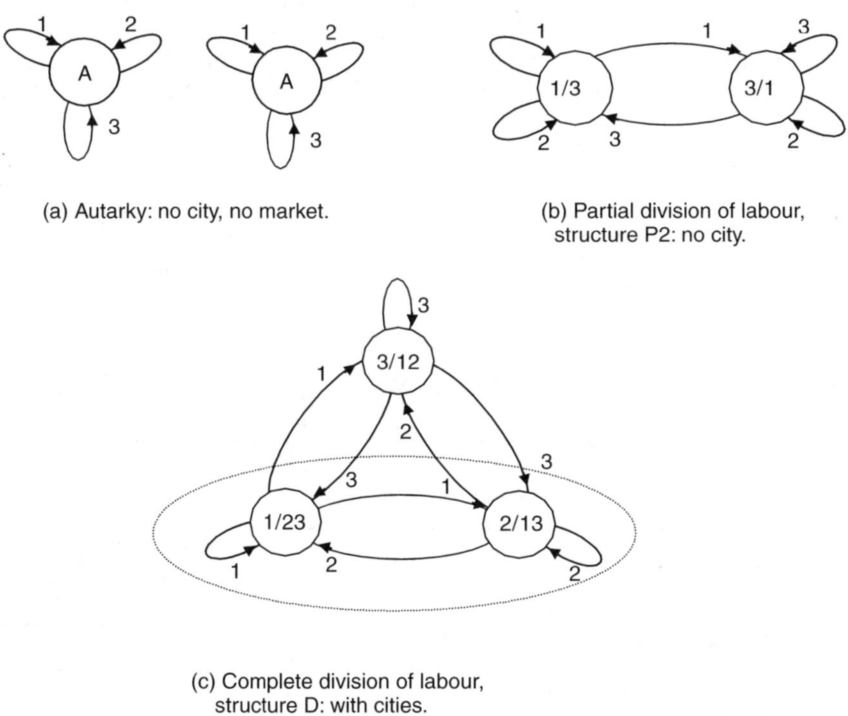

Figure 14.1 The evolution of the division of labour

will choose the latter geographical pattern of residence in order to reduce the transaction costs, implying that each partially specialized seller of an industrial good will reside next to a partially specialized farmer. Surely, there is no city formed in structure P2. For structure D, the division of labour between completely specialized manufacturers of industrial goods 1 and 2 can be organized in such a way as to save transaction costs by all specialist manufacturers residing in cities.

Under the assumption that each individual is *ex ante* identical and free to choose his/her occupation, we follow the inframarginal analysis developed by Yang and Ng (1993) to solve for the corner equilibria in the four structures, as shown in Table 14.1. Comparisons of per capita real incomes in the four corner equilibria yield the general equilibrium and its inframarginal comparative statics, as shown in Table 14.2.

The results in Table 14.2 imply that, as transaction efficiency increases from a low to a high level, the general equilibrium evolves from autarky, A, to the partial division of labour between farmers and manufacturers of industrial goods, such as structure P2 where no city exists, followed by the complete division of labour between specialist manufacturers of industrial goods and between professional farmers and the manufacturers, such as structure D. Cities emerge from this high level of division of labour. Note that as the general equilibrium changes from A to P2, the number of farmers decreases from M to $M/2$. As the general equilibrium changes from P2 to D, the number of farmers further decreases from $M/2$ to $(s/k)^{1/3}M/[2 + (s/k)^{1/3}]$.

Table 14.1 Corner equilibria in four structures

Structures	*Relative price*	*Number of different specialists*	*Per capita real income*
A			$[(1\square 3\alpha)/3]^3$
P_1	$p_1/p_2 = 1$	$M_1 = M_2 = M/2$	$[(1\square 2\alpha)/3]^3 r$
P_2	$p_3/p_1 = 1$	$M_1 = M_3 = M/2$	$[(1\square 2\alpha)/3]^3 s$
D	$p_2/p_1 = 1$, $p_3/p_1 = (k/s)^{1/3}$	$M_1 = M_2 = M/[2+(s/k)^{1/3}]$, $M_3 = (s/k)^{1/3}M/[2+(s/k)^{1/3}]$	$[(1\square\alpha)/3]^3(s^4/k^2)^{1/3}$

Table 14.2 General equilibrium and its inframarginal comparative statics

Parameter subspaces	$k\square k_0$			$k\square k_0$	
	$s\square s_0$	$s \in (s_0, s_1)$	$s\square s_1$	$s\square s_2$	$s\square s_2$
Equilibrium structures	A	P_2	D	A	D

Note: $k_0 \equiv [(1\square 2\alpha)^4/(1\square\alpha)^3(1\square 3\alpha)]^{1.5}$
$s_0 \equiv [(1\square 3\alpha)/(1\square 2\alpha)]^3 \square\ s_1 \equiv [(1\square 2\alpha)/(1\square\alpha)]^9/k^2$ iff $k\square k_0$.
$s_2 \equiv [(1\square 3\alpha)/(1\square\alpha)]^{9/4}/k^{0.5}$.

This theoretical discussion leads us to examine the following research hypotheses:

Hypothesis 1: Improvements in transaction efficiency will increase the level of urbanization and decrease the share of the labour force in agriculture.

Hypothesis 2: Improvements in transaction efficiency will raise per capita real income.

Hypothesis 3: Increases in per capita real income are systematically connected with economic structural changes including increases in the level of urbanization and decreases in the share of the labour force involved in agriculture.

Note that the positive effects of transaction efficiency on per capita real income are mediated by the extent of division of labour that is accompanied by urbanization and specialization. Therefore, we propose the following research hypothesis specifying the structural relationship between transaction efficiency, the level of urbanization, the share of agricultural, labour force and per capita real income.

Hypothesis 4: The transaction efficiency has direct positive effects on the level of urbanization, direct negative effects on the share of the labour force involved in agriculture, and indirect effects on per capita real income.

3 Measuring transaction efficiency

3.1 Data

This research adopts a cross-country data set for 1996. The data source is the *2001 World Development Indicators CD-Rom* published by the World Bank. This establishment-based data contains country information, including economic and social characteristics, the dissemination of communication technologies, and the transportation conditions. We employ the methodology of factor analysis. Because factor analysis requires the sample size to be no less than 100, the problem of missing values could be critical in some variables. Therefore, a simple moving average method was applied to predict the missing values.[1] Including values derived from the data interpolation, we achieved a valid sample size of 120 for the following factor analysis, from the 207 countries or economies in the database.

3.2 Factoring transaction efficiency

Because they are latent variables, it is difficult to directly observe the level of transaction efficiency and the extent of division of labour. Instead, they are indirectly measured using observable indicators. Our approach follows the tradition of indirect measurement of transaction costs (Hobbs, 1997), in which some parameters of infrastructure are employed rather than how much the marketing activity costs.

Responding to Cheung's (1998) call for a specification of transaction costs, we consider that transaction efficiency consists of two major dimensions: transportation efficiency (TE) and information/communication efficiency (ICE). As shown in Table 14.3, the level of transportation efficiency is measured by three observed variables: population density, passenger car density, and non-passenger car density. The level of information/communication efficiency is measured by four variables: fax machine density, mobile phone user density, Internet user density, and Internet host density.

The concept-related measurement variables were preprocessed by factor analysis. The principal axis factoring extraction method with varimax rotation was performed. After rotation, a factor structure was obtained with seven measurement variables which are converged to two factors. The two factors accounted for 83 per cent of the variance in the data. Table 14.4 shows the factor loading on each of the two factors.

It is apparent that the factor analysis produces a clean factor structure, or simple structure, with variables loading on appropriate factors. Three of the seven selected variables – passenger car density, non-passenger car density,

Table 14.3 Transaction efficiency constructs and measurement variables

Constructs	*Measurement variables*
Transportation efficiency (TE)	1. *Passenger car density*: The number of road motor vehicles, other than two wheelers, intended for the carriage of passengers, per kilometre of road. 2. *Non-passenger car density*: The number of road motor vehicles, including cars, buses, and freight vehicles but excluding two-wheelers and passenger cars, per kilometre of road. 3. *Population density*: Mid-year population divided by land area in square kilometres.
Information/ communication efficiency (ICE)	1. *Mobile phone user density*: The number of users of portable phones subscribing to an automatic public mobile phone service using cellular technology that provides access to the public switched telephone network, per 1000 people. 2. *Fax machine density*: The estimated number of facsimile machines connected to the public switched telephone network, per 1000 people. 3. *Internet host density*: The number of computers with active Internet Protocol (IP) addresses connected to the Internet, per 1000 people. 4. *Internet user density*: The number of people with access to the worldwide network, per 1000 people.

Table 14.4 The result of factor analysis

	Factor loading	
	Factor 1 Transportation efficiency	*Factor 2 Information/ communication efficiency*
Passenger car density	0.889	0.225
Non-passenger car density	0.837	0.006
Population density	0.725	0.010
Mobile phone user density	0.277	0.910
Fax machine density	0.276	0.725
Internet host density	–0.007	0.949
Internet user density	0.105	0.916
Total variance explained: 82.8%		

Note:
Extraction Method: Principal Axis Factoring.
Rotation Method: Varimax with Kaiser Normalization.

and population density – have significant factor loadings on one factor, factor 1, and insignificant factor loadings on the other, factor 2. The remaining four variables – mobile phone user density, fax machine density, Internet host density, and Internet user density – have significant factor loadings on factor 2 but insignificant factor loadings on factor 1. Therefore, the simple structure confirms the posited relationships between latent constructs and measurement variables as shown in Table 14.4, in which factor 1 is labelled as transportation efficiency and factor 2 as information/communication efficiency. Factor scores (using the Anderson–Rubin method for orthogonal scores) for the two transaction efficiency factors were applied for further examination of hypotheses in section 4. Each country's factor score of transaction efficiency can be estimated by the latent transaction efficiency construct in this study.

4 Results of hypothesis testing

Multiple regression analysis was used to test the research hypotheses. The share of the total population living in urban areas (URBAN), the share of the labour force in agriculture (LFAGR), and per capita GDP (GDPPCAP) were utilized as the dependent variables in three ordinary least squares regression equations. Each regression analysis includes two predictor variables: transportation efficiency and information/communication efficiency.

Consider that the values of URBAN and LFAGR range from zero to 1, and that of GDPCAP remains positive. We make a logistic transformation on

URBAN and LFAGR. The logistic transformation is useful when the outcome variable of interest is a proportion of a number bounded on the [0,1] interval. Without such transformation, the predicted value of endogenous variables from a simple linear model is likely beyond theoretical interval. In such a case, we may take a logistic transformation on URBAN and LFAGR.[2] Note that both URBAN and LFAGR are scaled by 100 in the regression models. GDPCAP is taken as a logarithmic value in order to make the predicted value greater than zero. The advantage of value transformation is that the fitted value of dependent variable will stay within its theoretical ranges.

Empirical results of the regressions are displayed in Table 14.5. Obviously, the empirical results on both transaction efficiencies are consistent with hypotheses 1, 2, and 3. In the first column, both transaction efficiency factors have substantial positive impacts on the level of urbanization, in which the coefficients are 13.03 and 9.86, respectively, and both are statistically significant at the 0.1 per cent level. The results basically underline the point that transaction efficiencies are capable of driving the urbanization of an economy. For the second regression, the coefficients of both transportation efficiency (TE) and information/communication efficiency (ICE) are significantly negatively related to the percentage of labour force in agriculture (LFAGR). This demonstrates a picture of structural transition along with economic development. In the third column of Table 14.5, the coefficients of both TE and ICE are significantly positive, showing that transaction efficiency is important in determining the per capita real income of an economy. The coefficients of URBAN and LFAGR in the fourth and fifth columns are statistically significantly positive and negative, respectively, to per capita GDP (GDPPCAP), indicating that the division of labour plays an important role in determining per capita real income. Therefore, all three hypotheses are substantially and significantly confirmed by our empirical analyses.

We in turn, examine hypothesis 4 claiming that the division of labour, characterized by both variables LFAGR and URBAN in this study, mediates the positive relationship between transaction efficiency and per capita real income. The above analysis only touches on the important correlation between transaction efficiency factors and URBAN, LFAGR, and GDPPCAP, but does not yet outline their structural relationship. Hypothesis 4 demonstrates a recursive system constructed by ICE, TE, URBAN (LFAGR), and GDPPCAP. Both ICE and TE determine the value of URBAN (LFAGR) and URBAN (LFAGR) further determines the value of per capita GDP. The recursive system is one of typical simultaneous systems. The following structural equations are employed to examine the hypothesis,

$$DL = a_0 + a_1 TE + a_2 ICE + \varepsilon$$
$$GDPPCAP = b_0 + b_1 DL + \eta$$

Table 14.5 The level of urbanization, labour force in agriculture, and per capita GDP on transaction efficiency: Ordinary Least Square Estimation Method

	Dependent variables				
Independent variables	(1) URBAN	(2) LFAGR	(3) GDPPCAP	(4) GDPPCAP	(5) GDPPCAP
Intercept	42.66*	20.51*	7.87*	7.39*	9.42*
	(4.90)	(11.09)	(88.37)	(71.43)	(55.67)
ICE	48.39*	–6.46*	1.09*	—	—
	(5.67)	(–4.30)	(12.52)		
TE	90.18*	–4.36*	1.29*	—	—
	(6.59)	(–2.66)	(9.23)		
URBAN	—	—	—	0.01*	
				(11.99)	
LFAGR	—	—	—	—	–0.06*
					(–9.38)
adj. R^2	0.37	0.23	0.66	0.56	0.54
Number of observations	115	73	115	115	73

Note: *denote the statistical significance at the one per cent level.

where *DL* is the level of division of labour, proxied by either URBAN or LFAGR. A Three Stage Least Square (3SLS) method is applied to estimate the systems of simultaneous equations in this chapter. The advantages of 3SLS are that its estimator is more efficient than 2SLS estimator (Fomby et al., 1980, p. 503), and 3SLS can provide the system-weighted R^2 to measure a goodness of fit for the whole system.

Drawing on the theoretical backdrop of our analysis, we applied a 3SLS instead of an OLS analysis to examine the structural relationship of variables. Table 14.6 shows the empirical results. For both regressions, the weighted system R^2 for the simultaneous solution is no less than adjusted R^2 for the two separate OLS solutions shown in Table 14.5. This implies that the simultaneous solution may provide a better way to examine the hypothesis than the OLS solution, and supports the conjecture that there exist systematic relationships between transaction efficiency, economic structural changes, and per capita real income.

As shown in Table 14.6(a), the coefficients of transaction efficiency (TE) and information/communication efficiency (ICE) on the share of the total population living in urban areas (URBAN) are statistically significantly positive, and the coefficient of URBAN on per capita income is also statistically significantly positive. The coefficients of TE and ICE on the share of the labour force in the agricultural sector (LFAGR) are statistically significantly

Table 14.6(a) The level of urbanization, and per capita GDP on transaction efficiency: the Three-Stage Least-Squares Estimation method (3SLS)

	Dependent variables	
	URBAN	GDPPCAP
Intercept	40.77*	7.15*
	(4.70)	(50.97)
URBAN	—	0.02*
		(9.85)
ICE	60.79*	—
	(8.73)	
TE	73.66*	—
	(6.13)	
System-weighted R^2	0.56	
Number of observations	115	

Note: *denote the statistical significance at 1%.

Table 14.6(b) Portion of the labour force in agriculture, and per capita GDP on transaction efficiency: the Three-Stage Least-Squares Estimation method (3SLS)

	Dependent variables	
	LFAGR	GDPPCAP
Intercept	–176.42*	6.06*
	(–13.53)	(19.50)
LFAGR	—	–0.01*
		(–7.86)
ICE	–70.23*	—
	(–7.34)	
TE	–50.18*	—
	(–4.74)	
System-weighted R^2	0.54	
Number of observations	73	

Note: *denote the statistical significance at 1%.

negative, but the coefficient of LFAGR on per capita income statistically significantly negative, as shown in Table 14.6(b). These empirical results strongly support hypothesis 4.

5 Conclusions

In this study we examined the hypotheses of Yang and Rice (1994) concerning the interrelationships between transaction efficiency, economic structural changes induced by the division of labour, and per capita real income. The method of factor analysis was employed to construct two transaction efficiency factors – transportation efficiency and information/communication efficiency. In this study, both the level of urbanization and the share of agricultural labour refer to the extent of division of labour. And a multiple regression analysis is employed. The empirical results show that both transaction efficiency factors have strong positive effects on the level of urbanization and on per capita real income, but strong negative effects on the share of the labour force in agriculture. A substantial positive relationship exists between the level of urbanization and per capita real income, but a substantial negative relationship is found between the share of the labour force in agriculture and per capita real income. These results validate the hypotheses.

This chapter also considered the important and systematic linkages between the transaction efficiency, division of labour, and the per capita real income of an economy. A 3SLS analysis was applied to examine the structural relationships between these variables. The empirical result indicates that we cannot ignore the existence of systematic relationships between transaction efficiencies, economic structural changes relating to the division of labour, and per capita real income of an economy. Both transaction efficiency factors are found to have substantially positive effects on the level of urbanization, and the latter has substantially positive effects on per capita income. Both transaction efficiency factors have substantially negative effects on the share of the labour force in agriculture, and the latter has a substantial negative effect on per capita income. Our empirical study provides strong evidence to support Yang and Rice's (1994) theoretical claim that division of labour mediates the positive relationship between transaction efficiency and per capita real income and induces economic structural changes, including increases in the level of urbanization and decreases in the share of the labour force in the agricultural sector.

Notes

1 That is, we measure the average value of y_{t-1} and y_{t+1} to predict the unknown value of y_t, where y_{t-1} and y_{t+1} are the values of observable variable y in year $t-1$ and $t+1$, respectively, and y_t is the missing value in year t.

2 A logistic transformation is defined as $Z = Ln(Y/(1 - Y))*100$ in this chapter where Y is the value of URBAN or LFAGR. And Z will be applied in the empirical examination. This transformation yields a boundless variable, because $Z = -\infty$ when Y approaches 0, and $Z = +\infty$ when Y approaches 1.

References

Cheung, S. (1998) 'The Transaction Costs Paradigm', *Economic Journal*, 36, 514–21.

Fomby, T., Hill, R. and Johnson, S. (1980) *Advanced Econometric Methods* (New York: Springer-Verlag).

Hobbs, J. (1997) 'Measuring the Importance of Transaction Costs in Cattle Marketing', *American Journal of Agricultural Economics*, 79, 1083–95.

Yang, X. (2001) *Economics: New Classical versus Neoclassical Framework* (Cambridge, MA: Blackwell).

Yang, X. and Ng, Y.-K. (1993) *Specialization and Economic Organization: a New Classical Microeconomic Framework* (Amsterdam: North-Holland).

Yang, X. and Rice, R. (1994) 'An Equilibrium Model Endogenizing the Emergence of a Dual Structure between the Urban and Rural Sectors', *Journal of Urban Economics*, 35, 346–68.

15

Endogenous Transaction Costs and Division of Labour

Xiaokai Yang and Yimin Zhao

1 Introduction

In the emerging literature of general equilibrium models of high development economics (see Fujita and Krugman, 1995 and Krugman and Venables, 1996) and in the growing literature of endogenous specialization (see Yang and Ng, 1998, for a recent survey and selected references), effects of transaction costs on the equilibrium network size of division of labour, the extent of the market, and productivity are explored by formulating a tradeoff between increasing returns and transaction costs. In these models, however, transaction costs are exogenous in the sense that they are not caused by conflicts of interest between players in the economic arena.

North and Thomas (1970) distinguish between endogenous transaction costs, caused by moral hazard, adverse selection, and other types of opportunism, from exogenous transaction costs. Williamson (1975, 1985) also draws the distinction between endogenous transaction costs caused by opportunism (for instance, opportunistic time delays, cheating, and making commitments that are not credible) and tangible exogenous transaction costs. At the same time, an extensive literature of formal models of endogenous transaction costs has developed.[1] Game theory has been extensively used in the literature to investigate endogenous transaction costs caused by strategic interactions. However, none of these models can analyse the effects of endogenous transaction costs on the development of division of labour that classical economists, such as Adam Smith, focused on. This chapter intends to fill the gap by developing a model with endogenous structure of division of labour and endogenous transaction costs.

As elaborated by Smith (1776), the division of labour and specialization are 'the mainspring of economic progress'. They are dependent on the extent of the market (chapter 3 of book I), and the extent of the market is determined by transaction costs (pp. 31–2). Allyn Young also noted that division of labour has positive network effects since 'not only division of labour is dependent on the extent of the market, but also the extent of the market is determined by the level of division of labour' (Young, 1928). Trading between different specialists, however, involves transaction costs which in turn deters the development of division of labour. The transaction costs include not only tangible exogenous transportation costs, but also endogenous transaction costs caused by strategic interactions. Since the network effect of division of labour is a general equilibrium phenomenon, the levels of endogenous and exogenous transaction cost, each player's decision in choosing a pattern of specialization, and the network size of division of labour are interdependent. If all players choose autarky, there will be no transactions or related costs, while players' decisions of the level of specialization are dependent on the equilibrium level of endogenous and exogenous transaction costs. In addition, all players' decisions about participation in the division of labour are dependent on the equilibrium network size of division of labour, while the equilibrium network size of division of labour and related trade are dependent on all players' decisions of participation. Hence, we need a general equilibrium model to investigate the interactions amongst all of the interdependent variables.

The present chapter specifies a general equilibrium model of an alternating offer bargaining game (Rubinstein, 1982, 1985) in which players compete for a greater share of the gains from division of labour, in order to study the impact of endogenous transaction costs, caused by opportunism, on the equilibrium level of division of labour. The players' choices of patterns of specialization are endogenized in the model. The main finding is that the players' strategic competition to gain a first mover advantage results in endogenous transaction costs, which generate a Pareto inefficient level of division of labour. If the game is repeatedly played and both players care about their reputation, it can be shown that a cooperative outcome may emerge from the interactions between noncooperative decisions, as such endogenous transaction costs can be eliminated.

The chapter is organized as follows. Section 2 specifies the basic model. Section 3 solves for the Nash bargaining equilibrium, and uses that as the benchmark case, in which the equilibrium level of division of labour is Pareto efficient. Section 4 analyses the endogenous transaction costs associated with Pareto inefficient level of division of labour by introducing the game where players compete for a greater share of the gains from division of labour (of which the alternating offer bargaining game is a subgame). Section 5 examines how the consideration of reputation can eliminate the endogenous transaction costs in a supergame. Section 6 concludes the chapter.

2 The model

Let us consider a simple economy with two *ex ante* identical consumer-producers. There are two consumer goods, x and y, in this economy.

Each individual can either self-provide both goods by himself or produce a good and then trade that good for the other good with another individual. The self-provided amounts of the two goods are x and y respectively. The quantities of the two goods sold by the two consumer-producers are x^s and y^s respectively. The quantities purchased by the two individuals are x^d and y^d respectively. The exogenous transaction cost is assumed to be of an iceberg type, which is proportional to the quantity purchased, so that the exogenous transaction cost coefficient for a unit of good bought is 1-k. Thus kx^d (or ky^d) is the amount an individual obtains when he purchases x^d (or y^d).

Assume that the utility function is identical for the two individuals:

$$u = (x + kx^d)(y + ky^d) \tag{15.1}$$

where $x + kx^d$ is the amount consumed by an individual of good x and $y + ky^d$ is the amount consumed by the individual of good y.

Each individual has a system of production functions and labour endowment constraint given by

$$\begin{aligned} &x + x^s = l_x{}^a \text{ and } a > 1 \\ &y + y^s = l_y{}^a \text{ and } a > 1 \\ &l_x + l_y = 1 \text{ and } l_x, l_y \in [0, 1] \end{aligned} \tag{15.2}$$

where $x + x^s$ and $y + y^s$ are the respective output levels of x and y, l_x and l_y are the person's respective amounts of labour allocated to the production of the two goods. When $a > 1$, the production functions display increasing returns to each individual's labour allocated to the production of each good. The parameter a represents the degree of increasing returns to specialization. From the utility function and the production system, we can see that the preferences for diverse consumption and specialized production generate a tradeoff between economies of specialization and exogenous transaction costs.

In such an economy, it can be proved that an individual's optimum decision can be achieved by avoiding the choice to sell and buy the same good, and by selling at most one good.[2] Thus, two feasible organization patterns, autarky (A) and division of labour (D), can be specified as illustrated in Figure 15.1.

Circles in Figure 15.1 represent the two individuals and lines with arrows represent the flows of good. Circle (A) denotes that individuals choose autarky and self-provide all goods. Circle (x/y) in the organization pattern of division of labour denotes the individual selling and self-producing good x and buying good y, while circle (y/x) denotes the individual selling and self-producing good y and buying good x.

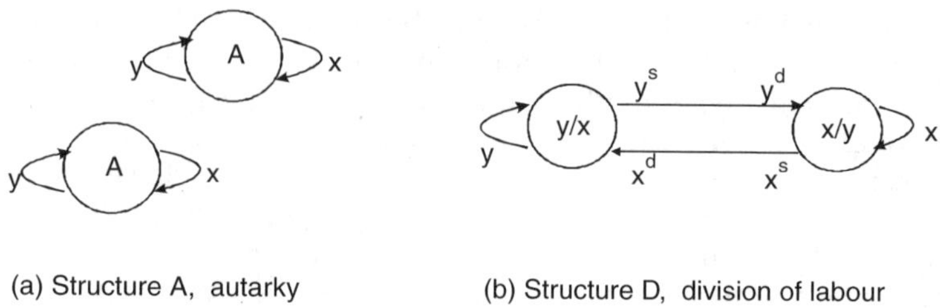

Figure 15.1 Autarky and division of labour

In autarky, $x^s = y^s = x^d = y^d = 0$, since each individual self-provides all goods and there is no trade. Assuming this in the decision problem (15.1) and (15.2) yields

$$\underset{l_x}{\text{Max}}\ u = xy = l_x{}^a(1-l_x)^a \tag{15.3}$$

which implies $l_x = l_y = 1/2$, $u_A = 2^{-2a}$.

With division of labour, each individual specializes in one good and buys the other good from the other individual. They bargain over the relative price of the goods to maximize their utility. For the specialist of x, $x^d = y = y^s = 0$. Substituting this into (15.1) and (15.2) yields

$$\begin{aligned}&\text{Max } u_x = (1 - x^s)ky^d \\ &\text{s.t.} \quad px^s = y^d \text{ (budget constraint)}\end{aligned} \tag{15.4}$$

where p is the relative price of x in terms of y.

For the specialist of y, $y^d = x = x^s = 0$. Substituting this into (15.1) and (15.2) yields

$$\begin{aligned}&\text{Max } u_y = kx^d\,(1 - y^s) \\ &\text{s.t.} \quad y^s = px^d \text{ (budget constraint)}\end{aligned} \tag{15.5}$$

The market-clearing condition generates that $x^s = x^d$ and $y^s = y^d$. To simplify notations, we use X and Y to represent equal quantities demanded and supplied for the two goods respectively. Then the utility for the player who self-produces x is $u_x = (1 - X)kY$, and the utility for the player who self-produces y is $u_y = (1 - Y)kX$. Both of their utilities are dependent on the relative price, $p = Y/X$. The two players sort out the relative price through a bargaining process. The two questions examined in the next section are: (1) what is the equilibrium organization pattern that develops? and (2) whether the equilibrium organization pattern is Pareto optimal.

3 Nash bargaining equilibrium

Let us first examine the Pareto efficient pattern of division of labour in the simple economy by solving for a Nash bargaining game. Suppose that each of the two players has complete information about his opponent's production and utility functions, exogenous transaction conditions and endowment constraints. Hence, he can easily find the opponent's threat point for refusing participation in the division of labour and trade.[3] A Nash product can then be defined as follows:

Denote the net gain that the specialist of x can receive from the division of labour as $V_x = (1 - X)kY - u_A$ and the net gain that the specialist of y can receive from the division of labour as $V_y = (1 - Y)kX - u_A$. The x specialist wants the relative price, p $(= Y/X)$, as high as possible whereas the y specialist wants the opposite. Nevertheless, both players are faced with constraints. The x specialist may be able to achieve higher gains once p is larger, but the probability of realizing the larger value of V_x gets smaller. If there exists any stochastic disturbance in the bargaining process, the probability of the x specialist realizing her net payoff V_x, which is an increasing function of p, is proportional to the y specialist's net payoff V_y, which is a decreasing function of p since the y specialist is less willing to be involved in the division of labour if her net gain from the division of labour is very small.

If we consider V_y as the probability that the x specialist can realize V_x, then the expected net payoff of the x specialist from division of labour (the Nash product) is

$$V = V_x V_y + 0 \times (1 - V_y) = V_x V_y \tag{15.6}$$

where $1 - V_y$ is the probability that the net payoff cannot be realized or that the net payoff is 0. Hence, the Nash bargaining equilibrium is given by maximizing the Nash product in (15.6).[4]

$$\max_{X,Y} : V = V_x V_y = [(1 - X)kY - u_A][(1 - Y)kX - u_A] \tag{15.7}$$

If the utility in an alternative occupation is considered as a threat point, while utility in autarky is just a bottom line, the Nash product becomes

$$V = (u_x - u_y)(u_y - u_x) = -(u_x - u_y)^2 \tag{15.8}$$

Maximizing the Nash product in (15.8) implies the utility equalization condition. The maximization of V in (15.7) with respect to X and Y subject to the utility equalization condition derived from (15.8) generates the Nash bargaining solution in (15.9).

$$X = Y = 1/2, \quad p = 1, \quad u_D = u_x = u_y = k/4 \tag{15.9}$$

where u_D denotes the per capita real income for division of labour in the Nash bargaining game.

Comparing the per capita real income in an autarky situation with that from division of labour in the Nash bargaining game, it is clear that

$$\begin{aligned} u_D < u_A &\text{ iff } k < k_0 \equiv 2^{2-2a} \\ u_D > u_A &\text{ iff } k > k_0 \end{aligned} \tag{15.10}$$

Hence, the Nash bargaining equilibrium organization pattern can be illustrated in Table 15.1.

From Table 15.1, we can see that the division of labour outcome occurs in the Nash bargaining equilibrium, only when the exogenous transaction efficiency coefficient, k, is sufficiently large such that the benefit from division of labour and specialization outweighs the exogenous transaction costs.

Since the maximization of the Nash product is equivalent to the maximization of a social welfare function, it is straightforward that the Nash bargaining equilibrium organization pattern is always Pareto optimal. Hence, in the model with endogenous specialization, the Nash bargaining process achieves the Pareto efficient organization structure and thus there are no endogenous transaction costs associated with the choice of organization pattern. It also ensures the resource allocation for a given organization pattern is Pareto efficient because no player can be better off without making the other player worse off.

A major shortcoming of the Nash bargaining model is that it looks like a simultaneous move game, which does not spell out the dynamic nature of the bargaining process. In the next section, we introduce the Rubinstein alternating offer bargaining game into our model in order to study the implications of such a dynamic bargaining process. The Nash bargaining equilibrium is used as a benchmark case to examine the endogenous transaction cost associated with a Pareto inefficient organization pattern.

4 Alternating offer bargaining games, division of labour and endogenous transaction costs

Similar to the Rubinstein (1982) game, the two players in our model alternate offers over the relative price of their product. Player 1, the first mover,

Table 15.1 Equilibrium organization pattern in the Nash bargaining game

k	$0 < k < k_0$	$k_0 < k < 1$
Equilibrium Organization pattern	Autarky	Division of labour

makes an offer in period 1. Player 2 can take the offer in period 1 and then terminate the game. Player 2 can also reject the offer in period 1 and make a counteroffer in period 2. Again player 1 can choose between accepting and rejecting player 2's counteroffer in the next round of bargaining. The game can go on indefinitely. Having a value placed on time provides players with incentives to seal the deal as soon as possible. This ensures a unique equilibrium.

Because of the symmetry between the two players, there are two subgame perfect equilibria: one with the x specialist as the first mover and the other with the y specialist as the first mover. How does one decide the first mover? Since, the first mover always has the advantage of exploiting the impatience of the second mover, there will be a competition to determine who moves first. In subsection 4.1, we first study the alternating offer bargaining game in which the first mover is randomly chosen by Nature. Then in subsection 4.2, we show that the competition for the first mover advantage between the two players generates endogenous transaction costs associated with inefficient pattern of division of labour.

4.1 The dynamic bargaining game without competition for the first mover position

Without loss of generality, we assume that Nature chooses the x specialist as the first mover (referred to as player 1, or he) and the y specialist is the second mover (referred to as player 2, or she). The two players have the same discount factor δ. $1 - \delta$ can be considered as the exogenous bargaining cost. Two players make offers and counteroffers following two rules. First, the player who makes an offer must ensure that the opponent will take the offer since it does not make sense to delay the game with the knowledge of complete information. Second, a player maximizes his utility subject to the acceptance constraint in his turn to make an offer. The first decision rule implies that the payoff for the opponent from rejecting a player's offer should not be more than her payoff from accepting the offer.

Let us use subscript to denote time dimension. Suppose that player 1 offers X_1 [equivalent to x^s in (15.4)] to exchange for Y_1 [equivalent to y^d in (15.5)] in period 1. This implies that he offers the terms of trade $p_1 = Y_1/X_1$ because of the market-clearing conditions $x^s = x^d = X$ and $y^s = y^d = Y$, and the budget constraint $p = Y/X$. According to the decision rules, the decision problem for player 1 in period 1 is:

$$\underset{X_1,Y_1}{\text{Max}} : u_{1x} = (1 - X_1)kY_1, \tag{15.11}$$
$$\text{s.t. } u_{1y} \equiv (1 - Y_1)kX_1 \geq \delta(1 - Y_2)kX_2 \equiv \delta u_{2y}$$

where u_{1x} is the x specialist's utility under the terms offered by him in period 1, u_{1y} is the y specialist's utility under the terms of trade offered by player 1 in period 1, u_{2y} is the y specialist's utility generated by her counteroffer in period 2, and δ is the discount factor.[5]

Similarly, player 2's (the y specialist's) counteroffer (Y_2/X_2) in period 2 is given by

$$\max_{X_2, Y_2} : u_{2y} = kX_2(1-Y_2) \tag{15.12}$$
$$\text{s.t. } u_{2x} \equiv (1 - X_2)kY_2 \geq \delta(1 - X_3)kY_3 \equiv \delta u_{3x}$$

where u_{2x} is player 1's (the x specialist's) utility under the terms offered by player 2 in period 2, u_{3x} is the *x* specialist's utility generated by his counteroffer in period 3. The bargaining process can go on ad infinitum. According to Rubinstein (1982), in a steady equilibrium, $X_1 = X_3 = X_5 \ldots, Y_1 = Y_3 = Y_5 \ldots, X_2 = X_4 = X_6 \ldots$, and $Y_2 = Y_4 = Y_6 \ldots$. Then the alternating offer bargaining equilibrium can be solved by replacing the constraint in (15.12) with the following constraint.

$$u_{2x} \equiv (1 - X_2)kY_2 \geq \delta(1 - X_1)kY_1 \equiv \delta u_{1x} \tag{15.13}$$

The subgame perfect equilibrium can then be solved using backward deduction.

$$X_1 = \sqrt{\delta}/(1+\sqrt{\delta}), \quad Y_1 = 1 - X_1 = 1/(1+\sqrt{\delta}) \tag{15.14}$$
$$X_2 = 1/(1+\sqrt{\delta}), \quad Y_2 = \sqrt{\delta}/(1+\sqrt{\delta})$$
$$u_x = k/\left(1+\sqrt{\delta}\right)^2 > u_y = \delta k/\left(1+\sqrt{\delta}\right)^2 \text{ for } \delta \in (0,1)$$
$$u_x = u_y \text{ for } \delta = 1$$
$$p = Y/X = 1/\sqrt{\delta} \text{ if } \delta \in (0,1); \quad p = 1 \text{ if } \delta = 1.$$

The dynamic bargaining generates unequal distribution of gains to trade. The equilibrium utilities and relative price indicate that the first mover's advantage increases as the discount factor falls (or as the degree of impatience increases). As the discount factor approaches 1 or as the time lag between offer and counteroffer is reduced, the two players' utilities converge to the same level and the equilibrium terms of trade converges to the Nash bargaining equilibrium level.

The above solution is relevant only if the utilities from division of labour are greater than those from autarky. If players have smaller utilities from division of labour than those from autarky, then their threat to choose autarky will be credible. Suppose $\delta \in (0,1)$, then from (15.14), we know that $u_y < u_A$ iff $k < k_1 \equiv 2^{-2a}\left(1+\sqrt{\delta}\right)^2/\delta$. If $k < k_1$ player 2's threat to choose autarky is then credible. For the case of $k < k_1$, the equilibrium can be solved as follows.

The decision problem for player 1 in period 1 is:

$$\underset{X_1,Y_1}{\text{Max}}: \ u_{1x} = (1 - X_1)kY_1, \tag{15.15}$$

$$u_{1y} = (1 - Y_1)kX_1 \geq u_A = 2^{-2a}$$

Solving for the above decision problem yields the following solution for $k < k_1$:

$$X_1 = 2^{-a}/\sqrt{k}, \qquad Y_1 = 1 - 2^{-a}/\sqrt{k}, \tag{15.16}$$

$$u_x = k(1 - 2^{-a}/\sqrt{k})^2 \qquad u_y = u_A = 2^{-2a}$$

Player 2 has no incentive to turn down the above offer from player 1 since rejection and counteroffers would drive the bargaining process going back to the solution (15.14) which incurs negative net gain.[6]

The solution in (15.16) implies that $u_x < u_A = 2^{-2a}$ if $k < k_0 \equiv 2^{2(1-a)}$). Hence, the players will choose autarky if $k < k_0$. For $k \in (k_0, k_1)$, the equilibrium is given by (15.16). For $k \in (k_1, 1)$, the equilibrium is given by (15.14). Summarizing the above results and comparing with the Pareto optimum Nash bargaining equilibrium, we have Table 15.2.

Table 15.2 Alternating bargaining equilibrium without competition for the first mover position

k	$k < k_0$	$k_0 < k < k_1$	$k > k_1$
Alternating bargaining without competition for the first mover position	Autarky $u_A = 2^{-2a}$	Division of labour $u_x = u_H' \equiv k\left(1 - \frac{2^{-a}}{\sqrt{k}}\right)^2$ $u_y = u_A = 2^{-2a}$	Division of labour $u_x = u_H \equiv \frac{k}{\left(1+\sqrt{\delta}\right)^2}$ $u_y = u_L = \frac{\delta k}{\left(1+\sqrt{\delta}\right)^2}$
Nash bargaining	Autarky	Division of labour $u_D = u_x = u_y = k/4$	Division of labour $u_D = u_x = u_y = k/4$

where u_H is the first mover's utility in the subgame equilibrium for $k \in (k_1, 1)$, u_L is the second mover's utility in the subgame equilibrium for $k \in (k_1, 1)$, and u_H' is the first mover's utility in the subgame equilibrium for $k \in (k_0, k_1)$. It is easy to see that $u_H > u_D > u_L > u_A$ for $k > k_1$ and $u_H' > u_D > u_A$ for $k_0 < k < k_1$.

It is clear from Table 15.2 that the subgame perfect equilibrium organization pattern is division of labour if and only if the Nash bargaining equilibrium organization pattern is division of labour. That is, the alternating offer bargaining does not generate endogenous transaction costs associated with organizational inefficiency. Furthermore, the subgame perfect equilibrium is also Pareto optimal in resource allocation since each player maximizes his own utility for a given utility of the other player, although it generates unequal income distribution. The result is summarized in proposition 1.

Proposition 1

Division of labour will emerge in the alternating offer bargaining equilibrium if and only if it occurs in the Pareto efficient Nash bargaining solution. The alternating offer bargaining with no competition for the first mover position does not generate endogenous transaction costs associated with a Pareto inefficient organization structure; neither does it generate allocation inefficiency.

The above dynamic bargaining model, however, does not endogenize the choice of the first mover.[7] Both players will actually compete for the first mover's position since they know the existence of a first mover advantage. Such competition for a greater share of gains from division of labour will generate endogenous transaction costs, as shown in the next subsection.[8]

4.2 Competition for a greater share of gains from the division of labour and endogenous transaction costs

Period 0 is added to the dynamic game in the previous subsection in order to allow the two players to compete for the first mover position. After period 0, the structure of the new game is the same as in the previous subsection. Hence, the alternating offer bargaining game in the previous subsection is a subgame of the new game.

Assume that each player has two strategies, tough (T) and soft (S), in period 0. Tough strategy implies that a player insists that it is he who should be the first mover and he will not accept any terms of trade that gives a lower utility than what the first mover receives. Soft strategy implies that a player accepts the second mover position if the opponent is considered tough, or that he agrees to a fair terms of trade given by the Nash bargaining solution if the opponent is considered soft.

Let us first consider the case of $k \in (k_1, 1)$, where both players receive higher utilities than in autarky in the subgame perfect equilibrium started from period 1. The game initiated at period 0 for the given subgame equilibrium in period 1 can be described in Table 15.3.

Table 15.3 Strategic form of the game to compete to be the first mover advantage as $k \in (k_1, 1)$

		Player 2	
		T	S
Player 1	T	u_A, u_A	u_H, u_L
	S	u_L, u_H	u_D, u_D

where the first term in an entry represents player 1's payoff (utility), the second term represents that of player 2. We know that $u_H > u_D > u_L > u_A$ from Table 15.2.

Table 15.3 implies that the two players receive u_A if both of them choose tough strategies, which means that autarky will be chosen as no agreement on terms of trade can arise. The two players receive the utility for division of labour that is given by the Nash bargaining solution and the gains from the division of labour is equally divided between them if both of them play soft strategies. If one player is tough and the other one is soft, then the tough one gains more than the soft one and mutually beneficial gains from division of labour are realized despite unequal distribution of income. The game in period 0 for given subgame perfect equilibrium in period 1 is a typical Nash game which has two *pure strategy* Nash equilibria, $S - T$ and $T - S$.

For the pure strategy Nash game, we cannot predict which one of the two Nash equilibria will take place. But if each player is allowed to choose a probability distribution for each strategy, we will have a unique mixed strategy Nash equilibrium. Suppose player i chooses soft strategy with probability q_i and tough strategy with probability $1 - q_i$. Since the purpose of a player's mixed strategy is to confuse his opponent, player 1 will choose q_1 such that player 2 feels indifferent between her choices of T and S. For a given q_1, player 2's expected utility for her choice of T is $(1 - q_1)u_A + q_1u_H$ and that for strategy S is $(1 - q_1)u_L + q_1u_D$. The two utility levels are indifferent iff

$$q_1 = (u_L - u_A)/(u_H - u_D + u_L - u_A) \tag{15.17}$$

The symmetry of the model implies that the mixed strategy of player 2, q_2, is the same as q_1. Denoting them by q, then it can be shown that

$$q \to 1/2 \text{ as } \delta \to 1; \quad q \to 0 \text{ as } \delta \to 0; \quad \text{and } \partial q/\partial \delta > 0. \tag{15.18}$$

Since $(1 - q)^2$ represents the probability that both players choose T strategy and the mutually beneficial gains from the division of labour cannot be realized, there exists organizational inefficiency in the game as long as $(1 - q)^2$ is greater than zero, which is obviously true from (15.18). Moreover, since $1 - \delta$ can be considered as the exogenous bargaining cost, (15.18) also indicates that endogenous transaction costs associated with organizational inefficiency are not zero even if exogenous bargaining cost tends to zero.

For the case of $k \in (k_0, k_1)$, since the second mover receives only u_A in the subgame started from period 1, u_L in Table 15.3 must be replaced with u_A. Also, the utility of the first mover from the subgame stared from period 1 is u_H' rather than u_H. The strategic form of the game to compete for the first mover advantage for $k \in (k_0, k_1)$ can then be described in Table 15.4.

Table 15.4 Strategic form of the game to compete for the first mover advantage as $k \in (k_0, k_1)$

		Player 2	
		T	S
Player 1	T	u_A, u_A	u_H', u_A
	S	u_A, u_H'	u_D, u_D

where $u_H' > u_D > u_A$ from Table 15.2.

It is easy to see from Table 15.4 that there exists a unique pure strategy Nash equilibrium, $T - T$, which implies that autarky is the resulting equilibrium organization pattern and division of labour will not take place for $k \in (k_0, k_1)$ in the game competing for the first mover position. In Table 15.5, we summarize the above results of the game (the competition for a greater share of gains from division of labour), and compare it with the Pareto optimum Nash bargaining equilibrium, as well as the results from the alternating offer bargaining game without competing for the first mover position.

From Table 15.5, we can see that for $k \in (k_0, k_1)$, division of labour is not the equilibrium organization pattern in the game to compete for the first

Table 15.5 Endogenous transaction costs associated with organizational inefficiency

k	$k < k_0$	$k_0 < k < k_1$	$k > k_1$	
			Organization pattern	*Probability*
Alternating offer bargaining game with competition for the first mover position	Autarky	Autarky	Autarky Division of labour	$(1-q)^2$ $1-(1-q)^2$
Alternating offer bargaining without competition for the first mover position	Autarky	Division of labour	Division of labour	1
Nash bargaining game	Autarky	Division of labour	Division of labour	1

mover position even if it is Pareto optimal. For $k > k_1$, division of labour is not the equilibrium organization pattern with probability, $(1 - q)$,[2] even if it is Pareto optimal. The results are summarized in proposition 2.

Proposition 2
The competition of both players for a greater share of the gains from division of labour generates endogenous transaction costs that can prevent the efficient organization pattern, division of labour, from realization.

5 Reputation and the elimination of endogenous transaction costs

If the pure strategy game in the previous subsection can be repeatedly played, then the endogenous transaction costs associated with organizational inefficiency may be eliminated due to consideration of reputational effects.

Let us first consider the case of $k \in (k_0, k_1)$. Assume there are infinite periods $T = 1, 2, \ldots$, and there is a stage game in each period, which is the same as the pure strategy game in Table 15.4, then there is a *supergame* in all periods. In the supergame, each player chooses a series of pure strategies to maximize his total discounted utility.

Suppose that each player's strategy is as follows. Each player announces that he/she always chooses a soft strategy as long as the other player does so, but he/she will choose tough strategies forever, if the other player chooses a tough strategy in the last period. Then given the above strategy of the other player, a player's total discounted utility with infinite decision horizon from a soft strategy series is

$$\underset{T\to\infty}{TU_s} = u_D\left(1+\delta+\delta^2+\ldots+\delta^T+\ldots\right)\frac{u_D}{1-\delta} \tag{15.1}$$

If he/she chooses a tough strategy in a period, his/her immediate utility is $u_H' = k(1-2^{-a}/\sqrt{k})^2$, which is greater than u_A when $k \in (k_0, k_1)$. His/Her utility afterwards, however, is always u_A because the other player will retaliate by always playing tough. Hence, the total discounted utility from being tough is

$$\underset{T\to\infty}{TU_{Tough}} = u_H' + \delta\left(1+\delta+\delta^2+\ldots+\delta^{T-1}+\ldots\right)u_A = u_H' + \delta u_A/(1-\delta)$$

It is easy to see that $TU_s > TU_{Tough}$ iff

$$u_D > (1-\delta)u_H' + \delta u_A$$

which implies

$$\delta > \delta_0 \equiv \frac{(2 - \frac{2^{1-a}}{\sqrt{k}})^2 - k}{4k - 2^{3-a}\sqrt{k}} \quad \text{as } k > k_0 \equiv 2^{2-2a}$$

From the above analysis for $k \in (k_0, k_1)$, we can see that, provided players are not very impatient and sufficiently value future utilities ($\delta > \delta_0$), both players will naturally choose soft strategies and cooperate with each other to realize the gains from division of labour. However, for the interval of $k \in (k_1, 1)$, the threat of a player choosing to play tough forever when the other player chooses tough in the last period is not credible because $u_L > u_A$ in Table 15.3 (the utility from choosing 'soft' is greater than the utility from retaliation). Hence, cooperation results will not emerge if $k \in (k_1, 1)$. The above results generate proposition 3.

Proposition 3
Under a certain condition of k ($k_0 < k < k_1$), if players are not very impatient ($\delta > \delta_0$), the consideration of one's reputation may facilitate mutual cooperation to emerge from noncooperative strategic behaviours and therefore eliminate endogenous transaction costs associated with organizational inefficiency.

The Folk theorem in game theory shows that, with the added assumption of a limited time horizon for punishment of deviation from a cooperative solution, there are many other Nash equilibria in the supergame that can generate cooperative results. For instance, when a player chooses a tough strategy in the last period, then his opponent chooses to play a tough strategy for three periods and then returns back to a soft strategy afterwards.

6 Conclusion

George Stigler pointed out:

> The last of Smith's regrettable failures is one for which he is overwhelmingly famous – the division of labour. The failure is ... almost no one used or now uses the theory of division of labour, for the excellent reason that there is scarcely such a theory. ... there is no standard, operable theory to describe what Smith argued to be the mainspring of economic progress. Smith gave the division of labour an immensely convincing presentation – it seems to me as persuasive a case for the power of specialization today as it appeared to Smith. Yet there is no evidence, so far as I know, of any serious advance in the theory of the subject since his time, and specialization is not

an integral part of the modern theory of production. (Stigler, 1976, pp. 1209–10)

The growing literature of endogenous specialization tries to tackle the challenge posed by Stigler by formalizing the tradeoff between positive network effects of the division of labour on both aggregate productivity and transaction costs. But it is not enough to bring a formal study of division of labour back to the core of modern mainstream without a further consideration of endogenous transaction costs caused by strategic interactions. On the other hand, the literature of endogenous transaction costs fails to capture the essence of classical mainstream economics: interdependence between network size of division of labour and total endogenous transaction costs. In this chapter we use a model with an endogenous structure of division of labour and endogenous transaction costs to investigate the interplay between them. Even if exogenous transportation efficiency (k) and/or exogenous bargaining efficiency (δ) are high, division of labour may not be chosen as an outcome because of the endogenous transaction costs caused by the strategic rent seeking behaviour of the players. Interesting implications for the role of trading rules, property ownership structure and income distribution from the model may be topics of future research.

As an interesting theoretical extension of the model, future studies can investigate the effects of information asymmetry on endogenous transaction costs associated with an inefficient level of division of labour, where the notion of sequential equilibrium may be used.

Notes

1 See Hart and Holmstrom (1987), Milgrom and Robert (1992), Hart (1995), Maskin and Xu (1999), and the references there.

2 See Wen (1998) for the proof. Though Wen's proof of this is based on price-taking behaviour, it is not difficult to show that her proof can be easily extended to the model here.

3 There are two threat points for each player in such a Nash bargaining game. The first is the bottom line given by the utility in autarky, u_A; Secondly, a player may use the utility for the occupation producing y as the threat point when he chooses the occupation producing x, since he can always change occupation configuration if the terms of trade are deemed unfair or if one occupation generates more utility than the other.

4 Although no risk is specified in the game, the players' attitude towards risk 'plays a central role' (Osborne and Rubinstein, 1990, p. 10). As long as there exists some uncertainty about other players' behaviour, there is a chance that the negotiation would break down, thus each player intends to maximize his *expected* utility gain in the negotiation. The Nash product can be interpreted as a player's expected utility gain, with the probability of reaching an agreement being approximated by the utility gains of the other player(s). For this reason,

Nash (1950) contends that the Nash bargaining solution is the outcome of a non-cooperative game despite the fact that the gains are shared fairly among players.

5 The bargaining cost here is a variable cost that increases with the number of bargaining rounds. Fixed bargaining costs are dealt with in Rubinstein (1982).

6 Binmore, Osborne, and Rubinstein (1990, pp. 4–18) present a general version of Rubinstein's original bargaining model (1982). In a sense the model here is a special case of that general alternating offers bargaining model. Hence, the proof for existence of subgame perfect equilibrium and the procedure for solving equilibrium here are the same as in that paper.

7 Binmore, Osborne, and Rubinstein (1990, pp. 20–4) address the concern with the endogenization of the choice of the first mover. Moulin (1984) develops a model that endogenizes the choice of the first mover by allowing for auction of the rights of the first mover. Also Perry (1986) has endogenized the choice of the initial proposer by introducing incomplete information into a bargaining model and Cramton (1992) randomizes the choice of the first mover in his model with two-sided uncertainty.

8 Gal-or (1987) has shown that the first mover may have a disadvantage if information asymmetry exists.

References

Binmore, K. (1987) 'Nash Bargaining Theory I, II, III', in Binmore and Dasgupta, *The Economics of Bargaining* (Oxford: Blackwell).

Binmore, K., Osborne, M., and Rubinstein, A. (1990) 'Noncooperative Models of Bargaining', mimeo, Department of Economics, McMaster University, Hamilton.

Coase, Ronald (1937) 'The Nature of The Firm', *Economica*, 4, 386–405.

Cramton, P. (1992) 'Strategic Delay in Bargaining with Two-Sided Uncertainty', *Review of Economic Studies*, 59, 205–25.

Fujita, M. and Krugman, P. (1995), 'When is the economy monocentric?: von Thunen and Chamberlin unified', *Regional Science and Urban Economics*, 25, 505–28.

Gal-or, E. (1987) 'First Mover Disadvantages with Private Information', *Review of Economic Studies*, 54, 279–92.

Grossman, Sanford and Hart, Oliver (1986) 'The Costs and The Benefits Of Ownership: a Theory of Vertical and Lateral Integration', *Journal of Political Economy*, 94, 691–719.

Hart, O. (1995) *Firms, Contracts, and Financial Structure* (Oxford: Clarendon Press).

Hart, O. and Holmstrom, B. (1987) 'The Theory of Contracts', in T. Bewley (ed.), *Advances in Economic Theory* (Cambridge: Cambridge University Press).

Hart, Oliver and Moore, John (1990) 'Property Rights and the Nature of The Firm', *Journal of Political Economy*, 98, 1119–58.

Helpman, Elhanan and Laffont, Jean-Jacques (1975) 'On Moral Hazard in General Equilibrium Theory', *Journal of Economic Theory*, 10, 8–23.

Klein, B., Crawford, R. and Alchian, A. (1978) 'Vertical Integration, Appropriable Rents and the Competitive Contracting Process', *Journal of Law and Economics*, 21, 297–326.

Kreps, D. (1990) *A Course in Microeconomic Theory* (Princeton, NJ: Princeton University Press).

Kreps, D. and Wilson, R. (1982) 'Sequential Equilibrium', *Econometrica*, 50, 863–94.

Krugman, P. and Venables, A. J. (1996) 'Integration, Specialization, and Adjustment', *European Economic Review*, 40, 959–67.

Laffont, J. and Tirole, J. (1986) 'Using Cost Observation to Regulate Firms', *Journal of Political Economy*, 94, 614–41.

Maskin, Eric and Xu, Chenggang (1999) 'Soft Budget Constraint Theories: From Centralization to the Market', Working Paper, Department of Economics, Harvard University.

Milgrom, P. and Roberts, J. (1992) *Economics, Organization and Management* (Englewood Cliffs, NJ: Prentice-Hall).

Moulin, H. (1984) 'Implementing the Kalai–Smorodinsky Bargaining Solution', *Journal of Economic Theory*, 33, 32–45.

Nash, J. (1950) 'The Bargaining Problem', *Econometrica*, 18, 115–62.

Nash, J. (1950) 'Equilibrium Points in N-person Games', *Proceedings of the National Academy of Sciences*, 36, 48–9.

North, D. and Weingast, S. (1989) 'Constitutions and Commitment: the Evolution of Institutions Governing Public Choice in Seventeenth-Century England', *Journal of Economic History*, XLIX, 803–32.

North, Douglass and Thomas, Robert (1970) 'An Economic Theory of the Growth of the West World', *The Economic Review*, 23, 1–17.

Osborne, M. and Rubinstein, A. (1990) *Bargaining and Markets* (Boston: Academic Press).

Perry, M. (1986) 'An Example of Price Formation in Bilateral Situations: a Bargaining Model with Incomplete Information', *Econometrica*, 54, 313–21.

Rubinstein, A. (1982) 'Perfect Equilibrium in a Bargaining Model', *Econometrica*, 50, 97–108.

Rubinstein, A. and Wolinsky, A. (1985) 'Equilibrium in a Market with Sequential Bargaining', *Econometrica*, 53, 1133–50.

Schelling, T. (1960) *The Strategy of Conflict* (Cambridge, MA: Harvard University Press).

Selten, R. (1975) 'Reexamination of the Perfectness Concept for Equilibrium Points in Extensive Games', *International Journal of Game Theory*, 4, 25–55.

Smith, Adam (1776) *An Inquiry into the Nature and Causes of the Wealth of Nations*. Reprint, edited by E. Cannan (Chicago: University of Chicago Press, 1976).

Stahl, I. (1972) *Bargaining Theory* (Stockholm: Stockholm School of Economics).

Stigler, George (1976) 'The Successes and Failures of Professor Smith', *Journal of Political Economy*, 84, 1199–1213.

Wen, M. (1998) 'An Analytical Framework of Consumer-Producers, Economies of Specialisation and Transaction Costs', in K. Arrow, Y.-K. Ng and X. Yang (eds), *Increasing Returns and Economic Analysis* (London: Macmillan).

Williamson, O. (1985) *Economic Institutions of Capitalism* (New York: The Free Press).

Williamson, Oliver (1975) *Markets and Hierarchies* (New York: The Free Press).

Yang, X. (1990) 'Development, Structural Changes, and Urbanization', *Journal of Development Economics*, 34, 199–222.

Yang, X. (1994) 'Endogenous vs. Exogenous Comparative Advantages and Economies of Specialization vs. Economies of Scale', *Journal of Economics*, 60, 29–54.

Yang, X. and Borland, J. (1991) 'A Microeconomic Mechanism for Economic Growth', *Journal of Political Economy*, 99, 460–82.

Yang, X. and Ng, Y.-K. (1995) 'Theory of the Firm and Structure of Residual Rights', *Journal of Economic Behaviour and Organisation*, 26, 107–28.

Index